Paying for Performance

Paying for Performance

A Guide to Compensation Management

Second Edition

Peter T. Chingos, Editor
and
Consultants from Mercer Human
Resource Consulting, Inc.

JOHN WILEY & SONS, INC.

ISBN 0-471-17690-7

Printed in the United States of America.

10 9 8 7 6 5 4 3 2 1

About the Editor

Peter T. Chingos

Peter T. Chingos is a principal in the New York office of Mercer Human Resource Consulting and a member of the firm's Worldwide Partners Group. He is the U.S. leader for the firm's Executive Compensation Consulting Practice. For more than 25 years he has consulted with senior management, compensation committees, and boards of directors of leading global corporations on executive compensation and strategic business issues. He is a frequent keynote speaker at professional conferences, writes extensively on all aspects of executive compensation, and is often quoted in the press. He has appeared before the Internal Revenue Service and the Securities Exchange Commission on a variety of regulatory issues related to compensation. He is a member of the advisory board of the National Association of Stock Plan Professionals and currently teaches basic and advanced courses in executive compensation in the certification program for compensation professionals sponsored by WorldatWork. In 1998 he received WorldatWork's prestigious Keystone Award for outstanding contributions in the areas of compensation and human resource management.

Contributors

John D. Bloedorn

John D. Bloedorn is a principal in Mercer Human Resource Consulting's Atlanta office. He has more than 30 years of experience as a consultant working on executive compensation projects on behalf of clients in all industries. He has authored numerous articles on compensation and related human resources topics, is a frequent speaker on pay and performance issues at national conferences, and has directed joint compensation research projects with WorldatWork on high-performing companies. He is a recipient of WorldatWork's Lifetime Achievement Award.

Steven L. Cross

Steven L. Cross is a principal in Mercer Human Resource Consulting's Houston office, where he leads the Reward and Talent Management Consulting Practice. He focuses on executive compensation program design, competitive evaluation, and regulatory issues and has worked with many compensation committees on executive compensation strategy issues. He often consults on compensation issues in the energy and mining industries and is a technical adviser to the firm's Data Systems Group on compensation and human resource issues related to these industries.

Janet Den Uyl

Janet Den Uyl is a principal with Mercer Human Resource Consulting in Louisville. She is the head of the Executive Benefits national resource group that specializes in the design and funding analysis of executive benefit plans. She has authored articles on executive benefits, split-dollar life insurance, voluntary deferred compensation, and the use of life insurance to fund benefit plans. She is a chartered life underwriter.

Donna L. DiBlase

Donna L. DiBlase is a consultant in the Orange, California office of Mercer Human Resource Consulting. Donna specializes in employee and executive communication on a broad range of human resources issues, including compensation, equity, and benefits. She works with clients to develop and implement communication strategies that motivate and create change. Donna has more than 15 years of experience as a communications professional.

Susan Eichen

Susan Eichen is a principal in Mercer Human Resource Consulting's New York office. She specializes in incentive plan design, option valuation, and accounting for compensation arrangements. Her clients include publicly and privately held companies, subsidiaries, and foreign-owned entities in a broad range of industries. She has written extensively on issues in incentive plan design and the impact of accounting rules on compensation policies and practice. She holds an MBA from the Wharton School of the University of Pennsylvania and is a CPA.

Vicki J. Elliott

Vicki J. Elliott is a principal with Mercer Human Resource Consulting in Munich, Germany, where she leads the firm's worldwide financial services network. She has more than 20 years of experience consulting on human capital strategy development, variable pay plan design, performance management, and executive compensation. Her clients include major commercial and investment banks, insurance companies, investment management firms, and diversified financial service companies. She has written extensively on performance measurement and pay-for-performance relationships, team management systems, and mergers and acquisition integration. She is a frequent speaker on strategic human resources issues.

Margaret M. Engel

Margaret M. Engel is a principal in Mercer Human Resource Consulting's New York office. She focuses on all aspects of executive compensation and has worked with leading companies on compensation strategy, annual and long-term incentive plan design, best practices research, and securities and tax issues. She worked closely with the firm's Data Systems Group to establish Mercer's *Survey of Long-Term Incentive and Equity Award Practices*.

Edward W. Freher

Edward W. Freher is a principal in Mercer Human Resource Consulting's New York office. He has extensive experience in executive and board compensation and has consulted with major companies in designing compensation programs to support their business strategy and build competitive advantage. He is a frequent speaker on executive compensation issues and is a faculty member of WorldatWork, where he teaches executive compensation in the certification program for compensation professionals.

Howard J. Golden, JD

Howard J. Golden, JD is a principal in Mercer Human Resource Consulting's New York office. He specializes in executive compensation design and compliance, and the interrelationship of compensation and benefits programs. Mr. Golden has been a contributing editor for many professional journals, a featured speaker at many national forums, and has testified before Congress. He is quoted often in the national media.

Loree J. Griffith

Loree J. Griffith is a principal in Mercer Human Resource Consulting's New York office, where she specializes in designing and analyzing client compensation programs related to salary management, performance management, incentive plan design, job titling, and compensation benchmarking. Her work has covered all employee groups, including executives, middle management, professional and technical employees, and nonexempt employees. Her primary area of focus has been within the financial services industry.

Steven E. Gross

Steven E. Gross is a principal in the Philadelphia office of Mercer Human Resource Consulting and a member of the firm's Worldwide Partners Group. He serves as leader of the firm's U.S. Employee Compensation Consulting Practice. He is an active speaker and seminar leader for WorldatWork and the Society for Human Resource Management and author of *Compensation for Teams* (Amacom, 1995). He is a Certified Management Consultant and holds an MBA from the Wharton School of the University of Pennsylvania.

Steven Grossman

Steven Grossman is a principal in the Chicago office of Mercer Human Resource Consulting, where he leads Mercer's U.S. Sales Effectiveness Practice. For more than 20 years, he has consulted on domestic and international sales force management as well as on marketing, competitive analysis, and organizational effectiveness. He is a frequent speaker on sales force management and compensation and a principal author of *The Sales Compensation Handbook,* (Amacom, 1998), a standard resource in its field. He has an MBA from Boston University and is a Certified Management Consultant.

Richard Harris

Richard Harris is a principal in Mercer Human Resource Consulting's Chicago office. He concentrates on executive compensation and has worked extensively in designing and implementing incentive cornpensation programs based on economic profit. He is a frequent speaker on linking compensation to economic value management principles and lectures on compensation at the Kellogg Graduate School of Management at Northwestern University.

J. Stephen Heinen, PhD

J. Stephen Heinen, PhD is a principal in Mercer Human Resource Consulting's Cincinnati office. He is an industrial/organizational psychologist and works with companies in the areas of organizational development and change and competency-based human resource systems, especially performance management and selection, talent management, and employee surveys. He has served on the faculty of the College of Business of the University of Minnesota and has a PhD in organizational psychology from Michigan State University.

Martin L. Katz

Martin L. Katz is a principal in the San Francisco office of Mercer Human Resource Consulting. He serves as the West Coast Executive Compensation Consulting Practice leader, consulting with Fortune 500 companies and their boards and the boards of large tax-exempt organizations. He has spoken at national conferences sponsored by WorldatWork, the Conference Board, Loyola Law School, and others. He is a CPA and holds a Masters in taxation from DePaul University.

Patricia Kopacz

Patricia Kopacz is a principal in the Executive Benefits national resource group in Mercer Human Resource Consulting's Louisville office. She focuses on executive benefit design and financing issues and has extensive experience in tax-exempt health care organizations as well as public corporations across a wide range of industries. She has earned the Certified Employee Benefit Specialist designation sponsored by the International Foundation of Employee Benefit Plans and the University of Pennsylvania's Wharton School.

Karyn Meola

Karyn Meola is an associate in the San Francisco office of Mercer Human Resource Consulting. She specializes in designing and analyzing executive and management compensation programs related to salary management, annual and long-term incentive program design, executive benefits, and board compensation. Her primary area of focus has been in the health care industry and the not-for-profit sector. She holds an MBA from Columbia University School of Business.

Haig R. Nalbantian

Haig R. Nalbantian is a principal in Mercer Human Resource Consulting's New York office and a member of the firm's Worldwide Partners Group. He is a founding member and research director of Mercer's Human Capital Strategy Group. He has been instrumental in developing Mercer's human capital model and measurement capabilities. He is a labor/organizational economist with special expertise in the economics of incentives and organization. He was on the faculty of economics at New York University and was a research scientist at its C.V. Starr Center for Applied Economics. He has MA and MPhil degrees in economics from Columbia University.

Colleen O'Neill, PhD

Colleen O'Neill, PhD is a principal in Mercer Human Resource Consulting's Atlanta office and a member of the firm's Worldwide Partners Group. She is the U.S. leader for the firm's Talent Management Consulting Practice. She has been a seminar leader and lecturer for various educational institutions and professional societies and is the author of numerous articles on performance and development issues. She holds a PhD in clinical psychology from the University of Georgia.

Peter J. Oppermann

Peter J. Oppermann is a principal in Mercer Human Resource Consulting's New York office. He has more than 20 years of consulting experience focusing on executive and board compensation. He has developed executive and management compensation programs for national and international clients in the manufacturing, services, e-commerce, and high-technology sectors. He is a frequent speaker at national and regional seminars on executive and management compensation.

Rose Marie Orens

Rose Marie Orens is a principal in Mercer Human Resource Consulting's New York office. She has more than 20 years of experience consulting in executive compensation, salary management, and variable pay. She is on the faculty of Worldat-Work, where she teaches executive compensation and alternative rewards in the certification program for compensation professionals. She is often quoted in the business press and speaks frequently on strategic compensation issues. She has been an adjunct faculty member in the Graduate School of Business of the New School for Social Research and has received the YWCA Academy of Women Achievers Award.

Anna C. Orgera

Anna C. Orgera is a principal in Mercer Human Resource Consulting's New York office. She focuses on the development of salary management programs, job evaluation programs, annual and long-term variable pay programs, and performance management and evaluation processes. She has conducted benchmarking and best practices studies and customized compensation surveys. She has worked with a broad range of financial services, manufacturing services, and public-sector organizations.

Dana Rahbar-Daniels

Dana Rahbar-Daniels is Asia Regional Practice Leader for Mercer Human Resource Consulting's Talent Management and Competency Applications Practice, headquartered in Singapore. He has extensive experience in developing and implementing performance management, leadership development, and total reward systems for global and domestic companies. His consulting engagements include aligning reward with competency development, organizational transformation initiatives, salary broadbanding systems, multisource performance feedback processes, and team-based incentive and recognition practices. He is a frequent speaker and writer on human resources effectiveness and competency program applications.

Donald T. Sagolla

Donald T. Sagolla is a principal in Mercer Human Resource Consulting's Los Angeles office. His consulting experience is extensive in both the United States and Canada and spans the entertainment, media, health care, high-technology, financial institutions, retailing, and manufacturing industries. He writes frequently on integrating executive compensation with business planning, organization change, and pay-for-performance. He is a frequent lecturer and workshop leader in compensation and human resource management and has particularly focussed on board of director compensation and governance.

Carol Silverman, JD

Carol Silverman, JD is a principal in Mercer Human Resource Consulting's New York office. She specializes in executive and director compensation strategy and design, with an emphasis on employment and change-in-control arrangements and equity programs. Ms. Silverman joined Mercer after practicing employee benefit law for nine years. She holds a JD degree from Columbia University School of Law, where she was a Harlan Fiske Stone Scholar.

William J. T. Strahan, JD

William J. T. Strahan, JD is the Office Leader for Mercer Human Resource Consulting's offices in Philadelphia and Princeton and formerly the head of Mercer's Philadelphia Reward and Talent Management Consulting Practice. He has worked with clients on a variety of strategic compensation issues. Before joining Mercer he spent more than 15 years in corporate human resources positions and practicing human resources–related law. He is a frequent speaker on compensation issues.

Craig Ulrich

Craig Ulrich is a principal in Mercer Human Resource Consulting's New York office and a senior member of the Sales Effectiveness Practice. He specializes in sales productivity, sales force deployment, organization design, and aligning human capital programs with sales strategies. He has been quoted in numerous leading business journals and has written extensively on sales productivity issues. Craig holds an MBA degree from Fairleigh Dickinson University.

Contents

Introduction: Paying for Performance—Best Practices
in a Changing Environment   xix
Peter T. Chingos

1 Looking at Rewards Holistically   1
   Steven E. Gross and Haig R. Nalbantian

   1.1 Why Is Reward Strategy Important?   2
   1.2 What Constitutes a Reward Strategy?   2
   1.3 How Corporate America *Currently* Looks at Rewards   5
   1.4 The Hospitality Company Finds Its Answers   7
   1.5 How Corporate America *Might* Look at Rewards   9
   1.6 How to Develop an Effective Program   11
   1.7 Case A: Implementing Reward Strategy to Stay Ahead
        in the Fast-Changing Technology Industry   13
   1.8 Case B: Utilizing Reward Strategy to Integrate—
        M&A Opportunities   15
   1.9 Case C: Creating an Effective Global Reward Strategy   17

2 Variable Pay Programs: Pay for Results   20
   Rose Marie Orens and Vicki J. Elliott

   2.1 A Process for Implementing Variable Pay   20
   2.2 Case Study: Gainsharing Plan   30
   2.3 Team Incentives   36
   2.4 Conclusion   42

3 Performance Management: Mapping Out the Process   43
   Loree J. Griffith and Anna C. Orgera

   3.1 Framework for Defining Key Elements of Performance Success 44
   3.2 Performance Management as an Ongoing Process   48
   3.3 Mechanics of a Business-Driven Objective Setting Process   49
   3.4 Multisource Performance Feedback as an Assessment Tool 51
   3.5 Maximizing Performance Through Feedback and Coaching   53

3.6   Performance Evaluation and Development   55
3.7   The Appraisal Interview   57
3.8   Development Planning   58
3.9   The Performance Management Framework in Action   60
3.10 Lessons Learned for Effective Performance Management
      Program Design   60

4 Competency-Based Reward Design Approaches   63
   Dana Rahbar-Daniels

4.1   Design Purpose for Competency-Based Rewards   64
4.2   Current Practices in Competency Linkages   65
4.3   Base Pay Applications of Competency Linkage   69
4.4   Variable Pay/Incentive Applications   80
4.5   Recognition Award Applications   84
4.6   Conclusions on Competency–Reward Linkages   85

5 Managing Talent to Maximize Performance   86
   J. Stephen Heinen, PhD, and Colleen O'Neill, PhD

5.1   The Business Opportunity for Talent Management   86
5.2   Aligning Talent Management and Business Strategy   87
5.3   Key Factors in Successful Talent Planning and Development   90
5.4   Conclusion   103

6 Getting the Most from Your Sales Compensation Plan   104
   Steven Grossman and Craig Ulrich

6.1   Why Change a Sales Compensation Plan? Is It Worth the Risks? 105
6.2   What Tells You the Sales Compensation Plan Really Is Broken? 108
6.3   How Do You Know When Your Sales Compensation Plan
      Is Really Broken?   113
6.4   Design and Implementation   122
6.5   Administration   126
6.6   Auditing and Modifying   127
6.7   Some Final Thoughts on Designing a Sales Compensation Plan   128

7 Pay for Performance in Not-for-Profit Organizations   130
   Martin L. Katz and Karyn Meola

7.1   Introduction to Tax-Exempt Organizations   131
7.2   Federal Tax Rules   131
7.3   Intermediate Sanctions   132

7.4   Determining Reasonableness   138
7.5   Private Foundations   139
7.6   Deferred Compensation in Tax Exempts   139
7.7   Typical Executive Compensation Programs   140
7.8   Designing Effective Incentives   141
7.9   Long-Term Incentive Plans   146
7.10 Developing a Pay-for-Performance Culture   148
7.11 Special Compensation Arrangements   149
7.12 Conclusion   152

8   Designing the Annual Management Incentive Plan   153
    Edward W. Freher

8.1   Role of Annual Incentives in Compensation Strategy   153
8.2   Influencing Management Behavior: Building a
      Line-of-Sight Relationship   154
8.3   Corporate and Business Unit Performance Measurement   155
8.4   Determining Participation and Size of Award Opportunities   158
8.5   Building Performance Scales   160
8.6   Assessing Individual Performance   164
8.7   Assessing Cost–Benefits of New Plans and
      Plan Modifications   165
8.8   Other Considerations   166
8.9   Final Checklist   167

**9   Designing Incentive Compensation Programs to Support
    Value-Based Management   169**
    Richard Harris

9.1   What Is Value-Based Management?   169
9.2   VBM Performance Metrics Differ from Other
      Financial Measures   170
9.3   VBM Implementation   171
9.4   Designing VBM-Based Compensation Plans   175
9.5   Establishing Performance Targets   178
9.6   Conclusion   185

10 Long-Term Incentives   187
    Margaret M. Engel

10.1 Long-Term Incentives Defined   187
10.2 The Most Common Approaches   188

10.3   Objectives of Long-Term Incentive Plans   188
10.4   Long-Term Plans and Compensation Strategy   189
10.5   Stock Options   190
10.6   Stock Appreciation Rights   195
10.7   Restricted Stock   195
10.8   Performance Plans   197
10.9   Private Company Long-Term Incentives   199
10.10 Increased Participation   199
10.11 Larger Awards   200
10.12 Investor Concerns   201
10.13 Responses to Market Volatility   202
10.14 Successful Long-Term Incentive Plans   204

11   **Broad-Based and Global Equity Plans**   **205**
William J. T. Strahan, JD

11.1   Prevalence   205
11.2   Tax, Accounting, Regulatory, and Legal Issues
       for Broad-Based Plans   207
11.3   Mechanics of Making Grants   208
11.4   Calibration of Individual Awards   208
11.5   Pros and Cons of Broad-Based Stock Compensation—
       Its Place within a Total Rewards Strategy   210
11.6   Global Stock Plans: U.S. Companies   220
11.7   Effects in High- and Low-Paying Countries   222

12   **Executive Benefits**   **223**
Janet Den Uyl and Patricia Kopacz

12.1   Core Benefits and Perquisites   223
12.2   Nonqualified Deferred Compensation   225
12.3   Executive Life Insurance   234
12.4   Executive Disability Benefits   237
12.5   Medical Benefits   238
12.6   Perquisites   239
12.7   Conclusion   240

13   **A Pay-for-Performance Model**   **241**
John D. Bloedorn

13.1   Guiding Principles   241
13.2   A Compensation Model   244

13.3 Base Salary Element 246
13.4 Annual Incentive Elements 247
13.5 Long-Term Incentive Elements 253
13.6 Other Compensation Design Considerations 261
13.7 Communications 262
13.8 Conclusion 263

14 Driving Organizational Change with Executive Compensation and Communication **264**
Donald T. Sagolla and Donna L. DiBlase

14.1 Types of Organizational Change 265
14.2 The Relationship Between Compensation Strategy and Organizational Change 266
14.3 Developing a Communication Strategy to Support and Drive Behavior 269
14.4 Communicating and Implementing an Executive Compensation Strategy 271
14.5 Linkage of Compensation to the Organization's Culture 273
14.6 The Message or Purpose of Compensation Elements 275
14.7 Linking Compensation Programs to Characteristics of Organization Change—A Readiness Assessment 277
14.8 Conclusion 278

15 Transaction-Related Compensation Arrangements **279**
Carol Silverman, JD

15.1 Overview of Transaction-Related Compensation Arrangements 280
15.2 Change-in-Control and Severance Programs 281
15.3 Retention and Transaction Bonuses 288
15.4 Treatment of Cash and Equity Incentives 292
15.5 Corporate Governance Issues 295
15.6 Conclusion 296

16 Director Compensation **297**
Peter J. Oppermann

16.1 Trends in Director Compensation 297
16.2 NACD Guidelines and Changes in Section 16(b) 298
16.3 Elements of Director Compensation 299
16.4 Developing a Director Compensation Program 307
16.5 Summary 312

17 The Role of the Compensation Committee **315**
Steven L. Cross and Donald T. Sagolla

17.1 Business/Competitive Environment 315
17.2 Shareholder and Regulatory Backdrop 315
17.3 Performance Benchmarking 322
17.4 Use of Third-Party Resources 325
17.5 Questions and Issues for the Compensation Committee 326
17.6 Summary 328

18 Accounting for Stock-Based Compensation **329**
Susan Eichen

18.1 Background 329
18.2 Understanding the Basics of APB 25 332
18.3 Understanding the Basics of FAS 123 347
18.4 Impact of Stock-Based Awards on Earnings Per Share 352

19 Selected Tax Aspects of Executive Compensation Plans **355**
Howard J. Golden, JD

19.1 Taxation of Equity Devices 355
19.2 Golden Parachutes 364
19.3 Section 162(m) Compliance 370

Index **373**

Paying for Performance— Best Practices in a Changing Environment

Peter T. Chingos

When we published the first edition of *Paying for Performance* in 1997, the business climate was very different than it is today. At that time, the U.S. financial markets were in the midst of an unprecedented multiyear boom. Many established companies were delivering record profits, but perhaps more important, a myriad of "new economy" marvels were rewriting long-standing rules about the relationship between earnings and market value, the relative importance of growth and profitability, and the definition of what constitutes successful business performance. Since then, the air has escaped from the Internet bubble and both old and new economy companies have been forced to wrestle with more fundamental business issues, including the long-term implications of a possible global economic recession.

This cooler climate impacts every aspect of a company's business and results in some compelling questions about pay programs in general and the pay-for-performance philosophy in particular. What is the proper role of equity in a compensation program, for those in the executive suite as well as the general rank and file? How can companies differentiate between outstanding, average, and below-average performers and ensure that they retain their key employees even when overall company performance is below expectations? And what should our time horizons be for both individual and corporate performance assessments, as well as wealth creation over the course of an employee's career?

While the previous questions are hardly an exhaustive list, they demonstrate that "paying for performance" can be far more complicated than the straightforward term suggests, especially in a rapidly changing economic environment. Even though the "pay-for-performance" concept has become widely accepted in corporate America (few public companies today do not at least pay lip service to the idea in their annual proxy statements), many companies have also discovered that the devil is in the details. Simply doling out stock options at all levels of the organization is hardly an effective long-term approach, even if it does appear (on the surface, at least) to tie pay explicitly to performance. Given this complexity, my colleagues at Mercer Human Resource Consulting and I believe it is an appropriate time to revisit the issues that we raised in the first edition of *Paying for Performance,* to expand on certain key points, and to refine other key messages based on our collective learnings in recent years.

As the title suggests, the emphasis of this book is on reward systems and how those rewards are linked to individual, group, and overall company performance. It is important to note, however, that paying for performance is just one piece of a much larger puzzle—namely, how can an organization best manage all of its human capital in order to build and sustain a long-term competitive advantage.

The notion of human capital as an investment to be cultivated, as opposed to a bottomless resource that can be tapped on demand, represents one of the most significant shifts in business thinking in recent years. In boardrooms around the country, I have seen firsthand how it is has become increasingly accepted that human capital is just as important as the more traditional forms of financial and physical capital to the long-term success of any business. As economic conditions continue to shift, effective human capital management may become the single most important driver of long-term financial success and shareholder value creation.

Of course, paying for performance is just one factor in the human capital equation. While this book touches on other aspects of human capital management, such as performance and talent management, it is first and foremost a book about designing compensation programs in a pay-for-performance environment. As such, one of its primary goals is to provide a broad overview of all of the elements of an effective pay-for-performance system, with each chapter constituting a guide to one specific part of the whole. These chapters can be read sequentially or referenced individually as needed and are designed to provide readers with a thorough understanding of the various pay-for-performance tools at their disposal, the advantages and disadvantages of certain approaches, and the tax and accounting consequences associated with specific compensation vehicles.

While *Paying for Performance* is in one sense a handbook that describes the nuts and bolts of an effective pay-for-performance system, underlying each chapter is Mercer's collective experience regarding "best practices" among high-performing companies in this area. This collective wisdom, obtained through decades of consulting experience with many of the world's most successful companies, as well as specific research projects on the topic, makes *Paying for Performance* more than a mere primer. There is no single "right" or "best" way to institute any of the approaches discussed in this book, but there are certain guiding principles that nearly all high-performing companies follow, either explicitly or implicitly, when designing and implementing their pay programs. These principles represent our understanding of "best practices" in this area and can help ensure that any reward program is properly aligned with a company's overall business objectives, measures the appropriate performance factors, and delivers meaningful rewards that support desired behaviors.

BEST PRACTICES IN PAYING FOR PERFORMANCE

While all of the following chapters reflect the "best practices" of high-performing companies, I'd like to focus on several key themes that Mercer believes should form the foundation of any successful pay program. Most of these principles can be applied to the various topics addressed in the body of this book. While their actual implementation can (and in fact should) vary considerably from organization to organization, the principles themselves should not. In short, they are a roadmap to the design and implementation of an effective pay-for-performance system.

Vision

Before any organization can hope to develop a successful pay-for-performance program, it must have a vision. While this may sound simplistic, without such direction, it is difficult to even identify the type of performance one should reward, never mind link that performance to various elements of compensation. What would success look like? And how would we know it if we saw it? Before we can begin to answer these questions, we must know what the organization is trying to accomplish. Put another way, a clear corporate vision is the foundation on which all effective pay-for-performance systems are based.

What exactly do we mean by vision? Without getting bogged down in semantic definitions of "vision" versus "mission" versus "strategy," we can perhaps best describe it as a clear sense of purpose. To be an effective part of the pay-for-performance process, a corporate vision does not have to be memorialized in lucite "tombstones" or posted above every water cooler; however, it does have to represent a high-level understanding within the organization of where it would like to be next week, next month, next year, and beyond.

When such a vision exists, the remaining elements of an effective pay-for-performance program can begin to be put in place. Without it, even the best-designed program will drift aimlessly. It may occasionally drive the correct behavior, but it will most likely be by chance rather than by design.

Alignment

If a company's overall vision represents a destination, it still must figure out how to get from Point A (where it is today) to Point B (where it would like to be). Proper alignment of the pay program is critical because it helps ensure that the behaviors the organization is rewarding are the same behaviors that will help achieve the desired results. We often see companies become frustrated when, after spending significant resources rethinking their business strategy, they are not able to make that new vision a reality. Upon closer examination, however, it becomes clear that the behaviors the pay program rewards (either explicitly or implicitly) and the behaviors required to achieve the vision are very different.

Alignment, however, goes beyond simply identifying desired behaviors. It also requires proper *calibration* of compensation programs, to ensure that the levels of pay delivered are in line with the levels of performance that are actually achieved. Mercer's research into the compensation practices of high-performing companies reveals that most use some sort of *external validation* in their pay programs. Such external validation is often both retrospective, to assess how the company actually performed compared to its peers, and prospective, to ensure that performance targets include an appropriate degree of "stretch."

Consider a company that as part of its pay-for-performance philosophy provides highly leveraged annual incentive opportunities with maximum payouts equal to two or three times an employee's "target" award. Theoretically, the company should only be paying out the maximum bonus amount when actual performance is outstanding. But how outstanding is outstanding? By comparing performance targets to both the recent and expected performance of relevant peer companies, we can begin to determine if the plan's definition of superior performance is, in fact, superior. Without such external validation, a company with a stated pay-for-performance philosophy risks overpaying for mediocre performance or perhaps underpaying for exceptional performance. In either case, pay and performance are not properly aligned, making it much more difficult for the pay program to drive the appropriate behavior and for the company to achieve its stated vision.

A Holistic Approach

As mentioned earlier, pay is just one aspect of human capital management. While proper alignment of a company's pay programs is critical, other factors in the human capital equation must not be overlooked. Even more important, however, they cannot be managed discretely. Effective human capital management requires a holistic reward strategy that links pay programs, benefits, and career opportunities and understands the relationships between these various reward components.

Mercer's human capital framework recognizes several elements that go beyond traditional compensation and benefits programs, including people, work processes, management structure, information and knowledge, and decision making. By understanding the role that each of these diverse elements plays in executing the overall business strategy, one can begin to develop an optimal rewards mix that motivates, develops, and drives an organization's talent as efficiently and effectively as possible. Such a holistic approach to reward strategy, in conjunction with a robust pay-for-performance program, can have a significant impact on both human capital decisions and overall business results.

CEO Commitment

Even a properly aligned, holistic rewards program will disappoint if it lacks commitment from the highest levels of the organization. When a CEO demonstrates, in both words and deeds, that he or she is truly committed to a pay-for-performance philosophy, that sense of commitment will cascade throughout the organization. If the CEO is not personally committed to the program, and his or her actions do not support its stated objectives (e.g., by not including senior executives in the same rigorous performance management process used at lower organizational levels), employees will quickly come to believe—and rightly so—that any talk about "paying for performance" is more about style than substance.

How do CEOs at high-performing companies demonstrate commitment to a pay-for-performance compensation philosophy? They begin by identifying and communicating the highest standards of excellence, not just on the basis of historical performance, but also on the basis of achieving breakthrough levels of performance in both financial and nonfinancial terms. When CEOs take the lead in identifying and communicating performance criteria, there is a clear understanding of how the organization will measure success and how specific individuals can contribute to that success.

An equally important element of CEO commitment is the CEO's willingness to drive change throughout the organization. As organizations continue to reposition themselves in light of changing economic realities, CEOs are spending more and more time on the performance management process, personally setting goals and evaluating performance for those who will carry out the new strategy. Importantly, this personal involvement is not limited to the CEO's half-dozen direct reports but extends to a broader group of executives and delivers a clear message to those executives that a rigorous performance management process is critical to the company's success. Those executives, in turn, can then drive that message even deeper into the organization.

Accountability

Personal accountability is in many ways the hallmark of an effective pay-for-performance program. A well-aligned program with a rigorous performance evaluation process means nothing if, at the end of the year, individuals are not held accountable for meeting agreed-upon goals.

Traditionally, a strong sense of accountability has meant that "the numbers tell the story." At the beginning of each performance period, companies set specific financial targets that support their overall business objectives. At the end of each period, actual performance is evaluated against the original target and individuals are held accountable for their performance through compensation and future career opportunities. While this notion of "black and white" results is common (numeric targets are either met or they are not), we increasingly see high-performing companies recognizing that shades of gray can also exist without sacrificing accountability.

One approach that is becoming more common is the use of nonfinancial measures in incentive plans. This can take the shape of a formal "balanced scorecard" in which performance is evaluated in specific areas such as financial results, people management, customer satisfaction, and intellectual capital development, or it can simply involve basing a portion of an annual incentive award on nonfinancial criteria such as quality or diversity. In either case, the measures remain quantitative, but they give a more appropriate picture of overall performance than rigidly adhering to a single financial metric such as earnings per share.

A second way some leading companies are moderating their approach to accountability is to continue to set specific, measurable targets in a variety of areas, but to refrain from attaching specific payout formulas and weightings to the various goals. Instead, they assess the various factors retrospectively, in light of the actual market conditions that existed over the course of the performance period. One company we have worked with describes it quite succinctly as a "qualitative assessment of quantitative performance."

To be effective, accountability does not have to mean rigid inflexibility, in which missing a target by one unit or 0.1% results in zero reward, regardless of any extenuating circumstances; however, there does have to be a clear cause-and-effect relationship between results and rewards. Strong performance should be rewarded; poor performance should not.

Balance

One of the most challenging aspects of any pay-for-performance program is striking the right balance among various compensation elements and performance measures. As organizations grow and become increasingly complex, their multiple objectives are not always compatible. In the short term, many companies believe that meeting or exceeding Wall Street's earnings per share (EPS) expectations each quarter is critical. But how can they balance that short-term focus with a long-term need for sustainable growth, some of which may require investments that will actually reduce short-term earnings? A clearly defined vision can help settle some of these differences, but tension inevitably exists.

When a company says it pays for performance, what type of performance is it talking about? Absolute performance? Or relative? If our share price rises 20% in a year in which our leading competitors all rise 30%, are we doing well or not? If our share price falls by less than the market average, is that cause for celebration? And more important, should our employees be rewarded for "beating" the market, even though our company as a whole is worth less than it was at the beginning of the year?

Similar issues exist in other areas as well. Over what time periods should we evaluate performance? While annual incentive plans are commonplace, many high-performing companies also have multiyear plans to ensure that key executives do not lose sight of their longer-term objectives. And what about the balance between cash compensation and equity? An over-reliance on equity can produce unintended consequences, such as retention difficulties in a declining market.

No single approach is properly "balanced" for every company or business situation, but the rationale behind the development of a holistic rewards program applies here as well. When evaluating any pay program, you must understand how the various pieces fit together and the types of behavior they will reward. If the pay program seems to support conflicting objectives, the correct balance has likely not been achieved.

Rewarding Top Performers

Another delicate balancing act involves rewarding top individual performers when the company as a whole is not doing well. While it may be tempting to argue that no single person should receive a substantial reward if some baseline level of organizational performance is not achieved, such an approach can be painfully shortsighted. When an organization is not performing well, the top performers of today are the ones who will drive overall performance improvements in the future. Failure to deliver rewards to top performers in difficult times can result in retention problems that exacerbate the problem even further, because those top performers are most likely to be coveted by the company's competitors as well.

In recent interviews with approximately two dozen Fortune 100 executives, all of them said that their companies have the ability to recognize top performers when company or business unit performance is below expectations. The actual approaches vary considerably from company to company (e.g., special grants of stock options, restricted stock awards, cash payments), but they universally recognize the need to reward top performers, regardless of overall business conditions.

In the chapters that follow, we discuss the various aspects of an effective pay-for-performance program in more detail. Many of these chapters will also expand on one or more of the aforementioned "best practices," and discuss how they can be applied to specific case studies or other real-world situations. Each chapter can be read as a self-contained overview of a specific topic, with the overall intent being to provide useful information on a broad range of issues related to people, performance, and rewards.

Chapter 1

Looking at Rewards Holistically*

Steven E. Gross and Haig R. Nalbantian

Imagine you are the Vice President of Human Resources at one of the world's largest hospitality companies, you hire 75,000 front-line workers every year in the United States alone, your corporation receives the highest ratings for employee and customer satisfaction, and you are weeks away from the grand opening of another top-notch resort. Sounds great, but there's one glitch . . . senior management is becoming concerned that you won't be able to find enough qualified associates to open the property. And, once you find them, you have trouble retaining them. This company was not alone in its challenge, but, unlike many other large corporations, the company was able to identify the problem, quantify its impact on the business, and implement remedies that would appreciably enhance its profits.

Since the 1950s, this hospitality industry leader has been building an impeccable international reputation for customer and employee satisfaction. Customers are extremely loyal, and employees rank the chain as a top employer in its industry. Still, there was a time when the company's senior management became concerned that it would not be able to open properties on time, not due to construction delays, but because there might not be enough hourly workers to provide the important services that its customers expected. To make matters worse, the company was having difficulties retaining its employees—the very people who said it was the best place to work. Under pressure to improve the situation, management proposed the typical solutions: pay higher salaries, increase incentive compensation, offer additional benefits, and so on. But at what cost? And which would solve the problem?

This chapter outlines a new way of looking at rewards—a holistic approach that uses measurement to:

- Determine what an organization *actually* values (in terms of skills, knowledge, experience, and behaviors).

*This chapter draws heavily on the work of the Human Capital Strategy and Reward and Talent Management Practices of Mercer Human Resource Consulting, Inc. Acknowledgments are also given to Ilse de Veer and Helen M. Friedman for their assistance in preparing this chapter.

- Analyze the impact of the broad spectrum of reward programs (pay, benefits, and careers) on human capital and, in turn, on an organization's profitability.

The authors guide readers through this hospitality organization's challenge — from problem to analysis to solution — and demonstrate how its new approach to rewards strategy can significantly add to the bottom line.

1.1 WHY IS REWARD STRATEGY IMPORTANT?

Today's competitive conditions make it more difficult for employers to acquire and retain experienced and productive talent. The growing awareness that finding, motivating, developing, and keeping employees is a key component of business success has raised expectations for human resource (HR) departments. Today, the HR function is being scrutinized more closely, with expectations that it will make a contribution to the business — just like finance, accounting, marketing, and sales. The reward programs that have been the traditional domain of HR (e.g., pay, benefits, training) represent a significant and growing investment for an organization. In general, these programs have been managed discretely rather than as part of an overall *strategy.* As leadership looks to HR to support the organization's business objectives and enhance profitability, some tough questions need to be answered:

- How can we attract and retain the *right* people?
- How do we motivate and develop employees?
- Do we know what skills, knowledge, experience, and behaviors we actually reward?
- How do we pay for performance?
- Are pay, benefits, and career investments aligned with each other — and with our business strategy?
- How do we measure the return on our investment in people?

A broader concept of rewards, and reward strategy, is needed to answer these questions effectively.

1.2 WHAT CONSTITUTES A REWARD STRATEGY?

Surely, an individual's evaluation of a job opportunity is based on more than just current *pay.* It also includes the *benefits* that a company might offer, as well as the opportunities for learning and advancement: the *career.* In assessing the rewards being offered by a company to its current and prospective employees, it is important to understand the relationship among these three important reward components (see Exhibit 1.1).

(a) Pay

Everyone, especially workers, knows the importance of *pay*. It includes base pay plus additional compensation in the form of incentives or bonus awards, stock options, and stock grants.

Many HR professionals believe that higher pay helps attract talent and reduce turnover. This is usually true, but it tells us little about the economics of the company's pay positioning. For example, let's look at TechCo, a high-tech firm that relies heavily on technology professionals. To attract the best and brightest, the company developed a pay package—including widespread use of stock options—which placed it at the 95th percentile. This upfront cost was expected to deliver a return in the form of lower turnover, particularly among high performers. But the strategy was not successful: turnover actually increased! Subsequent analysis of TechCo's business design and employee data revealed that TechCo's rewards were misaligned with its business strategy. The company was rewarding autonomy and innovation, whereas its business model required speed, consistency, and efficiency. Moreover, through its reward system, TechCo was attracting the wrong people. In the end, these people were still leaving the firm because the work—manipulating existing technology—was not motivating to the type of employees being hired. Unlike many of its competitors, the *right* people for TechCo were not "the best and the brightest" but rather were solid, homegrown performers. To retain these key employees, TechCo needed to focus more on careers, building a reward strategy that paid more for the development

Exhibit 1.1   Looking at Rewards Holistically.

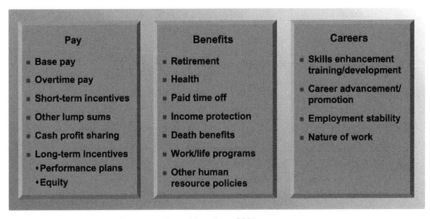

Source: © Mercer Human Resource Consulting, Inc., 2001.

of technical expertise over time. Organizations struggle to define "the *right* equation": how to pay the *right* people, the *right* amount, for the *right* reason at the *right* time. For TechCo, the right equation would have yielded a much less costly reward system with much larger returns.

(b) Benefits

Another key reward component is *benefits,* which, like pay, are measurable and can be valuable tools in attracting and retaining the right employees. But, the HR executive who looks exclusively at benefits, or only benefits and pay, may be short-changing his or her organization. Benefit plans have changed remarkably in recent times as companies move away from traditional pension plans, seeking out account balance plan alternatives designed to attract and motivate a "21st-century" workforce, which is generally older and has shorter service expectations. Newer programs like flexible benefits—allowing employees to choose their own benefit choices—as well as casual dress and more flexible hours have become standard in some industries. As benefits take on new characteristics, they become even more useful as a reward tool. But the picture is still larger.

(c) Careers

HR professionals, while trying to determine the right combination of pay and benefits, at times neglect an important component: *careers.* Careers represent the future value to employees of staying with an organization (i.e., what *will* they be paid and what jobs *will* they have). It is the opportunity to learn and grow; in many cases, employees forgo higher current salaries and better benefits for the prospect of career advancement. Have you or anyone you know turned down a higher-paying job offer? Our experience indicates that one-third to one-half of those turning down a higher offer state that higher current pay was important, but the opportunity for career advancement was even more important. We find that people trade off these reward components in different ways, depending on their stages of life. When people consider offers, they're considering both the current rewards and their expectations regarding the value of future rewards. For example, how many young adults join the Army because they're looking forward to a lifetime of low pay? Many dedicated soldiers choose a career in the armed forces, but most join the Army to learn valuable skills, to decommission out of the Army, and to use those skills for a more fruitful civilian career.

The role of careers in the rewards mix depends on many factors. A company in the high-tech industry is more likely to have young employees who are focused more on acquiring the latest skills than on growing their retirement savings. A company in an established industry that requires experienced (typically older) workers, however, might consider a reward mix that balances wealth accumulation through retirement plans with current cash compensation.

In the following sections, we show how a measured strategy that holistically looks at pay, benefits, and careers can become a driving force toward realizing your company's business objectives. After all, just as "you are what you eat," organizations "become what they reward."

1.3 HOW CORPORATE AMERICA *CURRENTLY* LOOKS AT REWARDS

Ask an HR executive: "Do you currently have a reward strategy?" In most cases, the executive will reply, "Of course." And indeed, most HR executives work hard to efficiently manage compensation and benefits programs. The question, however, is effectiveness: Does your company *maximize* its return on human capital? Are you getting the biggest bang for the buck? And, are you *buying* the *right* things? The current tools typically used to manage reward investments (e.g., employee sensing, industry benchmarking, "best practice" reviews) do not provide complete answers to these key questions. As a result, many organizations find themselves in the following reward strategy quandaries.

(a) Piecemeal Solutions

Given the day-to-day nature and structure of their jobs, many HR professionals spend the bulk of their time responding to specific tactical issues and crises. In fact, with the proliferation of the recent HR department downsizings, there is less and less time to invest in overall reward *system* innovation, management, and measurement; however, these factors generally are becoming more—not less—important as overall investments in people grow larger each year.

What's wrong with addressing issues as they come up? Let's look at an example. Because of the diverse nature of one global service company's operations, HR leadership gave significant autonomy to local HR managers in designing and managing its variable pay programs. This practice gave local operations the flexibility to address attraction and retention issues quickly and effectively, or so the company thought. The organization eventually realized that few employees were leaving the firm—not even the worst performers (see Exhibit 1.2). Why? Local managers had created so much complexity in overall reward program design that the company did not realize it had more than 300 separate incentive plans, which, in fact, were subsidizing many of the "subpar" performers. How was this discovered? In an effort to manage its soaring labor costs, HR leadership used innovative, quantitative methods to track where the reward dollars were actually going and measured their impact on turnover and business performance.

Exhibit 1.2 Percentage of Variable Pay Distributed to Subpar Performers as Related to Turnover Rate of Subpar Performers.

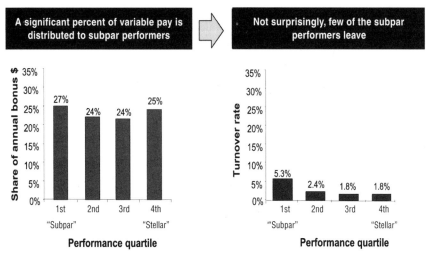

Source: © Mercer Human Resource Consulting, Inc., 2001.

(b) Cost Management

When all else fails, management often turns to HR and says, "We can only afford $X, so next year's compensation increase pool is $X." Or, "benefits can not increase by more than $Y." This approach can make HR executives tear their hair out; yet, most organizations are focusing to some degree on cost management.

As an example, a national medical services organization needed to trim costs. Most executives turned to health benefits as an ideal target. Employees were paid a slight premium above others in the industry; therefore, the executives did not think a reduction in health benefits would materially impact attraction and retention. By going beyond benchmarking and focus groups to analyze employee data, this organization discovered that employee turnover was highly sensitive to benefit reductions—significantly more than to pay changes. In fact, statistical modeling showed that the unanticipated turnover related to this cost management initiative would have had a substantial negative impact on five key measures of business performance, including customer retention, which would far outweigh any cost savings. Only by studying this organization's employee profile and conducting detailed statistical analyses of the business impact of different reward strategies were they able to avoid saving thousands to lose millions.

When you consider that service organizations have a payroll that may represent 40% to 60% of revenue, even small adjustments in rewards can mean an enormous loss or gain.

(c)   Look Inside and Out

How often has this situation happened to you? A member of the executive team enters your office first thing Monday morning and says, "I overheard that one of our competitors is going to pay a premium to attract the best workers in our industry. I want our firm to do that." An obvious problem with this approach is that what's best for one company isn't always right for your business. Best practices and benchmarking are useful tools, but should not be viewed as *the* answers. Best practices, or someone's judgment that what others are doing is the way to go, can serve as a good beginning, but what's good for other organizations—even in the same industry—is not necessarily good for your company. Benchmarking, or a review of what others are doing, is also a good start to determining reward strategy, but it should be just that—a start.

Organizations do look for answers internally as well by conducting interviews of executives, managers, front-line workers, and anyone else on the food chain. But, the information from those sources can be limited and potentially misleading. One problem with asking employees what they want is that their *stated* preferences may not match their *real* preferences. Ask employees if they want higher salaries, they say "absolutely." Statistically analyze the employee data, and often their "real" behaviors (i.e., their decisions to stay or leave) show other aspects of the employment relationship to be far more important.

(d)   Squeaky Wheel

For HR departments with reward strategies in place, politics and departmental turf wars often get in the way of fully executing these strategies. Many corporations throughout America experience a "squeaky wheel syndrome" in which managers who speak the loudest may have undue influence. The department manager who disdains turnover of any employees—good or not so good—shouts loudest at HR and potentially receives a greater bundle of cash with which to pay his or her workers. Because HR cannot respond for certain that the manager's plan does not provide a measurable positive return, HR may lose the case. Without good data to support its decisions, HR is forced to respond to squeaky wheels, often yielding suboptimal results.

1.4   THE HOSPITALITY COMPANY FINDS ITS ANSWERS

(a)   Rewards Reviewed

The hospitality company mentioned at the beginning of this chapter paid out billions to cover employee costs, which represented the largest single expense for the business. The question was how to best allocate annual increases to pay, benefits, training, and so on. For example, what would the company gain by putting another $50 million into benefits?

The organization's goal was to develop a comprehensive understanding of both its current and desired reward strategy, in support of its business objectives. To this end, key executives were interviewed to establish the business context—and related human capital implications—and five years of employee and organizational performance data were statistically analyzed to isolate drivers of employee behavior and property performance. Individual, organizational, and marketplace factors were evaluated independently and in combination. By connecting drivers of employee rewards to property performance, the key components needed for success from the people side of the business were isolated. The result: The company could identify the key skills and outcomes it was looking for and determine the rewards that could support their development (see Exhibit 1.3).

(b)   What Was Discovered . . . For Pay?

Although the organization was providing above-average pay opportunities for its employees in the aggregate, the company could improve its financial performance through additional performance-based pay differentiation. Increased incentive eligibility and opportunity also could lead to enhanced facility performance, generating $3 for every additional dollar paid out.

(c)   What About Benefits?

Analysis showed that the gains associated with higher rates of benefit program participation—particularly retirement and certain dependent health and welfare

Exhibit 1.3   Reward Strategy.

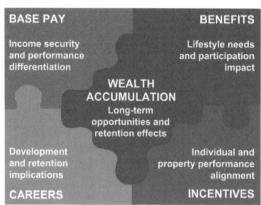

Source: © Mercer Human Resource Consulting, Inc., 2001.

coverages—could outweigh their cost by improving employee retention and property performance.

(d)   And . . . Careers?

The management training program (where managers moved from one property to another) was found to have a positive effect on employees' career opportunities without any negative impact on property performance. In addition, employees who were promoted from hourly to manager status were more likely to stay with the company, while requiring less training than new employees.

The new reward strategy designed as a result of this quantitative analysis would not only pay for itself but would also generate an additional return on investment (ROI) of tens of millions annually.

1.5   HOW CORPORATE AMERICA *MIGHT* LOOK AT REWARDS

The HR industry has traditionally looked at employee data from a "compliance" perspective. Today, it is possible to create much more value using this information—by connecting these data to operational, financial, and marketplace outcomes in order to link people practices to economic results. This section looks at how HR can leverage data to contribute to its organization's bottom line—through a combination of current techniques and some new tools.

(a)   Information Is Power

When your car's engine just does not sound quite right, you obviously know something is wrong. Furthermore, you know that the problem is under the hood or in the car body, and that there generally is a good explanation and remedy. All the information you need to diagnose and fix your car is right there at your fingertips. But where exactly do you look? What is the problem? How do you fix it? How can you make sure it remains fixed? For most people, a trained mechanic with diagnostic tools is the best answer. The good mechanic can study the "symptoms," diagnose the problem, make repairs, retest to be sure it was fixed, and, in the end, hand you the keys to a car that's "good as new." The only caveat to this analogy is that the mechanic must be someone with the integrity and know-how to offer you the best and most cost-effective solution.

An organization contains a vast amount of valuable information, but, like a good mechanic, you must know where, and how, to look. A good place to start is to ask people in the company two basic questions:

1. What is currently rewarded in our organization?
2. What *should* be rewarded to support our organization's business objectives?

Rarely is there complete agreement between the two or even clear concurrence on either point. For example, we often find that rewards emphasize current performance but overlook their influence in motivating and driving the development of the critical skills and competencies needed to meet future business demands; however, management must have perspective about what the root causes of the problem *are* before presenting a case for change. A good HR executive, like a good mechanic, needs to diagnose the problem, have an action plan for fixing it, and show that the resolution will create value—in this case, through better strategic alignment and a stronger ROI.

Not to mix metaphors, but, there's a treasure trove of information stored away about employees. The difficulty is finding, reading, and correctly interpreting the treasure map. This complex process requires a disciplined combination of content knowledge and statistical modeling expertise (linking and evaluating data from multiple sources) to identify untapped opportunities. But, the effort is well worth it when you can report to management that you have just saved your company 3% to 5% of annual labor cost through enhanced productivity and/or reduced expense.

(b)   People Create Competitive Advantage

Just as no two companies are alike, no two workforces are identical. And, different business strategies require different approaches to *human* capital. For example, a firm that needs employees who understand its products, services, systems, and procedures in order for its business to succeed may want to hire people and retain them over their careers. The more experience people have in such a company, the more valuable they may be to that company.

In a rapidly changing industry, however, an organization might want a significant and constant influx of new people because it seeks the latest expertise, which may require *buying* rather than *building* talent. Here, careers might not be as salient as short-term cash and equity. In industries such as aerospace, defense, and high technology, retention may not be as much a concern as attracting key professionals with the latest knowledge. For example, when the defense contract expires, your talent migrates to the next organization—that is, until you win your next big contract.

(c)   Perception Is Not Always Reality

While conducting employee focus groups and surveys is common, the information obtained by these kinds of analyses may only scratch the surface. Employee sensing can provide valuable information about what employees *say* they want, but the data also can be linked to actual employee histories to determine whether these perceptions match behavioral reality. For example, armed with information regarding the *real,* underlying root causes for employee turnover, a company can undertake targeted initiatives, based on:

- Return on investment (ROI)—net impact versus cost.
- Feasibility—how realistic would it be to implement (e.g., administration, management, and employee acceptance).
- Risk—how predictable and/or controllable are affected turnover drivers over time.

For example, a Fortune 500 commercial bank learned that, although exit interviews suggested that pay and workload were the primary drivers of turnover, the *real* factors that most influenced retention were promotion, job mobility, and retention of its better supervisors. The bank was able to use this information to develop a retention strategy focusing on careers and management stability. The results were quick and impressive. Similarly, a Global 500 manufacturing organization learned that, although its employees *perceived* little connection between pay and individual performance, the *real* relationship was consistent and strong. The company was able to use this information to improve communication about rewards and performance management, avoiding significant new—and unnecessary—reward investments.

1.6   HOW TO DEVELOP AN EFFECTIVE PROGRAM

A holistic approach to reward strategy, combined with comprehensive tools to connect employee data to economic outcomes, can have a significant impact on human capital decisions, specifically enhancing business results. This section lays out the process for developing a successful reward strategy by understanding the underlying human capital implications of a firm's business strategy and determining the return on rewards investment (rewards ROI). Three case studies are included at the end of this chapter to show the impact of this approach for three different organizations.

Rewards ROI involves the statistical analysis of employee, operational, financial, and marketplace data to determine the net effects of reward investments on human capital and business outcomes. The compilation, linkage, and analysis of data can save a company a lot of time, money, and headaches by evaluating reward choices *before* making the leap to a new reward strategy. The seven-step plan is detailed as follows:

1. *Review the business environment.* Understand the key factors outside the firm (economic, geographic, regulatory, political, labor, and supplier) that affect internal business and human capital decisions.

2. *Assess the organization's business design.* Establish the business goals, context, and key performance drivers (see Exhibit 1.4).

3. *Examine critical human capital implications.* Articulate the role of people and workforce practices (including rewards, managerial structure, work processes, information and knowledge flows, and decision-making practices) in executing the business strategy (see Exhibit 1.5).

4. *Measure internal human capital reality.* Determine what is rewarded, by qualitatively and quantitatively evaluating current human capital practices (i.e., to find out both what executives and employees *think* is rewarded and what actually *is* rewarded) and the degree to which the marketplace influences the effectiveness of those practices.

5. *Identify gaps and priorities for action.* Look at human capital practices holistically to create the optimal rewards mix to motivate, develop, and in fact drive the workforce based on business objectives (e.g., pay the *right* people the *right* amount for the *right* reasons at the *right* time).

6. *Develop an action plan.* Evaluate the ROI, feasibility, and risks associated with rewards interventions to create a sustainable reward strategy that will both generate bottom-line results and support future business needs.

7. *Implement and monitor results.* Guide communication, administration, and other implementation activities to ensure consistent messaging and strategic alignment (including the creation of a *human capital scorecard* to track progress).

Exhibit 1.4   Organizational Performance Model.

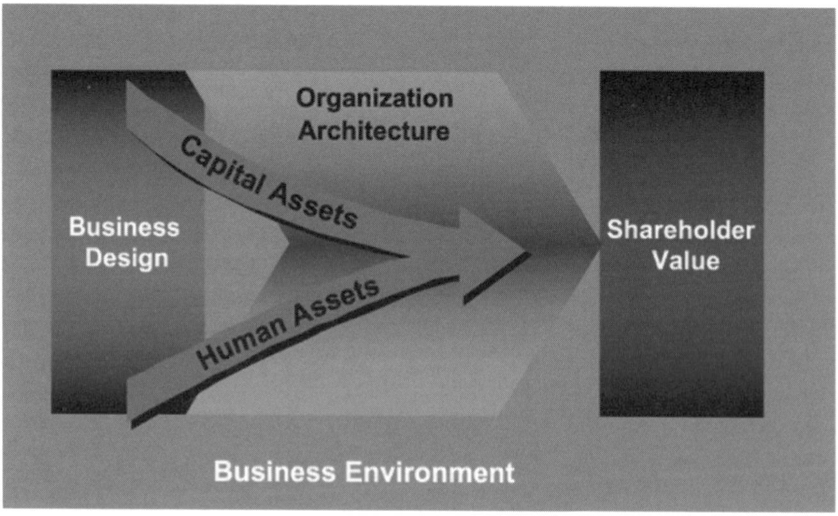

Source: © Mercer Human Resource Consulting, Inc., 2001.

Exhibit 1.5   Human Capital Strategy Model.

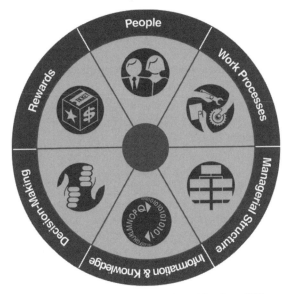

Source: © Mercer Human Resource Consulting, Inc., 2001.

1.7   CASE A: IMPLEMENTING REWARD STRATEGY TO STAY AHEAD IN THE FAST-CHANGING TECHNOLOGY INDUSTRY

(a)   Company

"Digitt," a leading global business services company

(b)   Situation

Digitt's compensation philosophy was to pay for performance. "If your performance helps build the bottom line, you will be rewarded," claimed senior executives. Line managers struggled to balance this pay-for-performance philosophy with a team orientation that was designed to encourage cooperation and innovation. Therefore, when allocating incentive dollars, these line managers did *not* weigh individual performance materially; instead they generally focused on group performance, resulting in minimal differentiation between star and poor performers. The unintended consequences: Digitt's revenues were sluggish, its new businesses were understaffed, few low performers left, and its stock price was plummeting.

(c) Research

How was this disconnect discovered? A quantitative analysis of historical employee, organizational, and external data revealed the following:

- An employee's bonus was more a function of the employee's business unit than his or her individual performance.
- Better employees were not being rewarded for superior performance.
- The bottom 25% of the employees were still receiving about 25% of the "pay-for-performance" pool.
- The company was paying out too much to the *wrong* people for what may— or may not—have been the *right* reasons.

Digitt believed that program *design* dictated program *delivery.* Our experience has taught us that many good plan designs fall short in the implementation stage. For Digitt, plan documents espoused pay for performance, but there was no individual performance management process to facilitate and support pay decisions. Without considering how the elements of rewards and human capital strategy fit together, Digitt was not able to achieve in reality what it had intended.

This rewards allocation issue restrained—and maybe even prevented— Digitt from addressing a critical business crisis. For years, Digitt had dominated its industry . . . until advances in technology shifted service focus from mechanical to digital. As a result, the business landscape changed and Digitt was competing against new technology firms for business as well as the *right* talent. The evolving businesses demanded that management change its talent mix and motivate employees in the new businesses without losing top-performing, long-term employees in the old businesses. Digitt needed to revamp its reward strategy to:

- Attract people with new skills in support of the future business design.
- Manage attrition of employees in the "cash cow" businesses—retaining top-performers but weeding out others, strategically reallocating the limited supply of reward dollars.

(d) Solution

Once Digitt realized that its reward strategy was misaligned (i.e., in and of itself, as well as with its human capital and business strategy), it was able to create an action plan to close the gap.

- *Compensation:* Digitt sought to reallocate compensation dollars from subpar performers in its traditional businesses to stellar performers in its new divisions by:

- Setting up a performance review process to track individual contributions.
- Enforcing performance gates for incentive distributions based on individual performance.
- Maintaining some degree of group incentives to continue to encourage its team orientation and culture.

- *Benefits:* Plans were reviewed by business unit in order to match benefit structures with desired workforce profiles (i.e., Did the human capital strategy rely on tenured employees?).

- *Careers:* The company used its strong reputation for developing talent to leverage its appeal to prospective employees of its fledgling businesses (in competing for talent with newer technology firms, Digitt's ability to offer added job security and broader technical exposure could give it an edge in the marketplace).

(e)   Results

This action plan is being implemented currently and is projected to save Digitt at least 6% of labor cost.

1.8   CASE B: UTILIZING REWARD STRATEGY TO INTEGRATE—M&A OPPORTUNITIES

(a)   Company

"BankCo," a Fortune 500 commercial bank

(b)   Situation

With more than 20,000 employees currently, BankCo had grown substantially in recent years, much of it through an aggressive mergers and acquisitions (M&A) strategy; however, beyond the postacquisition workforce reductions, BankCo had been experiencing an astounding surge in voluntary turnover that was well above industry benchmarks, exceeding 40% among some occupational groups. This trend was hurting the organization through higher labor cost, lost productivity, customer defections, and—most significantly—its inability to manage operations effectively during M&A transitions.

BankCo's HR department had been tracking turnover for some time to determine the extent of the problem. In particular, the HR staff gathered and reviewed reports from employee exit interviews. While the interviews revealed some reasons for departure, for the most part, they were inconclusive. HR needed substantive and precise information in order to move quickly to develop a retention strategy and rally senior line management for implementation.

(c) Research

BankCo accepted that it needed to track what people did—not just what they said—to find the root causes of employees' decisions to remain or depart. Employee, organizational, and marketplace data were statistically analyzed to identify factors that most affected BankCo's turnover. These factors fell into three categories: external market conditions, employee attributes, and organizational practices. The analysis quantified the impact of specific turnover drivers, allowing BankCo to prioritize interventions around those with the highest potential value relative to their costs.

BankCo found that factors relating to the strength and breadth of career opportunity far outweighed pay and other commonly suspected *culprits* as drivers of turnover. The research also showed that managerial turnover spawned great turnover among employees, particularly if those managers were high performers. Thus, focusing on managerial retention strategies would have cascading effects among the broader employee population.

(d) Solution

Interventions included:

- *Compensation:* BankCo had planned to invest in significant market price adjustments to reduce turnover but was able to save these dollars, given the relatively small retention effect.
- *Benefits:* No overhaul was needed in benefit programs either—the big potential retention payoff was in career rewards.
- *Careers:* Turnover could be reduced substantially through much less costly initiatives, including:
  - Improving communication about available career opportunities.
  - Expanding and accelerating promotion and transfer opportunities for high-performing employees.
  - Making more concerted efforts to expand training and broaden employees' job experience within BankCo.

(e) Results

This diagnostic work helped provide the factual basis for HR to make its business case; the hard data was compelling and galvanized CEO and organizationwide support for swift action. Within eight months of implementation of the new strategy, BankCo reported a 20+% reduction in turnover rates and estimated $50+ million in annual savings.

1.9 CASE C: CREATING AN EFFECTIVE GLOBAL REWARD STRATEGY

(a) Company

"EquipCo," a global manufacturer of factory equipment.

(b) Situation

EquipCo, a U.S. multinational company, had expanded its overseas operations significantly in recent years. As a result, HR leadership found itself struggling to apply U.S. policies and programs to non-U.S. operations with inherent and substantial cultural differences. Although there was a desire to maintain global consistency, the organization realized that some practices were not easily transferable across geographies. The company wanted to create a global reward strategy that would:

- Preserve overall *brand image*.
- Ensure critical *skill development* for the organization.
- Reinforce *performance management* standards and objectives.
- Offer a controlled degree of *local flexibility* to ensure market competitiveness and cultural sensitivity.

(c) Research

Through a combination of quantitative and qualitative analyses, looking inside and out, several potential factors were identified that could potentially impede the successful implementation of a global reward strategy at EquipCo:

- *Brand image:* Low levels of collaboration between business units, geographic locations, and functions.
- *Skill development:* Minimal recognition of individual accomplishments and weak long-term incentive compensation.
- *Performance management:* Disparate performance management practices, as well as skewed performance ratings and resulting merit increases:
  - — More than 50% of employees were rated above average.

— Fewer than 2% were rated below average.

— Only a 1% difference in average merit pay increases existed between "stellar" and average performance.

• *Local flexibility:* Inconsistent expectations with respect to risk taking, accountability, and attrition management (voluntary turnover was low overall, especially among "subpar" performers).

(d) Solution

A global reward strategy was designed to address these issues:

• *Brand image:* Establish key marketplace messages that distinguish both the organizational and employment brand across geographies.

• *Skill development:* Identify key individual competencies for future organizational success and build these factors (e.g., risk taking, personal accountability, innovation) into reward system design, particularly focusing on incentive plan improvements.

• *Performance management:* Support a performance culture through performance rating distribution guidelines (i.e., percent rated "stellar," above average, average, and so on), as well as associated dispersion in merit pay increases and transfer/promotion opportunities.

• *Local flexibility:* Provide broad guidelines and minimum compliance requirements globally, but also designate certain opportunities for reward program variation to accommodate differences in business environments, laws, cultures, and so on.

(e) Results

By bridging internal and external viewpoints and data, HR was able to establish global priorities and potential barriers. The new reward strategy is still in the implementation stage, but it is estimated to save 3% to 5% of payroll.

How Can You Tell If Your Reward System May Be Out of Alignment?

1. Reward elements are managed separately, particularly if you have several elements to consider (i.e., multiple incentive plans, independent benefit decision-making processes, decentralized training and development programs, and so on).
2. Reward programs are designed primarily based on competitive, industry, or "best" practices.
3. Reward programs send mixed messages.
4. Delivery of rewards is not tied to program intent (i.e., everyone in a division gets the same percent bonus payout even though the plan calls for dispersion based on performance).
5. There is difficulty in attracting and retaining key talent.
6. Pay, benefits, and career programs are not well integrated (i.e., there is no cohesive strategy).

Chapter 2

Variable Pay Programs: Pay for Results*

Rose Marie Orens and Vicki J. Elliott

Everyone seems to agree that linking employee pay to performance is the most effective compensation structure to encourage organizational improvement efforts, but in recent years, it has become increasingly difficult to build performance into the standard merit increase matrix. In the days when merit increases averaged 7% to 10%, high-performing employees could expect to receive bigger salary increases than their lower-performing peers. Today, with annual merit increases typically at 3% to 5%, it's almost impossible to significantly adjust the salaries of individual employees up or down based on high or low performance.

In order to replace, or augment, merit increases, many companies are implementing pay-for-performance incentive plans. These plans take many forms. Individual incentives, group or team incentives, management incentives, and sales incentives are most common.

Companies that have created variable pay plans have done so for good business reasons. They have found that a pay plan that pays for improved business results translates into more customers, higher profitability, and a more motivated workforce.

2.1 A PROCESS FOR IMPLEMENTING VARIABLE PAY

What's most important in formulating a variable pay reward system is to understand the key performance results and desired behaviors you seek to motivate. A plan can then be structured to encourage and reinforce those results and behaviors. The successful implementation of such a program is a multistep process that typically occurs in three phases:

*The authors wish to thank Melissa L. Burek and Kimberley N. Dabrowski for their assistance in preparing this chapter.

1. Awareness and understanding
2. Plan design
3. Implementation, feedback, and administration

Let us look in more detail at each of these phases and the various steps that constitute each of them.

(a)   Step 1: Develop Objectives, Including a Balanced Scorecard

The first step is to begin with a clear understanding of the organizational direction and preferred outcomes. By doing so we can develop a strategy and action plan to achieve the objectives. Most organizations have spent considerable time and effort in determining and codifying their mission and vision statements. Some organizations have even gone so far as to literally cast them in stone, so as to proudly exhibit them in their front lobby. Many have satisfied themselves with this herculean task. Others have moved beyond, going to the next step of developing a clear set of strategies to achieving each and every one of the visions and mission statements. The next critical step is to compare these strategies to the critical success factors ascribed to each area of the organization's supply chain. Once the critical success factors are known, the organization can set about determining the key performance drivers needed to be improved on and tracked for each layer of the organization. This can mean each division or each Strategic Business Unit (SBU), or each functional group, or even each functional and cross-functional team. A useful approach to identifying the key performance indicators (KPIs) is to use the four perspectives of the Kaplan and Norton Balanced Scorecard:

1. Financial
2. Customer
3. Process
4. Growth

From this myriad of segregated performance drivers, the few interlinked compensable factors can now be readily determined.

Typically, a project design team represents most of the key constituencies: major functional employee groups, finance, human resources (HR), management information systems (MIS), training, operations, and consultants. In many cases, the team is composed of line management, HR professionals, and the consultants. It has decision-making responsibility and oversight for plan design and administration, performance measurement, and communications. The team also determines the appropriate role of consultants and other facilitating resources. Finally, the team prepares a set of guiding principles by which it is chartered to perform its function and by which its success or failure will be measured.

(b)   Step 2: Conduct a Business Environmental Assessment and Feasibility Assessment

The business environmental assessment is typically done by the same project design team. Its job is to now oversee data collection and analysis. Using both internal and external data, the team determines how current performance compares with past performance and how the organization compares to others in the same industry. An environmental assessment is focused on economic, demographic, HR, sales and marketing, and technological trends. Once the external factors have been reduced to a workable analysis, the internal factors need to be addressed through a feasibility assessment.

The feasibility assessment is conducted to assess the appropriateness of variable pay in an organization or in any particular part of it. It is often used to identify the organizational, administrative, and cultural strengths and barriers within the organization. In addition, it is most often used to determine whether the potential exists for enough savings to justify the development costs of the plan—a concept known as *affordability*. The costs of correcting organizational weaknesses need to be calculated with respect to the potential savings generated by the plan.

Feasibility data can be collected by surveys, interviews, observations, reviewing records and data, and by focus groups. Typically, a combination of methods is used. Data collected during the process are weighed carefully to determine whether a variable plan will help the organization achieve its objectives and to determine the current organizational strengths and weaknesses with regard to sharing of gains from improved results.

(c)   Step 3: Conduct an Employee Readiness Diagnostic

Before designing a variable pay program, the project design team should determine that management and employees are indeed ready for variable pay. This involves gathering baseline data regarding employee perceptions of current processes that relate to a variable pay program. Typically a questionnaire is used that asks employees such questions as

• Do you understand the organization's direction, mission, and vision?
• Does management encourage employees to use initiative?
• Is the current compensation system equitable?
• Does it reward good performance?
• How do you evaluate the quality of current performance measurement?

Focus groups may also be formed to provide qualitative input on employee readiness for variable pay. In unionized settings, they can also provide information on how the union will react to the variable pay program introduction. Besides documenting employee perceptions and organization culture, the readiness diagnostic identifies issues relating to employee demographics, plan design, and implementation and initiates the communication process.

For instance, the following are typical areas of concern within the demographic framework:

- Average age, tenure, and receptivity to change of the employees
- Willingness to improve individual and/or group performance
- Willingness to share information
- Level of technical competence
- Ability to work as a team
- Belief that they can and should participate in the rewards
- Prior efforts to improve the organization/work group performance

(i) The "Must-Haves" There are only a few hard-and-fast requirements for a variable pay program to work:

- *Reliable performance data.* Before an organization can measure improvements in performance, it needs to know where it is with respect to that performance. This requires a sound database. If the data do not exist, the data collection process should continue until a database can be established. If the market is seasonal, growing, or shrinking, adjustments can be modeled, but only if one has sufficient data. Therefore, variable pay plans are not often implemented in startup situations.
- *Open sharing of relevant data.* Employees need access to the data that determine their payout. They need to trust that the data are fairly determined and administered.
- *A plan design that is viewed as fair by the employees.* Employees need to believe that the assessment of the performance results and the resulting payout is fair and not open to manipulation by management. Employee involvement in the development and administration of the variable pay plan is a way to achieve this.

(d) Step 4: Develop a Compensation Strategy Statement

The job of the project design team at this step of stage one is to identify the active barriers to success and to develop strategies to overcome or neutralize them. Strategies might involve the commitment of resources, time, or training. They also might involve recognizing that a culture change has to occur before employee involvement and a variable pay program can be fully developed. It may necessitate the identification of methods for supporting and facilitating culture change, while encouraging employees and managers to recognize the organization's evolution.

Because a variable pay program exists alongside other compensation and benefit programs, the organization needs to develop a statement of compensation strategy that defines the specific characteristics of the performance/reward structure and creates a framework for compensation decisions. As with steps 1, 2, and 3, such a strategy begins with the vision and mission of the organization, its business strategy, and its philosophy of rewarding employees or associates. The team correlates pay practices with performance by defining the role played by each element of compensation (i.e., base pay, merit pay, competency pay, special incentives, sales commissions, annual and long-term incentives) and analyzing its effect on the strategic goals of the organization or company. Any overlapping of roles and objectives should now be addressed. While variable pay should harmonize with the other elements in the reward system, it should not duplicate them.

Therefore, it is necessary to establish priorities based on the organization's business goals, employee groups involved, the organization's competitive pay position, and the desired mix of fixed and variable elements.

(e)   Step 5: Select a Variable Pay Program

Several plan designs may potentially meet an organization's or company's objectives:

* *Gainsharing:* Sharing productivity or profitability improvements with eligible employees.
* *Goalsharing:* Similar to gainsharing but emphasizing goals to be accomplished rather than past performance.
* *Profit sharing:* A percentage of income is shared across all employee groups, usually on a pro-rata basis.
* *Team/group incentives:* An incentive based on the combined accomplishments of a team or group, typically against specified goals.
* *Individual incentives:* An incentive based on achieving individual goals.
* *Competency-based incentives:* An incentive payment linked to achieving or applying new or critical competencies.

(f)   Step 6: Design the Plan

The team prepares a written document for senior management approval that addresses four major areas:

- Basic assumptions and constraints of the plan (e.g., eligibility, tie to business plan, costs, funding)
- Performance periods, measurement criteria, and goals
- Award levels (e.g., threshold, target, and stretch maximum awards paid as a percentage of salary or in specified proportions to all participants)
- Timing of the payment and type of payout (e.g., some plans pay in stock or combination of stock and cash, thus linking the reward to shareholder value creation)

There are no rules as to which factors should be included; however, experience and data drawn from independent studies indicate that the best approach is the one that will ensure that the plan's objectives are met, and any factors that help measure that are appropriate. It's also important to remember that the rule of thumb for variable pay KPIs, or what is sometimes called *metrics,* is "the simpler the better." There are three commonly used factors—financial, productivity, and quality.

(i) Financial Financial factors are typically those used in the internal management reporting processes and include various forms of sales/revenues and profitability (operating income margins or operating expense or value-based measures, including economic profit or cash flow). These metrics are aligned at the team or business unit level with those of larger business entities at the group or plant levels. Financial measures can also be used as overall "triggers" for funding incentive plans. In these cases a financial revenue goal is identified below which no incentives would be paid either to an individual unit or across a broader group. It is also common for each financial measure to have a stated threshold below which no incentive will be accrued for an individual measure.

(ii) Productivity There are many ways to calculate and measure productivity. Some organizations use a single ratio or metric to keep the formula calculation simple and easy to understand. Others use multiple ratios or metrics, with different calculations for different product or service lines. Whatever the calculation is, productivity in its simplest form is the relationship of input to output.

There are great variations in calculating the input side of the productivity formula. Variable pay formulas often include direct, controllable costs, such as labor, material, inventory, contracted services, and utility costs that participants can influence and in many cases control.

(iii) Quality It is important to include a quality measure along with the productivity measure in any variable pay formula. Without a quality component, the formula or metrics may encourage production or services that do not meet quality standards. For example, faster production of a manufactured item does not meet

organizational objectives if too many items are faulty. Providing quick response to phone calls is fine but the true objective is customer satisfaction, which is a measure of quality and not of productivity per se.

In some situations, quality measures cannot occur simultaneously. For example, in a computer service and repair operation, it may not be feasible to double-check each repair without doing double work; however, records can be kept for each technician reflecting the percentage of work that comes back, yielding a quality measure.

In some variable pay plans, the quality measure may function as a *trigger*. If the quality standards are met, the payment occurs as calculated by the formula. If quality standards are not met, then the payment is canceled or reduced. For example, a manufacturing company may adjust its payment according to the quality of the product at a final inspection point. If rejects per million are greater than 1,000, the payment is only 50% of what the formula calculated; if the rejects are 150 to 999, the payment is 75%; if the rejects are less than 150, the payment is 100% of what the formula calculated.

When identifying KPIs for variable pay, it is important to remember that the measurement of these indicators is openly shared between the organization and the participants. Experience shows that when this is a mandatory part of the program structure, any employee who wants to can calculate the potential payment by providing the relevant data. These metrics need to be from trusted sources that the participants believe are not vulnerable to manipulation.

(g) Step 7: Design the Plan—Participation and Frequency

All variable pay programs require organizations to generate data and calculate payouts within a relatively short timeframe. This is especially true of team/group incentives and gainsharing plans, which often pay out on a quarterly (and sometimes monthly) basis. The organization or company must decide how data will be tracked, who will have access to the data, and how payouts will be made. Effective administration is, therefore, critical to plan success and there are many issues to address and anticipate. These may include such issues as the impact of overtime on the plan payout, involvement of the payroll department, impact of the plan on benefits, and record keeping.

Administrative decisions are not limited to those mentioned previously. As examples, let's examine two other decisions at a slightly greater depth:

- Participation
- Frequency of payout

(i) Setting the Participation Policy   The appropriate policy regarding plan participation depends on the organization's situation. There is no "right or wrong" answer for all plans. It is important, however, that these issues be discussed, and

that a policy is set. A fundamental decision — one that affects participation policies — is the question of "what is the purpose of the payment?" Is it a payment to an individual for contributing to work accomplished? Is it a payment to all members of a team for accomplishing the work? Who needs to participate to ensure the objectives are reached? The answers to these questions will, in part, determine the type of policies that are set with regard to participation.

(ii) Deciding How Frequently the Plan Will Pay Out   Some variable pay plans pay out annually, whereas others pay out weekly. Most variable pay plans pay out quarterly or annually. As a general observation, the more frequent the payout calculation, the stronger the line of sight between pay and performance. How frequently to pay out is a decision governed by the organization's performance reporting and administrative conditions. The answer will depend on how often data are available, as well as the nature of the data themselves. If the data are highly variable, or if there is drastic seasonality in the data, then longer timeframes may be more appropriate.

(h) Step 8: "What-If" Testing

Testing minimizes the chance of any unexpected results once the plan is up and running. Testing a prospective plan involves developing retrospective and prospective "what if?" cost models at various levels of performance. For example, how would the plan have performed if it had been implemented last year? For the last two years? For the last three years? What would the payouts be under various scenarios based on achieving the threshold, target, and stretch goals?

Our experience has shown that in addition to the quantitative testing, it is often helpful to subject the plan to a reality test by asking focus groups of employees to review it and possibly even piloting the plan to selected groups.

(i) Step 9: Develop a Transition Approach and Pilot the Plan

Integrating the new plan with the existing compensation and reward systems must be carefully managed. Since the new plan will impact the company's base salary programs, total costs must be accurately anticipated, the switch to the new plan carefully timed, and the changes fully understood and communicated. Whether the transition is immediate or through a phase-in process, a temporary pilot program is highly recommended.

A pilot program permits the company or organization to evaluate performance measures, potential results, costs, and employee reaction to the new program. A pilot program can focus on a large group of representative employees within the entire company or on a smaller unit or department. While "greenfield" operations — those created within the past 1–2 years — may look suitable because there is no existing culture to change from, there may also be insufficient historical metrics from which to design improvements. By using a balanced business scorecard, one can mitigate some of these metrics problems. The focus can be shifted toward the fulfillment of service level agreements and away from incremental improvement; however, this judgment needs to be made based on observation and cultural assessment, as opposed to a "general rule."

Whatever pilot group is chosen, it should have the following characteristics:

- Enough critical mass to be meaningful
- Average performance, not the best or the worst
- Management that embraces the new plan
- Credibility within the organization as a whole

(j)   Step 10: Establish a Communications/Education Program

A communications/education program instructs employees on the purpose of the variable pay plan. It can serve to educate the organization in areas such as supply chain management, economic value added, and balanced business scorecard. Organizations have used this opportunity to provide employees with a grounding in business fundamentals, the importance of participation and teamwork, the mechanisms for sharing feedback, and the mechanisms of keeping participants informed.

It includes a strategy for plan introduction to give employees an immediate level of understanding and for ongoing communications explaining performance goals, payouts, and refinements to the plan, once it is implemented.

(k)   Step 11: Implement the Plan

The implementation phase of any variable pay plan is important to its success. This is the first time that employees will see it unveiled in its entirety. Implementation typically begins with an oral, written, or video communication to employees from the CEO or unit head. It is normally followed by rollout meetings and written communications explaining the details of the plan.

In addition to written communications, employees should have access to the formal plan document. The employee communications about the plan take many forms, but in general they should explain:

- The plan and its objectives
- How the plan will affect each employee in the long term and on a day-to-day basis
- How the plan works

- How the plan will affect parallel programs, such as existing incentives, base salary, skill-based pay, recognition rewards, or employee benefits
- The effective dates of the plan

Training is a major commitment on the part of the company and the project design team—training for the supervisors, employees, and teams. The following issues need to be addressed in the training sessions:

- Awareness of the business issues surrounding the business—would include ways in which employees can contribute to the success of the business
- What variable pay is and how it can help address the business issues raised earlier
- How the plan works
  - Review the plan and the feasibility study
  - Outline specific needs
  - Outline ways in which the KPIs and factors will address these needs
- Review the reporting system
  - What types of resources are available (understanding financial data, production data, and quality data)?
  - How will data be delivered to the employees?
  - How can employees analyze/interpret it?
  - What should they do with the information that they get from reports?
- How each employee can impact the factors that will influence the success of the company or business unit as appropriate
- Importance of employee involvement
  - Not individuals working harder, but groups figuring out how to work smarter
  - Individual roles
  - Team roles
  - Meetings
  - Involvement process
  - Administration

(I) Step 12: Integrate the Plan into the Organization

The company or organization develops management and employee initiatives that link the new reward program to other company or organization programs. These other programs may include the performance management system and other similar employee involvement programs. For example, if the new variable pay program is team-based, the company may have to modify an existing performance management system to accommodate team evaluations and other multi-source feedback systems. It may also be necessary to identify training and development needs and to redefine employee and supervisory roles.

(m) Step 13: Monitor the Program and Provide Feedback on an Ongoing Basis

To ensure ongoing plan effectiveness, the original goals, plan design, performance criteria, and employee understanding and acceptance should be monitored periodically. For example, many organizations and companies monitor their performance objectives quarterly to determine whether performance objectives are reasonable—that is, not so modest as to offer little or no motivation to employees and associates, nor so ambitious that employees become demoralized by their inability to achieve success. Financial results also have to be monitored to gauge the company's ability to make payments under the program and to determine the linkage to shareholder values at the business unit/corporate level.

The plan should be monitored on a regular basis. Many companies solicit feedback from employees about midway through the plan year. (Others gather information monthly or quarterly.) Some do this formally, with a survey, whereas others do it informally. This feedback serves as a source of information about the employees' views on how the plan is working. This monitoring is typically done by the variable pay leadership group (or the human resources department) and covers process issues, business issues, and administrative issues. The purpose of this monitoring is to identify any potential problems before they become impediments to the plan or to the day-to-day running of the business.

(n) Step 14: Refine and Continue the Variable Pay Program

Adjustments should be made to the variable pay program as the need arises. These changes may involve expanding the eligibility to new groups of employees, modifying the weighting of performance criteria, making a transition from macro to micro performance measures, and enhancing recordkeeping and administrative efficiency. Whatever the change, it should be logical, deliberate, rooted in outcomes, and fully communicated to employees.

2.2 CASE STUDY: GAINSHARING PLAN

Many organizations that implement variable pay/employee reward programs, particularly within a manufacturing environment, do so with the intention of improving productivity and/or reducing costs.

Organizations that have successfully implemented gainsharing, goalsharing, or team incentive plans attribute an equal share of the success to behavioral changes in employees, as well as to quantifiable improvements.

Such was the case with a private, nonunionized company, with approximately 300 employees. The company belongs to a consortium of suppliers for an American subsidiary of a foreign automotive company.

(a) Initial Situation

The company was in the midst of a critical situation with its inability to break even over the past several years. Quality had been suffering and, more important, morale was at an all-time low. The company did not have the infrastructure, including human resources, critical to surviving cyclical product demand cycles and increasing cost and quality pressures; however, management did feel that with increasing demand for plastics products, along with planned capital improvements and more strict adherence to quality control, the company had the potential to start making a profit. Management was also fully aware that employee relations problems would be instrumental to a turnaround.

Our overall approach to implementing a variable pay system included the following general steps:

- Develop a design team at the plant level.
- Conduct an environmental assessment, including an employee readiness diagnostic.
- Design a gainsharing program.
- Obtain employee feedback, train supervisors, and communicate the plan.
- Implement the plan.

(b) Incentive Plan Design

In the initial stages, the design team reviewed the company's business objectives, financial performance results over the past several years, and results of the employee readiness diagnostic. Based on the review, the team developed a set of objectives for the gainsharing plan to serve as the foundation for its design. The objectives were:

- Support and promote company goals of profitability, reliability, organization vitality, increased productivity, and safety.
- Achieve profitability and targeted performance levels.
- Reward productivity at the plant, above prior year performance levels.
- Provide opportunity for employees to share in increased earnings through improved plant performance.

- Maintain emphasis on quality, customer focus, and continuous improvement.
- Align the interests of the company and its employees.
- Contribute toward higher employee morale and foster team oriented environment.

(c) Plan Framework

The team worked through numerous design sessions to determine the framework of the plan, including key performance indicators, modifying factors, overall plan trigger, and funding/payout formulas, as well as sharing ratios and eligibility rules.

(i) Key Performance Indicators (KPIs)   At the heart of any gainsharing plan are the KPIs upon which improvements will be measured and financial gains shared with employees. It is imperative that KPIs are "self-funding" so that the plan will pay for itself through productivity gains and/or cost reductions. The KPIs must be measurable, with proper systems in place to track and communicate results. KPIs should also be independent of one another so that any improvements and generated gains will not be "double counted." Ideally, KPIs should be measured on an overall team (i.e., plant) basis to strengthen team-oriented behavior and not individual positions, departments, or groups against one another.

Given the lack of sophisticated accounting and management information systems in place at the plant, the design team was somewhat limited in selecting KPIs. The more commonly used productivity measurements, such as yield and material/labor cost per unit, were not well tracked, so the team finally agreed to the following KPIs: scrap/reject, supply expense, and gross margin. It was agreed that "gross margin" did not provide a very well understood or meaningful line-of-sight measurement for employees and that once the new accounting system was in place, a more direct productivity measurement would be incorporated into the plan.

(ii) Modifying Factors   The design team also determined that two other criteria were critical to the plant's performance and quality operations, yet these performance indicators did not directly generate funds based on their improvement. As such, both indicators were incorporated into the plan as "modifiers."

The modifying factors—safety (OSHA recordables) and back-ordered shipments—were designed to increase or decrease the overall fund of generated monies (from the three self-funding KPIs) based on the degree of improvement on these factors.

(iii) Plan Funding Formulas and Performance Thresholds   The next step for the design team was to develop performance thresholds for each

measure that would need to be met and exceeded before any associated gains would be contributed to the gainsharing pool. Because gainsharing plans are not budget-based plans, thresholds are typically developed based on historical performance levels and the premise that any improvement beyond the prior year's performance reflects gains to the company. In this case, the company set the performance threshold for every measure at the prior year's actual year-end level; performance targets established by the company's business plan were not used.

The next step required working closely with financial personnel to determine the exact funding associated with incremental improvements on each factor. The method to develop the "funding formulas" involves examining prior year cost and productivity relationships and forecasted spending in each area. It is important that the amount of dollar gains contributed to the gainsharing pool for associated levels of improvement on each measure (or KPI) can be clearly communicated to employees so that rewards are clearly linked with desired behavior and performance results.

(iv) Plan Trigger   The plan framework requires one additional element, the "plan trigger," which serves as an overall plan threshold or "yes/no" switch as to whether any gainsharing payouts will be made based on KPI improvements. The plan trigger functions as a safety net and ensures that the company can afford the plan and that the plan's cost comes from incremental gains.

At this company, the most logical plan trigger was profitability. Simply put, if the company did not break even (profitability > $0.01), "all bets were off," and the plan would not pay out. Examples of other plan thresholds may include return on sales, return on assets, or nonfinancial criteria such as quality.

(v) Other Design Criteria   At this point, the basic plan construct had been determined and the design team had to make decisions regarding eligibility, measurement periods, and sharing ratios.

It was determined that 50% of the gainsharing pool would be shared with employees and 50% would remain with the company. The sharing ratio may differ depending on the stage of the pay plan in the organization, and it may also differ for each KPI, although this will complicate the plan. It was also decided that performance would be measured and corresponding payouts made on a quarterly basis.

The final decision point focused on whether payouts would be made as a constant percentage of employee wages or as an equal amount shared with all eligible participants. The company decided to divide the gainsharing pool equally among all participants, thus reinforcing the message that success of the company is a result of overall team efforts and contributions and would be rewarded as such.

(d)   Plan Testing and Cost Analyses

At this stage, the plan design was integrated into a computer model and was tested using historical performance data and various prospective performance scenarios, to determine the plan's overall cost and award levels under each scenario. The design team needed to have a comfort level that employee payouts would be meaningful enough to influence behavior and reward for results. From the company's perspective, the plan had to provide sufficient performance improvements for the level of payout made.

Many sensitivity analyses were conducted to demonstrate the level of performance results that the company could expect compared to total payouts. Given years of zero profitability, management felt hard-pressed to reward employees if productivity gains did no more than offset the payouts. At the same time, management also knew that a different approach was needed to drive organizational change, embrace employees as viable team members instrumental to success, and challenge them to act as business partners.

After numerous plan refinements and testing, the design team obtained plan approval from top management and was presented with a mandate to ensure that the plan was well communicated and understood by employees before implementation.

(e)   Plan Communication

The design team was aware from the diagnostic results that communications were generally perceived as being very poor at the plant, and employee understanding of the plan and performance expectations would be critical. The team therefore implemented a thorough five-step approach to communications:

1.   Conducted a select number of employee and supervisor focus groups for feedback and reaction to the plan design.

2.   Developed a detailed information binder for all first-line supervisors (and their management) that included a summary of the plan design, employee readiness diagnostic results, and a slide show for the general employee population with detailed explanations of each slide and potential questions and answers that could be expected from employees.

3.   Conducted training sessions for all first-line supervisors, so they could educate their employees on plan mechanics and their role in contributing to company performance goals. It was important for supervisors to be able to field employee questions regarding the plan and serve as champions of the program on a daily basis. If the supervisor did not understand and support the program, we could not expect employees to commit to the program. Including supervisors in these communications efforts at the front end was one of the most effective elements of our implementation.

4. Introduced the plan to the general employee population through a slide presentation done by the company's HR manager that summarized the program in approximately 12 slides and lasted less than 30 minutes. The presentation was followed by a general question-and-answer session, and employees were provided with a brief foldout brochure that highlighted key program features.

5. Supported the plan with written communications material posted in the plant lobby and throughout the plant that summarized the program in a graphical chart format with attachments summarizing monthly KPI performance and award calculations.

(f)　Ongoing Role of Design Team Throughout Implementation

The charter of the design team for the first year was to meet at the end of each month to summarize performance results and monitor gainsharing program progress. The team was also responsible for quarterly payout determinations and ongoing communication efforts to employees and top management.

The team planned to meet again after three months of full implementation (the pilot period) and then again before year end, so the KPIs and performance thresholds could be revised for the second plan year.

(g)　Plan Results

The gainsharing program has been in place for more than two years. For the first two quarterly performance periods, no payout was generated from the program. Since that time, however, there have been six consecutive quarterly payouts. Performance in two areas has improved dramatically and had a significant impact on company results. Use of gross margin as a KPI continues to be suboptimal, but it will remain in place until the new accounting system is installed. The company has become profitable over the last fiscal year, and profits are now being projected to increase over the next three years.

Although the company does not have sophisticated management information systems, management notes that quality and productivity have, in fact, improved. Management attributes much of the improvement to capital investments and other plant initiatives but clearly acknowledges the role of the gainsharing program. Assessing the role of the gainsharing program, company management cites that the greatest benefit from the program thus far is the enhanced focus and understanding of business issues on the part of employees.

Management indicates that after a year and a half, employees have "bought in" to the program and have become interested in operating/financial information as it relates to plant performance and the gainsharing program. According to one executive, "The greatest benefit of our program is that associates are in tune with real business issues, and their energies, for the most part, have become focused on what employees can do to improve overall conditions."

While the company is still impacted by broader influences, such as foreign exchange rate fluctuations and Environmental Protection Agency (EPA) regulations, the program has impacted the organization from the bottom up, and employee morale and teamwork have noticeably improved. The company president made the following statement:

> Associates feel as if they have an inherent stake in the outcome of the business. The gainsharing checks have not doubled anyone's income, but associates feel a great sense of pride in our accomplishment. The gainsharing program has made great strides in improving morale and has contributed to our ability to double the size of our facility and better service customers through higher-quality products.
>
> Company President

2.3   TEAM INCENTIVES

The business strategies in most organizations today require people to collaborate on addressing the needs of their customers. The nature of work in the 21st century requires multiple skills, enormous speed, and innovation. This makes it imperative for individuals to share information and knowledge and collaborate to achieve the best result. Measuring and rewarding individuals for solo performances no longer makes sense if teaming is necessary.

Team incentive plan designs focus everyone on common shared goals. If the team wins together, everybody gains. These types of plans encourage people to be concerned about everyone's contribution, not simply their own. Thus, behaviors such as helping to train others, sharing valuable information, and accessing and introducing people with the most knowledge about the product/service and customer's need begin to take over instead of individually competitive, protective, controlling behaviors.

Because there are different types of team structures, team incentive designs vary depending on the team's role, purpose, size, and makeup. The line of sight to results, the time horizon, and the group dynamics of the team are impacted by whether the team is large versus small, has members at multiple organizational levels versus peers, is cross-functional in nature versus homogeneous, or is temporary/ad hoc versus longer term/permanent. Some organizations have even sought to design plans that work more like a true partnership with rewards shared among large numbers of participants based on the value created for the total entity or business (Exhibit 2.1).

Typical issues that arise in the development of team-based incentive plans include:

* *How to define the team.* Is the natural team the entire company, a large or small business unit, a staff function? Is the need for teaming fairly permanent,

Exhibit 2.1   Partnership-Like Incentive Design.

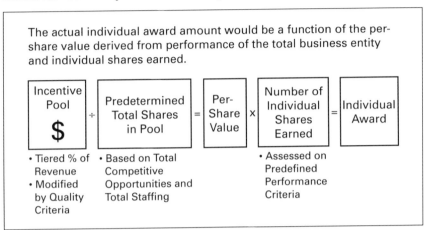

The actual individual award amount would be a function of the per-share value derived from performance of the total business entity and individual shares earned.

Incentive Pool $	÷	Predetermined Total Shares in Pool	=	Per-Share Value	×	Number of Individual Shares Earned	=	Individual Award
• Tiered % of Revenue • Modified by Quality Criteria		• Based on Total Competitive Opportunities and Total Staffing				• Assessed on Predefined Performance Criteria		

more annual in nature, or project driven. Defining the team is a critical part of the design phase. Clearly, multiple teams may exist within the company at any time. Some will stay, but others will come together and disband and come together again in a different form.

- *How to distribute team awards to team members.* One could argue that every team member should receive the same amount of reward if it's a true team incentive; however, it is also true that roles and levels tend to vary within the team, which also argues for aligning potential payout opportunities with those roles. A methodology that has proved useful in doing this is to pay all team members a competitive and equitable percentage of salary based on their role/level. This approach recognizes level differences. In other cases, flat dollar amounts are used to make equivalent awards where level has no distinct benefit to the process. It is important to state these opportunities upfront so everyone understands what they are.

- *How to recognize differences in individual performance among team members.* This is a delicate matter that, if not handled carefully, can be disruptive to the whole team approach. Some suggestions here include getting the team involved in evaluating each other's contribution to the team results either through a peer review process or open team discussion. Some have used a "most valuable player" approach to providing special recognition to key individuals, who then may receive an additional award (not always monetary) for their performance contributions. Others have chosen to base part of the incentive award opportunity on team performance and part of it on individual performance so that the evaluation is clearly twofold. Under this arrangement, it is important for the team portion of the award to be at least equal to, if not greater than, the individual portion in order to maintain the teaming behaviors and focus sought in the plan objectives.

- *How to deal with "free ride" employees.* Anyone who has implemented a team incentive plan has faced this question many times in the planning process. The reality is that generally the other team members take care of this problem through peer pressure and helping others to perform better; however, if the individual continues to be a nonperformer, the organization needs to be prepared to either coach the person toward improved performance or get them out of the role on a timely basis. As a failsafe, it is a good idea to require a specified minimum level of performance (e.g., satisfactory performance review) in order for an individual to be paid an incentive award for team performance.

- *How to handle changes in team membership.* The level at which "team" is defined should be examined carefully, so as not to discourage desirable movement and collaboration among the various groups. If, for example, it is important for staff in one area to be flexible and frequently help or work in other areas, the "team" should encompass the broader related areas. To the degree that changes in team membership naturally occur but on an infrequent basis, changes may be necessary in the performance expectations of the team until it has time to return to a more steady state.

- *How to strengthen line of sight.* Depending on the size of the team and the performance measures chosen to gauge performance results, education and communication may become important to getting everyone on the team to understand how they can impact the results. Larger, multilevel teams in particular need to have the picture painted more clearly because they are often less able to see their direct impact. This fact argues for a more "open book management" approach to sharing goals, results, and the details impacting them with all members of the "team," however it's defined. It helps if performance measures are not all financial in nature. A balanced scorecard approach that includes customer, process, and growth measures in addition to financial measures usually aids in getting people to more readily see how they can impact results.

Team reward approaches bring with them important implications for other management areas:

- Greater team participation in the goal-setting process
- Timely reports on team performance against goals
- Opportunities for regular group communication on improvement ideas, problem solving, and performance feedback
- Staffing criteria oriented to teamwork, mutual respect, and high achievement, as well as cross-functional/skill potential

- Opportunities provided for broader cross-functional knowledge and process skills training

(a)   Individual and Team Incentives

Some positions' roles and results are traceable primarily to individual effort. It may be the sales area, technology, or a staff function such as finance, legal, or human resources to name a few, where these individual contributors can be found. Identifying the right form of variable pay requires a fair amount of customization and understanding of the position's linkage to the organization's mission.

Individual incentives can have strong line of sight. The individual's influence is known, and measures of success can be fairly and easily identified. In some cases, other support positions participate in the program as well. The principles we've covered by identifying objectives, conducting interviews with management, creating focus groups with plan participants and support areas, determining the critical success factors, and other techniques are identical to the steps previously discussed for variable pay and team-based plans; however, the way the plan looks will differ.

(b)   Case Study: Individual and Team Incentives for Relationship Management

U.S. industry knows that the best customer any organization has is an existing one, that servicing a current customer is easier and cheaper than finding new ones; however, most individually driven incentive plans are based on new business or new clients. Companies have only recently become aware that they lose more business out their back door each year than they bring in the front door, thereby defeating their efforts to grow their customer base and accompanying revenues. Fortunately, incentive compensation—variable pay, well-designed— can help companies out of this dilemma.

This case study relates to a project undertaken for a financial services firm, but it is applicable to any organization that maintains sales and customer service as part of its sales organization and where responsibility for servicing and retaining accounts resides with individuals who are also expected to bring in new business.

A design team of senior management, human resources, finance, and regional managers was created. This group agreed that the current program's focus on new business (and corresponding lack of focus on existing business) was a major deterrent to reaching its growth goals. Focus groups were held with the individuals, whose feedback indicated that they had been doing what was valued by the organization, bringing in new accounts. They did not perceive that they were responsible for any ongoing involvement with clients unless they were contacted by them directly. Based on this feedback and the change in organizational direction, senior management implemented a reorganization. Large (or potentially large) relationships were assigned to individuals who were now retitled Relationship Managers (RMs). Books of business were calibrated, and RMs received in-depth information about their individual accounts—both size and the services currently being used. Staff were assigned to each RM to support the customer service aspects of the position (Relationship Associates, or RAs). Sometimes a staff member was assigned to multiple RMs or multiple staff to one RM depending on the size of their book of business. The design team met on several occasions to finalize the plan design. Specifically, it articulated the following guiding principles for plan design:

- Enable the business overall to grow by XX%.
- Demonstrate a higher retention of existing business through implementation of best practices research on customer service.
- Develop a relationship culture toward their clients and colleagues.
- Reward outstanding performance—financially and in service.
- Motivate teamwork.
- Provide opportunity for 75th percentile pay against a specific group of peers.
- Maintain costs to a reasonable amount of additional, incremental revenue.

(i) Incentive Plan Design Features   The incentive plan included the following design features:

- *Participation.* All relationship managers and relationship support staff were eligible for the plan.
- *Funding and award determination.* The framework created was a combination of a formula and goal attainment plan. The formula related to the new business developed from new or existing clients. The goal attainment framework related to the business retention achieved. Thus the plan blended features of a pure sales plan with a retention-based structure (Exhibit 2.2). Support staff were compensated based on the results of the team(s) they supported (Exhibit 2.3).
- *Award opportunities.* In determining the size of awards, the company's desired competitive positioning came into play. We arrived at opportunities at threshold, target, and superior levels, making sure that the award levels would allow for the desired 75th percentile positioning when results merited.
- *Performance measures.* Performance measures were clear and simple: (1) percentage retention of existing book of business (latest year is base year—could also be multiple year average), and (2) percentage increase of new business from existing or new clients. The new business from existing clients

Exhibit 2.2 Combination of Team and Individual Incentives—Relationship Manager Incentive Plan.

Retention	
Percent Retention of Current Book[a]	Incentive as Percentage of Salary
90 or less	5
95	10
100	15
105	20
110	25
115	30
120 and over	35

New Business	
New Business	Incentive as Percentage of New Business
$100,000 or less	0
100,000–200,000	3
200,000–300,000	5
300,000–400,000	10
400,000–500,000	15
500,000–and over	20

[a]Based on prior year's results. Achieving greater than 100% is based on additions to existing book, not new business.

must be a new service and therefore would not be double-counted (i.e., book new business and new business). Reports by client and product/service area would be provided monthly. Definitions for all terms were developed.

- *Performance and payout cycles.* After much discussion it was determined that the program would operate on an annual cycle. Performance goals are established for the year and formal reviews are made on a quarterly basis.

- *Plan communications.* The management team recognized the need for an in-depth communication program for both the business directional change and the introduction of the incentive program. It was determined that both could be done simultaneously with the participation of management and regional managers. Communication materials included a slideshow of business and incentive highlights, preparation of a detailed booklet describing the plan, and small group meetings to ensure that individuals fully understood the process. Examples of how they would have fared under the program in the prior year and potential for the current year were customized for these meetings. The response was highly positive.

Exhibit 2.3   Team Support Incentive Plan.

Retention	
Percent Retention (Team) of Current Book[a]	Incentive as Percentage of Salary
90 or less	2.5
95	5
100	7.5
105	10
110	12.5
115	15
120 and over	17.2

New Business	
New Business	Incentive as Percentage of New Business
$100,000 or less	0
100,000–200,000	1.5
200,000–300,000	2.5
300,000–400,000	5
400,000–500,000	7.5
500,000–and over	10

[a]Combination of RMs served or individual RM. Achieving greater than 100% is based on additions to existing book, not new business.

2.4   CONCLUSION

Incentives that are properly aligned with business strategy are extremely powerful. They encourage people to think "outside of the box"—not based on the way they have always done things—but rather on how their customers see them and the service(s) they expect to receive. Incentives change behavior, build teamwork, and encourage individual endeavors. Appropriately designed, incentives help organizations implement new approaches, reorganize, and set new directions in a much quicker timeframe. Incentives, variable pay, and team awards are not a panacea. Their presence does not make up for bad strategies, faulty implementation, or just poor management judgment; however, if you have a group of employees who you would like to think more like business owners, if being successful can be identified by key measures employees can see in their "line of sight," and management is committed to educating employees and providing commensurate rewards, you may just want to take a stab at it.

Chapter 3

Performance Management: Mapping Out the Process

Loree J. Griffith and Anna C. Orgera

As human resource professionals and executives, we recognize that performance management is critical to an organization's ability to be successful in an increasingly competitive and changing business environment; however, all too often firms devote considerable time and effort to the performance management process only to find that the system is not working as well as expected. Common problems we often hear include:

- Inadequate differentiation exists in ratings among performance levels.
- Employees lack full understanding of how to improve performance.
- Performance feedback lacks candor and constructive criticism.
- The "form" is too administratively burdensome.
- No consequences exist for poor performance.
- Employees do not see transparency between appraisal ratings and rewards.

This chapter addresses how performance management can be used as a tool to raise organizational and individual performance by aligning the process with broader business objectives and emphasizing performance improvement and development as prime objectives. On the performance management continuum, this is very different from the classic "performance appraisal" that typically involves an annual review of individual traits and goals tied primarily to merit increase determinations. The real objective of performance management, which is performance improvement and development, is often overlooked in the midst of completing forms and determining compensation actions.

A truly effective performance management process should enable an organization to articulate both business and individual objectives that are focused, meaningful, and clearly linked to broader business strategy.

3.1 FRAMEWORK FOR DEFINING KEY ELEMENTS OF PERFORMANCE SUCCESS

Exhibit 3.1 describes a framework that we have found useful for organizations to use in meeting the challenge of developing, implementing, and communicating an effective performance management process. The framework integrates the organization's mission and business strategy with its reward system. Clear articulation of business strategy enables an organization to foster employee identification with organizational values, as well as an understanding of the competencies or skill sets required to achieve performance levels consistent with those values. The linkage between business strategy and employee rewards centers on identifying, measuring, and communicating three broad performance categories: business performance results, technical/functional knowledge, and behavioral competencies.

(a) Business Performance Management Using Balanced Performance Measurement

The first performance category, business performance results, *highlights* both financial and nonfinancial performance objectives measured at the company, division, team, or individual organizational levels. In today's business environment, a Balanced Scorecard performance measurement framework has become a powerful tool to communicate critical outcomes necessary to attain strategic business objectives.[1] The Balanced Scorecard serves as a framework for addressing key strategic questions from a range of perspectives:

- *Financial.* How do we look to our shareholders?
- *Customer.* How do we look to our customers and targeted markets?
- *Internal.* What internal business processes must we excel at?
- *Learning.* Are we able to sustain innovation, learning, and improvement?

Broadening performance measurement beyond financial results creates awareness about how nonfinancial performance areas can impact financial success. It enables an organization to communicate the drivers of business strategy and clarify where employees should channel their energies, abilities, and knowledge for achieving those goals. A performance management process that incorporates

---

[1] The Balanced Scorecard is a concept developed by Robert S. Kaplan and David P. Norton. See Robert S. Kaplan and David P. Norton, *The Balanced Scorecard: Translating Strategy into Action* (McGraw-Hill, 1996).

Exhibit 3.1   Illustrative Performance Management Framework.

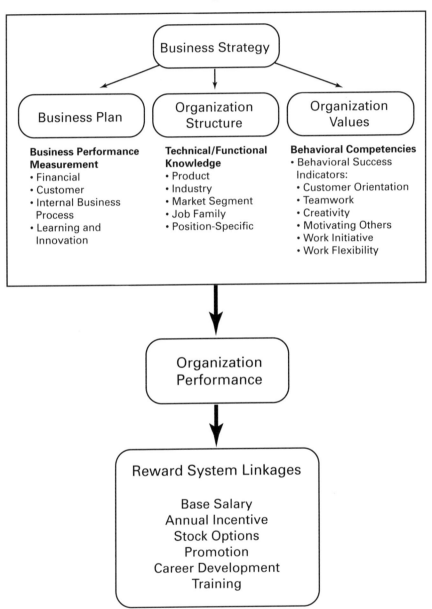

a Balanced Scorecard approach to performance measurement has many benefits, including:

- Serves as a tool for planning, assessing, and communicating the organization's performance objectives and results.
- Incorporates "leading" measures to characterize future drivers of successful performance in addition to "lagging" measures that report historical performance and merely keep score.
- Facilitates ability to monitor achievement of strategic plans.
- Helps identify and focus on customers and market segments through measuring satisfaction, product performance, and new development progress.
- Identifies critical internal processes that an organization must excel at to satisfy customer demands.
- Identifies infrastructure to improve people, systems, and internal procedures.
- Serves as a foundation for identifying goals and objectives within the employee goal-setting and compensation processes.
- Builds a rational and consistent framework for differentiating rewards between solid and outstanding performers.

The power of the Balanced Scorecard lies in mapping the strategic linkages between the four perspectives. It is important to ask a series of questions in a cause-and-effect manner:

- To succeed financially, how should the company appear to internal and external stakeholders?
- To achieve business vision and satisfy stakeholders, how should the company appear to customers?
- To satisfy customers and stakeholders, at what business processes must the company excel?
- To achieve business vision, satisfy stakeholders, and satisfy customers, how must the company improve the skills and capabilities of its people?

If the organization improves the right skills and capabilities, it will improve key internal processes, which will result in improved customer perceptions, which will in turn satisfy shareholder expectations. Exhibit 3.2 provides an example of a Balanced Scorecard measurement framework.

(b) Technical/Functional Knowledge

The second performance category, technical/functional knowledge, represents the skill, knowledge, or experience requirements necessary for effective job

Exhibit 3.2 Example of a Balanced Scorecard Measurement Framework.

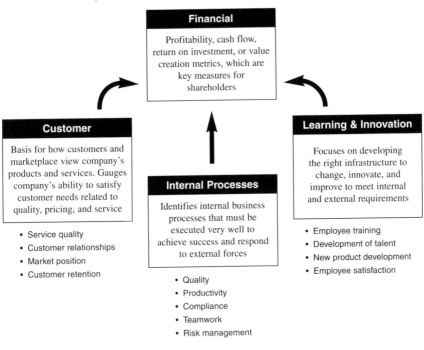

functioning. These skills generally result from specific organizational structure needs and typically reference specialized industry, product, market-segment knowledge requirements, or technical skills/expertise.

(c) Behavioral Competencies

The third performance category, behavioral competencies, emphasizes success indicators that are critical for employees to demonstrate in daily work situations. Behavioral competencies generally reflect important organizational values such as teamwork, innovation and creativity, work initiative, motivating others, or customer orientation. In some cases, a given set of behavioral competencies may apply to all employees in the organization. In other cases, a set of behavioral competencies applies to a subgroup of the employee population such as executives, managers, technical personnel, or administrative support personnel.

All these performance categories ultimately impact organization performance and therefore serve as viable linkages to employee reward systems. These linkages can include base salary progression, annual cash incentive payouts, promotion or career development opportunities, and enhanced training requirements.

3.2 PERFORMANCE MANAGEMENT AS AN ONGOING PROCESS

The prevalent view on the part of today's executives and human resource professionals is that individual performance management is not an appraisal event, but rather an ongoing process involving performance planning, feedback, evaluation, and development. The emphasis is now much more on providing employees with feedback on their success in achieving specific performance goals and expectations, as well as on their ability to develop core competencies and skills.

(a) Performance Planning

Performance planning refers to the confirmation of business performance goals, technical/functional knowledge areas, and behavioral competencies used to measure job performance. The planning phase commences before the performance period (the period over which performance is being measured). It involves identifying applicable performance criteria that link to the organization's business plan and defining success at varying organization levels. The planning process is most effective when there is broad employee participation so employees take responsibility for their development.

(b) Feedback

The feedback phase is ongoing throughout the performance period. It emphasizes opportunities for informal feedback and coaching by managers and/or peers to improve and develop employees' job performance. Feedback is important because employees want to know how they are doing relative to performance expectations. One significant aspect of the feedback phase is the opportunity for enhanced communication between work colleagues through informal discussions and coaching sessions that occur throughout the performance period.

(c) Evaluation and Development

The evaluation and development phase typically occurs at the end of the performance period. At this time, results on all pertinent criteria are evaluated relative to expectations, and a performance improvement plan is developed. The results assessment phase serves two main purposes. The first is to determine appropriate employee reward system linkages, such as base salary increases, annual cash incentive payouts, promotion or career development opportunities, and general training and development needs. Second, the assessment phase contributes to planning for the upcoming performance period by highlighting necessary adjustments to business performance goals, technical/functional knowledge areas, and behavioral competencies that may be necessary in response to changing job and organizational requirements. Exhibit 3.3 displays the cyclic nature of the performance management process.

3.3 MECHANICS OF A BUSINESS-DRIVEN OBJECTIVE SETTING PROCESS

Objective setting is an integral part of the performance management process, particularly to create an understanding of how individuals can impact broader business results. Objective setting creates an effective link between department, team, or individual goals and the organization's strategic objectives so that individual and team efforts are aligned with the organization's overall business plan. Without a formal objective-setting process, there is a greater chance that individual and team efforts may pull in directions contrary to broader organizational objectives.

The objective-setting process, whether at the individual or business unit level, can be facilitated by applying the following guidelines:

*   *Define specific goals that link to broader business strategy.* Goals that are specific to broader business objectives will better direct employees' attention to those critical few business objectives most important to achieving desired results. For example, the objective "maximize loan profitability" is appropriate for a bank lending department because increased department profitability

Exhibit 3.3   The Performance Management Cycle Is Continuous.

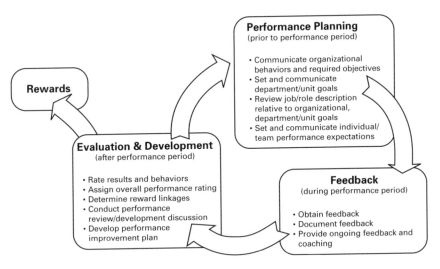

will contribute to increased bank profitability. Where possible, link individual or team objectives to functional accountabilities of the position or department.

- *Goal statements should identify a "yardstick" against which successful completion of attained results can be measured.* It is important to clearly define benchmarks as in this example: "Increase account balances by 20%, from $6 million to $7.2 million."

- *Goals can describe quantitative or qualitative results.* Quantitative measures reference financial, operational, or productivity-oriented items that are easily tracked through various management reporting systems. Common areas for quantitative goal setting include income generation, operating expenses relative to budget, customer satisfaction ratings, number of procedures or transactions completed, or processing times for specified transactions. An example of a quantitative goal is "By year-end, manage controllable operating expenses to $200,000 annually." Qualitative measures reference a variety of project-oriented activities such as new product development, systems enhancements, or staffing requirements. An example of a qualitative goal is "By the second quarter, develop systems and procedures manual for private issue function that would effectively familiarize all staff with pricing guides, audit guides, referrals, and individual risk assessment."

- *A well-developed objective should represent a statement of the end results intended, rather than the tasks or activities needed to attain desired results.* Unlike tasks, goals should not simply describe what is being done, but rather should define desired outcomes as in this example: "By year-end, design and test a financial forecasting model that reduces variances between actual results versus projection to 5% or less."

- *Objectives should represent challenging, yet reasonably attainable performance expectations.* A goal perceived as unattainable can be demotivating. An objective that expects an increase in product revenue by 15% over the prior year may be much more reasonable than one that would require a 100% increase in revenue.

- *In addition to specifying the expected performance level, it is sometimes useful to reference broader benchmarks that describe "threshold" and "superior" performance accomplishments.* "Threshold" performance levels should reference minimum results meriting recognition, particularly through the reward system. "Superior" performance requirements should describe distinguished performance results that far exceed expectations.

- *Address critical influences or constraints that may impact performance against the planned objectives.* Examples might include changing internal or market circumstances. The objective should be feasibly met within internal and external operating constraints and within established timeframes. The measurement process should take place without significant interference to the daily workflow. Appropriate resources such as time, money, people, or technology should be available. Should necessary resources be unavailable or obstacles realized, the objectives should be reviewed and adjusted accordingly.

- *The time period for achieving designated goals should be within the performance period (typically one year).* In some cases, the time period needed to achieve a designated objective may span more than one year. When this occurs, the objective can be divided into key milestones for partial completion during the year.

- *Identify a reasonable number of planned objectives that represent outcomes with the greatest impact over attainment of broader business objectives.* Consider the relative importance or weight of identified objectives; a typical guideline is for each goal to carry a relative weight of 10% to 40% of the total.

- *Employees should discuss the range of expected results with their managers.* In this way, they can arrive at a formal, written agreement about objective attainment.

3.4   MULTISOURCE PERFORMANCE FEEDBACK AS AN ASSESSMENT TOOL

Organizations have increasingly adopted multisource performance feedback programs, a powerful tool to solicit feedback from work colleagues regarding an individual's performance. Unlike traditional performance assessments, which concentrate on supervisory input only, multisource assessments consider feedback from a variety of inputs, including peers, direct reports, other work colleagues, key internal customers, or external customers. In many cases, the feedback is used as a tool to shape an individual's training, development, and performance improvement needs; however, mechanisms to link multisource feedback results to employee reward decisions are becoming increasingly important. The multisource feedback process is typically more complicated to administer and interpret than traditional systems, yet can have greater impact and meaning to individuals.

Our experience indicates several success factors for implementing a multisource appraisal process:

- *Secure management's involvement and participation to create employee buy-in.* Managers must demonstrate a strong willingness to receive performance feedback from sources other than direct supervisors and must take seriously the need to make behavioral changes based on the input received. Frequently, the program is first piloted with members of the management team and then filtered down to lower organizational levels as readiness occurs.

- *Clearly define and communicate the program.* The program's purpose, features, and anticipated outcomes must be clearly defined and communicated to employees.

- *Create a valid and sustainable process.* Many participants often express concern that the program will emphasize individual personality over job performance. Therefore, the evaluations typically specify common performance criteria that help concentrate the feedback provider on demonstrated behaviors and competencies over personality. Another concern centers around the phrasing of written comments and likelihood of a feedback recipient misinterpreting written commentary. Comments should be stated specifically and constructively to support specific rating decisions. Any comment should be supported with specific behavioral examples. For example, the comment "well liked by customers" would be more meaningful if expressed as "customers are drawn to the employee because he or she sees decisions through their eyes."

- *Preserve rater anonymity.* Initial implementation of a multisource feedback program may create anxiety for both employees and managers. Rater anonymity issues and the detection of negative feedback are of prime concern, particularly when departments contain a small number of staff or when employees are evaluating a supervisor. Therefore, rater anonymity is generally preserved through results analyses that are aggregated either across all feedback providers or across feedback provider categories (e.g., peers, direct reports) to arrive at a consensus opinion. Also, a minimum number of feedback providers (e.g., five) should usually be required before results are distributed to recipients.

- *Provide support and training to all users on how to provide feedback and how to use feedback.* The objective of the process is to eliminate assessment decisions that are based on personal preferences or biases.

- *Provide efficient, cost-effective data collection, processing, and reporting.* A well-designed system should consider several factors, including nomination and selection of raters, feedback tools, feedback collection process, compilation and analysis of results, and presentation of results to recipients. These processes should be designed to facilitate performance management, not add administrative burden.

- *Create necessary linkages to training, development, or rewards.* Too frequently, multisource feedback programs have low impact because of the lack of accountability for change on the part of the feedback recipient.

Multisource performance feedback can be applied in several ways depending on how the program is phased in. In the initial stages (typically the program pilot), the feedback is often used for individual or team development, primarily through enhanced managerial coaching or self-assessment. As employees become more familiar with the process, feedback results may be linked to formal training and development activities, career pathing, or succession planning. At this stage, some organizations use the results as a secondary management input when conducting the annual individual performance appraisal. In the advanced stages of program implementation, results can be formally factored into reward decisions such as salary progression, annual incentive determinations, or promotion considerations.

One interesting case is a financial services company that uses internal customer feedback for departments as a means of inspiring performance achievement, improvement, and development at the team level. Internal customers are defined as officers of the company who are responsible for assessing the performance of each department on a quarterly basis. Internal customers are asked to evaluate each department on specific performance criteria such as technical work quality, effectiveness of internal communications, timeliness/responsiveness of service, and service value. Departments use performance feedback as a foundation for developing and implementing quality improvement initiatives. The company also uses incentive compensation to reward departments for achieving internal customer satisfaction levels.

3.5   MAXIMIZING PERFORMANCE THROUGH FEEDBACK AND COACHING

The feedback phase of the performance management process emphasizes feedback and coaching to help employees develop to their full work potential. Feedback and coaching refer to the formal and day-to-day activities that managers and employees engage in to support individual and team performance improvement.

Feedback and coaching can occur in two ways: formal and situational. *Formal approaches* typically occur through regularly scheduled meetings or progress reports:

* Staff meetings to inform employees of progress made in achieving business objectives
* Management reports that communicate financial or operating results relative to objectives
* Annual or interim individual performance assessments

Situational coaching occurs on an ongoing basis throughout the normal course of work. It refers to frequent, informal discussions between managers and employees, or even between work colleagues, regarding feedback on daily work challenges. Situational coaching can be a powerful means of providing immediate performance feedback to employees to promote positive change.

Effective feedback and coaching serve multiple purposes, including:

- Motivating improved work performance by helping employees maximize their potential.
- Clarifying performance expectations.
- Responding to employees' need to know how they are doing relative to specified performance expectations.
- Identifying performance improvement opportunities.
- Recognizing accomplishments and achievements.
- Breaking down boundaries that prevent effective teamwork.
- Creating an environment that promotes open discussion and continuous learning.

Because feedback and coaching represent the least structured component of the performance management process, it is imperative that managers receive appropriate training on effective feedback and coaching techniques. Performance feedback is generally more effective when discussions encourage and manage employee participation.

Effective feedback and coaching techniques include the following:

- Solicit others' ideas by asking open-ended questions such as those that begin with "what," "when," "tell me," or "describe."
- React to ideas in a positive, constructive way.
- Encourage others to discuss immediately any obstacles impeding effective job performance.
- Listen actively and encourage repeated employee contributions.
- Help others discover their own solutions and lead them to make their own decisions.
- Clarify work expectations and priorities while offering suggestions to resolve problems.
- Relay past experiences that model effective work behaviors.
- Monitor performance against goals to spot opportunities for improvement.
- Praise good work and highlight successes as often and as publicly as possible.
- Confront when necessary on needed improvements using specific examples of performance or behaviors that did not meet expectations.
- Give feedback as soon as possible after a particular event has occurred.
- Commit to further action when giving corrective feedback.
- Express overall confidence and support in the employee or work colleague.

Employees will generally be more receptive to feedback if managers or work colleagues make a conscious effort to minimize feelings of defensiveness or discouragement. Be specific to results, rather than personal or general; try to manage the process using facts or data rather than being vague. For example, the statement "I have noticed errors in two particular sections of your weekly report" is less threatening than the statement "You are not doing a good job with documentation." Be descriptive about potential performance problems rather than judgmental. Ask for additional information when giving corrective feedback. For example, instead of saying "Your points do not make any sense," a more effective approach might be "I see the point you are making, but I am not sure how it fits here—can you help me further understand?" Above all, remember that the primary purpose of the feedback and coaching process is performance improvement. Take advantage of the opportunity to help maximize the potential of work colleagues.

3.6   PERFORMANCE EVALUATION AND DEVELOPMENT

The evaluation and development phase of the performance management process typically occurs through a formalized annual and/or midyear review of performance relative to specified performance criteria. Performance assessment serves multiple purposes:

- Provides an opportunity for employees and their managers to formally discuss position accountabilities to ensure a mutual understanding of expected work outcomes.

- Facilitates improved job performance by providing an opportunity for a comprehensive review of past performance on business results, technical/functional knowledge areas, and behavioral competencies from the point of view of the manager, the employee, and others with whom the employee regularly interacts.

- Offers an opportunity for employees to discuss and obtain assistance in resolving job-related obstacles to success.

- Provides an objective, consistent basis for determining employee reward decisions.

- Identifies development needs and determines a specific action plan for improvement.

Not surprisingly, companies have used a wide range of performance rating scales to varying degrees of success. Key decision points are whether to use a forced rating distribution and determining what elements of pay should be linked to the performance ratings.

Scales that do not force a distribution of performance ratings reduce or eliminate the problem of employees being arbitrarily assigned to a performance category; however, it is important to regularly monitor and test the relationship between the rating distribution, rewards, and business performance to ensure that the system results in adequate differentiation. Forced distribution rating systems discourage uniform ratings across employees and often help overcome the common complaint of a lack of rating differentiation. To the extent that the targeted distribution approximates the true distribution among high and low performers, a forced distribution can be more effective than a nonforced distribution.

Organizations may adopt a practice of developing an overall performance evaluation rating based on assessments of performance accomplishments with respect to job responsibilities/expectations, competency/skill development and demonstration, and team/individual goals. The overall rating may be derived either by equally weighting each performance assessment area to develop an average rating or placing more or less emphasis/weight on different areas to reflect organizational priorities and individual employee expectations for the performance period. Some organizations have also used separate ratings for each performance assessment area to facilitate and communicate performance/career development and pay for performance linkages, for example:

Performance Assessment Area	Primary Ratings Purpose
Ongoing job responsibilities and competencies/skills	• Performance improvement and career development • Merit and promotion increases • Threshold for incentive plan participation • Long-term incentive or stock option award determination
Results achievement	• Annual incentive award determination
Multiyear performance trend and/or rating of longer-term potential	• Long-term incentive or stock option participation • Promotion • Career development • Retention importance

An integral facet of the assessment process is the opportunity for employees to complete a self-assessment of their performance, allowing employees to share perceptions of their performance relative to the specified performance criteria. An employee typically submits the self-assessment to the manager before the actual appraisal discussion. In this way, the appraisal discussion will foster employee participation, which is important in gaining employee acceptance.

Additionally, the self-assessment allows managers to receive additional input about employees' perceptions of their job responsibilities, performance strengths, and potential problem areas. When using the self-assessment technique, a manager's communication and coaching skills become even more important to keep the appraisal discussion constructive and objective.

The result of the performance assessment process involves determining an overall performance rating for the employee. The following guidelines will help facilitate the assessment process for both managers and employees:

- When making rating judgments, consider performance over the entire performance period rather than emphasizing isolated incidents or the individual's most recent performance.

- Throughout the year, maintain a written log of interim performance achievements or development needs, including any progress made in designated development areas; reference these written performance comments to gain a better perspective on the year's overall performance.

- Complete any formal evaluation forms in plenty of time before conducting the actual appraisal interview to allow sufficient time to arrive at your conclusions.

- If any item is rated other than "fully meets expectations," make sure to provide specific behavioral comments to support the rating; this is especially important for facilitating employee understanding and acceptance when rating judgments impact employee reward decisions.

3.7 THE APPRAISAL INTERVIEW

Near the end of the performance period, the formal appraisal interview is typically conducted. Feedback can be represented from both the manager and work colleagues if a multisource feedback program is in place. During the appraisal interview, managers have key accountability for communicating relevant performance feedback and helping identify the cause of performance that requires improvement or is below expectations. Questions that need to be considered are: Does the employee have the ability to produce better results? Is the employee appropriately motivated? Is poor performance caused by a constrained supporting environment? Are new skill sets required?

It is important that managers communicate the details and supporting rationale for specific rating judgments. Communication should be two-way, with the employee encouraged to offer his or her perception and responses to the evaluation. Differences of opinion should be fully discussed and resolved, if possible. If disagreements persist, they should be documented on the appraisal form.

Many of the behaviors used for effective coaching and counseling sessions also apply to conducting the appraisal interview. The session is most effectively conducted in a private, comfortable, nonthreatening environment where outside interruptions are avoided. Encourage a two-way conversation, rather than a monologue. Ask the employee for comments based on her or his self-review. Use open-ended questions, and listen attentively. When giving feedback, be clear and to the point, drawing on comments written on the evaluation form.

Remain objective and nonjudgmental by accentuating job-specific behaviors and outcomes relative to stated business results, technical/functional knowledge areas, or behavioral competencies. Avoid attributing potential problem areas to the employee's personality. Never overtly compare an employee to other colleagues. If you want good performance repeated, call attention to it but ensure that expectations are clearly communicated.

It is also important to stress the continuous nature of the performance management process. Once the appraisal discussion is completed, it will frequently be necessary to review the position's job description, annual objectives, and other performance criteria to determine significant changes in position accountabilities. Any resulting changes should be appropriately reflected in the planning process for the coming year.

3.8   DEVELOPMENT PLANNING

Development planning is a key component of the performance management process because it motivates all employees to enhance personal effectiveness and increase contribution to the organization. It also provides the human resources department with a viable template for developing in-house training or career path programs. The first step in the development planning process is the identification of performance strengths and improvement needs.

Performance strengths can reflect several areas:

- Significant contributions or growth areas
- New skills acquired and job-related advances
- Individual or team goals attained beyond the expected level
- Exceptional performance on technical/functional skills or behavioral competencies

Development needs often reference the following:

- Skill or knowledge requirements for promotion or salary advancement
- A change in performance expectations driven by changing business objectives
- Goal attainment levels below expectation

- Technical/functional skills or behavioral competencies that are not met at full expectation

Once the major performance strengths and improvement needs have been identified, the employee and manager should agree upon, and formally articulate, a performance development plan. The key to defining a successful development plan is to stress those areas that have the greatest importance to job effectiveness. It is often useful to think about how the employee has demonstrated particularly effective or ineffective behaviors on key performance criteria, for example:

- *Customer orientation.* What difficulties has the employee experienced with customers and how has he or she handled them?
- *Communications.* In which situations was the employee able to explain a technical or complex issue in simple terms without losing content?
- *Teamwork.* How has the employee contributed to cross-sell efforts with other areas of the organization?

In most cases, it will be more effective to limit the development focus to a few key performance areas. The development plan should specify three components:

1. *Key action steps.* These should address a variety of activities that an employee can undertake for development. Traditional activities might include attending external training courses or participating in outside coursework; however, other activities can reference on-the-job development of a particular skill set, new and expanded work assignments, participation in joint projects with other departments, or enhanced coaching by a manager or mentor. Development activities should also recognize how an individual can better use performance strengths.
2. *Support/resources needed.* These should specify any assistance that the employee may need to complete each action step. Considerations should include cost constraints, time availability of others whose assistance may be necessary, or availability of relevant materials or supplies.
3. *Timetable for action.* This should indicate target completion dates or milestone achievement dates for completing each action step over the course of the upcoming year.

Once the development plan is drafted, both the manager and the supervisor should chart progress against the specified action steps. Monitoring progress can help heighten motivation by recognizing incremental achievements. Documentation of progress made will also prove useful when assessing performance achievements for the upcoming performance period.

3.9   THE PERFORMANCE MANAGEMENT FRAMEWORK IN ACTION

The performance management framework is a highly flexible tool because it enables a variety of reward linkages to those broad performance measures that best align with the organization's business strategy. The following case study illustrates how the reward linkage can work.

The company used the performance management framework to facilitate determination of annual incentive payouts. Business performance results were tied to financial and nonfinancial measures. Financial goals were developed at the corporate, division, and team levels. Nonfinancial goals reflecting customer, productivity, project-oriented, and business development measures were developed for individuals and groups. Annual incentive awards were determined on the basis of actual business performance results relative to goal. An individual's earned award was then modified by his or her individual performance on both the technical/functional skills and behavioral competencies. In this case, technical/functional skills referenced ongoing job responsibilities specific to individual position roles, such as client managers or marketing representatives. The job responsibilities described 5 to 10 key accountabilities most critical to effective job functioning that remained relatively constant from year to year. Behavioral competencies represented employee behaviors important to the company's success. These included teamwork/cross-sell, initiative, organization understanding, customer orientation, work flexibility, problem solving, communications effectiveness, business planning, budget management, motivating others, and providing performance feedback.

Individual performance evaluation results enabled the earned incentive award to be increased or decreased by a specified amount. Managers evaluated individual performance against a four-point rating scale. Additionally, a peer feedback component was introduced that allowed colleagues in other areas of the organization to provide feedback on an individual's performance along selected behavioral competencies that emphasized teamwork and cross-sell efforts. The results of the peer review process were aggregated and used as a management input when evaluating performance.

3.10   LESSONS LEARNED FOR EFFECTIVE PERFORMANCE MANAGEMENT PROGRAM DESIGN

A performance management program that does not effectively cultivate improvement and development can lead to an abundance of lower performers retained in critical jobs. The consequences of this include low job performance, blocked development and advancement opportunities, improper development of subordinates and peers, low productivity and morale, and difficulty attracting and retaining higher performers.

Our research and experience with high-performing companies indicates several important success factors for developing or refining an effective performance management program. These include commitment, alignment, integration, simplicity, and continuous improvement. We believe that by applying, these learnings to your performance management designs, the goal of raising organizational and individual performance will be more readily achieved.

Commitment

- Secure senior executive involvement and participation in the process.
- Foster employee involvement and ownership for managing and achieving high performance.
- Hold managers accountable for accurate performance feedback and coaching.
- Provide ongoing communication and training about the program to all stakeholders.

Alignment

- Align performance management processes with current business plans, culture, and strategy.
- Align individual performance elements with organizational values and priorities.

Integration

- Create transparency between performance and reward decisions.
- Build a system that recognizes, rewards, and differentiates top performers.
- Define consequences of consecutive poor performance periods.
- Define linkages to other "talent management" processes (i.e., processes to identify, assess, develop, and retain talent).
- Synchronize the performance planning cycle with the business planning cycle.

Simplicity

- Minimize administrative burden in both forms and process.
- Use technology to simplify administration.
- Develop simple documentation.
- Create clear, consistent, and value-added planning, feedback, and assessment tools.

Continuous Improvement

- Gather and analyze ongoing feedback to monitor the program's success.
- Adopt incremental change as needed rather than massive redesign.
- Establish ownership for maintenance and enhancement of the program and related processes.

Chapter 4

Competency-Based Reward Design Approaches

Dana Rahbar-Daniels

The linkage of competency models to employee reward programs represents a recent development in the formalized application of competencies within the human resource (HR) management field. While employee selection, personal development, performance evaluation, and training are well-established applications for competency programs, rewards are relatively novel offering both new opportunities and new challenges. Most companies have, of course, been paying for competencies for years, without recognizing this in an explicit way. For example, employers striving to compensate "top performers" at the upper end of their salary range, or paying with maturity curves or technical career ladders, and even making well-deserved promotional increases, have been implicitly paying for competencies. What is truly innovative, therefore, about the new models for competency–reward linkage? The following contrasts the areas of design innovation that will be discussed in this chapter:

Characteristics of Traditional Linkage Approaches	*Characteristics of New Linkage Approaches*
• Highly subjective process	• Explicitly defined process
• Unilateral from one's boss	• Mutually understood
• Little focus on future capacity	• Strong development focus
• Uncertain link to business success drivers	• Grounded in business success drivers

This chapter opens with a discussion of the forces that have led organizations to link competencies to rewards in a formal structure and outlines the specific "people management" benefits expected from this linkage. The rest of the chapter presents several types of working models for competency–reward linkages drawn from Mercer's client experiences and HR practice research. The administrative components of these models are described and illustrated with examples in order to give the practitioner a clearer sense of how these programs actually work. For organizations looking at the possible adoption of competency-based rewards, we have included a discussion of readiness criteria to examine what program approach might best fit a given business and its people management challenges.

4.1   DESIGN PURPOSE FOR COMPETENCY-BASED REWARDS

The reasons why organizations have formally connected their competency assessments to one or more components of their reward system include the following factors:

- Reinforcement of personal accountability for competency development
- Redesign of work that places greater emphasis on people's involvement in a broad process, rather than on individual contributions within narrowly defined jobs
- Desire to emphasize "how work gets accomplished" as well as "what gets accomplished"
- Support to a cultural transformation process across the organization

Different models for competency–reward linkage are better suited to accomplishing one or more of these design purposes. This chapter presents examples of how such linkages can be tailored to a particular design intent.

Certainly a formal connection to rewards raises the profile of the competency development process from a "nice thing to do" to a "basic expectation" for the relevant employees, whether they consist of executives, middle management, professionals, or nonexempt employees. For many of these organizations, competency development has become a basic driver of sustainable high performance, integrating into their performance evaluation process and related reward decisions. These companies are saying that they will directly compensate people for the time and energy they invest in competency development if measurable gains are made in this area, however it is measured.

Many reengineering and restructuring efforts have also led to a basic shift from work organized in stable, well-defined jobs, to work defined by dynamic processes focused on satisfying customers of the process. In these new work designs, companies have felt the need to redefine "performance" in a far more robust way that emphasizes employee contributions to a broad process, rather than narrowly defined jobs. Competencies provide this extra performance ingredient, matching well to flexible, cross-functional work structures. This is also consistent with the broader theme of "paying for the person" as measured by relevant capabilities rather than simply "paying for the job."

When an organization embarks on a cultural transformation process, a competency model can serve as a guide to the "transformed state" and stimulate change in this direction. The role of reward linkages is then to promote and embed the new behaviors that strategically support the cultural change process. The linkage communicates the company's full commitment to the new culture as a "new way of doing business" for future success, both as an organization and as individuals.

4.2 CURRENT PRACTICES IN COMPETENCY LINKAGES

Competencies have been formally applied to pay and other reward decisions through a variety of new approaches. We have observed companies linking competencies to a single component of compensation, such as their base pay system, or to variable pay awards like incentives or specialized recognition awards, as well as various combinations of these components. The most common linkage has been to base pay. This preference for base pay linkages is rooted in certain characteristics of salary management that seem to integrate particularly well with the characteristics of competency models and the competency development process itself. For example, many competency models created for professional and technical employees consist of a combination of behavioral attributes and relevant knowledges and skills. This blend of factors—critical behaviors, skills, and knowledge—corresponds well to the concept of demonstrated work capabilities that salary programs are often designed to reward. These capability factors are traditionally expressed as training, education, and experience specifications for a "job."

Looking at the fit between base pay movement and the competency development process, most people acquire competency at a gradual pace, depending on many cumulative learning experiences to reshape and enhance one's behavioral approach and to add important new skills and knowledge to one's repertoire. Because the salary growth process is also relatively gradual and cumulative for most people, this represents another natural fit. This process is unlike incentive or recognition awards that, inherently, do not accumulate and can vary considerably for an individual from one time to another.

Despite the clear preference for base salary applications in the rewards area to date, some organizations have implemented competency linkages for variable incentive awards and recognition awards. The following discussion of design models presents examples of each of these distinctive reward applications.

(a) Readiness Criteria for a Rewards Application

For an organization considering the application of competencies to a part of its reward programs, certain issues are well worth exploring to see how favorable the circumstances are to a particular use. A readiness assessment is particularly important given the heightened sensitivity that most employees have toward their compensation and the relative novelty of formal competency applications. Two broad categories of issues should be considered in this readiness assessment. First, has the competency model been defined and deployed in a way that supports sound reward decisions? Second, has the competency input to reward decisions been coordinated with other factors (e.g., business goal achievement, responsibility level, and/or competitive market practice) so that the company's overall pay policy remains coherent and fully understood? We will concentrate our attention on the first category but also touch on some points in the second.

(b)   Strength of the Competency Assessment System

In many ways a competency program that supports sound rewards decisions also meets the basic criteria of reliability, validity, and participant credibility desired for any performance evaluation system. In the area of reliability, client companies have included two features in their competency assessment process to add greater reliability to the evaluation ratings. One aspect consists of "anchoring" levels along a ratings scale with detailed indicators of behaviors (for behavioral competencies) or knowledge and skills (for technical/functional competencies) in order to distinguish each progressive stage on the scale. Exhibits 4.1 and 4.2 present examples of this "anchoring" concept for a behavioral competency assessment system (Exhibit 4.1) and for one involving knowledge/skill (Exhibit 4.2).

These descriptive "anchors" are meant to create a more consistent understanding of the ratings scale across a wide range of raters. This objective is particularly important given the multisource (so-called 360-degree) approach often used with these competency assessment systems. While developing staged anchors requires more intensive analysis and design work than a straight frequency scale, such as "rarely" to "nearly always," or a more traditional performance scale, such as "unsatisfactory" to "outstanding," the fuller definition of rating levels can add reliability to the system and, thereby, enhance its overall defensibility and credibility to participants.

A second program feature used to improve ratings reliability is formal training of raters in the evaluation process and instruments. Again, because these systems typically involve multiple raters for each participant, many of whom are co-workers, peers, and reporting staff with little or no experience in giving evaluative feedback, basic rater training can be a critical step in effective implementation. As an additional safeguard before linking competency assessments to reward decisions, we recommend that the assessment process be conducted at least once, and preferably several times, before the linkage is formalized. This approach allows for important rater experience and system refinement before the rewards application begins.

In the area of ratings validity, the methods and procedures used to develop the competency model or models can be decisive in achieving professional standards

Exhibit 4.1 Example of "Staged" Behavioral Competency Evaluation Format.[a]

Developing Stage	Effective Stage	Role Model Stage
• Responds to customers' needs promptly and courteously when asked to do so.	• Ensures that all customer requirements are met in the normal course of business.	• Makes customers' needs a top priority; takes any and all actions to meet these needs.
• Shows awareness of how his or her personal actions impact the customer's satisfaction.	• Acts promptly and takes strong measures to repair mistakes or service problems the customer has experienced.	• Takes responsibility for and deals effectively with the most complex and sensitive customer complaints.
• Shows a sense of urgency in referring difficult customer complaints or problems to senior staff, but does not "pass the buck" to avoid own involvement.	• Clearly communicates realistic expectations to customers of his or her ability to satisfy their requests.	• Anticipates customer issues and investigates the underlying causes of customer service problems to eliminate these difficulties in the future.

[a] Customer Focused—always keep customers (internal and external) as the focal point of one's work activities. Understands and responds to customer business issues, needs, and expectations. Develops strong personal relationships with customers to provide the highest level of customer service.

Exhibit 4.2 Example of "Staged" Technical Competency Evaluation Format.

Knowledge of Interface Design Element of Software Design		
Basic Stage	Accomplished Stage	Advanced Stage
Understands basic concepts of interface design in order to develop working software subsystem and user interfaces by using known tools and modeling techniques.	Applies in-depth knowledge of the interface design methods sufficient to create advanced software subsystem interfaces and user interfaces. May also use knowledge to present this design information (e.g., prototypes, design reviews, etc.).	Demonstrates an advanced understanding of interface design theories in order to develop and review complex software subsystem and user interfaces. Is expected to apply knowledge to critique interface designs presented by others for review.

for content and criterion validity. These factors influence the fundamental quality of the competency model. The model needs to be organic to the organization and not generic or off-the-shelf. The specific competencies need to be closely tied to the organization, its business challenges, and the type of work performed. The following model development criteria support competency rating validity:

- Multiple research protocols used to identify high-performance competencies (e.g., critical situation interviews of high performers, validation surveys, focus groups, expert panels)
- Multiple criteria used to select employees as "high-performance" subjects of the model research, with attention to avoiding sample bias from an equal employment opportunity perspective
- Competency model testing through field surveys of the covered population
- Competency categories analyzed for direct linkage to the organization's business strategy and relevant critical success factors

To address the factor of strategic linkage, Mercer employs a technique that we call *strategy visioning.* This technique is used to identify and confirm specific connections between a company's strategic priorities and behavioral competencies that can be vital to their achievement. Exhibit 4.3 shows an extract from a strategy visioning process, showing how linkages have been identified between a company's strategic priority to "rapidly increase market share" and a set of related critical behaviors.

Apart from an effective competency assessment system, another key element to preparing an organization for linking rewards to competencies is to decide how competencies will integrate with more traditional reward factors like business results achievement, job or responsibility level, and competitive pay standards.

Exhibit 4.3   The Strategy Visioning Process.[a]

Strategic Priority	Related Critical Success Factors	High-Impact Functions/ Processes	Points of Major Performance Leverage	Related Critical Behaviors
• Rapidly increase market share	• High responsive and reliable order fulfillment • Superior product reputation with multiuse flexibility • High potential distribution channels • Competitive pricing points	• Order processing • Marketing • Sales • Product engineering	• Embed preventive quality controls throughout order fulfillment process • Use fully integrated product development processes • Capture "most preferred" distribution channel prospects	• Analytical/ process thinking • Drive for improvement • Team orientation • Influencing • Results focused • Customer focused

[a] Extract from Mercer's strategy visioning documentation.

These integration issues, as well as how they can influence the selection of suitable competency–reward linkages, are discussed in the following section.

4.3 BASE PAY APPLICATIONS OF COMPETENCY LINKAGE

(a) Introduction

There are three types of working models designed to link competencies to base pay management. Each approach has been adopted in specific Mercer client situations with clearly positive results, as evaluated by the company's top management and the participating employees. These approaches vary considerably in their design emphasis on competency assessment results versus other decision factors such as the "going market rate" for jobs or individual performance against objectives. Because no single approach can work best in every situation, these three alternatives illustrate a range of working models for practitioners to consider. The challenge is to identify and tailor a "best fit" to one's own HR strategy, work process design, and business culture. Exhibit 4.4 presents several key factors that can influence the compatibility of the prototype models with a given business environment. This chart can be used as the starting point for an organization's readiness assessment. When used this way, it is important to look at the full set of factors under each type of model as interrelated characteristics, rather than as separate criteria for picking a suitable design approach.

Exhibit 4.4   Three Alternative Models for Linking Base Pay to Competencies.

Selection Factors	Base Pay Model 1	Base Pay Model 2	Base Pay Model 3
Nature of work roles	Stable, relatively routinized to specific functions Tight job definition	Some flexibility Some cross-functional responsibility Broader job definition	Very dynamic and adaptive Multifunctional Broad role definition
Lowest level of key business output measurement	Individual contributor	Group output	Process output
Work management structure	Hierarchical	More self-managed at individual and team levels	Group norms, overall process structure
Individual's career focus	Promotional ladders	Promotions and lateral development	Lateral development focus
Individual's performance focus	Fulfill job requirements	Achieve group's goals	Maximize personal and group value to the business

(b)   Overview of the Base Pay Design Alternatives

To a great extent, the design range for base pay linkage can be seen as an inno-vation continuum that ranges from relatively traditional to radically new. This design continuum begins with applications that remain close to traditional job-based systems. In these examples, competencies serve essentially as a fine-tuning mechanism, helping determine where each individual's salary level should be targeted within narrowly defined job salary ranges. The dominant salary driver in these situations remains the person's job assignment and the external "going market rate."

At the next level of design innovation, competencies are linked to base pay structures containing wide ranges generally called *broadbands* or *broad grades*. These broadbands are constructed from external job pricing, but the bands encom-pass entire job families or broad responsibility levels within an organization. From a competency standpoint, their innovative aspect lies in the tighter linkage devel-oped between competency assessment ratings and individual salary adjustments. This connection occurs through the organization's formal salary adjustment guide-lines. These guidelines are designed so that the size of salary increases depends largely on the person's competency rating. Other factors play a role in salary adjustment decisions as well, but the competency rating is used as a major deter-minant.

At the most innovative level, competency ratings are used as the driving force in setting the absolute level of an individual's base pay rate. The focus of these approaches is on paying the proper base pay level in absolute terms, rather than simply determining the next pay increase. These base pay applications structure the competency rating scale so that it runs parallel to each salary range, again defined as broadbands. Individual base pay levels are then established and adjusted to match the advancement or decline in a person's assessed competency level over time. For example, as a person's competency rating increases, his or her relative position in the applicable broadband increases similarly to maintain alignment between these two factors. A person may also experience interband movement, shifting from one broadband to another, but these shifts are relatively rare and are often accompanied by a change in the competencies for which one is being assessed. More specific details on these design parameters are presented in the following model descriptions.

(c)   Models for Base Pay Linkage

(i) Model 1: Competencies Within a Job Grade Structure   In this first model, the linkage between base pay management and competencies is struc-tured in a relatively simple format. The connection occurs through the company's performance appraisal process, with competency ratings introduced as an extra evaluation element and the overall appraisal then used to target a person's base

pay level within a particular job grade. The pay emphasis in this approach remains clearly on the market value of the job, with some narrow latitude in the job range to recognize differences in proficiency and results produced.

Implementation of this type of model can involve either of two alternative pay structures: a job range framework with three target segments in each range or a "position rate" system consisting of three preset rates. Exhibit 4.5 presents examples of these two approaches for a hypothetical pay grade, including the descriptive guides that help a reviewing manager decide what pay level within the job range is best suited to a person's proficiency and results. For both approaches, the role of competencies is generally a subjective one that combines with more results-oriented factors to guide the salary decision-making process.

(ii) Model 2: Competencies as a Salary Increase Factor Within Broad-bands   In the second model, competencies take on a larger, ongoing role in base pay decisions. This expanded role involves a variety of design features but typically centers on linking competency ratings explicitly to salary adjustment guidelines in a broadband structure. In these programs, broad salary bands represent a basic shift from a traditional hierarchy of narrow job ranges to a lateral progression opportunity structured by wide organizational layer or job family. As a result, while these salary systems still rely on jobs to price the bands and assign people into bands, competency ratings are given a major salary decision-making role.

Development of the Broad Pay Bands   When setting the minimum and maximum rates that define each broadband in this type of model, the minimum is

Exhibit 4.5   Two Examples of Competencies in a Job-Based Pay Structure.

Development Zone	Market Target Zone	Premium Zone
• Recent promotion or new hire	• Full mastery of assigned responsibilities	• Sustained exceptional performance
• Essential qualifications for position	• Performance consistently at or above expectations	• Continued stretch contributions
• Extensive development opportunities	• Effective in most critical competencies	• Role model in many critical competencies, strong in all

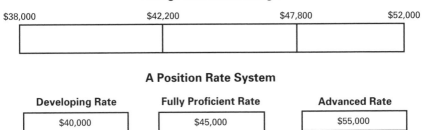

A Segmented Job Range

$38,000 $42,200 $47,800 $52,000

A Position Rate System

Developing Rate	Fully Proficient Rate	Advanced Rate
$40,000	$45,000	$55,000

typically intended to align with the average entry salary for the lowest-paid positions in the band and the maximum is matched to the 90th percentile of pay for the highest-paid positions in the band. This approach ensures that a fully competitive pay opportunity is available for all positions in a particular band.

Within the salary band structure, additional pay guidelines are typically defined by three sequential segments, or "zones," within each range. These are generally designated zones 1, 2, and 3. The purpose of these internal zones is to provide additional guidance for individual salary placement and periodic adjustments. To price the control points for these internal zones, the benchmark jobs within each job family or organizational layer are grouped into three levels that represent stages in the natural career path and progressive stages in knowledge and skill requirements for the function or layer. The three groupings consist of entry or basic jobs for zone 1, intermediate-level jobs for zone 2, and advanced jobs within the function for zone 3. The upper end of each zone is then priced to approximate the average median market rate for positions that match the knowledge and skills targets for that zone as the start of their pay range. For example, using the benchmark positions that are at the first level of a professional family, the top of the first zone of that pay band approximates the average of median pay rates for that set of positions. The one exception to this market relationship occurs at the top of each broadband, which coincides with the top of zone 3. To provide a fully competitive base pay opportunity at this advanced level, the top of the band is positioned using 90th percentile data for the advanced jobs in the applicable function. In most cases, the company has multiple functions or job families that are covered by one shared broadband. These zones are then priced as a blend of the applicable median market rates for that set of functions.

The basic structure of this model involves adding competency assessment results to the individual evaluation process and then using this broadened appraisal content to guide periodic salary review decisions. Exhibit 4.6 presents two examples of different salary adjustment guidelines developed by organizations that have adopted this model.

The first guideline in Exhibit 4.6 has been implemented in base pay programs that remain largely job based. Within this context, the pay controls for each job are derived from external market pricing (using benchmark matches), and the resulting market values are then used to construct broadbands distinguishing groups of jobs by job family or organizational layer. The competency linkage is then structured into the salary adjustment guidelines that cross-match a person's competency rating with a personal output rating for the same period. This cross-match generates a dollar adjustment guide for the person's base salary review. The relative weighting intended for competency and output measurement can be captured in the pattern of dollar values contained in the guideline matrix. Because the banding structures have relatively few levels, a dollar-based set of guidelines can be communicated and administered without undue complexity.

Exhibit 4.6   Salary Adjustment Guidelines—Two Examples.

Salary Increase Guidelines with "Core" and "Stretch" Zones

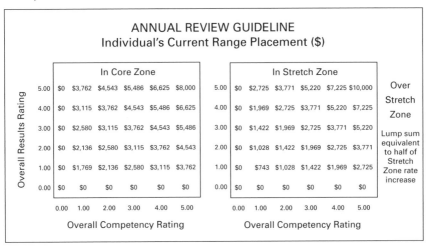

ANNUAL REVIEW GUIDELINE
Individual's Current Range Placement ($)

Salary Increase Guidelines with a Competency Indicator

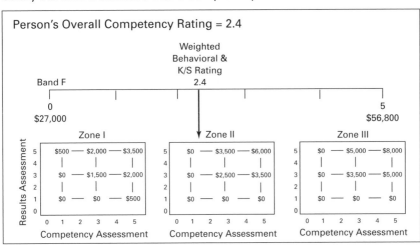

An additional policy concept reflected in the first guideline in Exhibit 4.6 is the concept of "core" and "stretch" pay zones. The "core" and "stretch" system divides the base pay opportunity for each job in much the same way as market midpoints have often been employed in traditional job grades. The "core" segment is intended as the pay opportunity for employees who are developing their performance in the basic job up to a fully proficient level. The "stretch" segment is for employees who are extending their job contributions beyond the basic job to achieve full mastery of a work role. When a broadband is constructed for a job family, the result is typically to have the "stretch" zone for one job in a career path overlap with the "core" zone for the next job in the career ladder. The structure of the salary adjustment guidelines links to this two-zone concept through the pattern of percentage or dollar increases within each matrix. The salary management principle they reflect is that pay advancement above a market average should involve competency and output levels clearly above the standards that apply below the market average for a job.

The second guideline in Exhibit 4.6 reflects an expansion of the role of competencies in base pay decisions. This approach replaces job-based adjustment guidelines with a policy structure that uses the employee's competency rating to indicate what increase matrix will apply to them in their band level. In essence, the competency rating is used as an indicator for the person's most appropriate increase opportunity. For example, a high competency rating leads to the largest increase opportunity, whereas a low competency coincides with the lowest opportunity, without regard to the employee's current salary position in the band. Organizations that use this guideline have included both behavioral competencies and knowledge and skill elements in their assessment model.

(iii) Model 3: Competencies as the Salary Placement Factor Within Broadbands Companies that adopt this approach typically have more generic work roles that are different from traditional job-based structures. Within these organizations, stable "jobs" have largely been replaced by a more diffuse and dynamic concept of "work roles" or "process roles." To align with these changes, base pay administration is reorganized around competency profiles that are customized for each work role. In some sense, competency profiles substitute for the traditional concept of a job. Each competency profile has two components:

1. *Technical or functional know-how categories:* primary area and collateral areas (typically 1 or 2).
2. *Behavioral attribute categories:* selected from the relevant behavioral model.

In this environment, people still possess a primary area of technical/functional expertise but also need one or more collateral know-how areas to handle their multifunctional roles. For example, mechanical engineering could be the primary expertise for a role, but the role would also require significant marketing know-how. At other times, the collateral know-how may shift to product design knowledge or involve purchasing and inventory management. People in this more flexible work environment are expected to steadily increase their core know-how, while also acquiring and applying skills and knowledge within relevant collateral areas.

The know-how portion of the competency profiles is typically defined by a job family or function to capture the distinctive skills and knowledge for that function. Other generic categories of skill and knowledge, such as computer literacy, relate to employees across multiple functions. In these competency-based programs, even managerial roles can follow the same structure. Exhibit 4.7 illustrates a complete set of technical/functional know-how areas defined by an industrial equipment manufacturer for one product line division, along with a sample of four know-how profiles adopted for specific work roles within that organization.

The model shown in Exhibit 4.7 combines the knowledge and skill components of the competency profiles with relevant high-performance behaviors. These behavioral competencies are as fundamental to the definition of a work role as the knowledge and skill categories. Through these high-performance behavioral attributes, the relevant knowledge and skills are integrated and applied for top performance in a given work role.

A work role (and corresponding competency profile) may apply to a single person or to several employees where there is a high commonality to their assignments. Unlike most job descriptions, these profiles are regularly rechecked, typically on an annual basis, to monitor changing work requirements. This does not mean that the competency profiles change annually, but there is an organizational commitment to keeping them up to date because they serve as the assessment structure for developmental feedback and eventual reward decisions.

Exhibit 4.7   Examples of Technical/Functional Competency Structure in Pay Model 3.

Technical/Functional Competency Areas

Product Design	Finance/Accounting
Shop Operations	Engineering
Administrative Support	Customer Service
Purchasing/Inventory	Sales/Marketing
Drafting	Production Supervision
Management	Drafting

Sample of Know-How Profiles
(single and multi-incumbent roles)

Primary Function	Collateral Function(s)
Work Role 1: Customer Service	Purchasing/Inventory
Work Role 2: Engineering	Product Design, Sales/Marketing
Work Role 3: Administrative Support	Customer Service
Work Role 4: Management	Engineering, Drafting

Linkage of Competencies to Base Pay Administration in Model 3 Approaches
The linkage of competency profiles to base pay decisions in Model 3 approaches occurs through three policy components:

• A set of salary broadbands covering all of the work roles in the program
• A shared linear scale for pay and competency progression (see Exhibit 4.9)
• The concept of "guideline salaries" as defined later

Development of Base Pay Bands   The salary broadbands serve as the external market connection for base pay administration in this model. Because of the nature of competitive pay survey practices and their continued reliance on job-matched data, rather than generic work roles or competencies levels, the development of base pay bands for the Model 3 approach must still rely on pay rates for benchmark positions in each job family or function to define the organization's pay bands. For matching internal to external pay practices, a set of "benchmark jobs" that have knowledge and skill requirements similar to the company's more generically defined roles are used as common points of comparison. The resulting competitive data include 25th and 75th percentile base rates for the benchmark positions, the average starting rate at entry level and top pay rates for the most advanced positions by work function. Exhibit 4.8 shows how these specific market reference points are used to develop and update each band in this type of linkage model.

Assignment to Broadbands   In this model, the assignment to a broadband is governed by the person's primary technical/functional area. If a person's primary area is the marketing function, the person's salary band is the band covering the marketing family of professional roles. As a result, the person's competencies can be assessed against the staged levels of marketing know-how, and his or her salary band covers competitive values for these skill and knowledge stages. This means that theoretically, a broadband could be established for each technical/functional area, but in actual practice the market pricing for different functions is similar enough so that one band can apply to several functions. This consolidating of functional areas (or organizational layers) into a few broadbands obviously simplifies the salary band framework. It also makes sense given the importance placed on collateral know-how (in addition to core know-how) in administering base pay under this model.

A Shared Linear Scale for Competency and Base Pay Progression   Exhibit 4.9 illustrates how this program model connects competency profile ratings to salary band progression through use of a shared linear scale of 1 through 7. To structure an overall competency profile so that it corresponds to this scale means that the rating scales for know-how competencies and behavioral competencies need to be formally weighted and blended. The typical approach used by

Exhibit 4.8   Market Pricing Benchmark for the Broadbands.

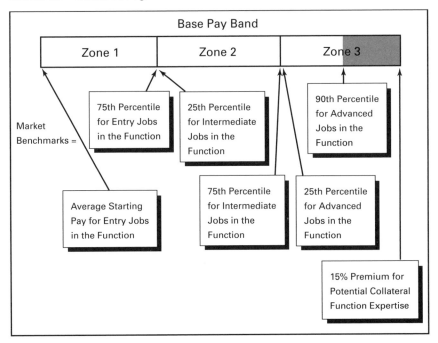

companies with this model sets the relative weighting at one standard for all participants (such as 50% for know-how and 50% for behavioral attributes), although there could be some benefit to varying the weighting for different broadband levels.

Within the know-how area alone, the ratings for one's primary area typically need to be combined with one or two designated collateral areas for a composite

Exhibit 4.9   Illustration of Competency-to-Pay Linkage in Base Pay Model 3.

Competency Profile Rating Scale

1   2   3   4   5   6   7

Salary Broadband

1   2   3   4   5   6   7

rating. Because a principle of this model is that collateral know-how brings extra value to the company beyond one's core expertise, the blended know-how rating needs to reflect this additive value.

To achieve this concept, the administrative structure for this model includes a shortened rating scale for the assessment of technical/functional areas. For example, the scale is structured as 1 to 6. In addition, the ratings for collateral areas are proportionally reduced in value before being summed with one's core rating. As a policy factor, this reduction amount reflects the relative importance given to collateral know-how versus core know-how and is standardized. For example, all collateral ratings would be reduced to 25% of their full rating value. Hence, a collateral rating of 4 is converted to 1 before being added to one's core rating.

As an additional policy control, a threshold rating of 2.0 or higher can be required in collateral areas before credit is given as extra know-how. Such a threshold requirement ensures that the collateral development is significant before it adds to one's overall rating. This approach emphasizes one's core knowledge and skills but also recognizes significant collateral development. Exhibit 4.10 illustrates two sample cases of this ratings calculation.

The Concept of Guideline Salary   In this model, the term *guideline salary* means the base pay amount that most directly aligns with a person's assessed competency level at a given point in time. In essence, it represents the approximate compensation value that the company targets for a given overall competency profile rating when it is tied to a particular broadband. Guideline salaries are expressed in full annual salary terms, not as increments or adjustments. Exhibit 4.11 displays a sample guideline salary of approximately $47,000, derived from a hypothetical competency profile rating and salary broadband.

Exhibit 4.10   Illustrations of Competency Rating Calculation.

	Rating					Additive Scores
Case 1						
Behavioral rating	=	3.2	×	.4	=	1.28
Core know-how rating	=	4.6	×	.6	=	+2.76
Collateral know-how rating	=	3.0 × .2	×	.6	=	+ .36
					Overall rating:	4.40
Case 2						
Behavioral rating	=	5.0	×	.4	=	2.00
Core know-how rating	=	5.5	×	.6	=	+3.00
Collateral know-how rating	=	4.5 × .2	×	.6	=	+ .54
Collateral know-how rating	=	4.0 × .2	×	.6	=	+ .48
					Overall rating:	6.02

Exhibit 4.11 Sample Guideline Using Hypothetical Ratings and a Salary Broadband.

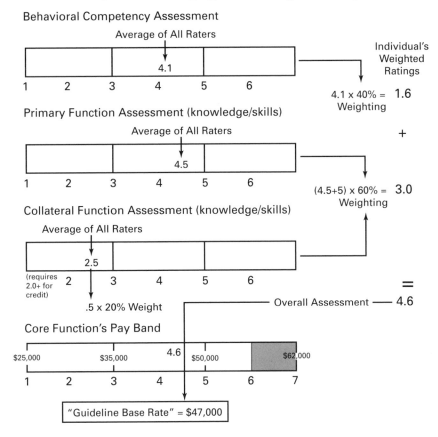

Behavioral Competency Assessment

Companies do not apply this guideline salary approach in a rigid, formulaic way, but rather use it as a policy guide in the salary review process. Other important policy factors enter into base pay decisions as well. These include the degree and direction of change in a person's competency rating (and corresponding guideline salary) from one assessment to another, any "macro" salary budget controls applied at the company or subunit level, and market-related movement in the established salary broadbands. Actual salary decisions are based on an interplay of these various policy factors. Each organization decides how it wants to weigh these factors in its base pay policy and in the training and direction given to pay decision makers.

Two common issue areas demonstrate how the policy factors interplay in actual practice.

Case 1: Applying the guideline salary concept in relation to current salary and prior competency assessments. The salary review process in this model is not formula driven but uses the guideline salary as a major reference point. Because an employee's overall competency profile rating can go up or down (or remain approximately the same) from one assessment to another, base pay decisions need to consider various scenarios. In practice, this is done through a set of review guidelines communicated to the pay decision makers. The following statements illustrate a set of salary review guidelines:

Guideline 1: Major upward movement in a person's competency profile rating (e.g., a jump of 0.4 or greater) that generates a corresponding major gap between the person's guideline salary and their actual salary would be addressed through phased adjustments spread over the immediate and next review. This would typically mean that a major part of the salary gap (between guideline and actual) would be addressed in the immediate review, but the full gap may not be addressed until the next review when the person's competency advancement has been reconfirmed.

Guideline 2: A decline in a person's competency profile rating would not typically result in a reduction in the person's salary, even where the guideline salary falls below the actual salary. In these cases, the individual's salary would be frozen and a period of time would be given (up to two years) to raise the assessed competency level back in line with the actual base rate. Only when the guideline salary is significantly below actual pay for a prolonged period would a reduction in the person's base pay be expected.

Case 2: Coordinating guideline salary levels with budget controls. The guideline salary approach is also typically integrated with a company's macro salary budget policies as an appropriate program control. This involves a two-step procedure. First, a "gap analysis" is conducted of the differences between the proposed new base rates (developed with consideration of the guideline salaries) and people's actual salaries. This gap analysis may be compiled at the departmental, business unit, or other organizational level, depending on how budget guidelines are managed within the organization. Once the total of all pay gaps has been identified for the group, this total is compared to the allowable budget control. If the budget will not fund all the proposed increases, then the increases are typically proportionally reduced (e.g., by one-tenth across the board) so that the new salaries can comply with the budget requirements. This uniform reduction keeps the focus on addressing individual salary gaps, while also giving balanced attention to the economic and competitive pay trends that also contribute to effective salary management.

4.4   VARIABLE PAY/INCENTIVE APPLICATIONS

As described in the previous section, several types of working models are in place for linking base pay management to competency assessment systems. By comparison, linkages of variable pay or incentive pay to competencies are less common and less developed as design options. The two basic concepts most widely used are:

1. Linking a person's competency assessment rating to a scale of modifiers that increase or decrease the person's incentive award that was funded by business goal achievement or a fixed financial formula.
2. Awarding one-time special payments to employees for acquiring and applying new competencies or demonstrating increased strength in a critical competency area.

This section illustrates the design components of these two approaches and describes the business purposes they are intended to serve.

(a) Competency as an Incentive Award Modifier

Companies that use competency ratings as an incentive award modifier are generally trying to achieve a healthier balance in the focus of their incentive pay opportunity. This healthier balance reflects dual attention to (1) generating the necessary performance results to fund incentives and (2) obtaining these results in "the right way," so that a positive, high-performance organization is encouraged and reinforced over the long haul. The competency model and related assessment ratings then serve as the company's monitoring tool for checking how results are being generated and what effect the incentive participants are having on the organization around them. In this variable pay application, the competency elements are typically behavioral in nature, rather than technical knowledge and skill competencies.

One important design option in this approach is what range of modifier to apply to the incentive award. For example, the modifier could range from +25% to −25% of the funded award, depending on the competency rating received by an individual. This range could also swing from +50% to −50%.

Clearly, the wider the modifier's range, the greater the company's emphasis on the competency component of performance contribution. In some programs, this emphasis is so strong that it allows for the funded award to be "zeroed out" if the person's behavioral impact on the organization is evaluated as deficient enough. In other cases, the competency assessment is used solely as a reduction factor when the person's competency rating is not at an acceptable level or above. This last approach provides no potential for increasing a funded incentive award based on a particularly high competency rating.

As with the range of base pay models for linking competencies to rewards, the suitability and type of incentive modifier that fit a particular organization or incentive plan implementation depend on several considerations:

- The relative importance placed on the employee's competency rating versus the business results used to determine incentive funding

- The degree to which incentive funding is based on group results or personal results
- The role played by competencies in other parts of the total rewards system, if any
- The company's strategy for deploying the competency model itself, in terms of whether the driving focus is on developing employees to the high-performance behavioral level or more on bringing everyone up to an acceptable benchmark of behavioral effectiveness

One other model used for incentive award linkage involves taking individual performance appraisal ratings that cover both competencies and personal work results and treating them as a separate and distinct incentive funding component. The remaining incentive opportunity is then allocated to group measures within the business. This design alternative can be particularly attractive where measurable individual results are closely tied to broader business success, but the company wants to achieve a balanced focus for individual performance as discussed above. As with base pay models that use competencies as part of a broader employee appraisal rating, this incentive model can involve a wide range of relative weighting of competencies, as opposed to the other appraisal factors.

(b)   Special Bonuses for Competency Acquisition

The second type of variable pay linkage identified in our practice research involves using special bonuses to reward the acquisition of targeted competencies. Although the use of this model is limited, it has been adopted by some companies as a design alternative to the base pay models described earlier. In essence, the linkage of competencies to special bonuses is used to reward competency development financially, without the perceived deficiencies of a base pay linkage. This variable approach is seen as a more effective means of addressing the following design issues:

- One-time bonuses can reward the acquisition of critical competencies without creating a "fixed" pay cost that is inappropriate, when a competency's value to the business will be foreshortened by frequent job transfers, constant innovation in technology, or the use of a noncore workforce that is intended to leave the organization after a few years.
- Measuring the value to a business of an acquired competency or a higher level of competency development is inherently imprecise and is therefore better rewarded through one-time payments rather than base rate increases that differentiate in individual rewards over the longer term.
- Because they are one-time, rather than "permanent," bonus payments can be potentially larger in immediate value than a base pay adjustment and, therefore, more dramatic in their reward impact.

- Individual performance results are the most appropriate driver of base pay progression, and competency developments that lead to stronger performance will inevitably carry over to base pay progression, without the need for an overt linkage.

Although these arguments certainly raise some important design considerations for base pay linkages, they have not influenced the general thrust of reward linkages to date. Base pay models have been at the forefront of linkage to competencies, and this pattern seems to be continuing.

(c)   Bonus Linkage Design Features

Among the design models now in place for linking bonuses to competencies, there are four basic design elements:

1. Competency-related certification standards
2. Guidelines for bonus award amounts
3. Timing of award consideration
4. Linkage to performance appraisal results

The competency certification standards used in these models have been structured in two different formats: (1) certification of newly acquired competencies at some qualifying level or (2) certification of the accomplishment of a personal development plan. The first approach provides a bonus award when the person meets the assessment qualifier for an additional competency category relevant to the work. This concept is used most commonly with technical knowledge and skills and is linked to a set of detailed knowledge and skill descriptors within a function or job family. Within these programs, the qualifying hurdles vary from simply the demonstrated acquisition of a higher technical stage within a particular competency category (e.g., for "trade promotion" within the marketing function) to the much tougher hurdle of advancing in all of the technical categories for a work function to the next higher stage (e.g., from a "basic" stage to an "intermediate" stage for all categories of marketing know-how). This latter requirement is similar to the promotional criteria traditionally applied in administering technical/professional career ladders. Behavioral competencies have also been included in these programs, but the qualifying standard takes a different form, involving a required increment along a linear assessment scale (e.g., advancing two or more points on an assessment scale of 1 to 6) to authorize bonus recognition. Both certification processes typically rely on multisource evaluations to add validity and credibility to the certification process. In the technical area, raters are selected as peers or technical leaders in the relevant work function. In the behavioral area, feedback comes from an assortment of contacts within the business who work extensively with the individual.

The second certification concept relies on a formal development planning and review process, where the individual documents a set of competency development objectives with guidance and approval from the supervising manager. Achievement of these approved objectives then becomes the standard for bonus recognition. The organizations using this format tend to rely heavily on the supervising manager to judge whether developmental objectives have been achieved or not, although multisource feedback can be used as an important guide in these decisions. The timeframe for development plan accomplishment is typically beyond one year so that bonuses are not an annual expectation but occur only when plan completion has been certified. Because the bonus payments linked to these plans are generally of uniform size (e.g., 5% of base pay or a fixed dollar amount), the need for consistent treatment across a participant group is of clear importance.

The bonus linkage models also typically include an administrative connection to performance appraisal results that add the appraisal rating as an additional qualifier for competency bonus awards. For example, a policy is established that employees have to maintain an appraisal rating of 3.0 or higher within a five-point scale to remain eligible for their next developmental bonus. Companies have viewed this control dimension as a way to ensure that participants stay focused on generating positive work results, while also addressing key developmental opportunities. As with many approaches to competency–reward linkage, the intended goal is to foster an optimal balance between meeting near-term performance requirements while building stronger, more flexible performance capabilities into the future.

4.5 RECOGNITION AWARD APPLICATIONS

Recognition awards are essentially nonmonetary forms of reward that emphasize public acknowledgment and honorary tokens of recognition, such as certificates and trophies. Although this vehicle would appear to offer considerable potential for competency-based reward linkages, there is even less use of this vehicle than with variable pay applications.

As with most recognition programs, competency-related awards are generally structured with specific nomination and selection criteria and with a variety of award types, depending on the relative importance and difficulty of the learning challenge. One recognition vehicle that has worked well in this area has been an educational grant concept that funds additional personal learning activities of the employee's choosing into the future. Given the caliber of employees who are most likely to take on these challenges, the organization's sponsorship of self-selected learning experiences can be particularly attractive to these employees.

4.6 CONCLUSIONS ON COMPETENCY–REWARD LINKAGES

While the use of competency-based rewards in business has been relatively limited as compared to other competency applications such as selection and personal development, the preliminary success of several working models, as described earlier, argues for continued efforts in this direction. The fundamental drivers in this innovation process will be the needs of business for HR processes that foster and sustain competitive advantage in the face of continually changing work requirements, processes, and organizational structures. Formal competency-based reward linkages now offer businesses a new tool with which to enhance their adaptability and cross-functional competence by stimulating and reinforcing ongoing improvements in their workforce capabilities. It is hoped that this review of current practice presents a clearer picture of the practical design options available to companies exploring this area, as well as a starting point to look at the potential fit of various models and approaches to one's own organization and strategic objectives.

Chapter 5

Managing Talent to Maximize Performance

J. Stephen Heinen, PhD, and Colleen O'Neill, PhD

5.1 THE BUSINESS OPPORTUNITY FOR TALENT MANAGEMENT

Although many sources of competitive advantage provide short-lived gains, talent management practices can create the most enduring competitive advantages. Financial capital is broadly available and no longer serves as a barrier that separates competitors. New technologies and process innovations typically can be easily replicated by competitors and generate only temporary competitive advantages. Sustained competitive advantage comes from an organization's talent management practices; however, the talent management practices that work for one organization may not create value in another. The most powerful talent management practices are firm specific and respond to an organization's unique business and human capital context. Once the "right" talent management practices are in place, they operate as a cohesive system and create a significant financial return that competitors will find difficult to replicate.

The companies doing the best job of managing their talent deliver better results for shareholders. For example, an often-cited study by Mark Huselid shows that a one standard deviation increase in high-performance talent management practices is associated with enormous economic returns.[1] These select companies, in the top 15% of all those in the study in terms of their use of high-performance talent management practices, were associated with the following financial advantages:

- A 7% decrease in turnover
- An increase of $3,800 in profits per employee
- Approximately $27,000 in sales per employee
- An increase of $18,600 in market value per employee

[1] Mark A. Huselid, "The Impact of Human Resource Management Practices on Turnover, Productivity, and Corporate Financial Performance," *Academy of Management Journal,* 1995, 38(3), 635–672.

The economic benefits of talent management are also demonstrated at the individual level. "A players," or the best 10% to 15% performers of an organization, have improvements in performance output ranging from 19% to 120% depending on the complexity of the job.[2]

The imperative to effectively manage talent is more urgent than ever. Despite the potential to deliver greater shareholder value and to realize the competitive advantage through better talent, most companies are not satisfied with their ability to develop talent quickly and effectively. Moreover, most companies are experiencing a shortage of top talent as well as increased competition for talent. In this chapter, we offer our recommendations for managing talent to maximize performance. Our talent management recommendations are based on Mercer's ongoing research on the "best practices" of leading companies.

5.2 ALIGNING TALENT MANAGEMENT AND BUSINESS STRATEGY

Talent management is a set of interrelated, workforce management activities concerned with identifying, attracting, integrating and measuring, developing, and motivating and retaining people. (See Exhibit 5.1.) Every organization has a talent management system—whether by default or by design. It is the people side of the business design.

Exhibit 5.1   Talent Management System.

[2] John E. Hunter, Frank L. Schmidt, and Michael K. Judiesch, "Individual Differences in Output Variability as a Function of Job Complexity," *Journal of Applied Psychology,* 1990, 75(1), 28–42.

Historically, organizations were concerned only with developing and replacing top executives. Today, organizations are increasingly putting intense focus on attracting and retaining the best talent at all levels of the organization. As companies question the effectiveness of their talent management systems, they need to address several questions, including:

- What capabilities do you need to successfully implement your business design?
- Are you attracting the top talent in your industry or is someone else?
- Are you recruiting and selecting "A players"?
- Can you clearly identify your top contributors—both current and future?
- Are you growing and developing the skills you will need to succeed in the future?
- Are your performance and development strategies aligned with your business strategies?
- Do your pay, performance, and career development programs work together to increase retention and commitment?
- Are you retaining your top performers at a greater rate than your low performers?

(a) Aligning Talent Strategies with Business Strategies

To address these questions, each organization needs to create its own unique talent strategy. To be successful, the talent strategy must be aligned with an organization's business strategy and human capital context. Aligning talent strategies with the business context is a frequently unmet challenge. Successful organizations often change their business models. With each evolution of business strategy, talent management practices need to be realigned and focused. As described in Exhibit 5.2, the alignment makes a difference. When aligned, the talent management practices work in unison to help drive company results. When misaligned, employee capabilities lag or are mismatched with market demands, and the organization lacks the skills and behaviors needed to implement and sustain the business strategy.

(b) Integrating Role of Competencies in Talent Management

A successful talent strategy is executed by designing and implementing the "right" talent management processes. Some of the processes associated with talent management include recruiting, selection, on-boarding, mentoring, performance management, career development, leadership development, succession planning, career planning, and recognition and rewards. Each of these talent management

Exhibit 5.2   The Impact of Alignment and Misalignment.

Misaligned TM Practices ⟶	TM Aligned with Strategy
Lagging or mismatched employee capabilities with market demands	Right workforce skills and behaviors in place to implement and sustain business strategy
Limited accountability or clear line of sight to business plan	Individual and team performance expectations aligned with organizational values and priorities
Lack of career roadmaps or limited and rigid career paths, undermining retention of top talent	Business success and diverse workforce supported by functional career path architecture
Disparate pay and career programs that fail to address retention issues	Integrated pay, performance, career development programs that improve on retention challenge and garner commitment
Conflicting processes and tools. Mismatched messages regarding identification, assessment, development, and retention of talent	Talent management programs work in unison to drive company results

processes must be designed to fit the strategic requirements of the business and to integrate with each other.

In many organizations, talent management processes are disconnected from each other. The disconnection among processes often results from each of the talent management processes having different "owners" who, in turn, focus on different priorities and drive different process outcomes. For example, an organization's selection process may focus only on acquiring talent with job-specific technical skills, whereas the organization's pay-for-performance programs focus on rewarding and recognizing people who innovate to achieve desired results. The lack of attention in the selection process to competencies such as results orientation, creativity, and problem solving may not yield sufficient talent to perform in the way the company desires. Even though disconnected talent management processes are sending "mixed signals" to employees, many organizations generally do not attend to the lack of synergy between talent management processes until significant problems have already developed.

If talent management processes are not well integrated, they will not operate as a cohesive system and they will not achieve the high performance required. In order to maximize performance and encourage employees at all levels to "pull in the same direction," talent processes should reinforce the same messages about performance excellence. Competencies are a critical lever for aligning and integrating talent management processes and practices; they are the practical tools for translating business and human capital requirements into specific behavioral requirements of high performance. When appropriately defined, competencies can align recruiting, selection, performance management, career development, and rewards to build and reinforce key valued behaviors and to provide a structured model to integrate the talent management processes. (See Chapter 4 for a discussion of competencies.)

5.3 KEY FACTORS IN SUCCESSFUL TALENT PLANNING AND DEVELOPMENT

Talent planning techniques have evolved significantly over the last decade. Exhibit 5.3 shows the shift that has occurred from traditional replacement planning to succession planning to the current more dynamic and integrated approach of talent planning and development.

Exhibit 5.3   Evolution of Talent Management.

Dimension	Replacement Planning	Succession Planning	Talent Management
Purpose	Risk management	Strategic staffing and development	Widespread sourcing and development
Target	Key executive jobs	High-potential pool	Broad organizational involvement
Assessment	Job-specific potential and performance	Performance trend and leadership competencies	All capabilities and outcomes that matter
Outcome	Replacement plan for critical positions	Development and staffing plan for high-potential pool	Development and deployment system fully integrated with HR processes
Career Path	Linear, mainly within function	Cross-function, some geography and division movement	Opportunistic, cross-function, geography and business
Implementation	Yearly review	Yearly review with development planning	Ongoing activities aligned with other HR processes
Ownership	Executives	Corporate	Shared: Employees, staff specialists, leadership, CEO
Participation	Compliance	Acceptance	Involvement

To optimize success for the individual and the organization, leading companies typically merge their workforce planning, career planning, and development processes. Mercer's ongoing research on best practices in talent management has identified 10 key factors for success. We offer the following factors as both a checklist for practitioners to test the success of their talent management efforts and a guide to their program development efforts.

(a)   Chief Executive Ownership

An organization's Chief Executive Officer (CEO) must be the "ultimate owner" of the talent management system and in so doing should personally drive the planning and development of the organization's talent, especially the top group of leaders. The CEO must also be held accountable for the overall results of the talent development effort. General Electric's celebrated CEO, Jack Welch, frequently and publicly says that his primary responsibility is ensuring that GE has the right talent in place to run the business.

The CEOs of leading companies understand that growing world-class talent and creating plans to help talent succeed in their career goals is both a strategic business need and a retention strategy. They create a shared set of leadership values around talent management and establish explicit guiding principles for acquiring, managing, developing, and rewarding talent. They communicate clearly that talent management is "business critical" by requiring business units to constantly reevaluate the health of their business regarding talent and ensure that adequate talent is available and ready to meet and execute the strategic challenges of their organizations. Specifically, they communicate that managers are directly accountable for ensuring that they have the talent in their respective business units sufficient to:

- Run their own business area.
- Fuel the growth of their business.
- Contribute to the growth of talent in the larger organization.

(b)   A Business Activity, Not an Administrative HR Task

Successful organizations view talent management as an ongoing strategic priority. It is also a critical business process, not an administrative HR practice. In today's world, people are the key competitive edge fueling business goal achievement. Thus, the talent planning process needs to be directly linked to the business and strategic planning processes.

At a corporate and business unit level, leading companies consider, at least annually, current and emerging business challenges and forecast talent needs. This forecast of required capabilities is used to assess the existing talent pool, identify gaps, and create individual and organizational development plans. Exhibit 5.4 illustrates the process organizations go through to link the business strategy and the talent strategy.

Each year the organization reviews its long-term strategy and annual goals to identify the talent issues that must be addressed for success and to determine the specific categories of talent or the competencies required for success. For the short term, it is important to flag talent issues or categories of people that may impede success (e.g., excessive management churn, lack of sophisticated marketing talent); however, it is equally important to identify the future talent gaps or new competencies needed 3, 5, or 10 years out. This will allow the organization to build for the long term and initiate the talent strategies that need to be addressed in advance. Leading organizations today are continually scanning their environment for both the short- and long-term changes they expect in their markets and industries, and building that information into their talent development strategies.

Once the talent needs are identified, attention is then given to analyzing whether the current talent practices are appropriately supporting the business strategy. This process leads to an overall identification of issues and gaps in talent needs and practices. After the identification of these various gaps, the specific talent issues are prioritized for attention in relation to their impact on business success. The outcome of that process helps set the agenda for talent review discussions. It can pinpoint talent categories that need to be spotlighted for attention or can identify talent practices that need to be improved. For example, companies

Exhibit 5.4   Linkage of Talent Strategy to Business Strategy.

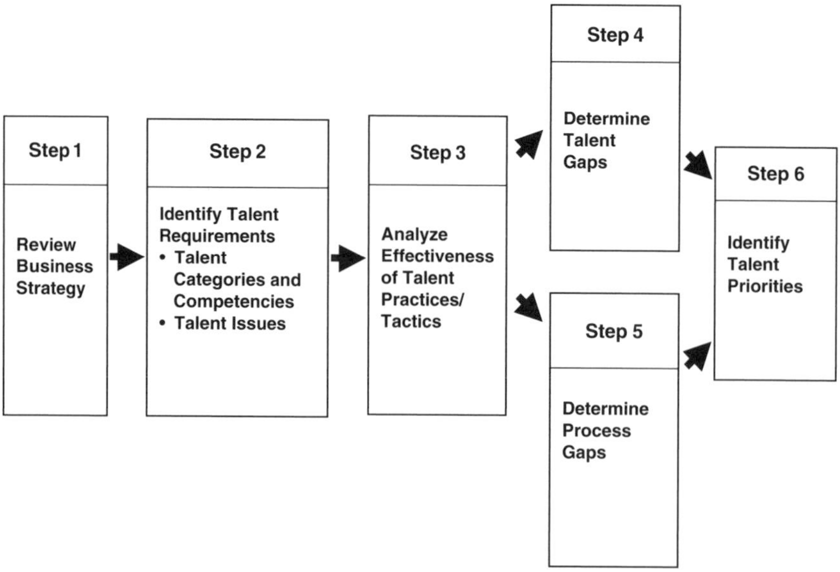

typically find that projection of the talent needs followed by an assessment of their internal and external labor pool to determine gaps allows them to strategically balance internal development and external hiring.

(c) Development Must Be Forward Looking

Given the rapidly changing environment in which most organizations operate today, a talent development plan must continually adapt to the changing business environment. The development process must focus on where the business is headed, not where it has been. It must not dwell on what was successful in the past, but what will be required to be successful in the future. Individual development for current job performance needs to be distinguished from longer-term development. Many performance management systems focus on what is needed to improve current performance. Often there is a lack of attention to what the individual will need to survive and perform productively in the future business environment.

Developing talent requires planned activities that concentrate on developing skills and abilities for future business needs as well as development of skills for current job performance. Successful programs identify strengths on which to build and development areas that need to be improved. The development activities generally include both on-the-job experience coupled with targeted educational/learning opportunities.

(d) Focus on Rigorous Candidate Assessment

Talent planning is based on candidate assessment. Successful development has as its foundation a strong and rigorous assessment of candidates' competencies. This includes assessing current performance, which is the starting point of all development; however, it also includes assessing the capabilities the person will need in future leadership or other targeted positions and creating development plans to help that person achieve those capabilities. Organizations today use a range of assessment tools to provide people with adequate feedback on their strengths and weaknesses so they can continue to grow.

Effective assessments generally include a range of different inputs. Employee career interests and aspirations are generally a starting point. Achievement records of past responsibilities, including performance ratings on different assignments or project activities, are another critical input. Many organizations have created competency models that can serve as another assessment criteria. The competency assessments for this purpose focus not only on the current role the person is in but also on other roles to which the person aspires. In some cases, personality assessments or other relevant personal data, for example, willingness to relocate, are factored into the assessment. Multiple assessment methodologies are generally used to provide a more thorough and accurate assessment of the individual. These assessments may include managerial assessments, multisource feedback, or even external professional assessments.

(e) Balance Organizational and Individual Needs

Talent planning and development must balance the needs of the organization with the needs of the individual. Addressing individual needs and concerns is a critical factor in attracting and retaining key talent. Individual employees need to be in charge and take ownership of their own growth and development; however, the organization must also deal with the reality of its own environment and address its key concerns for the future. This generally requires constant attention and continuous dialogue between organizational representatives and the individual employee.

Frequent movement is used as an approach for developing high-potential individuals. Furthermore, high potentials have an expectation that they will be frequently exposed to new challenges. If this does not occur quickly enough, high potentials are likely to leave the organization. In order to balance the needs of the organization and the individual, leading companies have either formal or informal guidelines that individuals are ready to move when they have transferred their expertise to others. These companies also reward and promote based on how effectively knowledge is shared. They establish developmental agreements at the beginning of assignments. These agreements make explicit developmental goals, expected contribution, and knowledge transfer expectations upon assignment's completion.

(f) Invest in Staff and Process Support

Although a CEO must play a pivotal leadership role in talent management, key staff roles are also needed to facilitate the talent management process and accumulate organizational learning. At many leading companies, corporate staff specialists focus on talent development, pipeline management, and talent growth. Corporate staff manage the talent review process, develop candidate slates, counsel line managers on pipeline issues, and assess and coach leadership talent. This group accumulates company learning regarding talent development and shares this knowledge with the various line managers. Corporate staff facilitates identification of talent across organizational boundaries. Often, each business unit also has a program manager who is responsible for supporting and facilitating the talent management process.

(g) Develop Multiple Talent Pools and Career Paths

In the past, managers often designated a specific person as their backup or replacement. In today's more ambiguous and uncertain world, emphasis is more on developing talent pools rather than a specific individual in order to ensure that an adequate supply of talent exists from which to choose when an opening occurs. Individual needs and organizational needs are not always directly aligned. Therefore, predicting specific successors is often unsuccessful, if not impossible. Also, organizations can be seriously damaged by investing in a "crown prince" (at the expense of others), who later leaves for opportunities elsewhere. Thus, by creating a pool of people who are given the development experiences to prepare them for future opportunities, the organization minimizes the risks of being unprepared to fill a key vacancy, yet provides opportunities for motivated high-potential talent. Leading companies designate multiple high-potential talent pools and attend to their growth and development. Examples of some of the high-potential lists often maintained by companies include:

- Early career high potential
- Sure bets for promotions to senior positions
- Employees one step away from officer
- Diversity: women/minorities
- Top 100 global talent
- "Black belts" in critical skill areas

Given the constantly changing business models and the limited supply of talent, companies also need to consider continually adding to their talent pool at different career stages. Talent strategies that are singularly focused on acquiring new graduates (i.e., talent just out of college or graduate school) and growing them throughout their careers are giving way to strategies that involve multiple entry points into the organization's talent pool and multiple career paths. Business success also depends on multiple career path options. Every business has multiple talent pools that it needs to develop simultaneously. Leading companies identify and communicate multiple career path options that strategically fit with the company's business needs and talent market dynamics. Through reviews of the business strategy, the organization may identify different or new talent pools that need special focus. Typical career paths include:

- Business unit leadership
- Functional leadership
- Technical/functional expert
- Project management expert
- Cross-function/expertise integrators

(h)   Focus on On-the-Job Learning

Job assignments and experiences are the best development opportunities. Because most development occurs on the job, many organizations have found that key positions offer rich learning opportunities for high-potential employees. Some organizations identify which positions have been particularly helpful in developing key executive or technical talent and ensure that high-potential candidates are placed in these positions to accelerate their development. These positions generally receive intense scrutiny, both in terms of staffing and ongoing monitoring of the incumbent's performance. Many organizations have found it helpful to identify specific positions that allow critical learning with minimal risk. Organizations have also identified specific types of project experiences or key mentors that can help accelerate developmental learning.

(i)   Conduct Regular Talent Reviews

Talent reviews are used to spotlight individual and organizational capability issues. Leading companies generally conduct regular talent reviews of all of their key people to plan and coordinate development activities and monitor progress. These reviews provide an assessment of an organization's aggregate talent, as well as an assessment of how well individuals are developing. The talent review process usually starts at senior leadership levels and, as an organization gains experience, cascades through other organizational levels. These talent review meetings generally work best if led by the line managers responsible for a business unit with support from Human Resources (HR) staff. Some organizations set up task forces in a business unit to guide the process, but this approach is not recommended. Separate talent review task forces often encounter difficulties because they separate ownership and accountability for talent development from the line managers.

The talent review process typically begins with individual employees preparing summaries of their career interests, aspirations, and constraints. (See Exhibit 5.5.) Typically, employees are asked to note the following:

* Summary of accomplishments over the past 12 months
* Areas of strength/growth
* Improvement/development needs and plans
* Job/career interests

Employees provide this summary of their accomplishments and development needs to their managers. Managers, in turn, assess employees' areas of strength/ growth and improvement/development and comment on the reality of employees' career plans. Managers also rate employees on their current contribution and career potential.

It is important to remember that the primary source of development for most employees is the relationship with their immediate manager. Employee commitment, growth, and development are highly correlated to the relationship the

Exhibit 5.5   Talent Review Process.

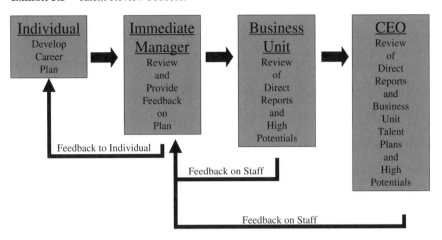

employee has with his or her immediate manager. The degree to which the manager is respected for his or her ability, models effective behavior, and provides coaching and guidance regarding careers are critical factors in the development process. High-performing companies have more managers with well-developed skills in identifying and assessing talent, providing effective feedback and coaching, and encouraging employees to broaden their skills and experiences. To facilitate this behavior, the organization needs to:

- Reinforce management's responsibility to grow and develop talent.
- Develop continuously managers' talent management capabilities.
- Provide the necessary support tools to facilitate the process.

Talent review meetings are then held at a business unit level to discuss the talent issues for that business unit and to review the managers' assessment ratings and development plans for these high-potential employees. Some of the questions usually considered during these talent review meetings include:

- Are the right people in the right jobs performing at maximum levels?
- Is this the right mix of talent necessary to drive the business?
- Who could be promoted to further career and organizational potential?
- Who needs to be reassigned to another position to improve results and/or behaviors?
- Does anyone need to be outplaced?
- What individual or group talent vulnerabilities exist?
- What actions need to be taken to improve talent development results?

Most companies rely exclusively on direct managers to identify high-potential employees during talent review processes. Because potential is most difficult to identify in early and midcareer employees, the opinion of a direct manager is not sufficient to identify high-potential talent. Leading companies include multisource feedback, reviews by next-level managers and HR representatives, and reviews at higher levels during the organizational talent review process.

Many organizations are not satisfied with their ability to adequately or accurately assess high potential. High potential is a rating based on an assessment of the employee's capability to perform at some higher level of responsibility in the organization. The rating is based on an assessment of the person's competencies or capacity to acquire the competencies needed in a targeted higher level of responsibility. Most organizations identify several targeted lists of high potentials to address their array of talent needs and multiple career paths. Leading companies do not merely focus on high potential for corporate leadership or general management roles. They also focus on high-potential professionals—those outstanding performers in a particular discipline who have the potential to deepen their skills portfolio and serve as functional leaders or technical experts.

Assessments of high potential consider both current and past performance, but the assessment is based on potential to perform significantly higher or more complex assignments. Because individuals have different capacities and develop at different rates, these assessments of high potentials are done at least annually, and individuals may be put on or dropped off the high-potential lists in subsequent years. High-potential identification criteria is typically defined as:

- High performance track record
- Early strength shown in "must-have" competencies, including demonstration of "active learner" characteristics
- Capacity to learn from experience
- If at entry or midcareer, seen as likely to succeed at least two levels up, given proper developmental support

Organizations often confuse "promotability" with "potential." Although the concepts are related, they are distinct and it is important to distinguish them. Promotability assesses readiness to move or timing to next job, whereas potential ratings should reflect the capability to demonstrate competencies required in an advanced role, and therefore, reflect the pace of progression. Most organizations consider potential in terms of the employee's ability to advance vertically in the organization. As a practical matter, it often gets expressed in terms of the number of organizational levels a person is expected to be able to advance. This can be done within a career or within a set period (i.e., three to five years). If it is based on a career, then generally "high potential" is expected to be two or more organization levels, and "potential" is considered one organizational level. This type of potential rating is used to help the organization determine the kinds and amounts of investments the organization makes in an individual. Potential ratings should be linked to development activities and plans. Because individuals grow at their own pace, accelerated development is likely to be more beneficial to the organization and the individuals, if they are high potential. Thus, segmentation of the employee population on potential can help guide the organization in how to tailor developmental plans, programs, and activities to the needs of the person with the greatest payoff to the organization. Because these judgments are fallible and employees actualize their potential at different rates, these assessments need to be continuously updated and actions modified based on actual results.

Because an individual could demonstrate high potential but still need more time in a current assignment to develop required skills, it is advisable to ask managers to delineate readiness to move or promotability from potential. Readiness is generally defined in terms of whether the person is considered ready or able to take on a new assignment and ready to be promoted to the next level or to a lateral assignment. Readiness is usually based on the fact that the person performed well in his or her current assignment and learned the important things he or she was expected to learn from that assignment. Thus, development is perceived to be enhanced by transferring to a new assignment rather than continuing in the present assignment. For planning purposes, most organizations determine whether the person is ready now, which generally means within the next 12 months. This allows the organization to orchestrate various activities to increase the chances for success of the promotion. Exhibit 5.6 is an example of rating categories that address both potential and promotability.

Exhibit 5.6   Potential and Promotability Rating.

High potential, ready now	Has the potential to progress at least two organization levels and is ready for a promotion now.
High potential, needs more time in assignment	Has potential to progress at least two organization levels, but needs more time in current assignment to develop his or her skills.
Potential, ready now	Has potential to move to next level and is ready for promotion now.
Potential, needs more time in assignment	Has potential to move to next level but needs more time in current assignment.
Irreplaceable pro	Is extremely valuable in current role, needs to continue to broaden current skills, and must be retained, but is not promotable to higher levels.
Meets expectations	Is performing satisfactorily in current role, but is not promotable to higher level.
Performance problem	Is not meeting expectations of current role and needs to improve performance.

The delineation of performance, promotability, and potential such as described in Exhibit 5.6 allows organizations to make appropriate development and compensation decisions. For example, although the "irreplaceable pro" should not receive the same development plan as the individuals with potential to advance, he or she should receive appropriate rewards to ensure ongoing motivation and retention.

Another area that often gives organizations difficulty in potential ratings is the person at the other end of the spectrum from the high-potential person, the "placement issue." Although these individuals lack the competencies to be promoted to higher levels, they still need to be moved from their present assignments. Possible actions include reassignment, demotion, or outplacement. Increasingly, organizations are learning that they cannot reach or sustain high performance levels by paying attention only to their high-potential employees; they also need to address "underperformers." Exhibit 5.7 shows the deleterious effect that underperformers can have both on attracting and retaining high potentials as well as on company performance and morale.

Some organizations design their performance management processes to specifically address concerns with underperformers. These organizations focus on identifying and addressing relatively low performance. Several organizations are also addressing concerns with underperformers in their talent review process. In the talent review discussion, some organizations simply flag individuals who are perceived to be weak performers or blockers of development. Other

Exhibit 5.7   High Cost of Underperformers.

organizations specifically identify anyone whose current performance results and competencies are not considered adequate for the company's new strategic direction or the performance standards required for the success of the company's new business strategy. Once these individuals are identified, some of the necessary remedial steps cannot be implemented immediately without severe disruptions, legal problems, or serious morale issues. Thus, broader planning in talent review sessions can be helpful.

Most organizations hold talent review sessions annually, but they are sometimes held more often. When organizations hold them more often, development plans are primarily focused on the people who are ready for immediate promotion. Whether talent reviews are held annually or more often, specific attention is devoted to identifying the actions that may help develop immediately promotable employees' capabilities. These actions would include new assignments or new responsibilities as well as all the supporting contingency planning around transfers, moves and reassignments, identification of backups for current assignments, and supporting resources needed for stretch assignments. For people whose potential is considered to be longer term, decisions will be made relative to what actions will be taken in the next time period that will further their development, such as a training program, a lateral assignment, or a project assignment.

At the same time, the organization's senior management will assess the talent gaps that exist throughout the organization and develop strategies to address those gaps. These may include creating or developing specific new capabilities or recruiting new employees with specific talents. In addition, management will analyze the success of its development strategies and the kinds of work experience and organizational activities that contribute to the effective development of people.

A byproduct of these talent review sessions is increased calibration among managers about their criteria and assessment of performance and value contribution. Over time, companies that discuss their talent in these "public forum" talent review sessions and pay attention to improving their process decrease their bias in evaluating and promoting talent and become more discerning in their talent development and deployment. The accumulated learning in talent management contributes to the long-term business success of the organization.

(j)   Leverage Technology and Measure Success

HR is in the midst of a technology transformation. There's a movement to leverage new technologies to automate talent management processes that previously had been done through manual processes. Today's new web-based software makes it easy for managers and employees to access online performance documents and gather comments and approvals. And modern HR information systems can provide a wealth of easily accessible data for managing talent to maximize performance.

Facts are key. Indeed, the right "dashboard" of metrics and measures helps leading companies accomplish two broad objectives: implementation and impact. Exhibit 5.8 shows some sample talent management metrics and measures.

Data in the service of the first objective—implementation—indicate the success with which talent management processes are being implemented as planned by answering questions such as: Are assessment practices netting the desired number and types of individuals? Are targeted career paths actually being

Exhibit 5.8 Sample Talent Management Metrics.

Tracking Metric	Definition	Comments
Voluntary turnover	Number quits/end-of-month headcount, annualized, by prior performance rating	Track overall trend and pay close attention to performance levels of voluntary exits.
High potential turnover by key area/attribute	Percentage of high potentials lost due to voluntary turnover in specified roles or by key characteristics	Data allow diagnosis and resolution of specific causes of high potential turnover.
Cross-functional experience	Number of managers who transfer in/out of functions or business units	The goal is to increase the flow of human capital among functions to develop talent and create cross-functional networks.
Promotion rate by level	Number of employees promoted/number of employees in level	Focus on rates of promotion out of career levels where there are career choke points; track rates at all levels over time.
Internal/external recruitment	Percentage of key positions filled by internal and external candidates	Companies should not attempt to fill *all* key positions with internal candidates because external hires can provide fresh perspective and skills.
Bench strength ratio	Number of high potentials per senior management position	Proper ratio of high potentials to upper-level positions facilitates effective succession management, helping to provide a sufficient number of candidates for key positions.
Development costs	Measurement of organizational resources devoted to development	Understanding of program costs enables a cost-benefit analysis of development activities.

followed? Are regular talent reviews being performed, and are developmental plans appropriately adjusted as a result? Impact, the second objective served by good data, concerns the link between talent management practices and business performance. What mix of homegrown and recently hired talent optimizes business performance? What is the impact of development programs on performance? To what extent is the loss of talent through turnover actually hurting business performance?

The best companies answer these difficult but critical questions and use measures and metrics to stay the course . . . or change it when new direction is needed.

5.4 CONCLUSION

Managing talent is difficult and time-consuming, but very rewarding. Too often, senior management has the best of intentions for developing people, but fails to invest the time and resources needed to realize the benefits. Organizations with long-term, sustained success are those that focus on growth and achievement by attracting and retaining the best talent. An organization can create the best business strategy, make the right acquisitions, and invest in the right programs; however, if the organization does not have the necessary talent, those strategies will fail to be implemented, the synergies from acquisitions will fail to materialize, and investments will not earn desired returns.

Chapter 6

Getting the Most from Your Sales Compensation Plan

Steven Grossman and Craig Ulrich

Imagine this: A Fortune 500 company looks to increase profitability and growth by revamping its sales compensation plan. Management sees a sales organization that's uninspired and not maximizing its potential. The company pulls together senior management, sales management, human resources—and even its sales-people—and *together* they develop a new sales compensation plan that helps double revenue growth.

This isn't some senior executive's active imagination, this is reality for several top corporations that have modified their sales compensation plans and today are enjoying increased profits from rejuvenated and redirected sales teams.

Why is this scenario unlikely in some executives' eyes? There exists a historical push and pull between management and its sales force, with each side not always understanding or trusting the other. Their traditional positions can be summarized as follows:

> We no longer have the right caliber of people. Costs are way out of line. Our sales-people spend more time on fairways than on highways and airways. And, we're losing good people to the competition, while keeping those who don't produce.
>
> *—Management*

> Management doesn't understand us. If it weren't for us, the company wouldn't make money. Just as we begin to make money with our customers, management wants to develop another new sales compensation plan that creates more work and offers less pay.
>
> *—Salespeople*

Often, the issue becomes even more complex with several additional players taking sides in this struggle, including sales administration, human resources, and even customers. With all this uncertainty and potential conflict, it's understandable that some companies ignore warning signs and delay developing a new sales compensation plan. By not redesigning a plan—or creating an ineffective plan—however, companies can find themselves behind the competition; losing precious market share, customer share, and high performers; and generating sub-par performance and results.

This chapter makes a case for effectively aligning the sales compensation plan with the business strategy and maximizing the company's growth potential. It further outlines the financial benefits of reworking a plan, demonstrates the importance of involving various constituencies, especially the sales force, and offers some tips for designing, implementing, and administering a new plan.

6.1   WHY CHANGE A SALES COMPENSATION PLAN? IS IT WORTH THE RISKS?

Companies that take a fresh look at their sales compensation plans and effectively design and implement their new plans can see a substantial impact on profitability. Mercer recently conducted a review of some of its clients that had just implemented a change in their sales compensation plans. Mercer wanted to determine the impact that the new plans had on the companies' results. The study looked at 18 companies representing a wide range of industries and found that in all cases, organizations saw a substantial improvement in profitability and in employee behavior. In fact, growth rates for the 18 companies doubled, on average.

Impact of Modifying Sales Compensation Plans

- Data was acquired from 18 companies in several diverse industries, including pharmaceutical, telecommunications, shipping and freight, retail, and resort and travel.

- All companies were seeking to create a more aggressive sales culture to drive sales and financial performance.

- All companies were transitioning from a low-leveraged plan (base/variable) of pay (85/15 to 100/0) to a more aggressive mix of pay (50/50 to 60/40).

Changes in plans included:

- Pay mix to include greater weight on incentive than base.

- Payout frequency of incentives from annual or quarterly to monthly with opportunity for annual bonuses.

- Tiered incentive structures (e.g., payouts at 75% of quota attainment).

(continued)

- No change in current salary levels (not lowered) where reps already were being paid below market.

- Suspension of merit increases while adding to incentive amounts where reps were being paid above market.

Design and implementation:

- Design teams included the CEO, director of sales operations, vice president of sales, regional managers, field managers, sales reps, HR, marketing, and systems people.

- In several cases, a full-time implementation team of sales management, HR, finance, and IT was dedicated for three to six months.

- Sales rep training was conducted directly by sales managers, who were first trained by consultants.

- Sales reps were involved from the beginning of the design process.

Behavioral results included:

- Companies attracted desired selling profile and talent.

- Reps were motivated by upside potential in earnings.

- Increased performance tracking resulted in better accountability and management control.

- Sales reps were focused on larger, more profitable accounts.

Financial results included:

- Growth rates doubled.

- First-year results were 18% above plan.

- After three years, sales increased 20% versus less than 10% the prior three years.

- Return on investment (ROI) was 25% to 30% over four to five years.

- Revenue increased 16% compared to 7% the previous three years.

As the Mercer study shows, modifying your sales compensation plan can be well worth the effort; however, company leaders often are averse to change or they become so frustrated with subpar sales performance that they make immediate, drastic decisions rather than take more thoughtful actions. Before management jumps to conclusions and instinctively cuts sales budgets, alters pay plans, modifies pay mixes, and more, they must first fully understand the complicated world of sales compensation. For starters, the sales compensation plan is much more than simply a pay document that states how much salespeople will be paid for making a sale. The plan must be viewed as a strategic tool that helps align the sales mission with the overall business strategy, that considers the best use of available resources, and that optimizes costs and maximizes profitability. *Essentially, the sales compensation plan should not be approached as a pay issue at all.*

The importance of an effective sales force is too great to ignore. According to *Selling Power* magazine, the combined sales forces of the 400 largest U.S. service and manufacturing companies total more than 1.5 million salespeople. This sales team generates $3.2 trillion in volume each year—close to the gross domestic product (GDP) of France, Germany, and Italy combined (on average, $2.1 million per sales rep/per year). Additionally, it is a direct result of this revenue that 13.3 million other people have jobs, since on average, one effective salesperson creates enough revenue to pay for nine other jobs within an organization.

Today, the sales world is evolving and management is not always in step with the changes. Customers no longer turn to hundreds of suppliers to provide their important resources; most have trimmed their supplier pools in exchange for a few loyal suppliers, who serve as strategic partners. These major organizations are serious about this new approach, and in fact, many have cut the number of suppliers by more than 50% and are demanding much more from those that remain. And, as if this were not enough to discourage sales organizations, many customer bases are diminishing as a result of significant industry consolidations, organizational and segment consolidations, fierce competition, and mergers and acquisitions.

Even with the stakes so high, many companies continue to take an overly simplistic approach to sales compensation, which often results in the following two situations:

1. *Lack of pay for performance.* There's little or no difference between the pay of the average seller, who performs just well enough, and the outstanding seller, whose performance far outdistances the others. The star performers attract the lion's share of business, and if they are not being rewarded for their efforts, they become difficult to retain. The ensuing effect is an environment that feeds on the adage that those who *cannot* leave remain, and those who *can* leave, jump ship.

2. *Too much pay for the wrong—or limited—performance.* At the other extreme, companies sometimes pay too much for what they believe are the star performers. Consider a company that pays a few "top performers" quite well. The company considers these few individuals as top in their field because they control the company's best customers. At face value this seems justified; however, at closer look many of these star performers are being rewarded for past accomplishments. For example, in many cases the top salespeople actually have built a pool of customers over the years, which guarantees the

salesperson a sizable commission based on continued sales. This is termed "shadow base salary" or "disguised base salary," and though the salesperson may be paid 95% commission, he or she in reality is working for base pay based on the constant flow of recurring business.

In addition, these top performers often enjoy the fruits of plum territories as a result of past performance or even "inherited" territories. This is not to say that these salespeople should not be rewarded for their contributions; rather, it is more a question of how much reward and for supporting which business objective—yesterday's or today's, and the company's or the salesperson's?

After reading the previous two examples, a reader may ask, "OK, so now what? I'm not sure if we're paying too little or too much." The ensuing sections will help answer this question by showing how to determine salespeople's actual contribution to the sales effort, how to motivate them, and how to make changes with their engagement and buy-in.

Purpose of Sales Compensation

- Motivate business and sales strategy execution
  - — Drive sales and service effort to achieve strategic objectives
  - — Drive business and customer priorities
- Support compensation philosophy
  - — Reinforce desired risk/reward culture
  - — Support organization and product/service life cycles
- Align with management interests
  - — Reinforce what executives want from the sales channel
  - — Sensitize sales channels to the messages sent to outside investors and analysts
  - — Support value/asset creation

6.2 WHAT TELLS YOU THE SALES COMPENSATION PLAN REALLY IS BROKEN?

Organizations are complex organisms in which the various functions need to share a common goal: to maximize profitability and increase shareholder value for the entire company and shareholders, not just individual functions or people. Often, however, functions begin to protect their turf and become distrustful of other functions within the company. This attitude is perhaps the greatest obstacle to creating a powerful sales compensation plan.

The successful sales compensation plan design process considers perspectives from all the key parties and includes them, especially salespeople, throughout the process. Salespeople and sales management may be afraid that change means less for them. Management and human resources may believe that the sales force is overpaid for their efforts. Sales administration may be frustrated because the salespeople do not listen to them. As the following section shows, however, the various key parties often differ on whether they believe the sales compensation plan is even broken.

(a) "Salespeople Are Overpaid: Change the Plan"

(i) Human Resources   The role of human resources is to oversee a company's talent base, including managing and collecting data, conducting annual satisfaction surveys, tracking turnover, and much more. But when it comes to sales, human resources often is uncharacteristically hands-off. If HR does conduct surveys of sales compensation practices, it may just skim the surface and look no further than benchmarks and basic industry practices. HR is likely to base sales compensation not on an in-depth analysis of the sales performance and the sales process but on where the company "feels" it should be compared to the industry. For example, the company may feel its salespeople should be paid in the 50th or 75th percentile. Often, HR would like to be more involved with sales force analytics but does not venture too closely because of historical differences between the two functions and sales management's discouragement of any "interference" from HR.

This lack of interaction and understanding between HR and sales management can create friction when considering changes to sales compensation, as depicted in Case 1 later. In that example, HR told senior management that it was paying too much for salespeople, as compared with the competition. HR did not understand the sales process, the sales rep's impact, and value to the sales process and to the customer, or the customer's perceived value of its salespeople. The design team brought together the key parties and studied customer needs so that everyone better understood the sales role and helped create a compensation plan that benefited all, and most important, the company.

(ii) Senior Management   Most companies are led by some combination of a CEO, COO, or CFO, who may have a particular bias toward sales. If the CEO climbed the company ranks from the sales organization, he or she may be more knowledgeable of and favorable toward sales. The CFO, however, rarely comes from a background in sales and is more likely to focus on the cost of sales and accounts receivable. The CFO may ask: "Why are we paying these people so much when we haven't even been paid by some of their accounts?" Senior management often views sales as an expense rather than an opportunity for greater profits.

(iii) Sales Administration   This unit, which answers to sales management, tracks data, oversees the operations of the sales force, and usually manages the pay plans. Often the sales force views sales administration with contempt for fear that sales administration and HR are creating yet another plan to reduce their pay. The salesperson may see the sales administrator as someone who continually

---

Case 1: Second Tier . . . and Climbing

A second-tier food ingredient company was competing heavily with the two major players in the industry. HR management saw a sales force that was overpaid and was not making inroads in catching up to the competition. Sales management just wanted senior management to leave the salespeople alone so they could remain content and not jump to the competition. The salespeople, of course, thought their pay was fair to slightly under market levels.

Along the front lines, sales reps for the first-tier producers "waited in line" to meet with the purchasing agent to sell their product. Their main sales pitch was to differentiate their products versus competitors' based on price, name recognition, and dependability of supply. The sales reps for the first-tier producers earned $75,000.

The second-tier company was paying its sales reps about $150,000, which concerned the corporate vice president for HR. "Why are *we* paying twice as much as the majors?" he asked. To find out, he created a design team, which conducted an extensive study including interviewing numerous levels of customers and potential customers. The team discovered that salespeople for the two largest competitors focused on purchasing, while its sales reps proceeded directly into the product development labs. There, they worked in partnership with the customer's technicians to help them develop the next blockbuster products. These sales reps were much more than salespeople; they possessed the right technical expertise to forge relationships with those creating the next big product lines. The team concluded that they may not be paying its people *enough!*

Lesson: A company cannot just look at market pay levels to target compensation; it must fully understand its salespeoples' role. It must also look at its strategy, compare and contrast it with the others' strategies, and think about what role the salesperson needs to play. Go beyond industry studies and benchmarks and actually talk with the customer. Analyze the buying process from a customer's standpoint, and find out the differences across customers. A company must decide: Is the salesperson an order taker or a market maker? As this case illustrates, sales compensation design goes well beyond market pay analysis.

studies the salesperson's performance results, looking to cut costs first, rather than increase sales. Some natural jealousies develop when sales administration reviews payouts to high-performing salespeople.

(b) "Don't Do Anything to Disrupt My Service"

(i) Customers   Many customers want close relationships with their suppliers' salespeople, but they don't want their salespeople to try to sell them products they don't want or need. While some customers want a close relationship with salespeople, others just want to know that their shipment will arrive at the same time in the same manner that it always does. The customer wants to be sure the company will come through; the product/service will be in-spec, meet its needs, and solve its problems; and it will arrive on time and at the agreed-upon (competitive) price.

Customers play a vital role in developing a sales compensation plan. Companies often overlook the important connection between the sales force, the pay plan, and customer perspectives of salespeople's behavior. A company and its sales force must understand the buying process and the selling process, which can be accomplished in several ways, including surveys, benchmarking, and face-to-face interviews with customers. Case 1 outlines the benefits of knowing, and establishing, the customer's needs.

(c) "Everything's Fine: Don't Change the Plan"

(i) Sales Management   Sales management often consists of former salespeople who have ascended the company ranks. They have strong loyalties to, and have camaraderie with, salespeople, and they tend to be averse to change because they don't want to rock the boat. To ensure that the salespeople are happy—and that they continue to keep customers content and drive revenue—some sales management teams often believe that salespeople are earning the right amount of money. Change the compensation plan, they figure, and the sales force will be demotivated, prompting them to leave the company and take their best customers with them. In Case 1, sales management thought the company was paying its salespeople the right amount and was afraid that HR would try to reduce it.

(ii) The Sales Force   Salespeople are different from most other employees. The salesperson typically isn't under the same roof as other employees and isn't as in step with company policies, procedures, and culture. These independent resources are vitally important to an organization. They are in the front-line trenches every day meeting with customers, creating value, witnessing new trends, suffering setbacks, hearing complaints about product /service offerings or deliveries, and driving their company's business. Many see themselves as the company's unsung hero, who is underpaid for bringing so much value to the company.

The typical salesperson also has a few fears: customers will leave tomorrow; the shipment won't get to the customer; the invoice will be wrong; management will anger the customer; the product won't be to specification; and HR and management will cut pay.

At the same time, many in management would be surprised to learn that salespeople actually understand the need for change long before company leadership gets wind of changing trends and customer attitudes. The salesperson may be more willing to change than what senior management and HR think because they are first to see shifts in the industry. Management is most often best served by attempting to better understand the salespeople—their roles and idiosyncrasies—and elicit their input and support in designing and implementing any changes, particularly a new sales compensation plan.

After reading about the characteristics of various issues, positions, roles, and personalities that may be involved with sales compensation, a reader may determine that creating a new sales plan is not worth the headache and effort. On the contrary, understanding the diverse positions and their roles, and including them throughout the process, is a major step toward designing and implementing the right sales compensation plan.

An effective plan does far more than efficiently provide pay to salespeople. It also should generate a measurable impact on financial performance; behaviors of sales and service people and executives, managers and staff; customer relationship, satisfaction, loyalty, and retention; employee satisfaction and retention; and business and employee performance and productivity.

Before designing a new sales compensation plan, management must first thoroughly articulate its own strategic business objectives and understand its own sales force, the customer buying process, customer needs, its current pay plan and its shortcomings, and the desired outcomes from a new plan.

First, to determine the need for a new plan, management should ask the following questions:

Does Your Pay Plan . . . ?

- Reinforce and drive behaviors that help meet management's overall strategic business objectives?
- Provide motivating, meaningful, and cost-effective rewards to the right people for the right results?
- Align with clearly articulated sales and sales management roles, prominence, and accountabilities?
- Align with other key sales management programs and practices, and reinforce the desired culture of the sales effort?
- Clearly communicate and reinforce desired behaviors to the sales force in an appropriately simple manner that is easily understood?
- Meet the changing needs of the business?

If you answered "no" to one or more points in the preceding list, perhaps it's time to consider a change.

Management is often well aware that its compensation plan is out of alignment with the company's strategy, but some managers are afraid to touch their plans for fear of "ruffling the feathers" of their salespeople. Just a slight modification, many fear, will create a rebellion in which the salespeople leave the company, with one or two of their best customers. Management also may acknowledge a deficiency in its sales force but reason that a slightly broken sales compensation plan is acceptable—at least the sales team is producing and bringing in *some* business.

6.3 HOW DO YOU KNOW WHEN YOUR SALES COMPENSATION PLAN IS REALLY BROKEN?

Problems or issues with sales compensation plans requiring plan redesign are usually not driven by typical compensation issues such as pay competitiveness or even pay levels. They are typically brought on by four types of sales or business issues, problems, or events.

(a) Key Elements of the Sales Model Are No Longer in Proper Alignment

As already highlighted, fundamental changes over time in any market drive changes in a company's business strategy and how it approaches and delivers value to its customers. All of the key elements of a sales effort are connected and need to be properly aligned (see Exhibit 6.1). A change in overall business strategy or customer segmentation ripples through a sales effort and requires an appropriate change in sales channels, account-level sales strategies, sales roles, coverage, goal setting/forecasting, and compensation.

Or, conversely, a change in customers' buying and decision-making processes (e.g., from customer consolidation or the development of buying groups) causes most salespeople to change how they approach these customers; the strategies they deploy to win, expand, or retain an account; and how they spend their time. If management does not change how it organizes/deploys, manages, and motivates its salespeople, then significant misalignments develop that severely compromise the effectiveness of almost every aspect of its sales management process, in particular the sales compensation plans.

It has become common for management teams to transition from one model—say, transaction selling, to another, such as consultative selling—in several segments of their customer base to move the company and its sales effort further up the "food chain" in terms of value and competitive positioning. Exhibit 6.2 portrays many of the key management practices typically associated

Exhbit 6.1   Aligning and Connecting All of the Key Components.

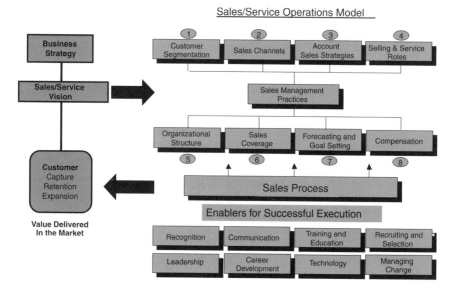

with the four generic sales roles or sales models—transaction, solutions, consultative, and partnership selling. Unfortunately, many management teams fail to make the appropriate changes to their pay plans to match how their roles, sales strategies, goals, and more may have changed.

The commission plan that had served the company and its salespeople well for the last several decades of "pure" transaction selling will probably produce improperly high (or woefully inadequate) earnings for a sales team that is now delivering the results in the new consultative model. Quite often, cultural legacies such as "We're a commission sales company" or "The only good salespeople are those on commission" prevent management from making the right changes as it modifies how it approaches each customer in order to continue to pay the right people for the right results. It's almost impossible to take a highly effective, transaction-oriented, "coin-operated" sales culture and overnight turn it into a highly effective, consultative, team-oriented, value-adding sales effort.

This comparison also emphasizes that if you are approaching each customer segment differently, then your sales management practices and your pay plans ought to differ as well. Too many companies are still mired in the philosophy of one pay plan for all salespeople, regardless of differences in roles and sales strategies across the sales effort.

Another perspective on this same phenomenon is how companies evolve (see Exhibit 6.3). Each stage in evolution requires different sales strategies, management approaches, and sales practices to operate effectively. Sales compensation plans also need to keep pace with this evolution.

Exhbit 6.2   Sales Roles Drive Key Elements of the Sales Management Process, Including Compensation.

Element/Sales Role	Transactions	Solutions	Consultative	Partnership/Alliance
Key Elements of Value Proposition	• Feature, function, benefit • Product cost • Availability	• Product sets/bundles • Operating costs • Dependability	• Creativity • Operating results • Profitability • Confidence, risk mgmt.	• Competitive advantage • Strategic positioning • Shared goals • Shared risks
Key Focus of Role	• Activities • Products • Programs	• Product sets • Solutions • Programs	• Diagnostics • Advice/counsel • Operations • Programs	• Business strategy • Organization integration • Collaboration • Resource sharing
Key Skills of Role	• Product knowledge • Pricing • Persistence • Numbers	• Product knowledge • Understand value • Creativity to see alternatives	• Business skills & acumen • Value creation • Political skills	• Strategic thinker • Leadership skills • Project, resource & budget expertise
Target Audience	Buyer, Anybody	Department Mgr.	Business Unit or Functional Head	Senior Mgmt.
Target Account Focus	A, B, C, D Accounts	A, B, C, D Accounts	A, B Accounts	A Account
Role of Field Sales Management	• Supervision • Recruiting • Expense management • Training • Territory management	• Technical resource • Relationships • Goal setting • Coach • Opportunity management	• Resource management • Senior management relationships • Strategist • Coach	N/A
Key Measures of Performance	• Orders • Revenue • Number of accounts	• Sales to quota/growth • Product and services sales	• Sales to quota/growth • Account profitability • Line expansion • Packaged services	• Performance-based agreements • Profitability • Value delivered, savings
Base/Incentive Pay Mix	0/100–50/50	50/50–70/30	70/30–80/20	80/20–90/10
Incentive Vehicle	Commission	Commission/Bonus	Bonus/Commission	Bonus
Pay Timing	Weekly/Monthly	Monthly/Quarterly	Quarterly/Semiannual	Annual

Finally, changes to the sales focus or objectives that companies pursue should have a correspondingly profound effect on how salespeople are paid to execute those strategies. Unfortunately, this is not always the case, and once again, a company's cost of sales and a salesperson's ability to earn desired levels of income can both be negatively impacted.

To determine if your existing sales model is aligned with your new business strategy, company leadership should ask the following questions to see where the organization currently stands and where it's going:

- How are your markets/customers changing in terms of how they buy, what they buy, relationships with suppliers, decision making, industry consolidation, etc.?
- What will your value-creation strategy be? Where are your profit zones?
- To whom do you sell today? To whom will you be selling in two to three years?
- What channels do you use to sell today (e.g., Internet, alliance partners, distributors, manufacturing reps, telesales)? What channels will you use in two to three years?
- How is your sales/service effort changing internally to capitalize on the external changes in your markets and customer base?
- What cost of sales issues are you facing?
- Is the sales/service effort consuming an increasing percentage of sales dollars?
- What's the financial difference to your organization between a superstar and a marginal salesperson? How much more do the superstars bring in?
- What is your recent turnover history? What impact is it having on achieving goals?
- Are you losing the "keepers" and keeping the "losers"? Why are they leaving? Where are they going?
- Are your current forecasting and goal-setting processes meeting expectations?
- How are goals set? By territory? By region? Who sets the goals? How often are goals met or exceeded?
- What are the real sales roles today?
- What relationship do salespeople have with customers?
- What steps is the management team taking to drive a true sales culture across the organization (when appropriate) and attract the right people into the sales/service effort? Is this area a competitive advantage?

Exhibit 6.3   Elements Should Evolve with Each Stage of Business Growth.

- Are the right skills and roles in place for the future or are you living in the past?

(b)   Mergers and Acquisitions of Companies with Different Sales Models, Cultures, and Pay Philosophies

Most companies that compete in the same industries or market segments have significantly different sales models, strategies, and cultures. It's not just differentiation in product/service offerings that distinguishes competitors; how they execute and how they manage their sales efforts also differentiate competitors. When two or more companies merge, or have multiple divisions in the same industry, these differences need to be addressed before "one" sales force can be created that represents the combined strengths of both companies or all divisions.

An interesting way to portray these differences is to position each business and sales effort in a grid that compares the relative prominence of the salesperson and the company, and the relative "value" being delivered. Is the customer "buying" what the individual salesperson can provide or what the "company" as a whole can provide? Are salespeople fulfilling the transaction or delivering value-added, "consultative" services?

Exhibits 6.4 and 6.5 are helpful in understanding sales roles and the nature of relationships with customers. Plotting where each sales unit (or competitor, division, or acquisition target) is positioned can reveal some significant differences (and key similarities) in sales approach, customer relationships, and cultures across sales efforts. Each quadrant represents differences in cost of sales, sales roles and overall sales models, and how each customer segment may require a different sales model and compensation strategy. Strategically, this process can help identify how each unit needs to change to execute the *customer relationship strategy* of the combined sales effort, including the compensation strategies and plans.

Units in the upper left quadrant have a relationship between company and customer. In the upper right quadrant, the company's brand name is driving sales of high volume, off-the-shelf goods. In the lower left quadrant, the individual salesperson drives the value-added service, serves as consultant, and partners closely with the customer. In the lower right quadrant, the salesperson often represents the one primary value the customer is buying, beyond the product or service. Furthermore, the type of sale and the selling approach (consultative or transactional) will have a significant impact on compensation.

(c)   No Longer Cost Effective for the Company

A fairly "clinical" review of sales performance and pay data can reveal how cost effective a pay plan really is and whether it's working for the company and its salespeople in the proper or desired balance, or for one stakeholder more so than the other.

With the appropriate information technology (IT) systems and databases, a multitude of analyses are able to be conducted quarterly and annually and tracked over several years. Each of these analyses can be as statistically sophisticated as the management team desires.

Although many analyses are interesting and helpful in assessing a sales effort, several in particular are revealing about the actual performance of the sales effort and the compensation plan(s).

(i) Performance and Pay Distributions How salespeople's performance and pay are distributed around medians, standards, or goals reveals how the pay

Exhibit 6.4   Different Sales Models and Pay Philosophies 1.

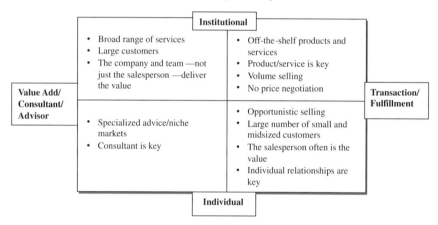

Exhibit 6.5   Different Sales Models and Pay Philosophies 2.

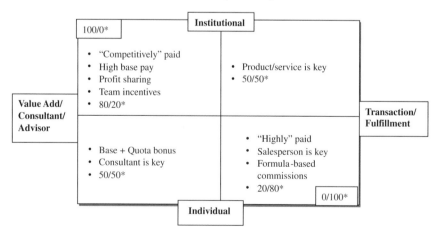

*Base/variable as percent of total compensation.

plans are really working in terms of delivering the right amounts to the right people for the right results (see Exhibit 6.6).

Is the shape of the distribution appropriate for your business? Your culture? How predictable are results every year? Every quarter? What drives that predictability, and can salespeople influence it? Are enough people "in the money" every quarter? Annually? Are your performance thresholds low enough? High

---

Integrating Diverse Sales Cultures

What happens when a major corporation acquires two smaller firms with completely different cultures and approaches to sales, customer relationships, and sales management? Friction.

In 2000, a leading business-to-business financial services firm, which formed institutional ties with customers, had just acquired two small companies whose sales forces took an individual transactional approach to selling. The acquirer placed greater emphasis on its organizational support and service offering, whereas sales teams from the two small companies being acquired typically earned large commissions for having close individual ties with customers. These relationships placed significant power in the hands of individual salespeople. The smaller firms were located in the far lower right corner of Exhibit 6.5. The acquirer was located in the far upper left corner, which was about as far from the others as possible. Sales organizations that are found in the upper left quadrant rely on more of a team sale and relationship with the customers. Organizations in the bottom right quadrant possess more of an independent, lone ranger approach to selling. The acquirer company concluded: "We need to quickly move the acquired sales forces from the lower right to the upper left to more effectively fit our sales culture and business strategy, without losing salespeople and customers."

Result: Salespeople in the lower right quadrant saw the change as management's taking away their hard-earned commissions. Many left the organization, and because of their close relationships with customers, they took some customers with them. Over time, the acquirer migrated the remaining accounts from the lower right to the upper left quadrant, where customers began to forge a relationship with the institution rather than with individual salespeople. Upon reflection, the large acquiring firm should have implemented a more careful change management approach in designing and implementing its sales model and new pay plan. Including salespeople early in the process may have enhanced buy-in. These losses could have been minimized; and the purchase price of the acquired companies was probably too high, in that it did not consider the loss of accounts.

enough? How effective is the goal-setting process? How current are standards of performance?

(ii) Key Drivers of Individual Performance and Earnings   Determining what drives differences in results across the sales effort (and across customer and product segments) is crucial in assessing whether your pay plans are driving the right focus and whether the actual focus of your salespeople is aligned with your current strategy. Is the plan encouraging the appropriate allocation of time, creativity, and energy across the sales organization? Is your strategy saying one thing and your pay plan rewarding something else? To quote one of Mercer's clients: "Are we putting the 'cheese' in the right place?"

(iii) Cost of Sales Curve   Perhaps most important is how cost effective the pay plan is in terms of cost of sales compensation as percent of revenue (or margin). The absolute value and the shape of the cost curve must be operating in the right balance between the company and the salespeople, particularly the high-performing salespeople.

Exhibit 6.6   Performance and Pay Distributions.

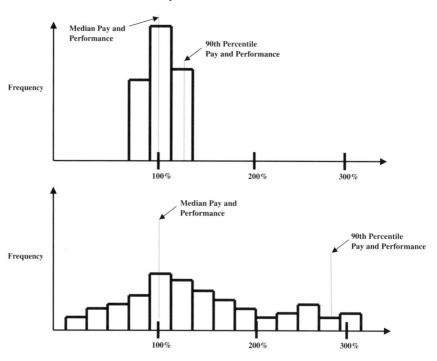

Ideally, incremental costs as a percent of revenue are declining while each additional sale or milestone provides the salesperson with sufficiently motivating and increasing levels of pay. This is highly dependent on the mix of fixed and variable elements in the pay program and the use of quotas, thresholds, gates, linkages, and so on. Many plans have cost curves that are not in proper balance, excessively favoring either the company or salespeople (see Exhibit 6.7).

(d)   No Longer Motivating

As noted earlier, how salespeople's performance and pay are distributed around medians, standards, or goals reveals how the pay plans are really working in terms of delivering the right amounts to the right people for the right results.

Even if someone lacks the necessary skills to significantly outperform the rest of the pack, just knowing that you can really "ring the bell" is often sufficient motivation to get someone to exert the effort required throughout the year.

Too many sales compensation plans simply do not provide sufficient motivation to excel. The "spreads" between median and high performers (e.g., 90th percentile) are well less than 200%, far too narrow to really drive outstanding performance.

Identifying and rewarding the real "stars" in the sales organization is one of the most critical activities management undertakes in every sales organization. The stars may be individuals, or in many cultures, teams of people. Regardless, the rewards must be sufficiently beyond the "average, solid performers" to drive everyone's behavior to excel. Senior management teams that systematically narrow the realistic range of earnings opportunities often compromise the overall effectiveness of their sales efforts.

Exhibit 6.7   Key Performance Drivers and Cost of Sales Curve.

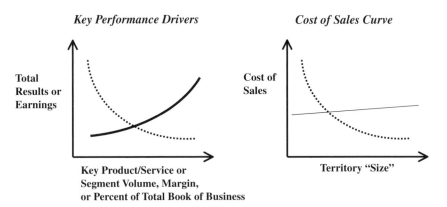

6.4   DESIGN AND IMPLEMENTATION

Design is the phase where all the pieces begin to come together. As you consider the following points, always remember to include salespeople and other key players early in the process. An effective sales compensation plan must work in concert with the company's overall goals, objectives, and strategy. Consider the following structural elements when designing the plan:

- *Determine eligibility.* Who should be in which plan? The plan should consider which employees are eligible, and may even include some people in customer service or technical support.
- *Set a target total cash level.* Based on the roles and relative impact (prominence), determine the annual level of total cash the position should earn in the external market when all expectations for performance are satisfactorily met.
- *Set the target incentive opportunity.* Set the proportion of target total cash that should be paid for reaching sales-related goals. The more direct influence the individual seller has in getting results (prominence), the higher the percentage the incentive component should be. As a general rule, if the incentive portion is less than 10% of target total cash, it's not enough to be a motivating incentive. You've created a communication plan, not an incentive plan. If necessary, reduce salary to accommodate an adequate proportion (mix).
- *Determine the overachievement incentive (OAI) opportunity.* Sales compensation plans should drive performance above expectations. If there is insufficient opportunity to earn additional money for exceeding goals, then most salespeople won't exceed goals. So, the opportunity is provided to earn more when goals are exceeded. Unlike other exempt positions, an OAI opportunity is usually greater for salespeople, often as a multiple of the target incentive opportunity. The ratio of OAI to target incentive dollars should be at least 2-to-1, 3-to-1, or even 4-to-1, depending on the industry and growth stage of the channel and business.
- *Select two or three performance measures and set their relative weights.* Ideally, one measure should have a relative weight of 50% or more to make it perfectly clear what management wants its salespeople to do. No weight should fall below 10%. No sales compensation plan can be expected to reward everything that must be done.
- *Establish standards for each measure.* After the measures and weights are selected, then set a range of performance around the expected or par achievement level for that measure. It is best to set minimum, par, and excellence levels for each measure at this point. If standards cannot be set comfortably for each measure, then that measure may not be a satisfactory measure on which to tie an incentive payout, unless it's carefully modeled and communicated.

- *Establish the simplest possible relationship between changes in each performance measure and changes in pay (payout curve).* Salespeople respond best to simple one-to-one relationships between single measures and the dollars that performance earns. Given the wider spans-of-control in most sales forces, complex matrix, multiplier, gated threshold plans developed 10 years ago that depend on overcommunication and frequent supervisory feedback can be cumbersome and not motivational for many sales forces; however, with the software tools available today, many plans that were viewed as too complex in the past may be manageable and motivating today.

- *Operationally define the compensable sales event for each measure.* A compensable sales event is the point in the sales process that when completed will trigger a specific sales incentive credit earned by the salesperson. It clearly specifies when a "sale" is a "sale" for compensation purposes. An elegant compensation design with all the right measures cannot be implemented unless the designer has clearly operationalized each compensable sales event so that finance, IT, and human resources can accurately track, record, and pay on all measures.

- *Understand the implications of payout timing.* If compensable sales events are operationally defined within the context of the sales process/cycle, generally the longer the sales cycle, the less frequent the payouts. The sales cycle is often the best gauge in determining whether payouts should occur monthly, quarterly, semiannually, or annually.

If these design elements are established for each compensation plan for each role, then the compensation plan design is complete. Next, the process moves on to cost modeling of the plan and evaluating the ROI from changing the plan (see Exhibit 6.8).

By now, you have a good idea about the business strategy, sales process, eligibility, expected behaviors you're looking to affect, target levels of sales growth, additional cost of sales versus new revenue created, and all the key components of an effective plan. Armed with all this data, management will proceed to the simulation stage, where it will run numerous performance scenarios to determine the effects on incentive payouts, and how these payouts affect company profitability.

Simulation can be quite complex and time consuming as designers run multiple scenarios on all performance measures under different market conditions, and even multiple what-if scenarios for each salesperson. Throughout simulation, companies will usually adjust the incentive schedule or commission rates in multiple combinations to study all possible outcomes. Simulation is often overlooked, but it is the best way to ensure that the investment in change equals the anticipated return in revenue and/or profits. It may take weeks to perform simulation tasks, but it will prove well worth the effort if the plan introduced considered all the possibilities.

Exhibit 6.8   Summary of Pay Elements.

Element	Purpose	Criteria
Base Salary	• Provides stable income to account for level of experience and skills needed to perform the job	• Prominence of sales role in customer buying decision • Competitive market practice • Strategic compensation positioning
Incentives • Commission • Bonus	• Secure commitment to critical outcomes • Provide motivation for results, particularly overachievement • Control fixed costs	• Prominence of sales role in customer buying decision • Sales cycle • Degree of risk taking, extra effort • Market practices • Profitability of sale
Stock	• Aligns economic interests of sales force and shareholders • Provides a retention vehicle • Provides future compensation that isn't expensed	• Industry practice • Stage of business's life cycle • Company philosophy
Spiffs/Contests	• Provide short-term incentives to encourage high-priority activities	• Introduction of new products or activities not contemplated at plan introduction
Vendor Payments	• Create extra vendor share of mind by providing a bonus/incentive for accomplishing key results	• Large percent of sales goes through an indirect channel
Recognition	• Celebrates top performers through non-cash rewards	• Highest performers (Top 5% to 10%) • Reinforces a culture of performance
Benefits	• Provide a level of low-risk financial security, such as 401K, medical, retirement, life	• Competitive practice • Compensation philosophy/culture • Stage of business life cycle
Perks	• Reimburse for out-of-pocket expenses	• Competitive practice

(a) Early Involvement Is Key

Although implementation physically occurs after design, planning associated with introducing a new plan needs to be initiated in parallel with the design effort.

As previously stated, it is beneficial to include salespeople and others early on so that they view any change in as positive a light as possible. If not, the odds for successful implementation are greatly reduced. A worst-case scenario is if salespeople were not included in the design of a new plan, and they first heard bits and pieces through the grapevine. Typically, their first reactions would be defensiveness, distrust, and fear that management planned to take something away from them. Once salespeople get into this frame of mind, it's difficult to change their first reaction.

A well-implemented plan will include salespeople in the beginning so they are participants rather than opponents. Communicating the change will be easier if they are involved from the beginning, have "spread the word" about the new plan in-process, have felt an ownership role in the plan, and have understood the benefits of the new plan. Other key players to include in design and implementation are sales management, sales administration, senior management, human resources, finance, and customer service. Rarely will all salespeople jump on board and fully support a new plan, but the ease of transition will be much smoother when at worst-case the "initially negative" salespeople are at least neutral to the change.

In addition to getting input from all salespeople early on, management must be particularly savvy in acquiring the support of its top salespeople. If the star performers understand that the new plan will benefit them (or they view it neutrally), they are more likely to support it. Furthermore, the remainder of the sales force often look to the stars for their reaction. Sales forces will generally support the new plan if the stars support it.

Case 2: Good Design, Poor Implementation

A large organization recently revamped its sales compensation plan after years of stagnant sales. Management created a sales compensation plan that on paper appeared to be a failsafe plan that would motive and fairly compensate its sales force, enhance revenues, contain costs, and retain its most effective salespeople.

The company made two serious errors, however: It failed to include salespeople early on in the design process, and it rushed through the implementation stage. Management was so excited about its new plan, which it believed would increase compensation for salespeople, that it mailed the plan overnight to its 1,000 salespeople, without any focus groups or one-on-one meetings. The result? Most of the best performers jumped ship when they learned the new plan was based on increased goals that had no credibility with salespeople.

Tips on Implementation

- **Do** view it as a change management process, no matter how insignificant the actual changes.

- **Do** communicate to salespeople one on one, between supervisor and salesperson, not just through the mail.

- **Do** provide what-if scenarios for all salespeople so they can see how the plan will affect them individually. This can be presented on a computer disk that has embedded in it the plan mechanics, the saleperson's past performance, and various scenarios for potential future performance.

- **Do** solicit quarterly and annual feedback from salespeople—either the entire sales force or a sample—to determine the level of success of the plan, the existence of glitches, and potential for modifications.

- **Don't** just enact the plan overnight. Give salespeople time to be involved, to provide feedback, and to understand the plan mechanics before unveiling it.

- **Don't** unveil it at a national sales meeting or in large groups. The larger the group, the greater the risk that pockets of negativity will develop.

Business change is not a one-time event; it is a continuous process. Sales force restructuring, creating a new culture, downsizing, process reengineering, or introducing a new pay plan does not happen overnight but over a period of time. No matter how compelling the need for change, the process elicits emotional responses from all affected. Correct implementation requires sales staff training, communications, early involvement from salespeople, and continuous auditing.

6.5 ADMINISTRATION

You have the perfect plan, you've run numerous macro financial and individual scenarios, and your sales force is on board. The last thing you now want is for the pay checks to be late or wrong. For years, companies have used spreadsheets to administer plans. Spreadsheets, although seemingly simple, still are powerful tools in administering even the most complex plans. There are some downfalls to using spreadsheets, however, including difficulty of acquiring the right data, data flow, conducting comparative analyses across the sales force, and re-creating the spreadsheet every year.

Today, a few software developers and plan administrators have created quality software packages and services that make the entire sales compensation administration process much easier, less painful, and more accurate and thorough. The new systems are tied to order entry or accounting processes and feed directly into the payroll system. The benefits of this new-age software include faster, more accurate information and better analytical tools.

It's important to note, however, that not all software is the same. What may be right for one organization could be completely wrong for another. In addition, some software developers and their packages are quite good and offer complete part-installation support, whereas others apparently end their service at the point of sale.

6.6 AUDITING AND MODIFYING

Now that you've designed and implemented a more effective sales compensation plan, you're all done, right? Well, not exactly. After all the effort of designing, simulating, implementing, and administering the sales compensation plan, the work is not complete, although it gets easier. The business climate is constantly changing, and just as business strategies change with evolving market conditions, the sales compensation plan should undergo periodic auditing and modifying.

The audit process should include financial analysis and interviews with salespeople and customers, and could very well show an effective plan that needs no adjustments. Chances are, however, that the plan will require at least minor adjustments. To remain on the cutting edge, a company should conduct an analysis—with potential modifications—at least once each year. For the company that recently underwent a major overhaul in its compensation plan, a monthly or quarterly audit over the first few years will ensure that the new plan has met or exceeded expectations.

Key factors that need to be monitored include:

- Financial performance (e.g., growth in revenues, profits, margins, cash flow)
- Pay and performance correlations and distributions
- Behaviors of sales/service executives, managers, and staff
- Customer relationship/satisfaction/ loyalty/retention rates
- Employee satisfaction/attitudes/retention
- Business and employee performance and productivity
- Communications process (better communications)

6.7 SOME FINAL THOUGHTS ON DESIGNING A SALES COMPENSATION PLAN

- It's about Sales and Marketing. It's not simply a Human Resources or compensation issue.

- It's about affecting day-to-day behavior, focus, time allocation, decisions and tradeoffs, not just pay delivery.

- It may appear as preferential treatment to the sales force, but it's more than a "special plan" for salespeople. It's about company strategy, direction, customer relationships, rewards, motivation, and so much more.

- It should always reflect the delicate balance of conflicting forces, such as stronger cultural norms versus strong management direction; using the pay plan versus strong managerial leadership to communicate priorities; management control versus sales rep independence; and the numerous perspectives and needs of senior management, sales management, human resources, sales force, sales administration, and customers.

- It's your strategy that counts. Understand the labor market and evaluate what the competition is doing, but don't imitate or assimilate—it's about your strategy and your sales effort.

- In the end, all of the elements of the sales strategy need to be properly aligned and connected, and often, sales compensation makes sure this connection is achieved.

Common Myths

Myth: A company must pay its salespeople at levels and in ways that are consistent or competitive with other companies in the same industry.
Truth: No two business strategies and no two sales efforts need be exactly alike. Each company must create a plan that considers its best use of resources to maximize profitability, in the context of its own business and sales strategy, and set pay levels accordingly.

Myth: A company must have one plan across all parts of the sales effort.
Truth: Too many companies are still mired in the philosophy of one plan for all salespeople, regardless of differences in roles and sales strategies across the sales effort. Significant differences in sales strategies and roles warrant different plans.

Myth: The sales compensation plan must be simple or it won't be effective.
Truth: With today's advanced software, you can have a more complicated plan that's effective and manageable, if it's communicated well.

Myth: Salespeople who are on 100% commission are the only effective salespeople.
Truth: Not true. Ninety percent of the sale forces that operate in the world today are not on 100% commission, and many are highly effective.

Myth: Salespeople who are 100% commission are the biggest risk takers.
Truth: These salespeople are often the last people in the world who'll take a risk because they don't want to adversely affect their compensation, especially when the commission is tied to an ongoing revenue stream.

Chapter 7

Pay for Performance in Not-for-Profit Organizations*

Martin L. Katz and Karyn Meola

This chapter explores designing compensation programs that link pay to performance in not-for-profit organizations. The focus of the chapter is on public charities and private foundations that are exempt from tax under IRC §501(c)(3).[1] These organizations present unique challenges when designing compensation programs. They often compete for talent with for-profit companies, yet they operate in a dramatically different environment. For example:

- Tax rules constrain the design of compensation programs.
- Organizational structure precludes using equity-based compensation, which is highly prevalent in the for-profit sector.
- Compensation strategy is often developed in the context of organizational mission and values, which may also constrain program design.
- Public perception and regulatory oversight strongly influence pay decisions.
- It can be difficult to identify appropriate performance metrics on which to base incentives, depending on the nature of the organization.

The chapter provides an overview of the federal income tax rules applicable to tax-exempt organizations generally, the elements of executive compensation typically used in tax-exempt organizations, and how to design incentive plans within these rules. We also discuss the new "intermediate sanctions" rules, which provide for significant penalty taxes if compensation is found to be unreasonable and how to protect the organization from sanctions. Finally, we highlight several

---

* The authors wish to thank Mercer colleagues who provided insight and peer review for this chapter, in particular Diane Doubleday, who made a substantial contribution to the chapter and the many technical aspects it touches.
[1] All section references, unless otherwise specified, are to the Internal Revenue Code (IRC) of 1986, as amended. These organizations may be subject to income tax on business activities that are unrelated to their exempt purpose (unrelated business taxable income). IRC §§511–512.

special situations, such as relocation, change in control or severance benefits, and executive fringe benefits.[2]

7.1   INTRODUCTION TO TAX-EXEMPT ORGANIZATIONS

When dealing with not-for-profit organizations, it is essential to understand the federal (and state)[3] tax status of the organization. Not all not-for-profit organizations are tax-exempt,[4] and not all tax-exempt organizations are within the scope of this chapter.[5] Public charities and private foundations that are exempt from tax under Internal Revenue Code (IRC) §501(c)(3) include organizations that are "organized and operated exclusively for religious, charitable, scientific, testing for public safety, literary or educational purposes."[6] Examples include hospitals and clinics, schools and universities, organizations devoted to research and treatment of diseases, museums, and foundations that support these kinds of organizations. Private foundations are distinguished from public charities based on their source of funds. Public charities receive at least one-third of their support from public sources such as gifts, grants, membership fees, donations, and contributions and not more than one-third from investment income and unrelated business activities.[7]

Organizations that are self-described as "not-for-profit" are often a combination of entities. For example, a health system may include tax-exempt hospitals and clinics, a foundation as a fundraising and investment management arm, and for-profit laboratories or physician management companies. The foundation may be a public charity—raising money from a variety of public sources—or it may be a private foundation organized by a wealthy donor to provide medical services to the community.

7.2   FEDERAL TAX RULES

The hallmark tax requirements for the tax-exempt organizations that are the subject of this chapter are that "no part of the net earnings can inure to the benefit of

[2] Compensating physicians is beyond the scope of this chapter. The chapter focuses primarily on the compensation of executives, and the principles outlined herein are generally applicable to other employees as well as to physicians who are employed as executives and compensated as such.
[3] The state tax laws defining and governing tax-exempt organizations are beyond the scope of this chapter.
[4] For example, Blue Cross and Blue Shield organizations, which can be organized as for-profit or not-for-profit, are taxable under IRC §833.
[5] E.g., state and local government entities.
[6] IRC §501(c)(3).
[7] IRC §509. Funds contributed by a disqualified person (defined in IRC §4946) are excluded. In general terms, a disqualified person includes substantial contributors (more than 2% of the contributions in any year), foundation managers, and related persons or entities.

any private shareholder or individual"[8] and the organization must be operated for the "exclusive benefit" of its exempt purpose. For prohibited inurement to occur, some or all of the earnings of a tax-exempt organization is provided to or used by a person (typically a director or officer) who is in a position to provide substantial influence over the affairs of the organization or influence his or her own pay. The magnitude and form of the benefit is immaterial in the determination of whether the prohibited inurement doctrine has been violated. Paying unreasonable compensation or providing a benefit without adequate consideration are violations of the principles of prohibited inurement and private benefit.

Until the Taxpayer Bill of Rights 2, enacted by Congress and signed into law in 1996, loss of exempt status was the only sanction available to the Internal Revenue Service (IRS) for violation of these doctrines. Because of the severity of this sanction, it was rarely enforced and therefore was not an effective tool for the IRS to combat abuses. Thus, the IRS and not-for-profit organizations joined to lobby for a less onerous penalty or sanction for violating these rules. The result was new legislation contained within Taxpayer Bill of Rights 2, often referred to as the "intermediate sanctions" law.

7.3   INTERMEDIATE SANCTIONS

The intermediate sanctions law imposes penalty taxes on "excess benefit transactions."[9] Under new §4958, an excise tax—rather than a loss of exempt status—is imposed on 501(c)(3)[10] organizations for transactions in which the economic benefit to a "disqualified person" exceeds the consideration (including services) received by the organization.[11] Compensation is an excess benefit transaction to the extent that the compensation is determined to be unreasonable.

A "disqualified person" is any person in a position to exercise substantial influence over the affairs of the organization. Examples would include the organization's top executives and Board of Directors. The penalty taxes are as follows:

- The penalty tax to the recipient is 25% of the excess benefit, which increases to 200% if the violation is not corrected within the prescribed period.
- Penalty taxes can also be imposed on the organization's trustees, directors or officers (referred to as "organization managers") who knowingly approved the excess benefit transaction.

---

[8] IRC §501(c)(3).
[9] P.L. 104-168, Taxpayer Bill of Rights 2 (1996).
[10] Organizations exempt under §501(c)(4) are also subject to §4958, but private foundations are subject to a different set of similar rules.
[11] IRC §4958(c). Note that tax-exempt organizations can still lose their exempt status under the prohibited inurement and private sanction doctrines.

- The tax on organization managers is 10% of the excess benefit up to a maximum of $10,000 per transaction. The organization may not be able to indemnify these managers.

The law contains an important protective provision, referred to as the "rebuttable presumption of reasonableness." If the requirements for establishing the rebuttable presumption are satisfied, the compensation paid is presumed to be reasonable, unless the IRS proves otherwise on the basis of sufficient contrary evidence. If the requirements are not met, the burden is on the organization to prove the reasonableness of the compensation. As a result, many not-for-profit organizations have restructured their compensation programs and decision-making processes to establish the rebuttable presumption of reasonableness. This requires three key elements:

1. The compensation arrangement must be approved in advance by a governing board (or a committee comprised entirely of independent directors) without conflict of interest.
2. The board or committee must obtain appropriate data as to comparability (e.g., compensation paid by similarly situated organizations for positions with a similar role and scope of responsibility).
3. The board or committee must adequately document the basis for its determination (e.g., the record includes a description of the decision made, the comparability data relied upon, and the basis for determining the compensation to be reasonable).

The IRS recently issued final regulations[12] which clarify questions raised by the original statute and earlier proposed regulations. For example, compensation is considered reasonable if it represents an amount that would ordinarily be paid for like services by similar enterprises under like circumstances. In addition, the timing of the determination of reasonableness was addressed. Specifically, the determination of reasonableness for "fixed payments" occurs at the time the contract for services is entered into. Discretionary or variable payments are generally determined when they are paid. The period over which reasonableness is measured generally follow these rules:

- For any period during which there is no discretionary or variable compensation, reasonableness can be determined at the beginning of that period based on circumstances existing at that time, and the determination will be good until the conclusion of the period (e.g., three-year contract with an executive).

[12] The IRS issued final regulations under IRC Section 4958 on January 23, 2002, replacing the proposed and temporary regulations issued on January 9, 2001.

- If the contract is amended during the period to provide for an increase in compensation not contemplated in the original contract, a new determination of reasonableness would have to be made for the remainder of the period.
- If, during the period, the contract is amended to include some form of discretionary compensation, a determination of reasonableness cannot be made until the discretionary compensation is paid (or at least declared).

There is an important exception for variable (incentive) compensation that is subject to a cap. The compensation, if considered at the maximum payment level, can be determined for reasonableness at the beginning of the period rather than when paid.

Compensation is defined as any compensation or benefit of value provided to a disqualified person, including but not limited to the following:

- All cash and noncash compensation, including salary, fees, bonuses, and severance payments
- Deferred compensation, including retirement and savings plans
- The amount of all premiums paid for liability or any other insurance coverage, as well as any payment or reimbursement by the organization of charges, expenses, fees, or taxes not ultimately covered by the insurance coverage
- All other benefits (excluding non-taxable fringe benefits under IRC Section 132), including payments to welfare plans, such as plans providing medical, dental, life insurance, severance pay, and disability benefits, and taxable and nontaxable fringe benefits or perquisites, such as forgiveness of debt and below-market interest rate loans
- Any economic benefit provided through another entity owned, controlled by, or affiliated with the applicable tax-exempt organization, whether such entity is taxable or tax-exempt

Another important exception to the intermediate sanctions rules is the "initial contract" exception. Fixed payments under an initial employment agreement with an individual who later becomes a disqualified person are treated as negotiated at arm's length prior to the individual becoming a disqualified person and are therefore exempt from excise tax. To qualify for the initial contract exception:

- The provisions of the arrangement must be documented in a binding written agreement.
- If the person fails to perform substantially the obligations under the initial contract, the exception does not apply.
- If later amended or canceled, the terms of the contract will no longer be exempt from excise tax.

Any payments or benefits provided to the individual under contract beyond those provided in the initial contract are subject to the same standards as payments that are not subject to the exception. Thus, the rebuttable presumption can be established and the compensation should be evaluated for reasonableness as additional compensation to the fixed payment arrangement.

As noted previously, organizations can meet three key requirements to establish the rebuttable presumption of reasonableness: comparability of data, approval by an independent board, and documentation of the decision. Tax-exempt organizations should establish a governance process or policy to ensure that these requirements are met for decisions on compensation arrangements with disqualified persons. The regulations provide guidance for each step.

(a)   Comparability of Data

In determining whether compensation is reasonable, the tax-exempt organization must compare its pay to pay provided by "similarly situated" organizations. Similarly situated in this context means organizations of comparable size and complexity of operations, and within a reasonable geographical range. A comprehensive competitiveness review should evaluate total compensation and include a composite of comparable market data. Comparability data can be selected from national and local published compensation surveys, a targeted group of comparable organizations ("peers"), and actual written offers of employment from like organizations. Collectively, these data are referred to as "market reference points" and can include the following:

- Published surveys
- Third-party "club" surveys
- Annual reports/proxy statements
- Association surveys
- Documented offers
- Form 990s

An organization should strive wherever possible to gather multiple market reference points in order to develop a full picture of the labor market. The more valid reference points an organization has, the more confident it can be in the comparisons it makes.

Once comparable organization data have been collected, organizations must then compare the market data for functionally equivalent positions. Using published compensation surveys, an organization can match the job responsibilities of its positions to the job descriptions provided in the surveys to determine the most appropriate match.

Comparability data will often not directly match the specific responsibilities and qualifications of the job incumbent who is being compared. Because of the unique duties and responsibilities of each position, and varying complexity among organizations, it may be appropriate to adjust the market data (up or down) to arrive at a more accurate match. For example, a Chief Financial Officer (CFO) who has responsibility for human resources may be entitled to a premium, whereas a CFO who does not have responsibility for the treasury function may require a discount to be applied to the market data. An adjustment of more than 20% generally should not be used. There may also be positions for which no appropriate comparability data are available. To assess the reasonableness of compensation provided to these individuals, the compensation can be compared to that provided to other positions of similar complexity *within* the organization for which adequate comparability data exist. Internal consistency versus external competitiveness has long been a factor used by the courts and the IRS in determining reasonableness of compensation.

Organizations may also adjust the data for differences in geographic location. For example, San Francisco has a higher cost of living than the national average. For an "apples to apples" comparison, national compensation data may be adjusted to reflect the higher cost of living in San Francisco. These adjustments should be reasonable in amount, not arbitrary, and the rationale well documented.

The regulations also provide that the compensation package should be evaluated *in its entirety* to establish the rebuttable presumption. It is not enough that the base salary is considered reasonable. The organization must take steps to ensure that the entire arrangement, including annual bonus, long-term incentives, benefits, perquisites, and any revenue-sharing arrangements, have been evaluated for reasonableness.

External consultants are often used to obtain comparability data for an organization. While independent compensation studies are not required, external consultants may have access to more comparability data, have more experience with adjusting the data for organization complexity or varying roles, can help justify extraordinary compensation (e.g., compensation that well exceeds competitive benchmarks, yet is justified based on organization performance), and, above all, offer an independent point of view.

(b) Approval by an Independent Board

Once the comparability data have been collected, the Board of Directors or a committee authorized to act on behalf of the Board must review the materials and approve the compensation arrangement. The arrangement must be approved either by the full Board or by a committee of independent directors who do not have a conflict of interest. Individuals who may have a conflict of interest include:

- Disqualified persons, or a family member of or an entity controlled by a disqualified person
- Those in an employment relationship subject to the direction or control of a disqualified person
- Those receiving compensation or other payments subject to approval by a disqualified person
- Those who have a material financial interest affected by the compensation arrangement or transaction at issue
- Those who provide benefits to any disqualified person who, in turn, has approved or will approve a transaction providing benefits to the individual[13]

If the compensation arrangement to be approved relates to a Board member, this individual should not participate in the decision-making phase of the meeting. For example, a Board member who is retiring should not participate in a decision to provide a "special recognition" payment to retiring Board members.

To secure the rebuttable presumption, approval must occur before the benefits are paid. If the Board approves the arrangement after the individual has already received some or all of the benefits, the rebuttable presumption cannot be established.

It should be noted that under the intermediate sanctions rules a Board *cannot* establish the rebuttable presumption of reasonableness with regard to directors' compensation because of the inherent conflict of interest. Thus, in making directors' compensation decisions, a Board should strive to ensure that it relies heavily on external market comparability data and an independent adviser on Board compensation. The decision should then be fully documented as described in the next section.

(c)   Documentation of the Decision

The third step in establishing the rebuttable presumption is adequate documentation of the compensation arrangement, the methodology used to gather comparability data, and the decision-making process. Adequate documentation must be in writing or in the electronic records of the approval committee and must note:

- The terms of the compensation arrangement that were approved and the date it was approved
- The members of the approval committee who were present during discussion of the arrangement and those who voted on it
- The comparability data relied upon and how the data were obtained

---

[13] Reg. §4958-6(c)(1).

- The actions taken with respect to consideration of the transaction by anyone who would have participated in the decision-making process but who had a conflict of interest

If the governing body or committee determines that reasonable compensation is higher or lower than the range of comparability data obtained, the records must include the basis for that determination.

In addition, documentation must be "concurrent." Specifically, the records must be prepared, reviewed, and approved by the governing body or committee as "reasonable, accurate, and complete" within 60 days or by the next regularly scheduled meeting, whichever is later.[14]

7.4   DETERMINING REASONABLENESS

Establishing the rebuttable presumption is an important governance process the Board should follow in order to protect itself and the organization. Nevertheless, Boards often ask the basic question: "What is reasonable?" Reasonableness is based on the facts and circumstances of each unique situation. Many factors can influence the determination of reasonableness. The IRS and the courts have used many factors over the years in their determination of reasonableness. Five key factors used by the Tax Court are described as follows[15]:

1. *Role and scope of responsibility.* Has the incumbent been compared to functionally equivalent positions in like organizations? Is the scope of responsibility similar to the position being evaluated? What adjustments were applied to the market data in an attempt to make the comparison more accurate?

2. *Character and condition of the organization.* How is the organization performing, both in absolute terms and relative to peers? Is the organization making or losing money? How complex is the organization, its operations, and structure?

3. *External competitiveness.* Does the compensation arrangement fall within a reasonable range of market practices? If the incumbent's compensation is higher than his or her peers, is it justifiable based on unique skills, experience, or the performance of the organization?

4. *Internal consistency.* Is a disqualified person receiving compensation that is greater than amounts received by comparable positions within the organization without clear justification (e.g., eligibility for incentives, special benefits, or perquisites)?

---

[14] Reg. §4958-6(c)(3).
[15] *Elliotts, Inc. v. Commissioner,* 716 F.2 and 1241 (9th Cir. 1983).

5. *Conflict of interest.* Has a disqualified person participated in or influenced the decision-making process with respect to his or her own compensation arrangement or exerted pressure on others to approve the arrangement? Is the approval committee composed entirely of independent members?

When making a decision about the reasonableness of compensation for a disqualified person, a Board would do well to think of the proposed package in light of these factors. Organization managers are often led to believe that market comparison is the only factor. On the contrary, it is an important factor, but it is heavily influenced by other quantitative factors such as organization performance and qualitative factors such as role and complexity.

7.5   PRIVATE FOUNDATIONS

The intermediate sanctions rules apply only to certain, but not all tax-exempt organizations. Private foundations that are not tax-exempt under IRC §§501(c)(3) and 501(c)(4) are not subject to intermediate sanctions, but are subject to a different set of rules with similar effect. Disqualified persons may not engage in acts of "self-dealing," and compensation for services must be reasonable. Although a full discussion of these rules is beyond the scope of this chapter, officers and Boards would be well advised to adopt the spirit, if not the letter, of the intermediate sanctions rules. Although private foundations cannot rely on the rebuttable presumption safe harbor, following the process by which it is established should provide reasonable protection.

7.6   DEFERRED COMPENSATION IN TAX EXEMPTS

Before designing compensation programs in tax-exempt organizations, it is also necessary to understand the special rules regarding income tax recognition applicable to tax-exempts. These rules are materially different from those which apply to taxable entities and directly affect compensation program design.

IRC §457(f) addresses nonqualified deferred compensation in tax-exempt entities. Under this section, compensation is taxable when it is no longer subject to a substantial risk of forfeiture.[16] A substantial risk of forfeiture exists when individuals' rights to compensation are conditioned upon performance of future services.[17] Section 457(f) applies to both elective and nonelective arrangements, such as salary or bonus deferrals and supplemental retirement plans. This standard

---

[16] IRC §457(f)(1)(A). This rule does not apply to qualified retirement vehicles described in §§401(a) and 403(b) or to transfers of property under §83.
[17] IRC §457(f)(3)(B).

is substantially higher than that which applies to taxable corporations, where compensation can be deferred as long as it remains subject to the claims of general creditors. This is not the case with tax-exempt organizations. For tax-exempts, such a provision would render the compensation taxable currently, even if deferred until retirement!

Thus, pressure exists on tax-exempts to provide competitive levels of compensation *and* competitive compensation vehicles. Given the fairly onerous rules regarding deferred compensation for tax-exempts, this represents a significant planning opportunity—and a trap for the unwary.

7.7 TYPICAL EXECUTIVE COMPENSATION PROGRAMS

Most executive compensation programs in not-for-profit organizations include base salary, performance-based incentives, health care and retirement benefits, and selected perquisites. The use of annual incentives is becoming prevalent, yet, unlike executives in for-profit companies, base salary continues to be weighted more heavily than incentives. Annual incentive awards among not-for-profits tend to be lower by one-third to one-half for similar positions in the for-profit sector. Additionally, not-for-profit incentive plans have less "leverage" because maximum award payouts are almost always capped. Long-term incentive plans are not widely offered, but are gaining favor, particularly among large health care systems.

To enhance the competitiveness of the total package, not-for-profits often focus on executive benefits and perquisites. Besides standard medical and dental, prevalent benefits include executive supplemental life insurance, long-term disability, and retirement plans. Supplemental executive retirement benefits often serve as a substitute for equity compensation (e.g., stock options) offered in the for-profit sector. Prevalent perquisites include, but are not limited to, membership in dining or country clubs, spouse travel, employment agreements, paid parking, cell phones, and a car allowance or company car.

To support their exempt purpose, not-for-profits strive to ensure that the compensation program is consistent with their mission. The organization's mission defines and communicates its exempt purpose, including the specific type of services to be provided, the intended beneficiaries, and the desired outcome in providing those services. A mission statement is often prepared, which can also communicate the values that the organization believes exemplify its exempt purpose. These values permeate an organization, embody its culture, and guide it in day-to-day operating decisions.

For example, a prominent health care organization defines its mission as providing quality health care to individuals who do not have access to health insurance and cannot afford to pay for medical treatment. The organization operates under the following values as part of its mission:

- *Dignity.* Respect each person as an inherently valuable member of the human community and as a unique expression of life.

- *Excellence.* Foster personal and professional development, accountability, innovation, teamwork, and commitment to quality.

- *Service.* Bring together people who recognize that every interaction is a unique opportunity to serve one another, the community, and society.

- *Justice.* Advocate for systems and structures that are attuned to the needs of the vulnerable and disadvantaged and that promote a sense of community among all persons.

The values serve as a standard for the quality of the organization's patient care, the type of leadership that is required to run the organization, and the expectations for the conduct of its employees. It is therefore important that the organization align its compensation programs with its mission and values to ensure that the desired behaviors are rewarded. A written compensation philosophy statement should reinforce the values and encourage employees to exhibit behaviors that are consistent with its exempt purpose.

The philosophy statement declares the organization's competitive market for employee talent, target competitive positioning with respect to that market, and the specific mix of compensation elements that are included in the total compensation package. An organization may craft separate compensation philosophies for executives and employees generally, or for selected functional positions depending on the nature of the competitive market. The philosophy statement should describe each element of the total compensation package, its role in the total compensation program, and the competitive standard being applied.

7.8 DESIGNING EFFECTIVE INCENTIVES

Until the last 10 years or so, tax-exempt organizations have underemphasized incentive plans because of constraints placed on them by tax rules and public perception. In recent years, however, an increasing number of tax-exempts have adopted a "pay-for-performance" approach to enhance competitiveness while ensuring their ability to provide community benefit. In this section, we explore how to provide compensation under incentive programs that minimize exposure to intermediate sanctions.

For an incentive compensation arrangement to be considered reasonable, there should be a valid business case for the plan, such as improved operating efficiency, providing greater community benefit, or both. The IRS looks closely at incentive compensation arrangements to ensure that they are not simply mechanisms for distributing profits to insiders and that the arrangement enhances the organization's ability to provide benefits or services consistent with its exempt purpose. As part of its review, the IRS will evaluate the amount executives can earn under the plan and the method used to allocate awards to plan participants.

Incentive programs should be designed to provide market competitive award opportunity at various levels of performance, yet minimize an organization's risk of providing excessive compensation. A well-designed incentive program would typically address the following key features:

- Eligibility
- Incentive Opportunity
- Performance Measures
- Performance/Payout Scale
- Funding Trigger
- Cost/Benefit Relationship
- Administrative Guidelines

For each feature, "best practice" designs that minimize exposure to excise taxes are explored in further detail.

(a) Eligibility

Participation in an incentive program is inherently discretionary but should include most or all positions of a similar level or function in an organization (e.g., vice president positions and higher). Incentive plan participation is often indicated by competitive market data, but can nevertheless be justified where there is a clear business purpose. Tax-exempt organizations should refrain from adopting incentive programs where there are no apparent criteria for inclusion, particularly at higher levels in the organization.

(b) Incentive Opportunity

The incentive opportunity is the amount that a participant is eligible to earn if performance goals under the program are achieved. This amount is typically expressed as a percentage of base salary. The incentive opportunity should fall within a range of competitive market practices and reflect the amount of "risk-based" compensation appropriate for the position. Both for-profit and not-for-profit organizations can be cited as comparability data with respect to incentive opportunity, provided the role and responsibility are similar.

A well-developed compensation philosophy statement will address the question of how much incentive compensation has been earned. In most cases, incentive pay at "target" or "expected" levels of performance is positioned at the 50th percentile of the market. Where "superior" or stretch goals are achieved, compensation can be allowed to rise above the 50th and perhaps to the 75th percentile. When comparing against for-profit data, a less aggressive competitive position is generally more appropriate due to the disparity between for-profits and not-for-profits on incentive compensation and, often, organization performance.

Again, it is important that an organization review the compensation provided to each participant *in its entirety* before setting the incentive award opportunity. A competitive and reasonable incentive opportunity is meaningless if the rest of the compensation (or even one element of compensation) is considered excessive.

(c)   Performance Measures

For many tax-exempts, it is difficult to identify performance metrics on which to base incentives. Best practices suggest using a "balanced scorecard" approach to select the performance goals for use in the incentive program. The balanced scorecard approach uses a mix of performance goals intended to balance all the important initiatives of the organization. Among not-for-profits, an optimal arrangement generally includes performance measures in three or four of these categories:

- Profitability/financial stewardship
- Growth
- Quality/customer satisfaction
- Mission/strategic
- Individual performance

Performance goals should be aligned with the long-range business plan or support a specific initiative or project that must be achieved within a predetermined timeframe. Having consistent, supporting goals aligns the interests of the executives with the mission and fosters teamwork. To improve the plan's focus, a "best practice" is to select no more than two or three specific goals in each category to ensure that each has a meaningful weight.

Specific goals and performance measures under the plan should be consistent with and supportive of the organization's exempt purpose. For many tax-exempts, setting nonfinancial goals such as the mission/strategic component is difficult because performance achievement may not be easy to quantify or measure. Organizations can, however, include mission-related goals in the incentive program by measuring the impact the activities have on the community and other beneficiaries.

For example, to measure mission performance, an organization could commission a professional "outcome survey" to track the impact of its activities on the specific individuals who are benefiting from the organization's services. For example, a not-for-profit organization has a mission "to empower low-income youth from diverse neighborhoods to strengthen self-esteem, self-discipline, and a sense of accomplishment through dance, academic, and family programs." Each year the organization conducts an impact study, which compares the success of its students to a national average. Their most recent study discovered that high school students who have continuously participated in the program "report statistically lower rates of risk-taking behaviors." These types of studies enable an organization to include mission/strategic performance goals in their incentive program and to measure the success of the goals in an objective fashion.

Measures that are difficult to define, overly complicated, or that require numerous adjustments cloud the issue of performance achievement and may call into question the amount awarded. Before the start of each performance cycle, the organization should document the measures, goals, and process that will be used to assess performance achievement and have the plan approved by its independent governing body.

(d) Performance/Payout Scale

Once performance measures have been selected, the Board of Directors and senior leadership team must set performance targets for each measure in the incentive plan. There are two general approaches to designing incentive compensation arrangements: year-over-year performance improvement or predetermined target goal achievement over a specific period. In order to ensure that clear and achievable performance targets are established, recent historical performance, the long-range strategic plan, and available benchmark data should all be considered. For example, looking back at the previous five years of performance is useful in determining a benchmark for an organization's performance levels. If the organization has achieved consistent revenue growth over the last five years, then it might be able to expect continued revenue growth in the forthcoming year. Nevertheless, as we have seen in 2000 in the technology sector and in 2001 across many industries, things can change quickly.

Looking ahead to the future can also be helpful in setting performance targets. From an organization's long-range strategic plan, shorter-term goals or "milestones" can be developed that support and reinforce the long-range plan. For example, an organization may have in its strategic plan an objective to open a new clinic in a less affluent area to help low-income individuals gain access to quality health care. In order to achieve this objective, the organization may need to secure additional financing, obtain permits, and develop the clinic within a predetermined budget. This may take more than two years to accomplish, but progress can be measured each year.

Tax-exempt organizations should never set performance requirements that can only be achieved at the expense of the organization's beneficiaries. For example, to achieve revenue growth of 15% per year, an organization should not be required to resort to price increases for its services to a level significantly higher than that of like organizations. Similarly, if an organization achieves its revenue growth goal but incurs significantly higher operating expenses as a result, the IRS may disfavor incentive compensation awarded under this arrangement. To justify the "pay for performance" relationship, the organization should also obtain comparability data regarding relative financial and qualitative performance. In the health care industry, these data can be found in nationally published compensation surveys or can be purchased from professional service firms that compile the data.

Once the organization has set its performance targets, the next step is to develop a payout scale. The scale should reflect a range of performance from a minimum acceptable level of performance, below which no incentives will be paid, to a maximum level of performance, above which the incentive award is capped. Whether to include caps on incentive award payouts is a philosophical decision for not-for-profit and for-profit organizations alike; however, for tax-exempts, capping award payments helps prevent excessive compensation by controlling the incentive award to a predetermined range for which the rebuttable presumption has been established. Caps are also helpful to avoid windfalls resulting from unforeseen business circumstances. For example, midperformance cycle changes in the economy or regulatory environment can impact a tax-exempt organization's performance with respect to an incentive plan goal (e.g., changes to Medicare reimbursements affecting the revenue goal in a health plan).

(e) Funding Trigger

A best practice is to require a minimum level of bottom-line organizationwide performance before the payment of any awards, even if superior performance is achieved on other measures. This design feature is called a "funding trigger."

The funding trigger ensures that the organization has met basic performance requirements (e.g., net income at least equal to the prior year) before any incentive award can be paid for the current year. The funding trigger also ensures that the organization can meet the needs of its beneficiaries before payment *and* that it has the necessary funds to pay the incentives. It discourages participants from losing sight of the mission and values of the organization in the pursuit of incentive plan goal achievement.

(f) Cost/Benefit Relationship

Incentive plans should have an appropriate relationship between the amount awarded to participants and the benefit generated for the organization. For tax-exempt organizations, this test is crucial because only a proportional amount of the profits generated by the incentive plan should be allocated to plan participants;

otherwise the incentive payments may be considered excessive.[18] Once this relationship is established, greater compensation can be provided for progressively higher levels of performance, thereby reinforcing a pay-for-performance culture.

(g) Administrative Guidelines

The incentive plan document should include an administrative section to establish guidelines for and minimize subjectivity when determining incentive compensation awards. The guidelines identify who administers the plan and provide instructions for the plan administrator in the event of midcycle changes to participants, such as termination of employment, retirement, death, or disability. Questions addressed in the guidelines include (1) What is the organization's obligation for payment if a participant terminates from the organization? and (2) How does the organization determine the award when year-end results are not available? The guidelines should also state that the governing body is responsible for approving the performance goals *each year* and the governing body's authority regarding plan amendments or plan termination.

Some plans allow for the governing body to make discretionary adjustments to the award payouts in a given plan year because of performance resulting from economic conditions outside of participants' control. Not-for-profits should use this authority sparingly or refrain from it altogether because it has the potential to put the Board at risk for approving excess benefit transactions.

7.9 LONG-TERM INCENTIVE PLANS

Long-term incentive (LTI) plans are most commonly used to reward executives for achieving long-term goals or completing multiyear initiatives. They are also used as retention devices because deferred compensation can serve as a strong motivator for staying with an organization. Organizational structure precludes not-for-profits from using equity-based compensation such as stock options or restricted stock; however, there are viable alternatives for not-for-profits that achieve the same objectives (i.e., to encourage retention and provide compensation for achieving long-term performance goals).

LTI plans are differentiated from annual plans on several levels: timeframe, performance measures, and basic strategy. Whereas annual plans are more tactical in nature and focus primarily on the income statement (revenue, expense control, net operating income), LTI plans are more effective when they reinforce strategic objectives and focus on income statement *and* balance sheet measures. More common measures in LTI plans include revenue and fund balance growth,

---

[18] Under the new temporary regs, revenue-sharing arrangements must be included in the overall compensation package and the determination of reasonableness.

operating margin, quality and service improvement, and other multiyear goals such as business expansion.

Designing LTI plans to minimize the risk of exposure to excessive compensation requires the same steps as outlined in Section 7.8, so they will not be repeated here; however, we briefly describe several forms of long-term compensation and suggest how they may best be applied.

- *Three-year performance incentive plan.* This is essentially the same as an annual bonus plan, but the goals established are three-year goals. The balanced scorecard approach is often used so performance goals can be established around financial, quality, mission/strategic, and individual objectives. This plan is best used when the organization has the financial systems to track performance over time and the ability to set long-range goals.

- *Cash retention incentive.* Where an organization does not have long-range goal-setting ability, an LTI plan can be established simply by offering a deferred cash payment. If the participant remains with the organization for three years, for example, a cash payment equal to 30% of base salary will be paid (the equivalent of 10% per year). If the participant leaves during the three-year period, the payment is forfeited. Because this type of plan is not performance based, it is even more important that the amount be reasonable and called for by competitive practices.

- *Value-based plan.* This LTI plan is more complex and can be used only when there is an operating company and similar types of organizations or services offered in the for-profit sector. For example, a health maintenance organization (HMO) owned by a not-for-profit organization can readily be compared to a for-profit, publicly traded HMO. By using the publicly available data, measures of value can be determined and a valuation formula created. The not-for-profit can then rely on that formula to measure whether new "value" has been created. As a not-for-profit, the new value created must be for the organization's exempt purpose, not the plan participants, so the amount of incentive sharing must be carefully evaluated.

- *Other long-term plans.* Many not-for-profits do not have the business operations to have a leading-edge incentive arrangement, nor do they have the type of three-year goals that are clearly measurable. For some, therefore, the main objective of the LTI plan is simply retention. For these organizations we typically see the adoption of a nonqualified supplemental executive retirement plan (SERP). This plan encourages retention by providing a better than average retirement benefit in lieu of a traditional LTI plan. For many, this incentive is enough to achieve the retention objective they seek.

As noted previously, all LTI plans and the participants' award opportunities (expressed as a percentage of salary) must be tested for reasonableness before adoption of the plan and in conjunction with all other compensation provided. The documentation of the plan, and the performance goals in particular, are essential to establishing the rebuttable presumption of reasonableness and a pay-for-performance culture.

7.10 DEVELOPING A PAY-FOR-PERFORMANCE CULTURE

Developing a pay-for-performance culture requires not only a well-designed plan, but also clear, measurable objectives and a strong communication program. Mercer has studied "best practices" in incentive plan design for several years. Many of the principles that are used in the for-profit sector can apply.

The following represent some common "do's" and "don'ts" that a tax-exempt organization can follow in the design and administration of a short- or long-term incentive program intended to help it maximize the effectiveness of the plan and minimize the risk of providing unreasonable compensation.

Incentive Program "Do's"	Incentive Program "Don'ts"
Establish a business case for the incentive compensation plan that supports the organization's tax-exempt purpose.	Avoid incentive plans that encourage actions inconsistent with the exempt purpose, such as reducing indigent care to increase operating performance.
Obtain comparability data on incentive opportunities to support the plan design and the range of compensation opportunity.	Avoid incentive programs that provide inequitable award opportunity among participants or that create the *perception* of inequity.
Select performance goals that are clearly measurable, easy to communicate, and consistent with the organization's mission and values.	Avoid incentive programs that are not performance-based (i.e., discretionary) or where the performance goals are routinely exceeded with little effort.
Ensure that performance goals are challenging, yet realistic, and prioritized according to the mission and strategy of the organization.	Avoid using solely financial performance goals by including quality, mission, and/or community benefit performance measures.
Create a minimum financial performance objective, or "trigger," that must be achieved before payment of any incentive award.	Avoid incentive plans with unlimited potential for award payout, using caps to prevent large payouts resulting from unforeseen circumstances.
Monitor the cost/benefit relationship to ensure that incentive payments are made after an appropriate return to the organization.	Avoid plans that provide a disproportionate share of financial results to plan participants.

Incentive Program "Do's"	Incentive Program "Don'ts"
Document the incentive plan, participant eligibility, performance goals, award opportunity, and administrative guidelines.	Avoid changing plan provisions or performance measures in the middle of the plan year or multi-year performance period.
Review potential incentive opportunity in the context of the entire compensation arrangement.	Do not ignore special compensation arrangements when reviewing total compensation (SERPs, housing loans, perquisites).
Develop a "pay-for-performance" culture encouraging personal accountability.	Discourage a culture of entitlement, particularly with performance-based incentives.
Protect the Board and the executives from sanctions by establishing the rebuttable presumption of reasonableness.	Do not add new compensation elements without reviewing the effect on the overall arrangement.

7.11 SPECIAL COMPENSATION ARRANGEMENTS

In addition to direct compensation (salary, bonus, long-term incentives), tax-exempts should also examine their indirect compensation arrangements, including executive benefits and perquisites. These elements of compensation are generally provided to "disqualified persons," thus it is important to monitor the benefit provided to ensure that it is reasonable. The following are some of the pitfalls and hidden minefields regarding executive benefit and perquisite arrangements.

(a) Relocation Expenses/Housing Loans

Relocation expenses are typically paid by organizations (both for-profit and not-for-profit) on behalf of an executive they are recruiting to join the organization. The organization will typically reimburse the executive for the cost of relocating from one area of the country to another. If the individual is relocating to an area with a higher cost of living than the previous residence, relocation expenses can be substantial. Many organizations will use relocation as a vehicle to "sweeten the deal." This action may create exposure to excessive compensation, so care should be taken.

For example, some organizations provide tax-free or low-interest loans to help an executive find an equivalent home in a higher cost of living area. Other organizations may forgive the loan obligation if the executive remains with the organization for a specified period (usually five years or greater). Relocation loans with these provisions provide indirect compensation to an executive, which must be measured and included in total compensation when testing for reasonableness. Even though "qualified home relocation loans" have preferable tax treatment under the IRC, the value must still be considered when determining reasonableness.

To properly structure a loan arrangement to an executive, tax-exempt organizations should strive to meet the following requirements:

- *Amount borrowed*—should be reasonable in relation to the value of the home.

- *Interest rate*—can be below market, or even interest free, provided that the value of the bargain interest is considered for reasonableness.

- *Length of the loan*—The loan repayment period should not be greater than the typical repayment period of similar loans found in the marketplace.

- *Secured loan versus an unsecured loan*—A loan to a disqualified person should be secured with a second mortgage on the residence.

- *Repayment*—The loan should be repayable in full at the earlier of when the executive sells the property or leaves the employment of the organization.

(b)   Change-in-Control and Severance Protection

Another type of special compensation arrangement involves executive severance and change-in-control protection. Change-in-control agreements have become popular to ensure management continuity and focus on the business during uncertain times, such as when an organization is considering a sale or merger. When a change in control occurs, executives often experience a significant change in their position responsibilities or are relieved from their duties as new executives are brought in.

To offer reasonable protection to these individuals, often as part of the recruiting package, many organizations provide change-in-control protection in the form of employment contracts with senior executives. Compensation arrangements typically include payment of a lump-sum amount equal to a multiple of base salary and bonus compensation, plus continuation of health and welfare benefits. Typical plans provide one to two years of severance benefit, with up to three years for the largest, most complex organizations. Some organizations provide top executives additional protection from golden parachute excise taxes. Great care should be taken before offering this benefit because it may create significant exposure to excessive compensation in all but a few cases. Other benefits provided, such as outplacement services and the acceleration of time-vested compensation and benefits, are fairly common at this stage and should provide little risk of exposure to excise taxes.

While change-in-control protection has become commonplace, the size of the package varies significantly based on the size of the organization and whether it is tax-exempt or not. Care should be taken to avoid using standard Fortune 500 market practices, when a lesser package is the competitive standard for smaller, tax-exempt organizations.

(c) Supplemental Executive Retirement Program (SERP)

Under current tax rules, employer-sponsored retirement plan contributions and the amount of compensation that can be included in the compensation formula are limited. To offset these limits, many organizations provide executives with "excess benefit" or supplemental retirement plans. These plans can take many different forms; however, the most common is to provide a supplemental contribution on top of contributions made under the organization's regular retirement plan, based on a percentage of an executive's salary (or salary plus bonus). The goal is to provide the executive with a postretirement income equal to a target percentage of final average income, upon meeting service requirements.

Crucial to the development of a SERP that will stand up to the test of reasonableness is to consider the following key design features:

- Eligibility limited to a select group of management or highly compensated employees
- Income "replacement ratios" that fall within competitive practices for the period of service provided to the organization
- Adequate vesting provisions so that the organization's assets are protected in the event the executive leaves, voluntarily or otherwise
- A benefit accrual rate that is sensitive to the organization's ability to fund (i.e., the benefit is proportional to the organization's ability to fund the benefit and support its exempt purpose)

As with other elements of compensation, market data on retirement plan eligibility, income replacement ratios, and required service periods can be found in nationally published surveys, custom surveys, Form 990s, and other data sources.

(d) Retention Incentives

Many organizations, particularly large tax-exempts with substantial operations, need long-term incentive arrangements to compete with the for-profit sector and retain talented people. Retention incentives can be a simple way to achieve the look and feel of a long-term incentive plan, without all the administrative complexity. A retention incentive can be as simple as an agreement to pay an executive 100% of his or her base salary at the end of five years. There are no business performance requirements for vesting. Rather, the amount vests at the end of five years if the executive remains employed by the organization over that period. In essence, this is the same as providing a long-term incentive plan that pays out 20% of base salary annually. If the 20% LTI plan can be considered competitive for the particular organization and marketplace, the retention incentive can also be an effective tool.

Retention incentives can also take the form of sign-on bonuses in a recruiting situation, or when an executive or other key employee is in a "hard to recruit, hard to replace" position and additional compensation is required to maintain competitiveness.

(e) Compensation Provided by a Subsidiary Organization

Other items often overlooked are compensation and benefits received from a subsidiary of a tax-exempt organization. If an individual is considered disqualified with respect to a tax-exempt parent organization, compensation arrangements provided to this individual from a subsidiary organization, whether taxable or tax-exempt, must be included in the assessment of reasonableness.

7.12 CONCLUSION

Compensation planning for tax-exempt organizations can be challenging. Not only do tax-exempts face issues of key employee motivation, retention, and competitiveness, which are experienced by all companies, but they also have the added problem of a complex set of tax rules and restrictions on how compensation can be delivered. Moreover, with a stated mission and exempt purpose, scarce funds must simply go further to meet the organization's needs. That said, there are many alternative ways to attract and retain key people, many ways to balance competitiveness with the mission and exempt purpose, and many ways to achieve pay for performance. We hope we have provided some additional insight regarding how to balance these competing objectives, while protecting the organization, its Board, and executives from intermediate sanctions.

Chapter 8

Designing the Annual Management Incentive Plan

Edward W. Freher

8.1 ROLE OF ANNUAL INCENTIVES IN COMPENSATION STRATEGY

(a) Primary Role as a Motivator of Management Behavior

Of all the compensation elements, the annual management incentive plan has the greatest potential to influence individual behavior and enhance business results. Unlike base salary, which focuses on core job responsibilities and the relevant external market for those responsibilities, or long-term incentives, which are often stock based and reflect the entire organization's success over a multiple-year period, annual incentives are determined by team and individual performance measures over which the individual manager has the most direct influence or control. The annual timeframe is sufficiently immediate to sustain attention, and the reward is generally paid in a lump sum in the form of cash or a combination of cash and stock. A properly designed annual incentive plan can assist an organization in achieving desired performance on critical tactical success factors—those success factors that can be measured and influenced within a one-year timeframe.

In summary:

- *Base salary* reflects core job responsibilities.
- *Annual incentives* recognize team and individual performance.
- *Long-term incentives* recognize corporate/organization performance.

(b) Annual Incentives Represent a Variable Compensation Cost

In addition to its motivational role in influencing management behavior, the annual incentive plan is usually the most potentially variable of the compensation elements, with the cost of the plan in a particular year flexing up and down with the aggregate achievement of incentive goals by participants. In fact, as discussed later, one test of a good incentive design is whether the total costs of the plan vary in a meaningful way based on overall organizational performance. In recent years, many organizations have limited base salary increases and moved more of their overall pay opportunities into annual incentive plans in order to have their compensation costs be more variable and affordable. These organizations are prepared to provide their managers with significant compensation opportunities, but only when they achieve the organizational results that support these opportunities.

(c) Annual Incentives Demonstrate Pay-for-Performance Linkage

A final role of the annual incentive plan is to support the belief that management pay, particularly that of senior executives, should vary significantly with the financial results achieved for shareholders over the performance year. Shareholder interest groups and the business press are sharply critical of executive pay that increases in the face of declining earnings. Since base salaries are generally considered fixed, and long-term incentives are by their nature multiple year and often tied to stock price, annual incentives must demonstrate the appropriate relationship between executive pay and the short-term financial performance of the organization.

8.2   INFLUENCING MANAGEMENT BEHAVIOR: BUILDING A LINE-OF-SIGHT RELATIONSHIP

(a) Performance Measurements Under the Control of Participants

In order for a management incentive plan to influence behavior, a *line-of-sight* relationship must exist between the participants and the plan performance measures. Accordingly, the performance measures that determine a participant's award should have the following key characteristics: (1) they must be under the direct control of the participant or of a team of which the participant is a significant member, and (2) they must be achievable within a one-year timeframe.

Let's look at some examples of the line-of-sight concept:

> An assistant plant manager participates in a corporate management incentive plan in which the awards to all participants are a function of corporate earnings performance. The corporation has eight manufacturing plants in the United States and two in Europe. There would not be a line-of-sight relationship between an assistant plant manager in this example and corporate earnings. Corporate earnings are not under the control of the assistant plant manager, and the management team would be too large for this position to be considered a significant member. To influence behavior, performance measures would have to be more specific to that particular plant and to the assistant plant manager's area of responsibility.

The manufacturing vice-president participates in the same corporate management incentive plan. The manufacturing vice-president is one of five key officers reporting to the chief executive. This position is a significant member of the management team that collectively impacts earnings. A line-of-sight relationship does exist. The motivational value of the plan may be improved by having a portion of the manufacturing vice-president's award based directly on manufacturing performance (the individual piece) and a portion based on corporate earnings performance (the team piece).

An industrial goods manufacturing company uses return on investment as one of its corporate performance measures in its management incentive plan. Most investments are capital expenditures for new plant and equipment, with the typical payback on such investments over five to seven years. Management incentive participants have little ability to influence return on investment in a one-year timeframe, and the plan could be improved by substituting more short-term tactical investment measures, such as inventory control.

(b) Differentiating Between a Management Incentive Plan and a Profit-Sharing Plan

Occasionally you will see a profit-sharing plan masquerading as a management incentive plan. In its simplest form, a profit-sharing plan allocates a percentage of corporate or business unit earnings to plan participants. These allocated dollars are distributed to participants based on salary or a combination of salary and position level. Unlike a management incentive plan, there is a limited line-of-sight relationship for many of the plan participants, since the only performance measure is typically corporate or business unit profitability. Also in a management incentive plan, the performance measures are not constant but will change periodically based on those tactical success factors that are most important in a given year; a profit-sharing arrangement uses the same success measure each year—earnings. There is nothing inherently wrong with a profit-sharing plan. It may have motivational value for senior-level participants, where the line-of-sight relationship does exist. It also represents a variable compensation cost that fluctuates with earnings. In its simplicity, a profit-sharing plan lacks the differentiating individual and team performance measures required to have the plan function effectively as a tool to influence participant behavior and help achieve organizational results.

8.3 CORPORATE AND BUSINESS UNIT PERFORMANCE MEASUREMENT

(a) Financial Measures

Exhibit 8.1 demonstrates the prevalence of varying financial measures used at the corporate level, based on a Mercer study. Here are some general conclusions from this and similar studies:

1. Almost all management incentive plans, at the corporate level, use some measure of profits. Earnings per share and net income are the most common.

2. Two or three financial measures are typical. The most common combination would be an earnings measure coupled with revenue growth, or an earnings measure coupled with a return measure.

3. A significant number of companies do not rely totally on accounting measures but also use economic measures such as cash flow and economic profit.

4. Different but complementary measures are used at the corporate and business unit levels.

(b) Nonfinancial Measures

At the corporate and business unit level, financial measures predominate, with nonfinancial measures more likely to be used to assess individual manager

Exhibit 8.1   Corporate Annual Incentive Plan Measures.

Measure	%
Earnings per Share	53%
Net Income	47%
Revenue Growth	47%
Cash Flow	35%
Return on Assets	24%
Total Shareholder Return	18%
Economic Profit	12%
Return on Sales	12%
Operating Income	6%
Return on Equity	6%
Return on Investment	6%
Return on Net Assets	6%
Other	35%

Number of Financial Measures Used to Fund AIP	% of companies
1	12%
2–3	47%
>3	41%

Source: © Mercer 350-Company Study, 2001.

performance. Where nonfinancial measures are used at the corporate and business unit level in management incentive plans, quality, customer satisfaction, or employee climate appear most often.

In an organization with multiple product lines, and perhaps international operations, frequently no single corporate measurements of quality or customer satisfaction can be used for all management incentive plan participants. Quality and customer satisfaction are more often line of business or team specific. For example, customer satisfaction may be an appropriate measure for an incentive plan covering employees such as tellers, customer service managers, and retail branch managers at a bank. It may not be an appropriate corporate measurement for senior executives of the same bank who are responsible for trading activities or corporate finance.

(c) Balanced Scorecard

In assessing corporate performance, compensation committees have historically been uncomfortable with performance measures that are not part of the statements of financial and operating performance found in the corporation's annual report. This view is changing, and some companies are using a "Balanced Scorecard" approach to assess corporate, business unit, and individual performance. A Balanced Scorecard recognizes that performance on key nonfinancial measures leads to future financial performance. These leading measures need to be part of the performance assessment process if we are to use effectively our incentive compensation program to drive business results. For example, new product development is often a critical leading measure for revenue growth. Chapter 3 includes a discussion of the Balanced Scorecard approach.

(d) Integration with Long-Term Incentive Plans

Most managers participate in both an organization's annual management incentive plan and its long-term incentive plans. Long-term incentive plans take various forms and may be based wholly on stock price appreciation measures, such as stock options, or may include plans whereby the rewards to senior managers are determined in part by financial performance over a three- to five-year period, such as performance unit plans, performance share plans, and their various derivatives (for a discussion of these plans, see Chapter 10, Long-Term Incentives).

The selection and weighting of performance measures for the annual incentive plan should balance with the shareholder value and financial measures used in the long-term incentive plan design. Considerations in this balancing include the desired tie to corporate success for all management participants, whether corporate long-term success is measured by stock price appreciation alone or a combination of stock price appreciation and three- to five-year financial performance and the most critical one-year business drivers at the corporate and business unit level. Some of the most typical combinations of annual and long-term incentive plan measures are shown in Exhibit 8.2.

8.4 DETERMINING PARTICIPATION AND SIZE OF AWARD OPPORTUNITIES

(a) Establishing Criteria for Participation

Determining cutoffs for management incentive participation is often one of the more vexing assignments for senior executives and human resource departments. For the individual manager, being selected to participate in the annual incentive plan is a key step on a career ladder. It has significant symbolic as well as monetary value. The result, regardless of the specific criteria selected, is constant pressure to include more and more managers so that participation in any management incentive plan invariably increases over time. A good rule for any organization establishing its first management incentive plan is to begin conservatively because you will inevitably expand your plan participation (and costs).

The following guidelines may help minimize your headaches on this issue:

• *Start with your organization's compensation strategy.* A key element in this strategy should be your emphasis on fixed versus variable compensation. An organization with a strategy favoring variable compensation should have lower base salaries and more incentive plan participants with generally larger

Exhibit 8.2   Balancing Annual and Long-Term Incentive Measures: Typical Combinations.

Example	Participant	Annual Plan	Long-Term Plan(s)
A	Corporate manager	Earnings per share and return on equity	Stock price appreciation (stock option plan)
B	Corporate manager	Net income and revenue growth	Stock price appreciation (stock option plan) and return on equity (four-year performance plan)
C	Business unit manager	Business unit operating income and return on assets	Corporate stock price appreciation (stock option plan)

incentive opportunities. The reverse strategy would suggest higher base salaries and fewer plan participants.

- *Assess which positions truly impact the performance measures in your plan.* A management incentive plan that measures performance at multiple levels in an organization (e.g., corporate, business unit, and department) should have lower participation cutoffs than an organization that measures performance only at the corporate level. This guideline is consistent with the line-of-sight relationship.

- *Consider the role of other organization incentive programs.* Most organizations have multiple incentive or bonus plans. There may be separate sales and sales management plans, productivity and quality-related plans for operations positions, and special award programs for outstanding individual achievements. A particular individual or position being considered for participation in a management incentive plan may better belong in one of these other programs in which the performance measures are more relevant.

- *Don't forget the market.* Management incentive plan eligibility is moving deeper into organizations across all industries. Specific market norms will vary by type of position, industry, and size of organization. Market norms need to be considered so that your total direct compensation program (i.e., base salary, annual incentive, and long-term incentive) is competitive. Market norms should not dictate participation, however, because you can frequently substitute somewhat higher base salaries for incentive participation and remain competitive.

(b)   Use of Target Award Opportunities

Most organizations assign some form of target award opportunity to each position in the management incentive plan. A target award is the percent of salary (or salary range midpoint) that the individual will receive if the organization achieves its goals and the individual achieves his or her goals. As organization and individual performance increases, the individual can earn more than the target award opportunity, generally as much as 150% or 200% of target award. Conversely, as performance deteriorates, the incentive award earned declines from target levels, with zero award below some predetermined threshold level of performance. We discuss aligning award opportunities with performance in the next section.

Target awards generally increase with position responsibility and salary grade. This conforms to market norms and reflects the reality that senior positions have more influence on organization goals; therefore, it is logical for a greater proportion of their pay to be at risk and tied to these goals. Organizations establish target award levels considering their compensation strategy and market norms for their industry. Exhibit 8.3 is an example of a target award schedule.

8.5 BUILDING PERFORMANCE SCALES

(a) Establishing the Standard

In designing a management incentive plan, the single most difficult and controversial task is aligning performance scales with award opportunities. If the level of achievement is too low, management is overcompensated for mediocre or poor results. Too high a performance expectation results in a demoralized management team who view their compensation as inadequate for the results achieved.

The four broad approaches that organizations use to establish performance scales are defined as follows. Exhibit 8.4 outlines the considerations in using each approach.

- *Basing awards on attaining the approved annual profit budget or business plan.* The budget becomes the performance standard against which management is measured, and budget performance results in payment of target incentive awards.

- *Comparing financial and/or operational performance against a defined group of industry peers.* For example, payment of target awards may require annual performance at or above the 60th percentile, with maximum awards payable at the 90th percentile and no award paid if performance is below the 30th percentile.

- *Establishing an expected level of earnings growth or asset utilization improvement over prior year's performance and linking target incentive awards to its achievement.* For example, the performance standard for each year's management incentive plan is based on a 15% growth in earnings over the

Exhibit 8.3 Sample Target Award Schedule (Expressed as Percentage of Salary).

Position	Salary Grade	Target Award (%)	Range Opportunity	
			Min (%)	Max (%)
President	25	75	0	150
Vice-president	21–23	50	0	100
Director	20–21	35	0	70
Director	18–19	25	0	50
Manager/Senior professional	15–18	15	0	30

prior year. Growth and improvement levels are usually established for multiple years and revised periodically as conditions change.

* *Developing a fixed performance standard that represents a level of excellence in the industry.* This "industry leader" standard is developed through competitive benchmarking. For example, the best performing companies in XYZ industry average a 15% annual return on assets. This 15% standard continues from year to year, unless modified according to changing conditions.

Exhibit 8.4   Determining Performance Standards.

Approach	Considerations
Budget or business plan	Requires well-established, credible budgeting, and goal-setting process.
	Allows business units to have different goals reflecting their economic conditions and stage in the business cycle.
	Can encourage budget gamesmanship.
	Works best with strong CEO involvement in budgeting process and performance benchmarking to test the stretch of budget goals.
Peer comparison	May be truest measure of management performance.
	Is often difficult to obtain timely and relevant peer data, particularly at the business unit level.
	Works best in cyclical industries in which key industry performance variables (e.g., interest rates, raw material costs) are outside control of management.
	Shareholders may be unwilling to pay significant incentive awards for excellent relative peer performance if it represents low absolute profitability or a decline.
Improvement over prior years	Consistent with continuous improvement culture.
	Straightforward and easy to communicate to participants and Board.
	Difficult to administer with business units at different stages in the business cycle.
	Does not recognize economic conditions or investments/ acquisitions that may depress short-term profitability.
Industry leader standard	Consistent with high-performance culture and performance benchmarking.
	May be consistent with shareholder expectations.
	May be difficult to develop and maintain for each business unit.
	Does not recognize economic conditions or investments/ acquisitions that could depress short-term profitability.

(b)   Target, Threshold, and Superior

The performance standard determines the level of organization performance required for target awards to be earned. A scale must then be developed, including a threshold below which no awards are earned and often a superior performance level that earns the maximum provided under the plan formula. Exhibit 8.5 illustrates a performance scale. Most organizations use two or three performance measures and have a separate scale for each measure.

   Approaches to establishing performance scales run from statistical (analyzing the volatility of past results) to management judgment. In an organization with multiple business units, the concept of target awards at achievement of the performance standard is generally a constant; however, the specific performance scale (80% to 115% in our example) should vary based on the size and maturity of the business unit and economic conditions in its industry.

(c)   Need for External Validation

The performance scales should not be determined without an external validation process that considers the competitive level of management and executive pay

Exhibit 8.5   Example of Performance Scale.

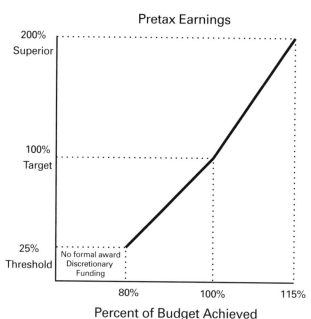

delivered at different points in the performance scale and the organization performance required for that pay. In the opening section, we discussed the important role of the annual management incentive plan in demonstrating a supportable relationship between pay and financial performance. In its simplest form, the market competitive position of base salary plus target incentive award should be consistent with the relative financial performance required by the performance scale to pay target awards.

An organization that performs in the upper quartile of its industry should have a performance scale that results in incentive awards that, when added to base salary, deliver upper quartile pay consistent with that performance. Conversely, if organization performance is in the bottom half of the industry, the performance scales on the management incentive plan should be aligned so that direct pay (base salary plus annual management incentive) is also in the bottom half. An organization's pay may lead its competitive position for a period of time (e.g., a turnaround situation with a new management team), but the compensation committee must see that the two are ultimately balanced.

(d)   A Word About Formulas

Organizations will occasionally establish a management incentive formula that limits the dollars that can be awarded under the management incentive plan.

Example: 10% of Pretax earnings that exceed a 6% return on capital

The formula in our example provides for an initial return to shareholders (6% of capital) before management can receive any incentive awards. Ten percent of the remaining earnings, if any, are reserved for management incentive awards. Formulas often provide for carryovers of any unspent amounts to future performance years. Carryovers provide the opportunity to make management incentive awards selectively or at modest levels in years in which no or minimal dollars are earned under the formula.

In some cases, formulas are intended primarily as shareholder protection against excessive amounts of earnings being committed to management bonuses. Incentive awards are determined by the same performance standards discussed earlier in this section. The formulas serve as an after-the-fact "failsafe" on reasonability. These organizations may regularly spend less than the formula amounts, and the formula exists primarily as shareholder optics.

In other situations, the formulas determine the specific management bonus fund for the performance year. This fund is then allocated to participants on a discretionary basis or using the approaches discussed in the next section. In general, bonus formulas leave something to be desired as a performance scale for a management incentive plan. Management incentive costs, as a percentage of earnings, tend to decrease with company growth. Therefore, the formula that is appropriate at one stage in an organization's development may not be valid at a later stage. It is also difficult to apply formula amounts to different business units, losing the line-of-sight relationship we discussed earlier.

8.6   ASSESSING INDIVIDUAL PERFORMANCE

(a)   Funding—Building the Incentive Pool

Management incentive plans almost always consider both business unit performance and individual manager performance. Business unit performance determines the overall approximate dollar amount of awards earned under the plan for the performance year (sometimes called *funding*), and individual performance impacts the specific amount an individual receives. Our discussion so far has covered funding.

(b)   Reliance on Goal Setting

Organizations that have been effective in using their management incentive plan as an important tool to help drive behavior frequently use goal setting as the basis for individual awards. Goal setting in these organizations is an integrated process that starts with the business unit's goals and then terraces down to develop supporting goals at the department and individual manager level. Business unit goals represent the collective accountability of the management team, and individual goals are the individual manager accountability. Effective goal setting is not an individual process with each manager recommending his or her own goals subject only to supervisory approval.

Organizations may divide the target award into two pieces, with a portion of the award based on business unit performance and a portion on individual performance (Exhibit 8.6).

A word of caution: Many organizations with less integrated goal-setting processes have found that individual awards do not vary up and down as expected with business unit success. Rather, individual awards follow a sort of a normal curve, with the total amount earned each year relatively constant, regardless of business unit performance. Thus, the concept of collective and individual accountability discussed previously is lost.

(c)   Other Individual Assessment Approaches

Such approaches vary from discretionary to formal, highly disciplined individual reviews. Increasingly, organizations are using such assessment tools as 360-degree feedback, balanced scorecards, and interdepartmental review teams to assess individual contribution and determine management incentive awards.

Exhibit 8.6   Target Awards.

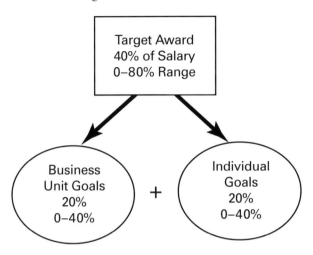

8.7   ASSESSING COST–BENEFITS OF NEW PLANS AND PLAN MODIFICATIONS

(a)   Concept of Self-Funding

Management incentive plans should be self-funding; that is, the profitability calculations used to determine awards earned under the plan should reflect (be reduced by) the cost of estimated management incentive payments. This method is consistent with other compensation costs such as salary and benefits, which are reflected in all profitability calculations. If the performance standard in the plan is operating earnings or return on assets, these measures should be calculated after all costs incurred in their achievement, including estimated management incentive payments. Self-funding is a key component in assessing the reasonableness of management incentive payments at different levels of organization performance.

(b)   Doing Due Diligence

A cost–benefit analysis should be completed when an organization considers establishing a new management incentive plan or significantly modifying an existing plan by adding new participants, raising target award levels, or revising performance scales. This analysis basically compares awards under the plan to the profitability required for those awards and ensures a reasonable balance. There are no absolute norms, but generally, management incentive payments, like all forms of executive compensation, should represent a relatively small part of total earnings. The exceptions to this statement are professional service industries, such as advertising, consulting, or investment banking, where compensation is the primary operating cost. Exhibit 8.7 is an example of a cost–benefit analysis.

8.8 OTHER CONSIDERATIONS

(a) Section 162(m)

Annual incentive plans should be designed so that the awards paid to the CEO and other named officers in the company proxy qualify for the performance-based exemption under Section 162(m) of the Internal Revenue Code. Compensation generally qualifies for this exemption if the following apply:

* Compensation is paid solely on attaining one or more performance goals established by a compensation committee consisting solely of two or more outside directors.
* The material terms under which the compensation is to be paid are approved by shareholders in a separate vote before payment.
* Before payment, the compensation committee certifies that the performance goals and any other material terms were in fact satisfied.

(b) Not-for-Profit Organizations

We are seeing an increasing use of annual management incentive plans by hospitals, colleges/universities, and health and welfare organizations. The basic rationale for establishing a management incentive plan is similar to that in for-profit organizations: a desire to link an element of management compensation directly to results achieved and to help foster a culture of accountability within the organization. While the performance measures selected will be different, reflecting the mission of the organization, all the principles outlined in this chapter are applicable. (See Chapter 7, "Pay for Performance in Not-for-Profit Organizations.")

Exhibit 8.7   Cost–Benefit Analysis of a Management Incentive Plan ($000s).[a]

	Threshold	Target	Superior	Incremental Target/Superior
Pretax earnings	16,000	20,000	23,000	3,000
Awards	225	900	1,800	900
%	1.4	4.5	7.8	30.0

[a]Award costs are included in calculating pretax earnings (self-funding).

(c) Holdbacks and Other Forms of Mandatory Deferrals

Most annual management incentive plans pay awards in cash (sometimes a combination of cash and company stock) early in the following year after final financial and operating results are known. Participants who terminate during the performance year forfeit any award for that year. The exceptions are death, disability, or retirement, in which case a prorated award is generally paid. There is no mandatory deferral of any portion of the award. The long-term incentive plan, through vesting schedules and multiple-year performance periods, encourages management and executive retention and provides the "golden handcuffs" element in the overall organization compensation strategy.

Mandatory holdback features are most likely in situations in which annual results may not be sustained by future events (e.g., credit losses) or when no separate long-term incentive plan is in place to encourage retention. It is also common in certain industries where annual bonus awards are very large and key employee turnover is a continual issue.

(d) Voluntary Deferrals

Many plans allow participants to make a voluntary election to defer all or a portion of any award to termination or retirement. The deferred award becomes part of a deferred compensation arrangement, and interest or other appreciation is credited annually. If the arrangement is properly structured, the participant can receive the benefit of tax deferral on both the deferred award and the interest credited. In order to qualify for the tax deferral benefit, the election to defer should be made before, or early in, the performance year, and the participant must have the status of an unsecured company creditor with regard to deferral balances. Voluntary deferrals and the related issues of constructive receipt and economic benefit are discussed in more detail later in this book.

8.9 FINAL CHECKLIST

We have reviewed several issues in designing or revising an annual management incentive plan. The following checklist is a summary of key concepts:

- Does participation represent the individuals who can truly influence, directly or as a significant member of a team, the plan performance measures?
- Are the performance measures the best short-term value drivers for the organization?
- Does the plan have the proper balance among corporate, business unit, and individual performance?

- Is the plan integrated with your base salary program to produce competitive cash compensation opportunities consistent with organization performance?
- Has there been an external validation of the performance scales to ensure both the right amount of performance stretch and award levels that are defensible considering your organizational performance?
- Does the plan provide sufficient upside potential to reward excellence?
- Is there a minimum threshold performance requirement below which no awards are earned (except possibly limited individual awards for truly superior individual performance)?
- Does the plan integrate with your long-term incentive plan in terms of award opportunities, choice of performance measures, and payout features?
- Is the plan self-funding, and have you performed a cost–benefit analysis to test the reasonableness of plan costs at different levels of plan performance?
- Does the plan have a voluntary deferral provision?

Chapter 9

Designing Incentive Compensation Programs to Support Value-Based Management*

Richard Harris

The purpose of this chapter is to provide compensation professionals with a practical understanding of compensation in a value-based management (VBM) environment. We address:

- What is commonly meant by value-based management.
- How VBM performance measures differ from other financial performance measures.
- The criteria for successful implementation of VBM.
- Design principles of VBM-based incentive plans.

After the conceptual discussion, we provide an example of one method for setting performance targets in a VBM environment.

9.1 WHAT IS VALUE-BASED MANAGEMENT?

VBM is an integrated approach to managing a business with the primary goal of maximizing long-term, sustainable value for the business's shareholders. It is a process that focuses on maximizing the value of investments made by suppliers' of debt and equity funding. It establishes an expectation that managers will operate in a manner that provides a return in excess of the cost of the debt and equity capital.

* The author wishes to thank Shelly Carlin, Senior Vice President Executive Compensation at Bcom3, for her valuable assistance in reviewing this chapter.

A VBM framework integrates a company's decision-making and behavioral processes and directs them toward the goal of creating shareholder value. The framework includes the following elements:

- *Business planning.* Developing a planning process that evaluates alternative decisions regarding strategy, investments, and human capital according to their potential to create shareholder value.
- *Target setting.* Establishing company performance targets at levels that create shareholder value.
- *Reporting and feedback.* Providing regular performance feedback at all organization levels (corporate, business unit, team, and individual) to improve decision making.
- *Rewards.* Rewarding managers and employees for long-term, sustained value creation.

9.2 VBM PERFORMANCE METRICS DIFFER FROM OTHER FINANCIAL MEASURES

VBM approaches are often described in terms of the various financial performance metrics used to drive shareholder value, such as Economic Value Added (EVA),[1] cash flow return on investment (CFROI), or total business return (TBR). These metrics reflect the true economics of business results better than accounting-based measures such as earnings before interest and taxes (EBIT), earnings per share (EPS), or return on investment (ROI).

VBM metrics have the following characteristics:

- Income is measured relative to the level of investment used to achieve the level of income.
- Risk is accounted for, typically by using a cost of capital to calculate the result.
- Generally Accepted Accounting Principles (GAAP) accounting methods are adjusted in order to:
  — Bring the measure closer to a cash basis rather than an accrual basis.
  — More accurately reflect the true level of capital invested in the business.

Value-based measures have all of these characteristics in common. While some accounting-based measures have some of these characteristics, none has all of them.

---

[1] EVA is a registered trademark of Stern-Stewart.

VBM metrics not only measure performance, but they also set a required level of performance. For example, having positive EVA requires that profits be greater than the cost of capital. Therefore, the cost of capital establishes a level of performance that is higher than simply achieving positive net income. When a business is not generating a return in excess of its cost of capital, value is being destroyed.

During the early 1990s, several research studies and media articles extolled the virtues of EVA and other VBM metrics for helping companies create value. More recently, the research and media have begun to question whether these metrics actually lead to higher levels of value-creating performance. Which position is correct?

The answer is "it depends!" While most financial experts agree that VBM metrics are theoretically superior measures of value relative to EPS, ROI, or other accounting-based measures, many companies reject these metrics because they are "too complex." We agree that value metrics are more complex; however, the failure of VBM efforts are not a result of the complexity of the metric but its implementation, especially in the area of incentive plan design.

In our experience, a successful VBM effort requires a company to:

• Evaluate its degree of readiness for VBM.
• Develop and execute an implementation plan founded on the three "Cs"— communication, compensation, and commitment.

9.3 VBM IMPLEMENTATION

(a) Readiness for VBM

Implementing VBM requires major organizational change. Well-designed incentive plans can be used effectively to support this change, but compensation is only one part of the story. Unfortunately, companies often attempt to use compensation plans to drive this change before the organization has fully embraced VBM as a management approach. For these companies, the VBM efforts often failed.

To make VBM successful, a company should first evaluate its readiness for VBM. Companies fall into one of the following three stages (illustrated in Exhibit 9.1 and described in Exhibit 9.2):

1. *Embryonic stage.* In this first stage, the company's top financial and operating management has committed to VBM but has not developed the supporting systems or broadly communicated the specific value metrics throughout the company.

Exhibit 9.1   VBM Maturity Curve.

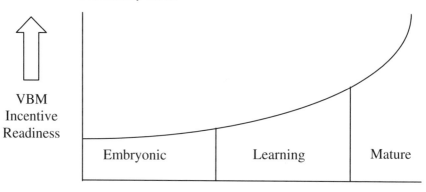

2. *Learning stage.* All the planning, financial reporting, and other necessary supporting systems have been converted to VBM requirements. Most employees have had initial education and training on the metric definition and how they can impact it. The VBM metric and/or the supporting value drivers are being measured and monitored; however, most employees have not had enough time to see how their decisions and actions impact the metric and are therefore not confident that they know how to "add value."

3. *Mature stage.* Decisions are consistently being made with the goal of improving value. Systems measure and report results by VBM centers, customers, and product lines. Training and ongoing education on VBM principles is in place for all employees.

It is difficult to predict how long each stage of development will last. The time-frame is affected by the commitment of the senior executive team, the resources devoted to making the change, and the economic environment impacting the company and its industry sector. There are, however, some rules of thumb to follow.

Exhibit 9.2   Characteristics of VBM Incentive Readiness Stages.

Embryonic	Learning Stage	Mature Stage
• Top management support • Desire to change • VBM centers identified • VBM metric (e.g., EVA) defined • Training started	• Broad-based introduction • Financial reporting to support measure (e.g., EP) • Preliminary education completed • VMB centers measured on metric	• VBM metric measured at product/customer levels • High level of organizational understanding • Decisions have become VBM based • Continuing education in place

The embryonic stage should be expected to be one to two years. If the VBM process is started within four to six months before the beginning of a new fiscal year, and enough resources are devoted to the effort, the company may reach the learning stage by the end of the next fiscal year. Conversely, if a company is in the embryonic stage for more than 18 to 24 months, it should reassess its commitment to VBM.

The learning stage may take an additional one or two years. The factors impacting the timeframe include the commitment of resources to the process and the rate at which employees adapt to the change.

A company will continue in the mature stage as long as it continues its commitment to VBM and periodically evaluates, refines, and refreshes its efforts. This stage can go on indefinitely.

(b)   Implementing VBM Through Communication, Compensation, and Commitment

Too many companies assume that a successful VBM implementation depends primarily on carefully selecting the best metric and tailoring the application of the metric to the company's needs. Defining the detailed calculation, they believe, is the hardest part. Once that is completed, communications efforts often consist of sending out a press release embracing value management principles. Unfortunately, it's not that simple.

Realizing value—creating performance improvements through a VBM effort—requires that the entire organization embrace the goals of VBM. Embracing the goals, however, is only the first step. Employees must understand how they create value, be rewarded for the right actions, and have the freedom to implement change.

Through our experiences with successful and unsuccessful VBM implementations, we have determined that three critical elements must be part of any VBM implementation:

1. *Communication* that gives employees the information they need to make good decisions
2. *Compensation* that rewards the right actions and results
3. *Commitment* to creating positive change

It is important to recognize that the impact depends on the product of these three elements: *communication* × *compensation* × *commitment* (see Exhibit 9.3). Communication in this context has a broad definition. The first part of the VBM communication effort is to articulate how a VBM approach will help the company achieve its business objectives, and describe in some detail the specific metric. Too many companies, however, stop communicating once the metric is explained.

Exhibit 9.3   Communication $\times$ Compensation $\times$ Commitment = Performance.

Communication

- Identify value-creating metric.
- Create connections to all employees: communicate and educate.
- Provide meaningful and timely data for decisions.

Compensation

- Align pay design and administration with performance.
- Use and connect all forms of rewards.
- Link company and employee interests.

Commitment

- Create a high-involvement environment.
- Remove influence barriers.
- Open communications channels.

Explaining the calculation is just the beginning. Creating the connections for each employee between his or her role in the company and value creation is the next step. This requires employees to understand how value is created in their company and industry. One effective way to achieve this is by developing a "value tree"(see Exhibit 9.4).

A value tree can be an effective tool because it breaks down the financial measure into its "value drivers"—those elements and actions that employees can recognize, relate to, and impact. Once the tree is defined, the company's reporting systems can be tailored to provide the meaningful and timely data required to manage value.

The compensation element begins with developing incentive plans linking pay with the level of performance achieved on the VBM metric. An example is provided later in this chapter. Successful VBM companies go beyond this and link all forms of rewards—cash, equity, spot bonuses, and recognition plans—to the VBM effort. In doing so, they create an unmistakable connection between the interests of employees and owners.

Commitment is the third element. Commitment in a VBM context is a two-way street. Clearly committed employees are more likely to take actions that create value once they understand their connection to it and know that they will be rewarded for their successes. The company's commitment is that it will provide an environment that encourages employees to manage for value. This requires creating a high-involvement environment where decision making is pushed as close to the activity as possible. It requires companies to remove influence

Exhibit 9.4   Financial Drivers/Operational Drivers.

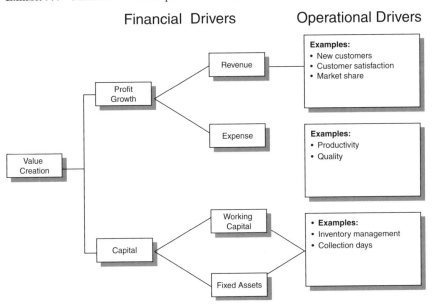

barriers, such as restrictive policies, and to eliminate being able to discuss things that were previously "unmentionables." Finally, it requires two-way, adult-to-adult communications to assess the VBM implementation and clarify questions regarding value creation.

Communication, compensation and commitment are necessary elements to the success of a VBM incentive plan. These three Cs create the connection between company value creation and employee actions. At least as much, if not more, resources should go into implementation as the incentive design effort.

9.4   DESIGNING VBM-BASED COMPENSATION PLANS

(a)   Key Principles

The objective of VBM-based compensation plans is to reward employees for acting like shareholders. Most often, this is achieved by designing cash and equity-based plans that simulate the risks and rewards of ownership. In these plans, a portion of the sustained value creation is shared with employees through annual and long-term incentives. From this philosophy, several key principles of plan design can be derived.

- *The "rewards of ownership" are measured in terms of absolute performance, not performance relative to an internal budget.* VBM-based incentives set performance standards that are empirically derived from shareholder expectations. This results in a system that no longer rewards the successful negotiation of lower budgets, nor penalizes managers for establishing "stretch" goals.

- *VBM plans reward sustained value creation.* This implies a long-term performance measurement period. VBM-based programs use design features that reward multiyear performance either through a "bonus bank" for annual incentive plans or through heavy emphasis on long-term performance plans.

- *The rewards of ownership are potentially unlimited.* Unlike most incentive plans, VBM-based plans generally have no cap or a very high cap on reward opportunities. This can be a powerful motivator.

- *VBM incentives incorporate downside risk as well as upside opportunity.* The methodologies used to ensure that sustainable performance is rewarded must allow for the reversal of accrued awards when economic value is destroyed. The plan's ability to produce large awards when substantial value is created and to reduce rewards when value is destroyed is critical to establishing an ownership mentality.

- *While not unique to VBM plans, measuring VBM performance at the lowest possible units of measure is a key success factor.* Measuring economic profit at a corporate level does not provide accurate line-of-sight for most employees. Incentives designed to directly measure the lowest appropriate levels improve line-of-sight while maintaining focus on creating value for the company as a whole. Where appropriate, the components of the chosen VBM metric value drivers may be used to fund or distribute incentives.

(b)   VBM Incentive Plan Design Features

There are several steps in developing VBM-based incentive plans. For ease of description, the remainder of the section will address incentive design using economic profit (EP), a simplified form of EVA. Incentive plans using CFROI or TBR have similar characteristics. The steps for VBM plan design are as follows:

1. *Determine mix of compensation elements.* The mix between salary, annual incentives, and long-term incentives needs to reflect VBM's emphasis on sustained value creation. A mix that reduces the emphasis on annual incentive opportunities and increases the emphasis on long-term opportunities is often appropriate.

2. *Establish performance targets.* Whether EP or its value drivers are the performance measure for funding incentives, empirical analysis should be used to determine the proper performance hurdle rates over a multiple-year period. One way to establish these targets is to use the company's market value as a starting point, as illustrated in Exhibit 9.5.

Exhibit 9.5   Deriving Expectations for Improvement.

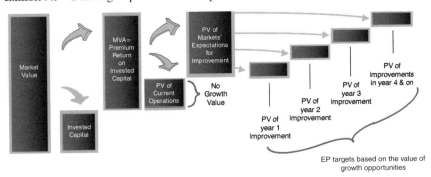

EP targets based on the value of
growth opportunities

Empirically derived goals provide tangible targets for operating managers.

3. *Establish the funding formula.* Once the targets are set, the next step is to establish the formula relating the change in pay to marginal increments of performance above or below the target. The variability of the business is a key factor impacting this pay-for-performance relationship. The greater the variability or cyclicality of business results, the wider the payout range. In this case, the payout curve should be flatter to provide rewards under a broad range of potential performance outcomes (Exhibit 9.6).

*   As the payout range narrows, the slope of the pay–performance line increases. Awards increase faster per increment of performance above

Exhibit 9.6   EP Incentives Reward Sustained Value Creation.

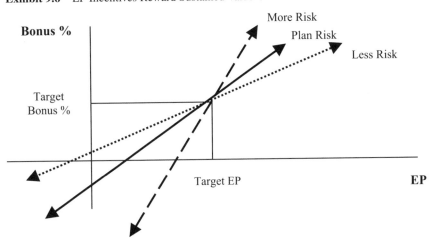

*   Target EP based on market expectations.
*   Variability of business results determines sensitivity of payout to deviations from target EP.

target, but they also decrease faster for performance below target. This increases the probability that no award will be earned.

- The slope of the lines can be set based on the probability of achieving 0% award and some multiple of target (typically 200%).

4. *Address the sustained performance requirement.* Being treated as owners of the business requires that if an employee is rewarded for value created, then the value must be sustained in order for that level of award to be realized. Therefore, VBM-based plans need to ensure that superior levels of incentive compensation earned by a given year's performance are offset by reductions in incentives if the level of economic profit decreases in the following years. This is often accomplished by using an annual plan deferral into a bonus bank arrangement. Another way to accomplish this goal is through a long-term incentive plan based on multiyear EP performance.

9.5 ESTABLISHING PERFORMANCE TARGETS

Target setting is hard; in fact, it is the most difficult part of designing a VBM-based incentive plan. Based on our experience, we've developed an approach that balances the need for a market-based, external standard of performance with the particular demands of a company's business environment. This section provides a numerical example of our approach.

For purposes of this example, the performance metric economic profit (EP) will be used. Economic profit as used in this book is a simplified form of EVA, defined as:

Net Operating Profit After Taxes (NOPAT) − a Capital Charge.

This EP definition requires adjustments to both NOPAT and Capital from Generally Accepted Accounting Principles (GAAP) that are used to produce audited financial statements. Typical adjustments are presented in Exhibits 9.7 and 9.8. The capital charge calculation is the multiplication of "Capital" and a weighted average cost of capital (WACC). WACC represents the combined costs of debt financing and equity financing. This portion of the calculation incorporates the concept that an economic cost of equity financing is not included in the definition of Net Income calculated on a GAAP basis. Exhibit 9.9 describes the WACC calculation.

Now that EP has been defined, how should EP targets be established and how should these targets be linked to competitive award opportunities? The goal is to develop an analytical approach that reasonably reflects shareholder's expectations for growth in EP. This approach helps to separate the target-setting process from the business planning process, thereby reducing the time and resources devoted to the "negotiation" of performance targets.

Exhibit 9.7   Defining NOPAT.

Net Operating Profit After Tax (NOPAT) represents the total profits from ongoing operations before noneconomic charges.

+ Sales
− Total Operating Expenses
= **Operating Profit**

+ Depreciation   } Potential Economic Adjustments[a]
+ Goodwill Amortization
− Changes in Capitalized R&D
= **Adjusted Operating Profit**

− Cash Operating Taxes ──────▶ Taxes relating to operating income
= **NOPAT**

[a] Company specific. Others include interest expense on noncapitalized leases, changes in LIFO/FIFO difference, etc.

Exhibit 9.8   Defining Invested Capital.

Invested capital represents the full amount that management has raised from investors that has yet to be recovered from operations.

──▶ + Current Operating Assets
    − Non-Interest-Bearing Current Liabilities ◀──────
    = **Net Working Capital**
    + Net Fixed Assets (Net P, P & E)
    + Goodwill (Incl. Accumulated Goodwill Amortization)
    + Intangibles
    + Operating Investments
    + Other Assets
    + Cumulative After-Tax Unusual Loss
    = **Invested Capital**

    Current Operating Assets
    + Accounts Receivable
    + Inventories
    + Prepaid Expenses
    + Other Current Assets
    Current Operating Assets

    Non-Interest-Bearing Current Liabilities
    + Accounts Payable
    + Notes Payable
    + Other Accrued Liabilities
    − Short-term Debt
    Non-Interest-Bearing Current Liabilities ──────

Exhibit 9.9   Determining Cost of Capital.

The weighted average cost of capital (WACC) is the total cost of all financing options. Typically the WACC includes the cost of equity and the cost of debt.

$WACC$ = Kd (debt/total capital) + Ke (equity/total capital)
   where: Kd = cost of debt
       debt = market value of debt
       Ke = cost of equity
       equity = market value of equity
       total capital = debt + equity

Cost of Debt (Kd)
   To approximate the cost of debt (Kd), assume book value and market value of debt are close. If firm has many issues outstanding and if any one deviates, on average, tends toward the market value.
   kd = interest expense/book value of debt from balance sheet
   debt = book value of debt from balance sheet

Cost of Equity (Ke)
   To approximate the cost of equity (Ke), use the capital asset pricing model (CAPM). The CAPM describes the expected return rates for a particular security.
   ke = Rf + beta (Rm − Rf)
       where: Rf = return on a riskless asset over the appropriate time period (e.g., 30-year U.S. government bond)
       beta = specific company's shareholder risk, or volatility of shareholder returns indexed to a marketwide equity risk. The beta statistic assesses the degree to which the value of stock parallels that of the stock market generally.
       Rm = Return on market (index such as S&P 500)
       Note that (Rm − Rf) is the expected equity risk premium, or the premium expected by shareholders for a risky asset to generate above the returns generated by a riskless asset.
   equity = market capitalization

Shareholder expectations establish performance targets designed to increase share price. While we recognize that other factors impact share price in the short term, we believe that a company's financial performance over time is the ultimate predictor of value creation.

A company's business planning process is key to its ability to create value over the long term. Our target-setting process brings together shareholder expectations and the results of business planning. When the EP projected by the business plan falls short of target, the shortfall must be addressed. Under our approach, the shortfall is added to the base EP projected by the business plan to derive the incentive plan EP targets. This approach helps preserve the underlying pattern of EP performance—an important consideration, especially in cyclical or capital intensive businesses. The business plan pattern of EP incorporates the management's best assessment of current industry and economic conditions, as well as planned capital expenditures and other major initiatives.

On rare occasions, the EP forecast of a company's business plan exceeds the market-derived targets. In these cases, the business plan targets should be used to motivate achievement of the targets established by the team and to reinforce the importance of establishing stretch but achievable business plans; however, the incentive plan award levels should be adjusted to reflect these higher performance targets. Without adjustment, managers would be penalized for setting aggressive business plans with lower incentive opportunities. Making the adjustment appropriately aligns pay and performance.

The target-setting approach illustrated in this chapter is a four-step approach. It is based on the following concepts:

- Annual EP targets should be derived from an evaluation of shareholder expectations over a three- to five-year period. Therefore, the annual targets are set currently for the next three to five years.
- The beginning point is a company's market value added (MVA), defined as the market value of equity (shares times share price) plus the market value of debt less the invested capital (as defined in Exhibit 9.10).
- Three- to five-year expected EP targets can be derived from MVA.

The following four steps illustrate the process. The numbers used are for a fictional company.

1. *Calculate MVA.* A firm's value is the market value of equity plus the market value of debt. MVA is the extent to which the market value of the firm exceeds the invested capital.

Exhibit 9.10   MVA.

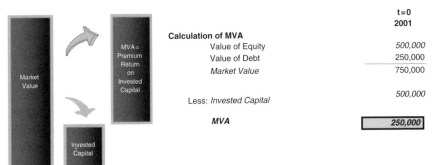

	t=0
	2001
Calculation of MVA	
Value of Equity	*500,000*
Value of Debt	250,000
Market Value	750,000
Less: *Invested Capital*	*500,000*
MVA	**250,000**

2. *Determine current business plan EP.* Economic profit is calculated for each year of the business plan.

	Year 1	Year 2	Year 3	Year 4	Year 5	Future Years
Annual Economic Profit	10,000	15,000	12,000	17,000	20,000	200,000

In addition to the annual EP for each year of the plan, all future years of EP are estimated using a simple perpetuity calculation.[2] This perpetuity represents the present value of ongoing EP beyond year 5.

3. *Compare business plan EP to MVA.* MVA, by definition, is the present value of all future EP and should equal the current business plan EP. If MVA exceeds the business plan EP, that means that the market's expectations for performance are higher than what management's current plans are expected to deliver. To compare MVA and the business plan EP, the present value of the forecast EP is calculated assuming a 10% cost of capital.

	Year 1	Year 2	Year 3	Year 4	Year 5	Future Years
Annual Economic Profit	10,000	15,000	12,000	17,000	20,000	200,000
Present Value of EP	9,100	12,400	9,000	11,600	12,400	124,200
Total Present Value of Future EP	178,700					

When the present value of the plan forecast EP is compared to the current MVA, the shortfall indicates that the market expects a higher level of performance than the business plans will deliver.

MVA	250,000
Present Value, Business Plan	178,700
Shortfall	71,300

4. *Allocate shortfall.* To set targets that reflect the return expected by investors, the shortfall must be added to the business plan forecast to create EP targets for the incentive plan. There are many ways to determine the allocation. In this example, we determine the annual annuity of the shortfall in perpetuity and add that to the business plan EP forecasts, as follows[3]:

---

[2] Calculated as follows: [20,000 × (1 + 0)] / (.10 − 0) or [Year 5 × (1 + growth rate)] / (Cost of Capital − growth rate).

[3] Calculated as follows: [((71,300 × .10) × (.10 − 0)) / 1.10 = 650; or [((shortfall × WACC) × (WACC − growth rate)) / (1 + WACC)].

	Year 1	Year 2	Year 3	Year 4	Year 5
Annual Economic Profit	10,000	15,000	12,000	17,000	20,000
Allocated Shortfall	650	1,300	1,950	2,600	3,250
Target EP	10,650	16,300	13,950	19,600	23,250

The addition of the allocated shortfall to the forecast EP yields the EP targets that are used in the annual and long-term incentive plans.

(a)   Evaluation of This Target-Setting Approach

The primary advantage of the MVA business plan approach is that it establishes performance levels that reflect investors' expectations, while setting VBM targets in a pattern that considers management's forecast of business conditions. By including the impact of known capital expenditures, this approach minimizes the disincentive to undertake value-creating opportunities that require large initial capital expenditures, but which may not generate positive VBM until several years in the future.

Because targets are aligned with the company's business plan, this approach can help foster ownership and support among senior managers in the organization. In addition, the integration of annual and long-term targets creates a consistent set of performance standards that can be easily translated into executive, management, and employee incentive plans.

The main disadvantage of the MVA business plan approach is the tradeoff between stability and flexibility. The establishment of targets over a multiyear time horizon provides the organization with a clear and stable performance benchmark; however, because the process does not contemplate changes to the targets absent significant unexpected events, it may be less flexible than other approaches, especially when the broad economy moves into a downturn.

(b)   Incentive Design Based on Stage of Readiness

As illustrated in Exhibit 9.11, as a company moves from one stage to the next, the incentive plan design should evolve in terms of:

- Specific performance measures used for incentives
- Performance targets
- Mix of fixed and variable compensation
- Amount of leverage designed in stock-based incentives

In the embryonic stage, most employees have not been introduced to the economic profit definition, and they do not have the tools to help them manage this

Exhibit 9.11   Stages of Readiness: Impact on Plan Design.

	From Embryonic ———➤	To Mature
• Measures	Combination of Traditional Measures	Directly Measure EP and Value Drivers
• Standards	Single Cost of Capital (COC)	Business Unit Specific COC
• Sharing Ratio	Modest	Substantial
• Equity Incentives	Traditional	Leveraged

metric. Therefore, companywide use of incentive plans that directly reward economic profit may not be appropriate; however, it is important that top executives lead the EP effort by agreeing to put a significant portion of their compensation in a plan linked to EP results. The following framework can be used in the compensation design for the *embryonic stage:*

- Annual incentive plan
  - Select traditional financial criteria that, in combination, approximate economic profit, such as return on capital plus earnings growth or net income, plus measures of asset utilization, such as inventory turns or working capital ratios.
  - Use external, market-based analysis to determine the required standard of financial performance in the company's industry.
  - Establish an incentive plan for top executives linked to EP.
  - Begin to use value drivers as measures for individual performance management objectives and team incentives.
- Long-term incentives
  - Use stock options as the core long-term compensation plan.
  - Introduce a long-term performance plan measuring corporate economic profit for a limited number of senior executives.
  - Consider taking options deeper into the organization.
  - Consider share ownership guidelines for senior executives.

During the learning stage, the compensation plans move toward direct measurement of EP for a broader group of employees. The following framework can be used to guide plan design during the *learning stage:*

- Annual incentive plan
  - Measure and reward EP performance at the corporate level.
  - For business units, assess readiness for measuring unit-specific EP goals; however, even if traditional performance measures continued to

be used, apply a unit-specific cost of capital to establish performance standards.

— Provide high maximum award opportunities or eliminate caps, but carefully calibrate the performance–award formula to ensure that awards are consistent with level of EP created.

— Consider deemphasizing annual incentive opportunities for senior executives and increase the opportunities under the long-term, economic profit-based performance plan.

- Long-term incentive plans
  — Expand eligibility in corporate economic profit-based long-term plan.
  — Adjust the size of equity grants, such as stock options, within competitive guidelines, for EP performance.
  — For executives, consider leveraging a portion of stock option awards through performance options.

- Team incentive plans
  — Make financial measures and standards consistent with the EP of the business unit.
  — Provide ownership to employees by contributing stock to qualified retirement plans.

In the mature stage, all incentive participants should be rewarded for economic profit performance. The following framework can be used to change plan design to move to the *mature stage:*

- Annual management incentive plans
  — Measure EP for all participants at the lowest organization level possible.
  — Eliminate gaps on award opportunities through incentive bank or integration with long-term incentive plans.
- Long-term incentive plans
  — Add business-unit-specific long-term performance plans.
  — Consider extending application of performance stock options.
  — Increase emphasis of long-term performance plan opportunities relative to annual opportunities.

9.6 CONCLUSION

Value-based management is not simply a performance metric—it is an integrated management process focused on increasing long-term shareholder value.

VBM can lead an organization to act in the interests of its shareholders; however, not all organizations are equally ready to implement VBM. Successfully implementing VBM requires that in addition to selecting a VBM metric, companies must manage the three key elements of communications, compensation, and commitment.

VBM-based compensation plan design should follow the four principles of:

1. Setting absolute performance standards based on shareholder expectations, not relative to an internal budget.
2. Rewarding sustained value creation.
3. Providing unlimited upside potential.
4. Incorporating downside risk in incentives.

Incentive design should be consistent with the level of readiness for VBM. In each stage, design features need to address:

- The mix of compensation elements.
- The establishment of performance targets.
- The appropriate pay-performance relationship.
- The need to reward sustained performance.

Chapter 10

Long-Term Incentives

Margaret M. Engel

Equity and long-term incentives figure as the single largest component of senior executive pay. Most important, equity and long-term incentives are the mechanism companies use to link executive pay to the fortunes of shareholders. In a properly designed executive compensation program, superior shareholder value creation results in executive wealth; over time, poor shareholder returns correspond to below-par compensation for executives.

This chapter discusses the role of equity and long-term incentives within the executive compensation program. We examine each of the major approaches companies use to provide long-term incentives, including stock options, stock appreciation rights, restricted stock, and performance awards. Current practices for participation criteria, award guidelines, and performance requirements are described for each. Finally, we discuss major trends related to long-term compensation observed over the last decade.

10.1 LONG-TERM INCENTIVES DEFINED

A long-term incentive is an arrangement for providing variable compensation for performance during a period that extends beyond one year. Long-term incentives can involve either stock or cash. These arrangements provide executives with a capital accumulation opportunity accompanied by generally favorable accounting, tax, and cash flow ramifications for the company. Participating employees may be awarded:

- Capital stock or the right to purchase or receive capital stock under specified terms and conditions
- The right to receive cash under specified terms and conditions
- A combination of any of the foregoing

10.2 THE MOST COMMON APPROACHES

Stock options, restricted stock, and performance awards consisting of shares, units, or cash figure as the primary forms of long-term incentive and capital accumulation plans. Other approaches, such as phantom stock, are far less prevalent.

As Exhibit 10.1 indicates, company size has relatively little impact on award practices. The prevalence of incentive stock options (ISOs), performance shares, and phantom stock is similar in both general industry and in large companies with market capitalization of $10 billion or more. Only a few differences related to company size are observable. For example, large companies are more likely to grant nonqualified options in addition to ISOs. Large companies are also more likely to grant performance shares, rather than performance cash or units. In addition, large companies use restricted stock more often.

10.3 OBJECTIVES OF LONG-TERM INCENTIVE PLANS

Long-term incentives create an identity between the interests of executives and shareholders. Executives whose actions affect the value of the company are provided with a direct financial stake in increasing that value. Importantly, value is measured by total shareholder return, with stock price appreciation and dividends used as the primary performance measures for long-term incentives. When total shareholder return performance is strong, long-term incentives provide a significant opportunity for executives to build wealth.

Long-term incentives also encourage stock ownership. Companies began to implement policies that required executives to achieve defined levels of stock ownership in the 1980s. Ownership requirements address one of the underlying flaws of stock option plans: While options are intended to create shareholder

Exhibit 10.1   Use of Long-Term Incentives.

Percentage of Companies Granting	General Industry Practice (n = 322)	Large Company Practice (n = 57)
Incentive stock options	30%	39%
Nonqualified stock options	73%	93%
Restricted stock	38%	54%
Performance shares	16%	19%
Performance cash/units	30%	12%
Phantom stock	13%	9%

Source: © Mercer 2001 Executive Long-Term Incentive and Equity Survey.

identification, executives do not actually lose anything if options expire out of the money. Shareholders make their purchase upfront, facing the risk that their capital investment may depreciate in value.

An executive exercises a stock option when a positive spread exists, and in the absence of an ownership requirement is likely to sell the shares acquired immediately. The transaction lacks a risk element unless the shares from option exercise are retained over time. Stock ownership guidelines help create true parity between the executive and the shareholder. Today about one-third of major companies use these guidelines.

Long-term incentives also help retain executive talent. Three to five years of service are commonly required before long-term incentive awards vest. Other employers seeking to recruit executive talent must be prepared to buy out long-term incentives, which can substantially increase recruiting costs.

Finally, long-term incentives are cost effective for the company and may offer tax advantages to the executives. Stock options, the most common form of long-term incentive, generally do not result in any compensation expense. The impact on the financial statements is limited to additional dilution arising from issuance of shares. Therefore, companies can use stock options to provide potentially greater levels of compensation at a lower cost than would be possible with cash.

10.4   LONG-TERM PLANS AND COMPENSATION STRATEGY

When companies establish an overall compensation strategy, definition of the role of equity and long-term incentives is essential. Decisions on appropriate pay positioning relative to the competitive marketplace and how to best achieve the desired competitive position will greatly impact long-term incentive plans.

Mercer's research indicates that most companies target senior executive and CEO total compensation between median and 75th percentile levels, but salary is not used to achieve premium compensation positioning. Most companies pay median salaries. Companies typically provide higher total compensation opportunities by combining above-average annual and long-term incentive opportunities with median salaries.

In addition to serving as an important component of total compensation, long-term incentives balance annual incentive programs. Companies weight annual and long-term incentives differently, varying the weighting according to the level in the organization. Mercer's research indicates that the annualized value of long-term incentives awarded to CEOs is almost four times the size of the annual incentive. Long-term incentives for senior management are about three times as large as annual incentives. At middle management levels, long-term incentives range from about one to two times the size of annual incentive awards (see Exhibit 10.2).

Exhibit 10.2   Median Annual Incentive and Long-Term Incentive Awards.

Salary Level	Median Annual Incentive (% of Salary)	Median Long-Term Incentive (% of Salary)
$1 Million or More	135%	525%
$750,000	85%	250%
$500,000	70%	200%
$300,000	50%	140%
$200,000	40%	80%
$100,000	25%	30%
$75,000	15%	20%

Source: © Mercer 2001 Executive Long-Term Incentive and Equity Survey.

This shift in emphasis gives executives with direct impact on long-term company performance and shareholder value the biggest stake in that success. As one moves down the hierarchy, an executive's ability to impact long-term corporate performance diminishes; his or her actions tend to have a greater impact on short-term results. Accordingly, in a well-designed executive compensation program, the mix of award opportunities shifts in like manner.

10.5   STOCK OPTIONS

A grant of stock options provides the optionee with the right to purchase a given number of shares of common stock at a fixed price for a defined term, usually 10 years. The option exercise price, or strike price, is normally set equal to the fair market value of a share on the date of grant, but may be set above fair market value ("premium-priced options") or below fair market value ("discounted options"). Today most companies use stock options priced "at the money" as their core capital accumulation plan.

Assume an executive is granted an option to purchase 1,000 shares at a strike price of $15.00 per share for a 10-year term. Eight years later the executive exercises the option and purchases the shares from the company for $15,000. At that point, the shares are trading at $75.00 per share for a total value of $75,000. By purchasing the shares, the executive recognizes a gain of $60,000 (taxable as ordinary income, if the option is a nonqualified option). The executive may either sell the shares to obtain a like amount of cash or hold the shares as an investment.

Most companies use stock options as the core long-term incentive. Stock options offer many advantages. First and foremost, they are relatively simple to understand and to communicate, and they do not require companies to develop a complicated performance measurement process. Stock options are also the most cost-effective form of compensation available, given that options continue to enjoy a favorable accounting treatment under Accounting Principles Board (APB) Opinion 25. Finally, they offer a participant considerable upside potential based on increases in the market price of shares, substantially exceeding the amount of cash compensation that a company is realistically able to pay.

From a corporate perspective, the most important decisions related to stock option plan design involve setting participation criteria and establishing guidelines for size of awards. Competitive practice and a company's compensation strategy should provide a framework for these decisions. The resulting dilutive impact should be assessed to balance shareholder concerns, and decisions on other issues, including the type(s) of options granted, vesting requirements, and exercise provisions, are needed to complete the plan design.

Mercer's research indicates that median eligibility for stock options begins at the $75,000 salary level. Among the companies surveyed, the 25th percentile for stock option eligibility is the $50,000 salary level and the 75th percentile is the $92,000 salary level. When the stock option-eligible population is expressed as a percentage of total employees, we find that 7% of employees are eligible for stock options at the typical company; however, considerable variation exists depending on the size of the company and its industry.

Under the current tax rate structure, nonqualified stock options are more cost effective than incentive stock options (ISOs). The tax benefit to the company from nonqualified options is more valuable than the reduction in income taxes paid by an employee under an ISO. Accordingly, more companies grant nonqualified stock options today. Our data indicates that 30% of companies grant ISOs and 73% of companies grant nonqualified options.

Smaller companies are more likely to forgo the tax deduction available from nonqualified stock options. Among companies with fewer than 1,000 employees, 34% grant ISOs. At companies with more than 1,000 employees, only 27% grant ISOs. ISOs should be considered when the company is not in a tax-paying position because of net operating loss carryforwards or other factors. ISOs may also make sense when stock ownership requirements or a lack of a public market for the stock prevent executives from selling option shares to cover the tax liability created by exercising a nonqualified option.

The term of a stock option is almost always set at 10 years. A few companies grant nonqualified options with shorter terms, such as five years, but this is uncommon. A shorter option term also substantially reduces the fair value of an option under Black-Scholes and makes the award less competitive unless more shares are provided. Longer option terms, such as 12 or 15 years, are also rare.

Most companies make regular annual grants of stock options. An annual grant schedule allows the optionee to obtain the benefits of dollar cost averaging over time. A policy of larger, less frequent grants exposes the executive to the risk that the option strike price represents a market high, but also provides management with the opportunity to leverage a favorable price.

We see a great deal of variation in how companies determine the number of shares to grant. Four approaches are commonly used: (1) Black-Scholes type model, (2) face value as a multiple of pay, (3) fixed share guidelines, and (4) discretion. Most commonly, companies try to deliver a given amount of compensation with a stock option grant. The number of shares depends on the present value of a stock option under an option-pricing model such as Black-Scholes. Using an executive with a $200,000 salary as an example, assume the company wishes to make a grant equal to 100% of salary. Assuming the stock price is $60 and the Black-Scholes value of a 10-year option is $20, the company would grant 10,000 stock options. Award guidelines that express the face value of a stock option (i.e., number of shares times current stock price) as a multiple of pay are also common. For example, the company could establish a face value multiple of 300% of salary. Using our example, the company would grant options with a face value of 600,000 (i.e., 10,000 options at a price of $60 per share).

Both of these techniques result in smaller option grants as stock price increases. This result is counterintuitive and difficult to communicate to participants. Also as stock market volatility increases, increasing the risk of underwater options, companies are reluctant to cut the number of shares granted. As a result, fixed share guidelines and discretionary grants have gained popularity. Today only 30% of companies adjust the number of options to reflect changes in stock price.

Option vesting schedules typically range up to five years, with considerable variation across industry lines (see Exhibit 10.3). For example, three-year vesting is common in manufacturing companies, whereas service companies commonly require four years of future service to vest. Companies may use either "cliff vesting," where the entire award vests at the end of the period, or a vesting schedule based on annual installments. In general, installment vesting is most popular, with 83% of companies vesting in installments and 17% reporting cliff vesting.

If voluntary termination of employment by the executive or involuntary termination without cause by the company occurs, unvested options are typically

Exhibit 10.3   Stock Option Vesting.

Percentage of Companies	Option Vesting In:
9%	2 years or less
41%	3 years
24%	4 years
17%	5 years or more

Source: © Mercer 2001 Executive Long-Term Incentive and Equity Survey.

forfeited. Vested options normally expire within three months of the date of termination. The three-month grace period tracks the ISO regulations and is justified by the argument that an executive planning to quit will exercise all vested options anyway before giving notice; however, provision for immediate expiration of unvested options should be considered and is clearly more performance-oriented.

Some companies have tightened up the rules affecting post-termination exercises by providing for a clawback feature. Under a clawback, the company requires that all option profits from exercises taking place within say, 12 months of the date of termination, must be returned to the company. Use of a clawback in the event of a termination for cause also makes a lot of sense. Other features designed to protect corporate interests against departing executives include non-compete provisions and provisions disallowing option exercise for inimical conduct by the executive.

When termination of employment occurs because of death, disability, or normal retirement, approximately 60% of companies allow unvested options to vest according to the normal schedule or on an accelerated basis. About 45% of companies allow options to vest after early retirement. Companies also provide longer post-termination exercise periods than seen in the past. Companies now commonly provide a one-year period after death for the estate to exercise stock option, and in some option plans the estate has longer periods to exercise (see Exhibit 10.4). In the event of disability, a one-year period is also commonly provided. Upon retirement, periods ranging from three months to the remainder of the option term are provided, indicating a wide range of practices.

(a) Variations on the Basic Stock Option

Companies have developed a several variations on the basic stock option. The rationale for these approaches involves raising the performance hurdle implicit in stock options. Larger award sizes are a common byproduct. In general, these approaches are limited to senior management and rarely extend to lower-level option plan participants. While they can increase performance requirements, these options have achieved only limited acceptance.

Exhibit 10.4 Common Post-Termination Exercise Periods.

Death	1 year
Disability	1 year
Retirement	3 months to remainder of option term
Termination for cause	None
Involuntary termination without cause	3 months
Voluntary termination	3 months

Source: © Mercer 2001 Executive Long-Term Incentive and Equity Survey.

(i) Premium-Priced Options   A premium-priced stock option is an option with an exercise price set above the fair market value of the stock on the date of grant. Less than 5% of the Fortune 1,000 have adopted this approach. The size of the premiums applied is often modest, commonly ranging from 10% to 30% above fair value. Over the 10-year term of an option, such premiums should have relatively little real impact on option gains. Assuming a 5% compound rate of appreciation over 10 years, the spread from a traditional option equals 63% of the face value, so substantial option profits can still accrue even when options are issued at premium prices. In addition, companies typically grant more shares so that compensation opportunities for strong performance are actually enhanced.

(ii) Performance-Contingent Options   Options that vest only when performance goals are achieved are known as performance-contingent options. If the goals are not met within a defined timeframe, the options expire. The most common approach is to provide that options vest when a pre-established stock price is achieved. Once the performance target has been met, the executive is free to exercise at a traditional strike price set equal to the fair value on the date of grant. While stock price is the most common performance target, and is favored by shareholders, any financial measure can be substituted.

   The major negative associated with performance-contingent options is the accounting treatment. Use of a performance requirement makes the number of shares ultimately issued uncertain and triggers variable accounting. Companies must then accrue compensation expense equal to option profits until the performance requirement is satisfied and the number of shares is fixed.

(iii) Options with Performance-Accelerated Vesting   Options with performance-accelerated vesting requirements avoid the negative accounting treatment that applies to performance-contingent options. Options with performance-accelerated vesting are normally granted at-the-money with a longer vesting schedule (e.g., seven years). If defined performance objectives are achieved, vesting is accelerated. If performance requirements are not met, conventional wisdom is that executives are unlikely to be employed that far out into the future.

(iv) Reload Options   A reload option provides an executive with a new option grant after an existing option is exercised by tendering previously acquired shares. The number of options granted under the reload option equals the number of shares tendered; advocates of this approach argue that reloads encourage ownership without contributing to dilution. Of course, exercise of an option for stock without a reload feature reduces dilution, so incremental dilution does occur. Reload options typically carry the same vesting requirements and extend for the remaining term of the original option. The executive can exercise an existing option, converting option gains into shares owned, and obtain a new option that maintains his or her carried interest in the underlying stock by

allowing for an interest in future appreciation. Reloads have become reasonably common, with about 20% of companies granting them.

10.6   STOCK APPRECIATION RIGHTS

A stock appreciation right (SAR) provides the executive with the right to receive a payment equal to the appreciation in the fair market value of a given number of shares for a fixed period, normally 10 years. From the executive's perspective, exercising nonqualified options is comparable to exercising SARs. The key difference is that the executive actually makes a purchase when exercising an option, receives shares, and has the opportunity to maintain an investment in the company by holding the shares. When an SAR is exercised for cash, a transfer of shares does not occur. While options and SARs have reasonably similar financial consequences for the executive, the financial impact on the company differs markedly. Unlike options, SARs result in a charge to earnings equal to the appreciation embedded in the underlying shares.

SARs were used extensively as an alternative to stock options until the Securities Exchange Commission (SEC) revamped the insider trading rules under Section 16 of the 1934 Securities Act in the early 1990s. Under the old rules, corporate insiders were required to hold shares acquired from the exercise of options for six months to prevent a matching buy/sell transaction subject to profit recovery. During this holding period, insiders were at risk because the fair value of shares acquired from option exercise could depreciate. As a result, most companies granted SARs in tandem with options to corporate insiders. Exercise of SARs was exempt from the insider trading rules, provided the SARs were exercised within a specified window period. Insiders were therefore able to exercise SARs, capture option profits, and avoid the six-month holding period applicable to options under the old Section 16 rules.

Under the simplified insider trading rules, corporate insiders were allowed to exercise options and sell the shares acquired immediately, provided the stock option was held for at least six months after grant and certain other conditions related to the option plan itself were met. The need for SARs disappeared, and most companies stopped granting them to avoid the onerous accounting and cash flow implications.

10.7   RESTRICTED STOCK

Restricted stock involves an outright award of shares to the executive. Normally the executive does not pay for the shares, although in some states and in certain mutual organizations, a nominal consideration, often the par value of the shares, is required. The executive enjoys the rights of a shareholder immediately, including voting and dividend rights, except that the right to sell or transfer the shares is restricted for a fixed period. If the executive leaves the employ of the company during this restricted period, the shares are forfeited, making restricted stock an effective retention device.

Today about one-third of companies using restricted stock awards build regularly scheduled awards into the core long-term incentive program (see Exhibit 10.5). In these companies, restricted stock is normally granted in combination with stock options at more senior levels. More commonly, companies use restricted stock sporadically, as a special recognition and retention tool.

Because awards of restricted stock result in a compensation expense, participation tends to be limited to more senior executives in most companies. Mercer's research indicates that median eligibility for restricted stock begins at the $92,000 salary level. Among companies surveyed, the 25th percentile for stock option eligibility is the $80,000 salary level, and the 75th percentile is the $130,000 salary level. When the population eligible for restricted stock is expressed as a percentage of total employees, we find that only 1% of employees are eligible at the typical company.

Restricted stock has received poor publicity in the business press. The thinking is that outright awards of shares put the executive in a position that is out of sync with shareholders. Even if the stock depreciates sharply, the executive reaps potentially high levels of compensation. Furthermore, under Internal Revenue Code (IRC) Section 162(m), restricted stock does not qualify as performance-based compensation. Nevertheless, only about 10% of companies attach performance requirements to restricted stock. Future service is typically the only condition on vesting.

Practices regarding the length of restriction periods vary, but both three-year and five-year periods are commonly seen. Practices also split on the use of cliff or installment vesting schedules; both approaches are common.

Exhibit 10.5   Restricted Stock Awards.

Grant Practices	Percentage of Companies
Regular schedule of awards	44%
Sporadic retention awards	19%
Special recognition program	17%
Recruiting	9%
Employee stock ownership	4%
Other uses	8%

Source: © Mercer 2001 Executive Long-Term Incentive and Equity Survey.

10.8   PERFORMANCE PLANS

Performance awards provide a participant with the opportunity to earn units, shares of common stock, or cash based on achieving performance objectives set over a multiyear performance period, normally three years in length. Performance unit plans involve an award denominated in fictional units. The value of a unit can equal a fixed dollar amount (e.g., $1,000), with the number of units actually earned contingent on performance. Alternatively, the number of units can remain constant, with the unit value fluctuating with performance. Performance share plans involve awards denominated in shares. In addition to the number of shares earned varying with performance, the value of each share will rise or fall with the market price of the company's stock, providing additional leverage. Performance cash plans involve a contingent cash award (e.g., 50% of salary). Depending on performance, the actual award might range down to 25% of salary, or zero for unacceptable performance, and increase to 100% of salary for outstanding results. Performance units, performance shares, and performance cash may all be paid in cash, stock, or a combination of the two. The real differences depend on how the award is denominated and on the accounting treatment that applies.

Participation in performance award plans is more restrictive than participation in stock options. Mercer's data indicate that median eligibility is at the $130,000 salary level. The 25th percentile extends participation to the $90,000 salary level, and the 75th percentile eligibility is at the $180,000 salary level. Clear line-of-sight between employee performance and a multiyear performance objective normally does not exist at the lower levels of the organization.

In practice, performance awards normally supplement stock option plans and serve as a hedge against volatility in the stock market. The performance measures normally consist of corporate financial goals judged to support total shareholder return. If financial goals are met, and company stock performs well, performance awards and options will pay off handsomely; however, if financial targets are achieved, but company stock fails to appreciate with options accruing little value, executives will receive a performance award payment.

While performance award plans can be effective, they are often plagued by difficulties related to setting meaningful longer-term performance targets and by poor communications. Companies using these plans need to give them careful attention to avoid common pitfalls.

Most companies make annual performance plan awards. A three-year performance period has become the norm, as companies found that four- and five-year financial forecasts were often impossible to make with any precision. The resulting overlapping award cycles support retention. An executive who leaves the company after a cycle is completed will forfeit the compensation potential from partially completed performance cycles.

Larger awards made every second year, combined with a four-year performance period, also provide this retention element. This schedule is sometimes preferred because it avoids making performance plan payouts an annual event. Discrete, heel-to-toe performance periods are not common because, if the performance targets become unachievable early on, companies have to wait too long to reset targets; however, discrete performance periods should be considered in turnaround situations where management must achieve the performance targets.

Companies use the long-term financial plan to establish performance targets (see Exhibit 10.6). While some companies define more absolute targets based on shareholder expectations, or measure performance versus peers or prior years' results, it is more common to factor these considerations into the business plan and rely on the plan to set performance targets.

When defining performance requirements, companies identify two or three important financial performance measures, which should support stock price performance. Earnings per share and net income are seen most often, and profitability measures combined with growth measures, such as return on equity combined with cumulative earnings per share, represent best practice. Total shareholder return is also commonly used as a measure.

Reliance on multiyear business plans creates many of the problems associated with performance award plans. Companies find it difficult to develop precise plans three years out, and a credible planning process is essential when compensation is attached. Compensation Committees may also have difficulty assessing the underlying difficulty of targets when asked to approve plans.

Approximately 60% of companies pay performance awards in cash; 20% of companies pay awards in stock; and the remaining 20% pay awards in a combination of cash and stock. Seventy-five percent of companies pay the entire award at the end of the performance period. Approximately 15% of companies make payments at the end of each year of the performance period, and 10% make payments after an additional mandatory deferral period.

Exhibit 10.6   Approaches in Establishing Performance Share/Unit Plan Measurement Criteria.

Measurement Basis	Most Important Factor (Percent of Companies)
Budget/Strategic plan	51%
Absolute goal	17%
Peer group comparison	26%
Formula	16%
Other	10%

Source: © Mercer 2001 Executive Long-Term Incentive and Equity Survey.

10.9   PRIVATE COMPANY LONG-TERM INCENTIVES

Private companies face special impediments to implementing effective long-term incentive plans, primarily because of the lack of a ready market for company stock. The first issue a private company faces is whether to use real equity or to provide long-term incentives in cash, without providing an actual ownership potential. If a company intends to go public, real equity should be considered; however, if the company intends to stay privately held, phantom arrangements that pay out in cash are often most suitable.

If actual equity is used, companies need to address two basic issues: a credible mechanism for establishing a fair market value and a strategy to provide liquidity. Stock options can be effective in a private company, but companies need to price grants at fair market value to avoid compensation expense under APB Opinion 25 accounting. An independent appraisal is the most common solution and satisfies the accounting considerations, but an appraised price may lack credibility among option plan participants. Regular appraisals, generally performed once a year, also entail an expense. Many companies use a formula, such as book value, to establish prices, but the accounting literature clearly discounts formula pricing unless a pattern of transactions support the formula as an accurate representation of fair value. Without evidence to support a formula price, companies are exposed to variable SAR accounting for formula-priced options.

Upon option exercise, the executive faces two hurdles: obtaining funds to exercise options and paying the taxes due at exercise. Techniques such as cashless exercise are not open to employees of a private company. ISOs make sense in this situation because the executive's tax event is delayed until the shares are sold, unless the executive is subject to the Alternative Minimum Tax. But the executive must actually buy the option shares to preserve the attractive accounting treatment available to the company under APB Opinion 25. Furthermore, the executive's investment must be at risk for at least six months or the accounting treatment is at risk.

Performance shares and restricted stock are valid alternatives to stock options in a private company because the executive does not need to make a purchase. Companies will generally set up a loan program through a bank to help finance taxes due at vesting. Of course, cash awards, on a phantom option basis or through a more traditional performance award program, address the liquidity question. Nevertheless, cash does not normally provide the upside available through stock-based programs. The private company removed from the public equity markets inevitably faces tradeoffs when designing long-term incentives.

10.10   INCREASED PARTICIPATION

One of the most significant trends observed in the competitive landscape is an increase in participation in long-term incentive plans. Over time, companies have extended eligibility for stock options and other long-term incentives deeper into the organization. Today, many companies offer stock options below the management ranks to the professional/technical population, and some companies offer stock options to all employees.

Several considerations are responsible for the increase in stock option plan participation. Companies have become increasingly sensitive to the importance of total shareholder return and are using equity compensation programs to establish and reinforce this mindset among employees. The thinking is that when an employee is an owner, that employee will perform differently, leading to enhanced shareholder value. Increased participation in stock options is also an extremely cost-effective method of providing additional compensation linked to results. Stock options continue to enjoy a favorable accounting treatment that allows companies to grant options, provided certain conditions are met, without incurring any expense for compensation.

10.11 LARGER AWARDS

Not only are companies extending participation in long-term incentives deeper into the organization, but the size of long-term incentive awards is also growing substantially. An analysis of CEOs in a group of the largest 350 companies tracked by Mercer illustrates the point (see Exhibit 10.7).

At median, the value of long-term incentives increased by more than 15% annually between 1996 and 2000, far outpacing the rate of increase in cash compensation. While industry differences exist, the trend is clear: Option grants are a larger and more significant piece of the total compensation package of senior executives than ever before. Certainly the most dramatic increases in long-term incentive award practices have occurred at the most senior levels; however, the phenomenon is not limited to the highest-paid officers. Stock option awards have increased throughout the ranks.

Exhibit 10.7   Median Value of CEO Long-Term
Incentive Awards.

Year	Median Award	As % of Salary
2000	$3,830,419	449%
1999	$3,543,448	408%
1998	$3,178,837	374%
1997	$2,547,514	327%
1996	$2,149,993	240%

Source: © Mercer 2001 CEO Compensation Survey.

10.12   INVESTOR CONCERNS

The expanded use of equity programs has increased investor concerns about dilution and overhang. Shareholders, particularly institutional investors, have become more sophisticated in assessing management equity proposals. For many years, shareholders tended to look only at the proposed share reserve when deciding whether to vote for or against an equity program. Newly authorized shares for reserve under a new or amended plan would be expressed as a percentage using shares outstanding as the denominator. When the percentage dilution equaled 5% or less, approval tended to be virtually automatic.

Given mounting institutional concern over the levels of executive equity awards, many institutions have revamped their voting guidelines to take a more comprehensive look at total overhang from all stock options. This includes three components: (1) all options granted and outstanding under existing arrangements; (2) the number of shares available for future grants of options; and (3) the proposed increase to the share reserve; with the sum of these expressed as a percentage of common shares outstanding. Mercer research indicates a steady increase in overhang has occurred over the last five years (see Exhibit 10.8).

Today many institutional investors instruct portfolio managers to vote against equity plans when the total overhang created by management equity awards exceeds 10 to 15%. While most proposals to expand equity plans continue to pass, these proposals garner significantly more opposition than in the past.

Various surveys of institutional investors indicate that several other long-term incentive plan features often fail to pass voting guidelines. Long-term incentive plan features viewed negatively by institutional investors include:

- The ability to grant discounted stock options, where the strike price is set below the fair market value on the date of grant.
- The ability to reprice or cancel and reissue underwater options.
- "Evergreen" option plans, which make a fixed percentage of shares, such as 1% per year, available for grant in perpetuity.

Exhibit 10.8   Median Overhang Among
350 Large Public Companies.

Year	Median Overhang
2000	13.3%
1999	11.8%
1998	11.3%
1997	10.7%
1996	10.7%

Source: © Mercer Proxy Analysis Database.

- Omnibus plans, which allow for a broad portfolio of awards without placing specific limits on a company's ability to grant restricted stock.

In short, a number of the bells and whistles that companies may attach to equity plans tend to draw fire from institutions because they are seen as potentially creating additional dilution and running counter to a pay-for-performance philosophy.

10.13   RESPONSES TO MARKET VOLATILITY

In 2001, the stock market's 14-year climb ended. Since then, market performance has been uneven. Stock prices of technology companies depressed, and many other sectors have experienced declines in stock prices. With the economy subject to recessionary pressures, significant stock appreciation may not be realized in the near term.

Recent option grants at many companies are underwater. How are companies reacting to this upheaval? Several alternatives are available:

- Take no action
- Issue additional options
- Issue truncated options
- Reprice options
- Cancel underwater options and grant new options after six months
- Cancel underwater options and grant restricted stock
- Use cash

Among large, well-established companies, particularly those operating outside of the technology sector, the most common response to the decline in stock prices has been to take no action. Companies are allowing previously granted stock options to run their course, reminding employees that the options have 10-year terms and still have the potential to become valuable. These companies realize that they would incur severe criticism from shareholders if they repriced options or canceled and reissued options.

When more dramatic responses to the downturn in market prices are required, mainstream companies are most likely to issue additional options. The regular annual grant of options can be accelerated to make grants at a more attractive stock price or the size of the grant can be increased. The most important financial consequence of this approach is an increase in potential dilution because new options and older, underwater options remain outstanding; however, this is not a major stumbling block, assuming sufficient shares remain available in the equity plan.

One approach that can help companies manage option overhang is the grant of truncated options—those that have a shorter term. For example, they may expire five years after grant rather than after 10 years, or they may expire six months after (a period of at least six months is required to avoid a variable accounting charge) a certain stock price hurdle is achieved. This type of option can be used to fill in the gap caused by stock price declines resulting in underwater options; however, because these options will expire more quickly, option plan participants are unlikely to be able to "double up" by receiving large gains from replacement stock options and original underwater options after stock prices recover.

Repricing outstanding option grants amounts to a far more aggressive response to underwater options. Under Financial Interpretation Number (FIN) 44, issued by the Financial Accounting Standards Board (FASB) in 2000, companies that reprice options are required to apply a variable accounting treatment to the new options until they are exercised or expire. This creates a potentially severe and unpredictable impact on future earnings. As a result, only a handful of companies have repriced options since the new accounting rules came into effect.

Instead, companies are more likely to cancel options and either wait six months to issue new replacement options or replace options with a grant of restricted stock or cash. Companies that cancel and reissue are likely to have most options underwater, with little or no opportunity for gains in the near future, encouraging aggressive action to retain staff. Many technology companies have canceled and reissued options, but the technique is relatively rare outside of the technology sector.

Companies that have canceled options and issued replacement options after six months commonly offer a one-to-one exchange, with the number of new options equal to the number of canceled options. All option plan participants are normally eligible, except that companies often exclude officers, Section 16 insiders, and members of the Board of Directors from these exchange programs. New replacement options receive a favorable accounting treatment provided the six-month waiting period is met and participants are not compensated for increases in the stock price during this time. While the financial consequences of canceling and reissuing options after six months are attractive—no compensation expense, no increase in potential dilution from options—communicating to option plan participants can be tricky. In addition to the risk of changes in stock price, replacement grants may not materialize if an employee terminates during the six-month waiting period or if a change in control occurs.

As an alternative, options can be canceled and replaced with restricted stock or cash. These vehicles provide immediate value and will likely increase retention; however, these approaches are not well received by shareholders, who prefer approaches that depend on increases in stock prices.

10.14   SUCCESSFUL LONG-TERM INCENTIVE PLANS

Sponsoring a successful long-term incentive plan depends on several critical factors. Senior management, the Board of Directors, and human resources professionals need to take the lead in communicating shareholder expectations and creating a sense of urgency around the subject of stock price. Organizations with successful plans take responsibility for shareholder value creation; it is part of the underlying culture. Stock price performance is crucial, and company strategy is continually evaluated for impact on stock price. Management and outside directors perceive a line-of-sight relationship between corporate performance and stock price performance. In companies with weaker performance orientations, the sense that the market fairly values corporate performance is often missing. Instead, the market tends to be viewed as arbitrary and irrational, creating a disconnect between stock options and corporate performance.

So creating a successful long-term incentive plan starts with creating a culture of accountability for shareholder value. Regular corporate communications of shareholder value performance should occur. In addition, executives should be provided with an understanding of the strategic framework shaping stock option guidelines. Discussion of the fair value of a stock option and how it relates to base salary and annual cash bonus, as well as to competitive norms, is appropriate. Finally, regular communication of stock option values, preferably as part of an integrated compensation and benefits statement, should be sent to individuals so that executives are aware of the build-up in value over time.

Chapter 11

Broad-Based and Global Equity Plans

William J. T. Strahan, JD

Equity-based compensation (stock grants and stock options) can be among the most powerful compensation devices available to a company. Companies are seeing tremendous return on investment from their broad-based plans at the same time that employees appear to be highly motivated by them and seeking employers offering these plans. Applied broadly, beyond the executive and management ranks, equity compensation can magnify and focus attention on an otherwise well-designed compensation program and human resources strategy. These plans can be important parts of a total reward strategy and can help the organization compete more effectively in both the internal and external labor markets as well as in the capital markets. Because stock options are overwhelmingly the most popular form of equity compensation, this chapter focuses on the adaptation of options from traditional executive programs to a wider participation base.[1] For our purpose, a "broad-based" plan is a plan whose eligible participants include most, if not all, employees of an organization. This is in contrast to an "executive-only plan" or even a management plan. Exhibit 11.1 gives the various device types used in broad-based plans. (A discussion of stock options, restricted stock, and performance units can be found in Chapter 10, "Long-Term Incentives.")

11.1 PREVALENCE

Use of broad-based equity compensation plans has been growing dramatically over the last several years both inside and outside the United States. Among

---

[1] This chapter also does not include information on stock purchase plans (plans where employees pay full or substantially full price for shares of stock). These plans, while potentially important parts of a total reward strategy, are more of an investment plan than a "pay-for-performance" incentive arrangement.

Exhibit 11.1 Devices Used in Broad-Based Equity Plans.

Source: © Mercer Survey of 308 Organizations, 1999.

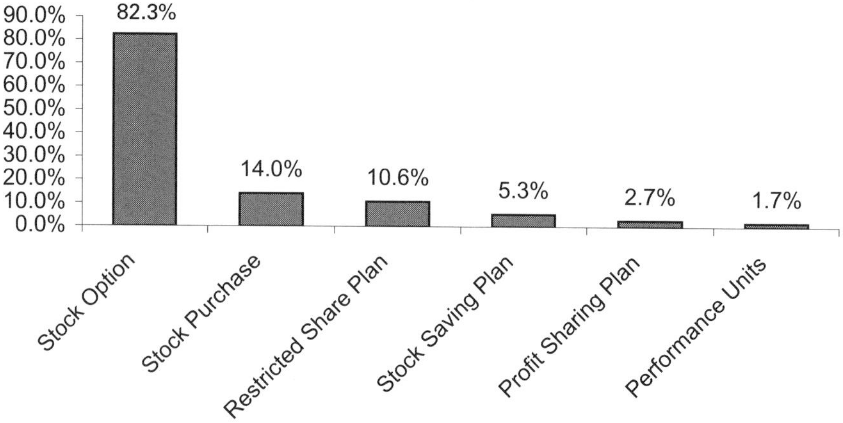

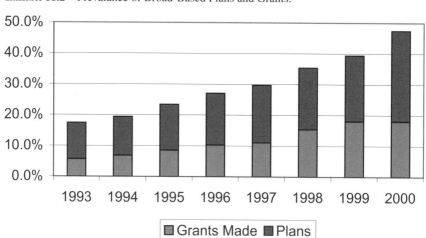

large public companies, the use of broad-based equity has been growing even more quickly and has reached substantially higher levels. During the period from 1995 to 2000, the companies whose plans allow for broad grants have increased from about 23% to 48%, and those actually making grants have doubled from 9% to 18% (see Exhibit 11.2).

This growth in prevalence is important to employers. A company may find that within its relevant labor market, the prevalence of broad-based plans is high. Use of these plans by even a few important competitors for talent, capital, or

Exhibit 11.2 Prevalance of Broad-Based Plans and Grants.

Source: © Mercer Proxy Analysis Database.

customers can make using them worth considering. It is relatively easy to find evidence to justify offering such a plan for purely competitive labor market reasons. Being able to do so for the right total reward reasons and doing so while maintaining a strong link between pay and performance requires more work but can be well worth it.

11.2 TAX, ACCOUNTING, REGULATORY, AND LEGAL ISSUES FOR BROAD-BASED PLANS

The tax, accounting, and legal issues related to the use of stock options in broad-based plans are generally identical to those created by use of these devices for executives. For more information on these topics, please refer to Chapter 18, "Accounting for Stock-Based Compensation," and Chapter 19, "Selected Tax Aspects of Executive Compensation Plans." One area where broad-based plans differ from executive plans is the issue of shareholder approval.

Most stock option plans for executives are submitted for shareholder approval. The decision to subject the plan to a vote is made to secure a corporate tax deduction for grants, to comply with rules imposed by the various stock exchanges, and to grant incentive stock options (ISOs). In 1996, the Securities and Exchange Commission (SEC) eliminated its requirement that all plans making grants to executives be subjected to shareholder approval. Whether the SEC will maintain its current position is in doubt at the time of this writing. Public statements by SEC members have periodically indicated that they are not satisfied with the oversight of stock exchanges concerning executive compensation.

Under current NYSE rules, broad-based plans generally need not be approved by shareholders if most full-time U.S. exempt employees are eligible to receive shares and if most of the shares granted over a three-year period are awarded to nonofficers and directors. Other exceptions cover grants to new hires and plans that restrict the percentage of shares that can be acquired by officers and directors to specified amounts. NASDAQ's broad-based plan exception is substantially the same. There have been several proposals to limit or eliminate these exceptions. Companies need to verify the rules of their exchange before acting.

Some organizations use two plans to make grants. One plan is reserved for executive grants and submitted for shareholder approval. The second is for non-executives and is not submitted for approval. Organizations make decisions about submitting plans for shareholder approval for many reasons, including administrative ease, the complexity of shareholder communication, or even the likelihood of the plan being approved if submitted.

ISOs are rarely used in broad-based plans because by definition an ISO will not generate a corporate deduction for compensation expense when the stock option is exercised. Few organizations, if any, are willing to lose such a deduction for a broad-based plan. Further, because of the different patterns in holding stock acquired through exercise, the value of an ISO to individual employees is usually limited. When an ISO is exercised, there is no recognition of ordinary income as there is for a nonqualified stock option (NQSO). Rather, the individual recognizes a capital gain if the holding period requirements are met. Because many rank-and-file employees will not hold the stock for the required one-year period, the use of ISOs is somewhat moot. Going to shareholders for a vote in order to potentially grant ISOs is therefore unnecessary. The other reasons for a shareholder vote are also absent. The deduction for compensation over $1 million is not an issue for rank-and-file employees, and the stock market requirements for executive grants are not applicable by definition. Therefore, the use of a stock option plan that is not submitted for shareholder approval becomes potentially attractive.

11.3   MECHANICS OF MAKING GRANTS

One significant difference between using equity compensation broadly for rank-and-file employees versus executives is the mechanics of making the grants. The actual grant usually is conveyed with the same type of agreement that would be used to convey an executive grant. The terms of the grant may even be similar or identical to those of the executive group regarding option term, vesting, and treatment of vested and unvested options in case of death, disability, or termination. The company's culture may require similar treatment of all employees. The difference in a broad-based versus executive plan usually comes in the methodology used to set the magnitude of the grant and potentially the frequency of the grant.

11.4   CALIBRATION OF INDIVIDUAL AWARDS

Executive grants are typically set by targeting a dollar value of long-term compensation. Using some valuation technique (e.g., Black-Scholes, binomial), the number of stock options needed to convey that amount of value is determined and granted. The target amounts are typically calibrated to base salary levels for the executive or manager (e.g., a CEO earning $500,000 annually might have a long-term incentive target equal to 200% of base salary or $1,000,000). If the award is being made in the form of stock options and each one is determined to have a Black-Scholes value of $50 per option, then 20,000 options would be awarded. The specific target is generally determined by consulting with market data to determine what is the competitive level of long-term incentive compensation being delivered for a given pay level or functional position.

Rank-and-file grants typically are not directly calibrated to a target dollar level. Rather they are set on a "number of stock options basis" for large tiers of employees. There certainly is some recognition of the value being conveyed, but that is not the specific criterion for calibrating individual grants. In other words, a sample schedule of grants by level might read: Level 7—100 stock options; Level 8—500 stock options; Levels 9, 10, and 11—1,000 stock options. More than 60% of organizations making broad-based equity grants use this method.[2] The proportion of awards granted to each level can be made based on various criteria that are associated with value creation.

Ideally, an organization will have a clear understanding of its value drivers. Value drivers are "the operating factors with the greatest influence on operating and financial results.[3] These value drivers are critical financial and operational measures. Typically they are the factors that when successfully managed result in successful "bottom line" measures of growth, return, and strategic success. By understanding the critical points at which value is created or destroyed in a given organization, the allocation of a broad-based plan can be tailored to retain and provide incentive for those who are most likely to create that value.

A first important decision is the determination of who the decision maker will be regarding the allocation of shares. Some organizations treat all stock-based compensation as a corporate asset and determine share allocation at the corporate level. The allocation formula may be standard across all lines of business or more specifically tailored against criteria created at the corporate level. A second approach is for the corporate group to allocate a pool of shares to the business units, allowing each business unit to determine its own allocation. The right decision is the one that best mirrors the overall rewards strategy of the organization and aligns with the way the organization is managed and measures performance.

Once the decision maker is identified, the next step is to determine the relative contribution levels of employees. Does the first-level supervisor contribute the same value as senior researchers? Do they contribute less? Is it even productive to make a distinction? Which levels of the organization need to be aligned better with value creation? Once the relative value of the various employee groups is known, it is often a matter of basic algebra to determine the number of shares available to that group and by extension to each of its members. A more difficult question is what number of discrete tiers should be used to set these amounts. Generally, fewer bands produce better design. Fine distinctions are difficult to justify if the criteria is long-term value contribution. Exhibit 11.3 shows market data on the frequency and method of allocating broad-based equity compensation.

---

[2] *2000 Stock Plan Design and Administration Survey.* National Association of Stock Plan Professionals/PriceWaterhouseCoopers (Concord, CA: 2000).
[3] Knight, James A. *Value Based Management* (McGraw-Hill, 1998), pp. 166–67.

Exhibit 11.3   Grant Frequency and Size.

Frequency of Grant	% of Companies Disclosing
Discretionary One-Time	41.3
Discretionary Periodic	23.8
Discretionary Biannual	1.6
Discretionary Annual	11.1
Automatic Annual	4.8
Not Specified	15.5
Grant Size	
100 Shares/Employee	23.8
200 Shares/Employee	4.8
300 Shares/Employee	7.9
400 Shares/Employee	4.8
Another Fixed Number	6.3
Based on Performance	3.2
Based on Compensation	3.2
Based on Grade Level	1.6
Not Specified	42.9

Source: © Mercer Survey of 308 Organizations, 1999.

11.5   PROS AND CONS OF BROAD-BASED STOCK COMPENSATION—ITS PLACE WITHIN A TOTAL REWARDS STRATEGY

There are many good reasons to consider a broad-based stock option plan.

(a)   Stock-Based Compensation Aligns the Workforce with the Interests of Shareholders

When companies grant stock options or other forms of equity-based compensation to large numbers of employees, it might reasonably be expected that they would become more interested in the performance of the organization in the capital markets. When employees are—or could be (through options)—shareholders, their interests and those of the other shareholders come into closer alignment. To some extent, this connection is made through financial interests; it might also be made through the psychological impact of being paid partially through stock.

Achieving a tangible sense of shared destiny among shareholders, executive management, and rank-and-file employees is very powerful. Many CEOs have sought to "make employees think like owners," or "act like it was *their* company." Providing a broad base of stock option grants can be one tool among many necessary ones to attain that level of commitment.

(b)   Stock-Based Compensation Is Required to Be Competitive with Other Employers in the Labor Market

Competitiveness of compensation is classically measured in terms of economic value. The question is how the dollar value being conveyed compares to the value being provided in the market, for providing like services. With the diversity of ways to compensate employees now available (cash, equity, benefits, retirement arrangements, career progression resources, and perquisites), there is sometimes confusion about providing more or less devices versus more or less value. In other words, two companies may each compensate a given job family $30,000, but one does it all in cash, whereas the other with $25,000 in cash and the remainder in stock options worth, on a risk-sensitive basis, $5,000. Each conveyed the same value but through different vehicles, suggesting different compensation strategies and risk profiles.

Knowing whether a given company needs to provide broad-based stock for competitive reasons begins with understanding the value of compensation being delivered in the marketplace. Second, it may require testing employee *perceptions* about compensation. In technological fields or job functions, employees may think that they are "due" stock options. Reacting most effectively to employee perception should begin with testing why employees think that they want stock options and communicating with employees the value of the package being provided already.

The sublabor markets where broad-based plans are a necessity to compete are relatively few. Certainly in the "dot.com" or digital business community and in much of the high-technology area, stock options are normative and part of a standard pay package; in most other parts of the labor market, they are not.

A different way to look at competitiveness involves the business model of the company. The more "knowledge workers" a company employs, or the greater the reliance of the company on widely dispersed intellectual capital, the more likely that people need to see a share in the potential return on that personal investment. Equity compensation works well in these circumstances to provide a well-calibrated reward to long-term performance. Typical performance measure programs cannot adequately "predict" what will drive shareholder value in the long term accurately enough for compensation purposes. In addition, the contributions made by individuals occur at different times and may not be clear regarding the impact on ultimate shareholder value. Therefore, providing equity compensation allows for competitive compensation in a situation where the link between performance and shareholder value may be difficult to see. Essentially all employees make their contribution, receive their appropriate share of the equity stake (priced along the way by the capital market), and then everyone takes a share of the returns. Essentially, the compensatory nature of the device becomes consumed by the investment nature of the device. A knowledge worker invests his or her intellectual capital or interpersonal resources and reaps a return, along with those who invested financial capital. Part of being competitive, in the minds of these knowledge workers, is competing with all the other places where they might deploy their ideas and invest their time and attention.

(c) Using Stock in the Compensation Program Provides a Platform for Business Education for Employees

When large numbers of employees receive incentives based on stock price appreciation, there is a special opportunity to communicate with employees about what drives share price. Information on such issues as earnings per share, analysts' expectations, working capital, cost of capital, and P:E ratios can be made more relevant because of their relationship to this compensation vehicle. Stock price movement becomes less of someone else's scorecard and more part of "my" financial planning and compensation.

What is unlikely to occur is that simply granting equity compensation to employees will result in their becoming financially astute about the organization or even knowledgeable about public information beyond share price. Equity compensation becomes the theme and the focus for a broader business education and human capital strategy, not a replacement for them.

Privately held companies that would not ordinarily disclose financial information publicly may find the use of broad-based stock options, or broad-based *phantom* stock options, to be a useful way to convey the importance of increasing shareholder value to employees. A well-crafted plan can convey information about the increase or decrease in value of an organization, without disclosing too much detail of particular transactions or complete public company level reporting.

(d) Stock Options Are a Low-Cash Flow Alternative to Cash Compensation

The broad-based use of stock options by startup organizations is widely known. Organizations that do not have a good deal of cash can use equity-based compensation to convey real value to employees who share the founder's vision of the company growing and prospering. Unlike cash, which has the negative effect for the company of being "gone" once it is paid out, stock options retain after grant an incentive value as long as the option or the underlying share is held by the employee. As the company's situation changes and more cash from operations becomes available, the decision to use broad-based stock options can be revisited or the practice may be continued because of its inherent alignment with the strategy of the firm.

Stock options typically do not result in a charge to earnings. This fact needs to be balanced against the dilutive effect of issuing additional shares to satisfy options being exercised. It is undeniable, however, that a company can, under current accounting rules, provide employees something of value for services rendered without having to take a corresponding charge to earnings.

(e)   Stock-Based Compensation Can Be Designed Specifically as a Retention Device Through Vesting Periods

Because the potential value of stock compensation can be high, there is a clear retentive value for stock options that remain "in the money," that is, the exercise price is less than the current fair market value. Retention value is a function of (1) the employee's perception that the payoff will occur and (2) the employee's estimate of what the payoff will be, versus (3) what the employee has to "endure" to obtain the perceived payoff. Companies can increase the retention value by raising employee awareness regarding the likelihood and magnitude of a payoff. A consideration in estimating the payoff of such a plan should go beyond just financial payoff and include the psychological payoff of participation in such a plan. For many employees, other aspects of retention, such as career development, mutual respect, and meaningful work, will dwarf the economic value. Improving job satisfaction so that there is little to "endure" ensures that the maximum value of the stock options is realized.

Many companies find that granting equity compensation has a positive effect on retention because the binding nature of a long-term vesting schedule is viewed positively. That is, "I want to stay, because you want me to stay." One company finds that "employee owners" stay at a rate 2.5 times greater than nonowners do. Importantly, the company finds that the effect is only created by employees who buy stock and not for those who are "given" it. They use stock options as a means to facilitate such purchases.[4]

(f)   Company Culture Requires That There Be Some Commonality Between Executive Incentive Schemes and Compensation for "Rank-and-File" Employees

One of the labor markets in which a company needs to compete is the internal labor market. Competition in this internal labor market centers on the company getting good value creation from employees for the total rewards value

---

[4] B. Parus, "We've Finally Got a Piece of the Pie—Building a Company of Owners." *ACA News,* January, 2000, p. 36.

that it conveys to them. Signs that a company is doing well in its internal labor market are reflected in measures such as productivity, low turnover combined with robust performance management (i.e., keeping the right employees), alignment of its workforce with its business strategy and business model, and flexibility and adaptability on the part of the workforce to changing business conditions.

One of the more important things that a company can do to compete in the internal labor market is to maintain a fair and rational rewards structure that stands up to employee scrutiny. The reward structure will always be understood in the cultural context of the firm. Given the culture, use of "executive-only" compensation devices may be perfectly appropriate or may strain the notion of fairness. Granting equity compensation to large numbers of employees (albeit, even at much lower levels) can improve the sense of fairness in the overall perception of the rewards program and support the overall impact of the rewards program on participants.

(g)   Such a Program Allows the Company to Signal to the Capital Markets Its Interest in Shareholder Value Creation

Many companies go to some effort to publicize to Wall Street the fact that "every employee is a shareholder" or to announce the launch of their global broad-based equity compensation plans. Their message in effect says, "If every employee is motivated through equity compensation to drive stock price and total shareholder return, then investors will benefit directly from the employees' enthusiasm and efforts." This can be a positive message to send to investors.

A recent Rutgers University study examined the relationship between broad-based equity plans and several financial performance measures, including total shareholder return.[5] Results indicated that broad-based equity plans result in productivity "pop" immediately, but the effect quickly plateaus. The researchers conclude that productivity gains are largely offset by the added dilution of shareholders' equity by the broad-based plans themselves.

Perhaps the real advantage in an organization's communication with the capital markets regarding use of broad-based equity plans is not in suggesting any "silver bullet" to greater shareholder return, but rather as a means to explain to investors that the company has a thoughtful business strategy and business model that include an equally thoughtful human capital strategy and the role of the equity compensation plan in that overall strategy.

There are also reasons why an organization may decide not to offer a broad-based stock option plan.

---

[5] J. Blasi, D. Kruse, J. Sesil, M. Kroumova, "Public Companies with Broad-Based Stock Options: Corporate Performance from 1992-1997." The National Center for Employee Ownership, 2001.

(h)   Rank-and-File Employees Have Limited Personal Impact on Stock Price for Their Employer

It can be difficult to see the personal impact, of even a CEO, on the stock price of some organizations. For an individual rank-and-file employee to see his or her direct impact is virtually impossible. Classic compensation theory tells us that to achieve real motivation with incentive plans, the employee must have "line of sight." That is, the employee must be able to understand the connection between his or her work, the variable quality of his or her performance, and the level of payout that he or she receives. With equity-based compensation, this is impossible without a performance-based feature in how the grants are calibrated originally or in how they vest. Most companies do not use any individual or team performance criteria and, as we have seen, make grants based on a fixed schedule by tier or level in the organization up to the senior manager level.

Performance-based grants and performance-contingent vesting can create variable accounting (see Chapter 18, "Accounting for Stock-Based Compensation," for more information). Typically, this is a nonstarter. Performance can be a consideration in the making of awards and will likely not trigger variable accounting, if the link between performance and grant levels is not formulaic. For example, promising that if an employee achieves four of five critical success factors (goals) then 100% of a target number of stock options will be granted, and that if five of five are achieved then 150% of the target will be granted, would likely trigger variable accounting. The promise that "we will consider your performance in how we set grants" is not likely to trigger such accounting. The more formulaic or specific the expectation, the better the line-of-sight, but the greater the accounting risk.

Some organizations will allocate pools of shares to business units based on that unit's contribution to shareholder value and the overall business strategic plans. The unit then determines allocation of the individual shares to employees through the set tier/grant level method or through individual discretion/performance. The overall impact is that while the goal of individual linkage to performance may not be fully achieved, there is a link at the unit level.

When tested through econometrics, in many industries the impact of all of management action on stock price (as opposed to overall movement in the stock market and movement of the industry as whole) is less than 30% of all of the movement. In other words, the stock movement is more affected by factors external to the company than internal to the company. If this is the case, then use of stock options for rank-and-file employees may not be justifiable based on incentive motivation at all. Looking at peers in the industry and understanding any trends regarding broad-based plans can be useful. Look beyond the labor market competition (who is granting equity to whom) and include the capital market analysis as well (who is granting equity, why, and how).

(i)   A Significant Increase Occurs in the Aggregate Dilution and Overhang for Shareholders, Yet the Financial Impact for Any Given Participant Is Relatively Small

The point here is that if you provide even a modest number of stock options, for example, 1,000 each to 2,000 to 5,000 employees, a range of 2 to 5 million options would be needed. This is in addition to senior manager and executive grants that could easily double or triple the aggregate number granted. The analysis of whether this is good stewardship of shareholders' equity is of course specific to any firm. The common question for all companies making broad-based grants is finding the balance between a large aggregate expense (dilution) that typically has modest impact on the individual employee; it is analogous to a tax cut. There can be billions or trillions in tax cuts that result in the average tax-payer getting only several hundred dollars in tax relief over a year. The aggregate expense is high, but the impact on the individual is modest. To know whether the value is balanced, it is important to return to first principles of asking what was the goal of the program. Is it primarily a signal to Wall Street? Or to have a communications platform to talk to employees about shareholder value? Alternatively, is the plan intended to modify behavior and provide incentives for individual employees? No specific answer indicates whether a broad-based plan should be adopted, but it may help frame the discussion.

(j)   Administering These Plans Requires Considerable Cost, Resources, and Distraction for Corporate Human Resources and Finance Functions

Administering a workable equity compensation plan includes maintaining written agreements with all participants, providing them with copies of the governing plan documents, and educating them on their choices within the architecture of the plan. There is also a need to maintain accurate records for the number and ownership of stock options outstanding (e.g., shares issued and not exercised, vested and nonvested shares, and contingencies related to option termination). There should be coordination with the corporate secretary to maintain an accurate account of shares available for grant or to be issued as options. For grants of shares or stock options already made, there needs to be coordination between the plan administrator, the corporate secretary, and the accounting department. These three functions need to collaborate on fulfilling the requirements under Financial Accounting Standard 123 for disclosing the actual or hypothetical impact of grants made on earnings per share and for some rendering of the value of the shares previously committed to compensation.

Many organizations use the administrative services of their investment bankers or their deferred compensation administration vendors to support large broad-based equity compensation plans. In a survey of broad-based plan sponsors,

45% used such an outsourced administrator. These vendors supply everything from administrative recordkeeping-only arrangements to full turnkey operations. There is no hard and fast rule as to how large of an employee group or participant group is needed to justify use of an outsourced vendor. Looking at the volume of activity in other financially based plans and benefits can give some idea about the level of questions and transactions from employees. A planning point is that the activity may be highly seasonal. If large numbers of employees are vesting in broad-based grants simultaneously, much of the activity might come in the days and weeks immediately following vesting dates. The decision to outsource might be influenced one way or the other based on these peaks and valleys. Some companies can pull financial or HR resources in for short bursts of activities and eliminate the need for outsourcing, whereas others are staffed for lower levels of activity and always outsource heavier transactional needs. In market practice, about half of plan-sponsoring organizations use at least one full-time stock plan administrator.

(k)   Plans Themselves Are Sometimes Not Well Understood by Rank-and-File Employees

Employees generally are able to understand a simple time vesting scheme for both stock grants and stock options, but getting lower-level employees to understand or manage the value of those grants is much more difficult. Survey results indicated that about 1% of respondent companies thought their nonexempt employees had a thorough understanding of the value of stock options, and only just under 10% indicated that nonexempt employees understood how options worked. The levels only rise to 3.8% for exempt employees and about 25% for middle managers who thoroughly understand stock option value.[6]

Companies can essentially never give advice to employees about when to hold equity or when to exercise stock options. Employees receiving these grants look for signs about how to use them to create wealth. In the absence of such information, the equity grants that management intended to be long-term incentives and ties to the company become viewed as short-term cash equivalents by employees.

Just as difficult is when employees ask questions about the tax impact on their personal circumstances. Rank-and-file employees may also not understand clearly how the details of administration work. (Will I need to open a brokerage account? Will I be sent actual shares? How can I sell the shares? Do I get dividends?)

Development of a professional communications plan to accompany any equity compensation plan is useful to ensure that this valuable compensation

---

[6] *2000 Stock Plan Design and Administration Survey.* National Association of Stock Plan Professionals/PriceWaterhouseCoopers (Concord, CA: 2000).

resource attains its objectives. Administration outsourcing firms generally provide communications materials on the mechanics of exercise and redemption. The company needs to supplement these materials with information on how grants were made, the specific terms of the company's plan, and how this impacts the total reward structure for the employee. (Do amounts earned from stock options come in lieu of other compensation? Do those amounts enter into calculation of other benefits? When, if ever, will employees receive grants again?)

Getting the communications aspects of a broad-based equity compensation plan wrong can result in the most frustrating complaint possible to a beleaguered compensation manager who just slaved over bringing a plan to life. "Why didn't they just pay us more cash? I would have rather had cash."

(I) In a Down Market, or Worse, When the Company Alone Is Suffering from a Languishing Stock Price, a Broad Group of Employees Can Be Disenfranchised

Employees who own shares suffer when a company's stock price declines. Any HR manager reading this can imagine the water cooler conversation where Mary Loyal is speaking with her co-worker Joan Freeagent. Mary is bemoaning that her shares are down 30% this year, and her stock options are underwater. Joan gloats that she would never buy a share in this company because the managers are all incompetents or the stock price would not be in this situation. Joan goes on to point out that people like Mary were just putting money into the CEO's pocket with their investments because after all wasn't it just a year or two ago that he exercised stock options for millions of dollars in gain? The price a company pays for the communications, alignment to shareholders, and motivational advantages of a broad-based equity plan on the upside is that when the downside comes, and it will, employees can amplify the negatives.

When stock options go underwater, many companies consider some kind of relief for employees so that the underwater options do not become a catalyst to precipitate employee turnover or apathy. In 2000 when technology stock plummeted, Microsoft chose to double its grants to employees with underwater stock options with grants at the new lower price. Microsoft already had equity compensation overhang approaching 50% of all shares outstanding and used an additional 70 million shares to make this relief grant. The telecommunications giant Sprint used a recently devised accounting structure to effectively cancel underwater stock options and issue new stock options six months after the cancellation at what was then a lower exercise price than the ones cancelled. This resulted in new grants of 17.8 million shares and 14.3 million shares of two Sprint securities, respectively. In these and other cases, the actions of the firms were justified with strong arguments; however, both companies also faced some shareholder dissent.

Any reasonable planning for development of a broad-based stock option plan should consider what the communications, finance, and HR implications could be if the stock price were to take a significant decline either alone or as part of a general industry or market correction.

(m)   Lower Levels of Employees Are More Likely to Cash Out from the Equity Compensation Immediately upon Vesting

The fact that lower-level employees are more likely to sell their shares as soon as they vest may or may not be a material consideration. If the company intends to make a series of grants, each with vesting schedules that overlap, any detrimental effect of quick cash-out becomes masked by the next schedule. Any loss of retention value is likely mitigated in the same way by multiple vesting schedules. The goal of focusing employees on building wealth through acquiring employer equity or of aligning employees to shareholder value may not be met in an environment where employees frequently sell stock as soon as possible.

In addition to our own experience with clients who report the immediate sale of equity by lower-level employees, the available research supports this observation.

In their article "Employee Stock Option Exercises," Steven Huddart and Mark Lang focused on the exercise patterns of almost 60,000 employees from seven different companies over 10 years.[7] The study ranked individual stock options holders in order of the speed with which they exercised after vesting. By looking at both employee rank and number of days (30 to 365 days) since the vesting date, the authors found that 64% of exercises for lower-level employees occur within six months of vesting, whereas only 35% of senior executives' exercises occur in the same timeframe. Employees typically exercise stock in large blocks of 50% to 100% of options granted.

This pattern indicates that broad-based plans may only focus employee attention on stock price for a short period after vesting when a quick exercise is planned. Because of the large number of lower-level employees exercising, it would appear that they are less concerned about "timing" the exercise and more concerned with merely cashing out. Huddart and Lang went on to find that employees generally sell their shares at the time they exercise their options. Employees often use the cashless exercise feature of the stock option plan to sell their shares. This means that they have a brokerage firm purchase and sell the shares and then receive the difference between the exercise price and market price (minus any other fees and/or commissions). Research concludes that this was consistent with employee motives to reduce risk through early exercise as well as being bearish on the stock.

---

[7] Steven Huddart and Mark Lang, "Employee Stock Option Exercises," *Journal of Accounting and Economics* (1996) pp. 5–43.

11.6 GLOBAL STOCK PLANS: U.S. COMPANIES

Stock plans are an important element of compensation in U.S. multinationals. Companies have used them for many years to compensate their U.S. employees but have been exporting this concept to operations around the world only for about 10 years. Human resource professionals are often surprised by the complexities they encounter. One reason is that few countries have legislation specific to stock plans as an employee benefit. Therefore, a prospective plan sponsor must research securities, tax, labor, foreign exchange, and other laws in each country to develop a legally viable plan. Another challenge lies in the fact that most stock plans are developed at corporate headquarters on the basis of a certain philosophy and certain objectives. Their concepts may be alien to other countries' local national employees, so companies need to expend much time and effort on communicating the plan.

(a) Eligibility

Only half of U.S. companies with global stock plans extend them to all their foreign operations. The reasons for not doing so are that, in some countries, (1) legislation is not conducive to such plans; (2) the company does not have a sufficient number of employees in all its countries; or (3) business conditions do not justify a plan.

(b) Use of Locally Tax-Qualified Plans

Only a handful of countries have legislation that provides tax-effective vehicles for employee stock plans. Less than 25% of U.S. companies with employees in Western Europe are providing stock options. One explanation may be that the administrative burden of qualifying plans locally, monitoring legislative changes, and adjusting the plans accordingly outweighs the tax advantages. When plans do exist, they are typically purchase plans and not stock option or stock grant plans.

(c) Satisfaction with Plans

In the United States, companies rank their satisfaction with global stock plans (on a scale of 1 to 10) as 7.2 for stock option plans and 7.4 for stock purchase plans. Overseas, these ratings are 6.5 and 6.6, respectively. Reasons cited for the lower satisfaction ratings overseas are lack of understanding of the plans by employees and the complexities of local tax laws. Still, these ratings may be considered very favorable, since most companies say they would repeat offering these plans in the future.

(d)   Global Stock Plan Considerations

(i) Taxation from the Employee Perspective   In some countries, stock options are subject to tax at grant—before the employee realizes any financial benefit. Many employees feel this tax treatment is burdensome and have asked their employers to provide some relief. Others have even rejected their stock options because of the tax. Actually, this tax treatment of options is favorable as compared with some other countries, which tax options at exercise. The treatment is good if the price of the shares increases and the employee remains with the company, although employees who leave before their options are vested will have paid the tax and not received any benefit. The benefit arises from having paid taxes on potentially a lower fair market value at the point of grant, rather than on the actual gain at the exercise of the option. This is analogous to the effects of a Section 83(b) election in the United States.

(ii) Labor and Data Protection Issues   Labor and data issues are not unique to stock plans, but they can easily be overlooked if corporate headquarters is unfamiliar with local-country issues.

- *Acquired rights.* In many countries, particularly in Latin America, an employee's regular pay is an acquired right that cannot be reduced. To deal with this issue, companies have had employees sign waivers that they understand that the remuneration from stock plans is not to be expected as regular pay. This issue deserves close, expert attention.

- *Severance pay.* In many countries, severance pay is legislated. For example, the proceeds from stock options can potentially be included in the basis for calculating severance. Again, companies have tried to reduce this risk by asking employees to sign waivers acknowledging that their options will not be taken into account for severance purposes. In addition, plan documents and communications should contain statements to that effect; however, because there are no guarantees that this approach will be honored, it is important for companies to anticipate this added liability where it can occur.

- *Data protection laws.* In some countries, notably those of the European Union (EU), recent legislation prohibits transferring employee data to countries without the same privacy standards for employee data as their own. At this writing, U.S. standards are different from the EU's. In some countries an employer must obtain the employee's written consent to the transfer of data or notify the local data protection agency of the transfer. In others, agency approval is required. In addition, the parent company and any third-party administrator that receives the data must agree to follow various rules relating to its use and storage. Alternatively, the company can attempt to use an administrator that can handle plan transactions through an operation in an

EU country. Companies have been dealing with this issue by having employees sign waivers to allow the transmittal of their data to the United States as a condition of eligibility for the plan.

(iii) Regulatory Issues   Several countries have currency controls that inhibit the operation of global stock plans. The controls restrict the amount of foreign cash that can leave the country. With stock options, this issue can sometimes be dealt with by offering the plans on a cashless exercise basis, eliminating the outflow of cash. Companies using stock purchase plans likely have a much more complex situation because the employee must contribute to the plan, and those contributions may need ultimately to leave the country.

(iv) Securities Laws   Securities laws generally apply when an offer is made to purchase stock, whether publicly or through a company stock option or stock purchase plan. These laws can change fairly quickly. Generally speaking, a prospectus should be filed and the shares registered. In some countries, this can be a slow-moving process.

(v) Impact on Local Nationals' Pay   Global stock plans have a significant effect on the total remuneration packages of local national employees. This effect should be the first aspect examined when considering a plan, yet many companies do not examine it until a problem is perceived.

11.7   EFFECTS IN HIGH- AND LOW-PAYING COUNTRIES

Even relatively small grants can provide gains that are substantial, perhaps larger levels of compensation than annual cash compensation. If share offers are repeated frequently, other forms of remuneration might lose motivational force — or perhaps the worker would simply retire after several offerings! At the other extreme, the offer can represent an insignificant value at the managerial or professional level in countries with U.S.-like pay levels; however, several companies successfully offer such grants in these countries, as a matter of simple competitiveness, a globalization message, or as a celebration of a milestone.

Chapter 12

Executive Benefits*

Janet Den Uyl and Patricia Kopacz

As more organizations adopt a pay-for-performance compensation philosophy, it becomes increasingly important to properly align the benefits component of the total compensation package. A much greater portion of the executive management team's pay is subject to meeting performance goals, making the provision of a core level of benefits more critical than ever before. A core level of benefits provides a degree of income security to executives, thereby enabling them to afford more pay at risk. This chapter explores the elements of a core executive benefits package, which creates the needed safety net for executives.

12.1 CORE BENEFITS AND PERQUISITES

Core executive benefits consist of a combination of nonqualified deferred compensation plans, supplemental executive life and disability insurance, and executive perquisites. Each component plays a role in fashioning the total compensation package for a company's executives.

Most broad-based employer retirement plans qualify for tax advantages under the Internal Revenue Code (IRC). These qualified plans must meet many ERISA (the body of legislation that governs retirement plans) and IRC requirements. For example, they must not discriminate in favor of highly paid employees, they must be funded, and they must have vesting provisions. Deferred compensation plans that do not meet these requirements are nonqualified, and they are not eligible for tax-favored treatment. When participation is restricted to a select group of management or highly paid employees, nonqualified deferred compensation plans are exempt from most ERISA requirements, which gives sponsors a great deal of flexibility in deciding what benefits to offer. As a result, a wide variety of nonqualified deferred compensation plans are designed to meet specific benefit objectives.

* The authors would like to thank Ann Egan of Mercer Human Resource Consulting for her help in preparing this chapter.

Although there are many ways to describe nonqualified deferred compensation plans, we have categorized them into the following types:

- Supplemental executive retirement plans (SERPs), which provide additional retirement benefits to a qualified retirement plan. The type of retirement plan can be either a defined benefit or a defined contribution plan.
  — Defined benefit plans, which provide a specified level of retirement income, based on the employee's pay, service, or both.
  — Defined contribution plans, in which contributions are determined either as a specified amount or as a percent of compensation. The contributions accumulate with interest or at specified investment returns. At retirement or termination of employment, the employee is entitled to his or her vested account balance, which can be distributed under various payout options.
- Elective deferral plans, which allow employees to defer either base salary or incentive pay, or both.
- 401(k) mirror plans, which refer to plans that combine both the restoration of employee savings opportunities and corresponding employer matching contributions lost because of tax limitations under a qualified 401(k) plan.

Most broad-based employee insurance plans provide uniform life, disability and medical coverage to all employees. Often, carriers will place limits on the amount of coverage provided. Many employers choose to supplement this coverage for select groups of executives. The major types of supplemental insurance plans include:

- Executive life insurance, which provides benefits in excess (or in lieu) of group term life insurance provided to all employees.
- Executive long-term disability income benefits, which provide benefits in excess of the broad-based disability plan covering all employees.
- Supplemental medical reimbursement plans, which provide additional medical coverage to executives to reimburse them for medical expenses not covered by broad-based plans.

Many organizations also provide various perquisites to the entire employee group such as paid parking and mileage reimbursement; however, the typical perquisites offered to executives go well beyond these fringes. They are often used to round out the total compensation package. The more common executive perquisites include:

- Company car or car allowance
- Club membership dues

- Financial counseling
- Physical exams
- Home or laptop computer

This chapter explores in greater detail the key elements of these executive benefits and perquisites, why they are used, prevalent practices in their use, typical design issues, and tax, legal, or other considerations that must be weighed when crafting or evaluating a specific executive benefits and perquisites program.

12.2 NONQUALIFIED DEFERRED COMPENSATION

(a) Supplemental Executive Retirement Plans

(i) What Are SERPs and Why Are They Used? SERPs meet a variety of needs and generally fall into two categories: restoration plans and target plans. Restoration plans "restore" benefits that are lost to an executive because of IRS limitations on compensation and benefits under a qualified plan. Target plans provide benefits beyond simple restoration. Typically, target plan benefits are more generous in some manner and are often provided to a more select group of executives than those affected by the IRS limitations.

Companies use SERPs as a means of maintaining competitive retirement benefits for the executive group. In organizations where the qualified plan is already competitive with the market, a restoration plan making up for lost benefits is sufficient; however, for those organizations that do not provide competitive broad-based retirement plans, target plans are used to fill the gap, thereby raising this component of the total compensation package to competitive levels for critical executives. Published survey data show that most companies sponsor restoration plans and roughly half sponsor a target plan, with many companies offering both.

Companies may also use SERPs to provide more generous early retirement benefits, making it more attractive for executives to consider an earlier retirement than would otherwise be possible under the qualified plan. SERPs often provide full retirement benefits at an earlier retirement age, such as 62 or 60, while qualified plans more typically have a normal retirement age of 65.

SERPs are also used as a recruiting tool. This is particularly true when organizations are trying to recruit a senior-level executive who would lose significant retirement benefits by changing jobs. Special consideration for benefits lost as a result of a change in employment are often handled separately through an employment contract instead of through the SERP plan.

(ii) What Are Typical SERP Designs?

Restoration Plans   For a restoration plan, the design is simply an extension of the qualified plan. The plan restores benefits lost under the qualified plan because of compensation and benefit limits imposed by the IRC. Eligibility usually is defined as including any person who is impacted by these limits, rather than persons meeting some other type of criteria, such as position or salary level. Vesting, early retirement provisions, and distribution options mirror those found in the qualified plan.

Target Plans   Target plans provide more generous benefits than a simple restoration of lost benefits. This may be accomplished in several ways, such as using a more favorable definition of compensation or a more generous formula for calculating benefits. Target plans usually cover a more select group of executives than restoration plans. It is common for eligibility to be limited to those executives who are direct reports to or specifically designated by the CEO.

The benefit in a typical target plan is based on a percentage of final average pay and years of service, and is payable at normal retirement. For example, a target plan might provide 50% of final five-year average compensation for an executive with 20 years of service. Typically, the benefit would be prorated for an executive with less than 20 years of service. SERP benefits are generally offset by any qualified defined benefit plan benefits and Social Security benefits. If qualified defined contribution plan payments are used as an offset, normally only the portion attributable to employer, not employee, is deducted from a SERP benefit.

Vesting provisions in target plans are often more restrictive than in a qualified plan, serving as a form of a golden handcuff. Target plans, as a rule, delay vesting until the executive is eligible for early retirement. The exception would be in the event of a change in control, when accrued benefits become immediately vested. Some plans also provide for the credit of additional years of service upon a change in control.

Target plans often provide enhanced early retirement benefits. The plan may permit the executive to receive an unreduced benefit at an earlier age than permitted in the qualified plan. Or, the plan may provide some other type of early retirement subsidy.

Benefits in target plans are often distributed in the same manner as the qualified plan; however, many organizations will permit executives to take their benefit in the form of a lump-sum payment even when it is not allowed under the qualified plan. There are two good reasons for allowing a lump-sum payment under the nonqualified plan: (1) because nonqualified plans are paid out of the general assets of the company, it gives the retiring executive the security of receiving the full value of his or her retirement benefit, and (2) the company accelerates its tax deduction for payment of the benefit. Of course, a good reason for an executive not to elect a lump-sum option is that the benefit would be taxed immediately.

(iii) What Are the Tax and Legal Issues with SERPs? SERPs must be limited to a "top hat" group to be exempt from ERISA's Title I participation, vesting, funding, and fiduciary rules. Nonetheless, SERPs are subject to the reporting and disclosure requirements of ERISA; these requirements are satisfied with a simple one-time statement submitted to the Department of Labor (DOL), which enforces ERISA. SERPs must also include a written claims procedure.

Plans that restore only IRC Section 415 limits can extend beyond the "top hat" group; however, these plans are virtually extinct because most plans restore a combination of IRC limits. Employers want to avoid the burdensome ERISA requirements when at all possible, most important because the application of ERISA's vesting and funding requirements to a nonqualified plan would cause vested benefits to be taxed before receiving them.

A "top hat" group is a select group of management or highly compensated employees; however, the DOL has never provided explicit guidance on what that means. Its position is that top hat employees can negotiate for themselves and do not need the protection of the DOL. Each organization must determine who meets this definition based on its specific facts and circumstances.

Besides being limited to a top hat group, SERPs must remain "unfunded." Although companies may set aside funds to cover SERP benefits, any funds set aside must remain subject to the company's claims of general unsecured creditors to avoid current taxation of SERP benefits to the executive when they vest and to preserve the SERP's ERISA exemptions.

An executive is not taxed on SERP benefits until they are actually or "constructively" paid, at which time they are taxed as ordinary income. The company will receive a tax deduction at the same time and in the same amount as the ordinary income recognized by the executive. To preserve this favorable tax treatment for the executive, the executive cannot have access to the benefit until it is paid (which would result in "constructive" payment and receipt of the benefit).

Benefits from a SERP are subject to FICA taxes when vested and ascertainable. Generally in the case of defined benefit plans, benefits are not ascertainable until they are actually paid. This usually means that the lump-sum value of SERP benefits are subject to FICA in the year an executive retires. In the case of defined contribution plans, vested contributions are subject to FICA tax when accrued. With unvested contributions, the account balance (i.e., contributions plus interest) is subject to FICA tax when vested.

SERP benefits may be included in the same pension table in a company's proxy statement that is used to declare retirement income from its qualified plan. From an accounting perspective, the company must accrue the pretax liability under Financial Accounting Standards (FAS) 87. A corresponding and offsetting deferred tax asset equal to the future tax savings results from deducting benefit payments also can be accrued.

(iv) Are There Other Considerations? First, in determining the appropriate level of benefit, consideration should be given to the other components of executive compensation. The value delivered to an executive from a target SERP can be a key component in the executive's total compensation package. As illustrated in Exhibit 12.1, the lump-sum value from a target SERP providing 50% of final average cash compensation is significant (e.g., more than $11 million for an executive retiring at age 62 with 20 years of service and final average cash compensation of $2 million). The guaranteed retirement benefit provided by a target SERP may be viewed as "too much" when combined with pay opportunities under stock option and other long-term incentive plans. Therefore, for companies with significant incentive opportunities, the SERP benefit objective may be simply to provide a core level of benefit, such as restoration of lost benefits under the qualified plan; however, for companies that provide below-market cash compensation, the total compensation structure may be boosted with higher target SERP benefits. In actual practice, it is not uncommon to see companies with high target SERP benefits have lower incentive opportunities. As companies move to a pay-for-performance philosophy, it is important to revisit the SERP benefit component of the total compensation package because a SERP represents "pay-for-showing-up."

Second, with a greater portion of executives' retirement income coming from nonqualified plans, more employers are choosing to finance these benefits. The most common alternative is a rabbi trust, in which nonqualified plan assets remain general assets of the employer, subject to claims of its general creditors and, therefore, not protected against insolvency. There is no current taxation to the participant, and the employer's deduction is postponed until benefits are paid. A rabbi trust primarily secures executives against the company's breach of its promise to pay, to the extent funds are held in the trust. A rabbi trust also provides flexibility in determining a funding strategy: it may be funded upon a

Exhibit 12.1   Lump-Sum Value of Target SERP Benefit.

Final average pay	$ 2,000,000
Target benefit (50%)	1,000,000
Qualified plan benefit[a]	51,000
Social Security	16,000
Net SERP benefit	933,000
Lump-sum value at 5.5%[b]	11,100,000

[a] Based on 1.5% × service, reduced for commencement before age 65.
[b] Based on Group Annuity Mortality factor for life income.

trigger event such as a threatened change in control, or advanced contributions may be made to the trust based on specific funding targets. Other alternatives, such as purchasing deferred annuities or establishing a secular trust for executives, provide security from company creditors as well as from the company's breach of its promise to pay, but the benefits are taxed currently to the executive to the extent funds are placed in the annuity contract or trust.

(b) 401(k) Mirror Plans

(i) What Are They and Why Are They Used? 401(k) mirror plans are designed to closely resemble the qualified 401(k) plan because the primary purpose of this type of plan is to supplement the qualified plan. 401(k) mirror plans are used for two primary purposes: (1) to "restore" benefits lost to executives under IRC limitations or qualified 401(k) plans and (2) to defer receipt of income, and the taxation of that income, until some time in the future.

Three different types of IRC limitations under qualified 401(k) plans result in 401(k) mirror plans. There are limits on (1) compensation ($200,000 in 2002), (2) deferrals ($11,000 in 2002), and (3) total annual additions (lesser of 100% of pay or $40,000 in 2002). In addition, the nondiscrimination testing required for qualified 401(k) plans can further limit deferrals and employer matching contributions. 401(k) mirror plans are used to restore lost opportunities because of these qualified plan limitations.

(ii) What Are Different Designs and Why Are They Used? Eligibility for 401(k) mirror plans is generally extended to those executives who are restricted in the qualified 401(k) plan because of the various limitations mentioned earlier; however, sometimes these limitations can affect a broad group of employees—a broader group than might be construed a top hat group. In these situations, other criteria, such as position or salary levels, are used to determine eligibility. Of course, the same issues discussed in Section 12.2(a)(iii) regarding top hat employees must be heeded when designing a 401(k) mirror plan.

Most 401(k) mirror plans permit executives to defer compensation up to the same percentages as allowed in the qualified plan. Some 401(k) mirror plans will allow executives to defer compensation at higher percentages or permit deferrals of incentive compensation even when the qualified plan does not, blurring the lines between 401(k) mirror plans and traditional elective deferral plans.

Typically, 401(k) mirror plans make up for any lost matching contribution under the qualified 401(k) plan because of the restrictions on the discrimination tests or compensation limits. It is common for a 401(k) mirror plan to match deferrals at the same rate as in the qualified plan. In some cases, the 401(k) mirror plan may provide higher matching contributions when there is no other executive retirement plan. If this is the case, the higher rate is generally restricted to a small group of top executives.

Most often, 401(k) mirror plans offer executives the same or similar investment choices as are offered in the qualified plan. Some employers will provide additional investment options that may be more diverse.

(iii) What Are the Tax and Legal Issues? Many of the tax and legal issues noted in the previous section on SERPs are the same for the 401(k) mirror plans discussed here; however, a few important differences between qualified 401(k) and nonqualified 401(k) mirror plans should be noted.

Distributions from qualified plans are eligible for rollover into an IRA. Distributions from nonqualified plans are not, nor are loans permitted from nonqualified plans. Withdrawals from nonqualified plans must be limited to unforeseen financial emergencies and must be limited to the amount necessary to satisfy the need. Care should be taken to ensure that the executive understands these differences. These differences make the 401(k) mirror plan somewhat less flexible from the participant's viewpoint.

As with SERPs, the reporting and disclosure requirements of ERISA are satisfied with a one-time notice submitted to the DOL. A 401(k) mirror plan must also provide a claims procedure that includes a reasonable opportunity to get a review of any claim denials.

(iv) Are There Other Considerations? Two primary additional issues should be taken into consideration when designing a 401(k) mirror plan: administration and financing.

In many cases, the qualified plan administrator may administer the nonqualified plan as well; however, administratively there are key differences between nonqualified plans and qualified plans: (1) the timing of the deferral election is more restrictive; (2) the actual daily balancing of funds does not need to occur, unless the company chooses to finance the benefit with a corresponding asset; (3) in-service distributions must be tracked separately; and (4) the investment choices may be different from those in the qualified plan. Because there is much latitude in designing a nonqualified plan, companies should weigh the objective to offer a wide array of options and to provide flexibility against the practical reality of administering the plan.

Many companies choose to finance 401(k) mirror plans because the participant is given investment options. The company hedges the liability created by these plans by investing in assets that correspond with the growth in the deferred compensation. By hedging, the company is able to put in place an arrangement in which the after-tax growth in the assets matches the after-tax growth in the liability, thereby reducing its exposure to investment fluctuations and stabilizing the program's costs. The cost of the program becomes the cost of financing the investment used to hedge the liability (to the extent the amount exceeds the after-tax deferral amount) and to pay taxes, if any, on the growth in the assets.

(c) Elective Deferral Plans

(i) What Are They and Why Are They Offered? With elective deferral plans, the primary objectives are typically postponement of taxes and enhancement of capital accumulation. Some deferral plans will also restore lost deferral opportunities under a qualified 401(k) plan and will enable employees with compensation in excess of amounts that are deductible under IRC Section 162 (m) to defer these amounts until retirement. Tax deferral is the traditional reason for a nonqualified deferred compensation plan. In the past few years, variable pay has become a larger portion of an executive's overall compensation package. Executives tend to view their variable pay as a source of savings; as it grows, so does the desire to set it aside, hence the increased popularity of elective deferral plans. Even with the lowering of tax rates, the deferral of compensation and the deferral of taxation on investment earnings continue to be advantageous. Exhibit 12.2 illustrates the relative gain of deferred compensation over the current receipt of compensation, assuming the same tax rate.

(ii) What Are the Different Designs and Why Are They Used? Most employers offer an elective deferral plan to at least senior management and often to a larger group of highly paid employees. Here again, care must be taken to limit the eligible group to top hat employees to maintain the status of the plan as exempt from most ERISA requirements. Alternatively, if the employer wants to extend eligibility beyond that group, the deferral period can be restricted to a

Exhibit 12.2 Comparison of Deferral to After-Tax Investment— One-Time Deferral of $10,000.

| Year | Lump-Sum After-Tax Value | | $[(a)/(b)-1]$ |
	(a) Deferral	(b) No Deferral	Relative Gain
5	9,551	8,375	14%
10	14,033	10,791	30%
15	20,619	13,904	48%
20	30,296	17,915	69%
25	44,515	23,084	93%
30	65,407	29,743	120%

Assumptions:
• 8% investment earnings
• 35% personal tax rate
• Earnings taxed as ordinary income

specific number of years (e.g., three to five years), rather than until retirement, and thereby avoid ERISA's restrictions on retirement plans.

Deferral plans generally allow executives to defer both base pay and annual incentives. It is common for plans to allow the deferral of all incentive pay while limiting the deferral of base pay. By limiting base pay deferrals, the employer ensures that there is sufficient pay to cover all necessary withholding requirements (e.g., FICA tax).

Most plans allow participants to defer compensation only until retirement or termination of employment; however, there is a growing trend toward allowing an election to defer for a specified period to enable participants to accumulate funds for a specific purpose, such as college tuition. Some plans allow participants to re-defer to a later distribution date, provided the election is made sufficiently in advance to avoid risking current taxation.

Historically, these plans have credited a fixed rate of interest to amounts deferred; some plans even offer an enhanced rate, such as Moody's average corporate bond rate plus 2%, when there is no alternative long-term incentive plan or attractive equity accumulation program. In recent years, the trend is to credit an interest rate tied to the performance of selected investment funds. Employers are giving executives the opportunity to select from an array of funds to satisfy the executive's desire for diversification. Although companies may also offer a credit rate tied to company stock performance, executives may feel that they have "too much" of their capital accumulation in other plans invested in company stock. Nonetheless, these plans can help executives satisfy stock ownership guidelines.

(iii) **What Are the Tax and Legal Issues?**   To qualify for an advance ruling, deferral elections in nonqualified plans must be made in the calendar year before the compensation is earned to avoid current taxation on the amounts deferred. There are two exceptions to the rule: (1) for new plans, the deferral election must be made within 30 days of the effective date of the plan, and (2) for newly eligible participants, the election must be made within 30 days after the date the participant becomes eligible; however, many plans allow for elections for bonus deferrals during the calendar year in which the bonus is earned, but before the amount is ascertainable. Although such provisions would not qualify for an advance ruling, the courts have been more lenient in such instances. Elections are irrevocable for a plan year, whereas with a qualified plan, elections can be changed prospectively throughout the year.

Unless it qualifies for an exemption from registration under the Securities Act of 1933, an elective deferral plan must be registered with the Securities and Exchange Commission (SEC) when the interest credited under the plan is tied to investment fund performance selected by the participant. For public companies, the registration is simplified using a short form; private companies will usually try to qualify for an exemption to registration.

(iv) Are There Other Considerations? Most companies do not realize that there is a cost to the company associated with the provision of a voluntary deferred compensation plan to its executives. As illustrated by Exhibit 12.3, the company has only the after-tax deferred pay to invest and receives only an after-tax return on these funds while it is crediting a pretax return to the executive's account balance. In essence, the tax advantage that inures to the executive is subsidized by the company. The subsidy increases with the duration of the deferral and the interest rate credited. See Exhibit 12.4 for an example of the company's cost measured as a percentage of the deferral amount.

Exhibit 12.3 Cost of Deferral.

Company Cost of Benefit to Participant		Company Assets	
$100,000	Deferral	$100,000	Deferral
(107,000)	Pre-tax payment	(40,000)	Forgone tax savings on current compensation
42,800	Tax savings at 40%		
($64,200)	*After-tax* payment	60,000	*After-tax* cash to invest
		2,520	*After-tax* investment earnings at 4.2%; 7% pre-tax
		$62,520	Accumulated asset at end of year

After-tax payment	($64,200)	
Asset	+	62,520
Net Cost	**=**	**($1,680)**

Exhibit 12.4 Increase in Cost of Deferred vs. Current Compensation.

	Rate Credited to Deferrals	
Deferral Period	4.2%	7.0%
5	0%	8%
10	0%	16%
15	0%	25%
20	0%	34%

Assumptions:
- Annual deferral as level percent of pay
- 4% annual pay increases
- 40% corporate tax rate
- 7% (pre-tax); 4.2% (after-tax) opportunity cost rate

Elective deferrals have administrative and financing issues similar to 401(k) mirror plans when investment options are allowed. Otherwise, if a fixed interest rate is credited, these plans are typically not financed and are administered in-house.

For proxy disclosure purposes, the investment earnings credited on elective deferrals must be reported when an enhanced credit rate is greater than 120% of the long-term Applicable Federal Rate. In the case of a variable credit rate that is tied to the performance of investment funds, it does not have to be disclosed, even though the return may be greater than 120% of the Applicable Federal Rate.

12.3 EXECUTIVE LIFE INSURANCE

(a) What Is It?

Many companies provide basic group term life insurance to all full-time employees. A typical amount of coverage equals 100% of base pay, until retirement. They may also provide employees an opportunity to purchase additional coverage (for example, up to 500% of base pay) on an elective basis. Because of underwriting limitations on coverage that can be provided by group term plans, as well as for competitive reasons, many companies provide additional life insurance protection to their executives through a separate program.

(b) Why Is Additional Life Insurance Provided to Executives?

The primary reason for providing additional executive life insurance coverage is to ensure adequate survivor benefit coverage for an executive who may die prematurely while actively employed. Another key reason is to permit executives to continue the life insurance coverage after termination of employment as a part of their estate planning. Also, it is not unusual for life insurance to be used to provide cash at retirement. In the latter case, additional life insurance coverage may be a secondary benefit objective to the use of the insurance to finance retirement or deferred compensation benefits.

(c) What Is the Typical Plan Design?

Most executive life insurance programs provide a lump-sum benefit that is a multiple of pay. Coverage for executives commonly ranges between 200% to 400% of pay, depending on whether pay is defined as base or total pay. This amount includes the basic amount of group term coverage; however, it is not unusual for the executive group to be carved out of the basic group term plan for amounts in excess of $50,000 (which is the amount of tax-free group term coverage for plans that do not discriminate in favor of officers or highly compensated employees).

When postretirement coverage is provided, the amount typically reduces to half the level of preretirement coverage. If possible, the coverage increases with pay increases; however, it is not always possible to track pay increases because of underwriting requirements, which vary significantly by the size of the group and the type of insurance product utilized.

There are three basic approaches to providing life insurance benefits: (1) policies owned by the executive, (2) split-dollar life insurance, and (3) self-funded arrangements, commonly referred to as death-benefit-only (DBO) plans.

- *Executive-owned life insurance plans* are plans in which the company purchases insurance owned by the executive, who is taxed on the premium contributed. The insurance can be supplemental term insurance, if the goal is to provide additional coverage only to active employees, or it can be a universal life policy. The level of company funding can be minimal, which provides a vehicle to which the executive can contribute additional premiums to accumulate cash value, which can be used to supplement retirement savings or to purchase paid-up insurance.

- *Split-dollar life insurance* is an agreement between the participant and the company in which the premiums, cash value, and death benefits of a permanent insurance policy are split according to the specific objectives of the plan. Generally, the company pays all or most of the premium, which it recovers at the executive's death or from the cash value upon termination of the agreement. The share of the death benefit going to the executive's beneficiary typically is a scheduled amount; however, under some agreements, the insurance beneficiary receives all proceeds in excess of the company's premium. The accumulated cash value of the insurance policy is split between the company and the insured based on the terms of the agreement. Under an "endorsement" agreement, the company owns the cash value, whereas, under a "collateral assignment" agreement, the executive owns the cash value in excess of the cumulative premium paid by the company. The cash value can be used to provide supplemental retirement income or paid-up insurance when the agreement is terminated.

- *Self-funded death benefit plans (DBO)* are plans in which the company pays death benefits directly from general assets, instead of through a life insurance policy. As a result, there is much flexibility in how the benefit is structured. Often these benefits are paid in the form of annual installments to the surviving spouse. It is not uncommon for these plans to be financed by corporate-owned life insurance (COLI), even though the benefits are paid from general assets.

(d) What Are the Tax and Legal Issues?

The tax and legal issues vary depending on the method used to provide the death benefit, as follows:

- *Executive-owned life insurance* provides income tax-free death proceeds; however, the premium is taxed currently to the executive (and is deductible to the company). The death proceeds can be assigned to a third party outside of the executive's estate and can thereby escape estate taxation. When the insurance is assigned, any accumulated cash value plus the future premium could be subject to gift taxes. Otherwise, any cash value accumulates on an income tax-deferred basis. If the insurance is provided through the group term plan, amounts in excess of $50,000 are taxable to the executive based on the Table I term rates published by the IRC. If the coverage is discriminatory in favor of the executives, then the entire amount is taxable to the executive, based on the greater of the Table I term rates or the actual cost of the insurance. Because the actual cost of the insurance increases with age, discriminatory coverage that continues after retirement would become costly to the retiree as he or she reaches life expectancy.

- *Split-dollar life insurance* is taxed in various ways. Under Notice 2002-08, the IRS sets forth how split-dollar will be taxed under future regulations. Basically, the taxation will depend on whether the policy is owned by the company or the executive. Under the endorsement method, in which the company owns the cash value of the policy, the executive has imputed income based on the lesser of the carrier's term rates or table 2001. However, if the executive owns cash value (the "collateral assignment" method), the split-dollar life insurance arrangement will be taxed as an interest-free loan to the executive, in which case interest on the cumulative premium is imputed income to the executive. In any event, the company does not receive a deduction for payment of premiums. The IRS also provided safe harbors for existing split-dollar arrangements as well as those established before final regulations are issued. A discussion of the safe harbors is beyond the scope of this chapter.

- *Self-funded DBO benefits* are taxable income to the beneficiary (and deductible to the company) when received. In contrast, the executive has no imputed income on the value of the death benefit. Because the death benefits are an unsecured promise to pay by the company, and are paid from general assets of the company, the executive cannot assign the death benefits outside his or her estate.

Premiums for an executive-owned life insurance policy are included for the top five highest-paid executives in a company's proxy statement under "other compensation" in the cash compensation table, as is the imputed income for a split-dollar life insurance arrangement.

(e)   What Are Other Considerations?

Underwriting is one of the key considerations in developing an executive life insurance program. If only a small group of insureds (generally less than 25) is covered, then the executives must qualify for the insurance by submitting medical evidence. Therefore, the covered group of executives is often larger than the group covered under a SERP. Even when the group is larger, guaranteed issue (i.e., no medical questions asked) may be limited to less than the full amount of the benefit.

Insurance products vary tremendously in the manner in which the cost of the coverage is assessed. As a result, a simple comparison of the price for insurance rarely is sufficient to make a well-informed decision. Products also vary significantly in how they accrue cash value. It is usually advisable to use the services of a qualified insurance consultant when purchasing executive life insurance coverage.

12.4   EXECUTIVE DISABILITY BENEFITS

(a)   What Are They and Why Are They Used?

Executive disability benefits protect the executive and his or her family in the event that he or she becomes disabled. Typically, the executive is covered by a salary continuation plan for short-term disabilities. For long-term disabilities, some organizations provide their executives with supplemental disability benefits in addition to any disability benefits provided to the general employee population through a group plan.

The disability benefits provided to the broad-based population of an employer may not sufficiently protect highly compensated executives. Group plans that cover the entire employee population generally have maximum monthly benefit limitations that prevent the executive from receiving an adequate benefit or may use only base salary as the defined pay. Supplemental plans extend coverage beyond these limits and may include bonus pay in the definition of pay. Organizations also use supplemental plans to provide a program with more liberal provisions, such as reducing the waiting period or extending the benefit period. Supplemental plans can be tailored to meet the specific needs of the executive.

(b)   What Is the Typical Design?

Eligibility for supplemental disability benefits is usually determined based on those executives who are impacted by the benefit limitations of the group plan. In some organizations, those impacted may be only a handful of executives, while in large organizations, they may include a much larger group, such as vice presidents and above.

Benefits are generally expressed as a percentage (e.g., 60% to 70%) of salary or total compensation. Some plans will cap monthly benefits (at higher levels than the group plan), but others may not. Those employers who cap supplemental benefits typically limit them to $12,000 to $15,000 per month. Often supplemental plans are structured so that benefits are not reduced by benefits from other sources.

Under basic plans, long-term disability is usually defined as the employee's inability to perform his or her own specific occupation for the first consecutive 24-month period. Thereafter, the disability benefit is paid only if the employee is unable to perform any occupation. Executive plans generally use the more generous "own occupation" definition of disability for the duration of the disability. In any case, benefits usually cease when the employee reaches age 65.

(c)   What Are the Tax and Legal Issues?

Disability benefits provided by the employer are fully taxable to the executive as ordinary income, whether the plan is insured or self-insured. If the employee pays the premium with after-tax dollars, then that portion of the benefit is received tax-free; however, most employers do not require employee contributions for supplemental disability benefits.

(d)   Are There Other Considerations?

More often than not, employers purchase disability insurance policies to insure the risk because of the potential for high-cost claims. The group policy, which the organization has for the general employee population, is typically supplemented with either group or individual disability insurance policies for the executives. As with life insurance, underwriting is a key consideration, regardless of whether group or individual policies are used. An equally important consideration is the cost of the coverage. Group coverage usually will be more cost efficient if a large group of executives is covered by the supplemental plan.

Individual policies will generally provide a specified dollar amount, which can be increased with additional purchases of insurance coverage as salaries increase. Unlike group plans, individual policies do not normally offset the disability benefit with benefits received from other sources, as group plans do.

12.5   MEDICAL BENEFITS

(a)   What Are They and Why Are They Used?

Supplemental executive medical benefits generally take the form of a medical reimbursement plan, which is designed to reimburse the executive for specified medical expenses not covered by the employer's group plan. In addition, some employers waive any contributions to the broad-based plan.

Medical costs are constantly on the rise and can represent a significant expense to an individual in any given year, particularly if sizable expenses are incurred that are not covered. The primary goal of most supplemental medical plans is for the executive to avoid any out-of-pocket expense. Therefore, reimbursement plans can make employment with companies that offer this type of supplemental plan more attractive. It should be noted, however that most surveys report that a relatively small percentage (less than 15%) of employers offer supplemental medical plans to executives.

(b)   What Is the Typical Design?

A typical arrangement reimburses the executive for premium contributions to the broad-based plan, for either the executive or dependents. It is also common practice to reimburse the executive for copayments, deductibles, coinsurance, and expenses not covered by the basic group plan, such as vision care, annual physical exams, dental care, and so on. Most employers who provide reimbursement programs place a cap on the annual amount of reimbursement, with the median amount equal to $5,000.

(c)   What Are the Tax and Legal Issues?

Under current tax laws, the value of any self-insured discriminatory medical benefits is included in taxable income for the executive. Insured benefits are not taxable. Therefore, when possible, this type of benefit is provided through an insured plan.

12.6   PERQUISITES

(a)   What Are They?

Executive perquisites represent another component of the total compensation package. Perquisites are generally cash, property, or services that an organization provides to executives in addition to salary. For purposes of this chapter, we define executive perquisites as items such as cars or car allowances, club memberships, physical exams, and financial counseling. Perquisites are distinguished from core executive benefits that supplement income at death, disability, or retirement.

Perquisites are included in taxable income unless specifically exempted. The exemption from taxation would generally apply only if the perquisites are provided on a nondiscriminatory basis or are used exclusively for business purposes. For example, the cost of a company car is tax deductible for the company. The executive is not taxed to the extent the car is used for business; but personal use would create taxation. Amounts paid by the company for financial planning, however, would be treated as taxable income for the executive and as a tax deduction for the company.

(b) Why Do Organizations Offer Perquisites?

In tight job markets, companies use perquisites as a means of differentiating themselves from their competitors. Increasingly, perquisites are seen as a way to enhance an executive's quality of life. In recent economic boom times, employers became more creative and liberal with perk offerings, such as the personal use of company aircraft, interest-free home loans, on-site massages, personal trainers, and concierge services. More commonly, however, perquisites are used to enhance an executive's working environment so that he or she can be more productive.

12.7 CONCLUSION

When base pay constituted the primary source of income for an executive, benefits (such as supplemental retirement income and deferred compensation) played a greater role in the accumulation of long-term financial security. The shift to greater emphasis on pay-for-performance and stock incentive plans has made executive benefits more of a safety net for executives. They provide core coverage for risk-taking executives who look to equity-based capital accumulation as their primary source of long-term financial security. Nevertheless, the cost of executive benefits can be greater than many companies may anticipate (for example, when higher-than-expected cash incentives are included in the definition of pay in a target SERP plan). When a company's executive compensation strategy is to reward for performance, it is important to review the structure of various executive benefits to avoid unexpected increases in cost and unnecessary subsidization of benefits to executives.

Chapter 13

A Pay-for-Performance Model

John D. Bloedorn

This chapter presents a pay-for-performance model intended to provoke new thinking and encourage those responsible for compensation programs to take a forward look, consider some new emphases, and perhaps take new directions. While not a blueprint for any company, it is based on our own work with many companies to enhance their pay-for-performance position.

13.1 GUIDING PRINCIPLES

We believe that the following 10 principles provide a solid foundation on which to build a compensation program. Support for each principle was found in various research studies we have conducted over the past decade.

1. *Start with a compensation strategy.* It establishes a foundation for the compensation program, addresses the role compensation should play within the company, and helps determine the desired competitive position for the total compensation program and its various elements. It should reflect on the company's objectives, the industry in which it operates, and the economic challenges the company must face. It also should consider and support the organizational structure, decision-making process, and the company's risk/ reward orientation. Once the compensation strategy is determined, the primary elements of the executive compensation package—salary, annual incentives, and long-term incentives—can be tailored to meet the company's unique needs.

2. *Reinforce your company's desired culture orientation.* Companies have different values and strategies for success. Determining your prevalent or preferred company culture orientation is an important step toward that success, so too is reinforcing your preferred values and orientation through your compensation program. Higher-performing companies are more likely to provide high reinforcement for their desired culture orientation.

3. *Involve the CEO, management, and compensation committee.* Good design isn't enough; "buy-in" is essential on the part of those most affected by the compensation plans. The compensation expert who designs alone stands alone. Our best practices research found that involvement of the chief executive officer (CEO) was a major contributing factor to the success of the executive compensation program.

Also, a constructive change has occurred in that compensation committees are doing a better job representing the interests of shareholders. Compensation committees have become more proactive in developing the compensation strategy, determining award/grant levels, and reviewing and approving the performance measures used to fund incentive plans. The primary catalyst for their increased involvement is the Securities Exchange Commission (SEC) disclosure rules pertaining to reporting of compensation in the proxy statements of all publicly traded companies. Their increased review should be viewed as constructive inquiry, and a strengthening of the pay–performance relationship is the natural result.

4. *Take incentive eligibility deep.* Companies should consider taking both annual and long-term incentives deeper in their organizations in terms of eligibility. Incentives can expand the team committed to delivering results. They can cause employees, individually and collectively, to focus their attention on the company's goals and identify with shareholder interests.

With annual or even shorter timeframe incentives, it is important for participants to understand how the plan works and how they can affect results favorably. This is helped by keeping the plan simple and within the participants' "line-of-sight" in terms of their ability to have an impact.

5. *Leverage incentives.* The relationship between performance results and pay will be strengthened if the incentive opportunity is substantial for performance excellence and minimal if performance is below standard. By leverage, we mean the payout variability based on performance. We find that higher-performing companies usually provide more leveraged annual and longer-term incentives than do lower-performing companies.

6. *Make shareholder value creation a top priority.* Total shareholder return (TSR) is the sum of the appreciation realized plus the dividends received or reinvested divided by the shareholder's original investment. It also is the principal element in the performance graph in proxy statements. Why? Because over the long-term, TSR is the best expression of the shareholders' interest. Therefore, TSR should be given primary consideration in the design of long-term incentives. The term *shareholder value creation* is overworked. It seems that almost everyone toting a particular measure, financial or otherwise, or management theory claims to "create shareholder value." They are also devoting a lot of energy trying to correlate their favored measure or theory (independent variables) with that of total shareholder return (the dependent variable); however, nothing correlates better with TSR than, of

course, TSR. Thus, directly rewarding the creation of shareholder value will be the primary goal for several of the alternatives described in the long-term element section of this chapter.

7. *Emphasize the long term for executives.* As relates to senior management personnel, higher-performing companies give greater emphasis to longer-term results than annual results. Just the opposite is the case for lower-performing companies. Thus, the annualized target value for long-term incentives should be greater than the target for annual incentives as pertains to these employees.

8. *Benchmark long-term performance through comparative measures.* Most of the companies that have goal-based long-term incentives struggle with setting goals, the attainment of which will determine the compensation payment. Quite simply, companies have difficulty setting accurate performance targets for three years or more because of external forces such as economic, political, and regulatory trends or mandates.

   Our solution is to stop using long-term goal-based financial measures in isolation from competitive norms. Instead, we suggest using comparative measures. This is in keeping with a growing desire on the part of many compensation committees to obtain external validation of success before large incentive payments are made.

   We also suggest considering a broad-based sample group such as the Standard & Poor's 500 (S&P 500). A selected industry grouping runs the risk of changing during the performance period because of mergers, acquisitions, leveraged buyouts, and other restructurings. A broad-based sample group is particularly appropriate if shareholder value creation is the goal, since shareholders are not limited to investing in only one industry.

9. *Communicate initially and regularly thereafter.* Those eligible for incentives need to know how compensation plans work and what the plan can mean to them. This means providing them with both reader-friendly plan descriptions at time of rollout, as well as periodic (i.e., quarterly) statements about incentive performance results and projected award levels.

10. *Do not reward poor performance.* Investors are not forgiven for a bad investment, and executives should not be forgiven for poor performance. While the business press is on target when they highlight significant rewards to top executives whose companies do poorly, this can reflect negatively on those companies that are trying to link pay to actual performance results. We believe this is what most companies want to do.

Most companies indicate that they anticipate future changes in their executive compensation programs; their number one reason for making a change is a desire to strengthen the pay–company performance relationship. This is a positive sign, and we are convinced that if shareholders see the value of their investment increase substantially, they will not object to significant rewards for executives.

13.2   A COMPENSATION MODEL

With these guiding principles in mind, the purpose of our compensation Model is to ensure total compensation opportunities substantially above those of competitors when performance is above competitors and substantially below competitors if performance is below that of competitors. This can be accomplished with the following strategy:

- Conservative salaries with midpoints set at 95% or 90% of market, except for the CEO and chief operating officer (COO), set at 85%.
- Substantial annual incentives for all exempt personnel based on attaining planned operating goals, with increased proportional funding above-goal performance.
- Very substantial long-term incentives for all exempt personnel, for which the top priority is shareholder value creation on a comparative basis.

Exhibit 13.1 reflects this strategy and contrasts it with that of the typical company. The various tiers represent descending responsibility levels. Exhibit 13.1 indexes all salaries for the typical company at 100, which can be considered a competitive salary.

The CEO of the typical company has a base salary of 100, an annual incentive target of 90% of a competitive base salary, and a target annualized long-term incentive with an estimated value of 225% of a competitive salary, for a total compensation of 415 (100 + 90 + 225). Reading down the tiers for the typical company, we see that the annual incentives decrease, but not as quickly as the long-term incentives. This occurs because the ability of employees to influence results decreases as one moves from tier to tier. This is even more the case relative to long-term incentives.

The targeted total compensation mix in the Model is consistent with its stated compensation strategy and is quite different from the typical targeted total compensation mix. It features lower salaries at all tier levels. It is also more leveraged because both annual and longer-term incentive amounts are larger than those offered by the typical company. Finally, the Model's targeted total compensation is higher at all tier levels than for the typical company, although our fixed cost commitment (base salary) is always less than that found in the typical company. Exhibit 13.2 displays the Model's target annual incentives and target annualized long-term incentives as percentages of the Model's salaries.

No doubt, some readers will be concerned with the idea of establishing salary ranges that are intentionally below those in other organizations. Others may be concerned with incentives being as large as those suggested by the Model. While the degree of emphasis may be beyond the comfort level of some, the direction in which higher-performing companies are pointing toward is clear—relatively

Exhibit 13.1   Contrasting Compensation Strategies.[a]

	Base Salary	Annual Incentive	Long-Term Incentive	Total Compensation
CEO	100 / 85	90 / 100	225 / 300	415 / 485
COO	100 / 85	80 / 90	170 / 225	350 / 400
Tier II	100 / 90	60 / 70	100 / 135	260 / 295
Tier III	100 / 90	45 / 55	50 / 75	195 / 220
Tier IV	100 / 95	35 / 40	35 / 50	170 / 185
Tier V	100 / 95	25 / 30	15 / 25	140 / 150

Typical

Model

[a] All numbers indexed to competitive salaries.

Exhibit 13.2   Target Annual and Long-Term Incentives as a Percentage of Model Salaries.

	Annual Incentive (%)	Estimated Value of Long-Term Incentives (%)
CEO	118	353
COO	106	265
Tier II	78	150
Tier III	61	83
Tier IV	42	53
Tier V	32	26

conservative salaries coupled with more substantial incentives. Let's now return to each of the elements in the Model.

13.3   BASE SALARY ELEMENT

Of the three primary forms of compensation addressed by the Model, the base salary element may have the least significant consequence. Most companies, however, devote a greater amount of time to salary administration than is needed, without much effect on salaries or work behavior.

Most companies assign positions to responsibility groups. Each responsibility group is then given a salary range with a spread of 50% or more from its minimum to its maximum. The company's base salary structure is composed of the various salary ranges it uses and is adjusted periodically to reflect general market conditions.

The midpoint of each range is typically differentiated from the range midpoints immediately above and below it by 10% to 15%. Virtually all companies would benefit by expanding this differential to 20% to 30%. This would eliminate approximately one-half of their existing salary ranges, while still providing substantial range overlap. This simpler approach eliminates wasted time evaluating jobs to a degree that is neither necessary nor defensible. Each employee's salary should fall within the range of his or her position. The individual's advancement within the range should reflect his or her performance value over time. Most companies will use some form of performance appraisal to rationalize any differentiated salary treatment.

The problem is that most companies have too many rating categories with too little salary discrimination based on performance. Thus, a lot of time is spent spreading the dissatisfaction evenly among employees.

It is better to start with a simple set of rating categories associated with performance improvement over time. As shown in Exhibit 13.3, only three rating categories are needed: above, at, and below expectation.

Our Model eliminates the practice of granting an annual, modest performance-differentiated increase. Instead, individuals would receive adjustments consistent with annual or biannual range changes. Thus, employees would maintain their position within a range, unless they move significantly up the expectation curve, in which case they would be adjusted to a new level. The first level change would likely occur in a year or two, with succeeding level changes taking longer. Thus, getting to the top of one's range would take at least 10 to 15 years. Exhibit 13.4 reflects this guideline.

This approach has not generated a following because it is radically different from the current salary increase practices of virtually all companies; however, the approach has three advantages over traditional practices. First, salary administration

Exhibit 13.3   Expectation Concept, Showing Performance
Improvement Over Time.

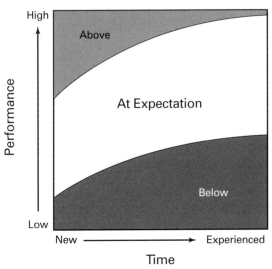

Exhibit 13.4   In-Grade Progression Guidelines.

Level	1	2	3	4	5
Probable years to attainment	0–1	1–3	3–6	6–10	10–15
Salary	$80,000	$90,000	$100,000	$110,000	$120,000

time and expense are reduced. Second, level adjustments make a meaningful difference in one's pay. In a sense, they represent mini-promotions within a grade as a form of recognizing advancement in job proficiency. Third, the cumulative earnings of those who advance rapidly will be substantially greater than the earnings of slower-tracking employees.

13.4   ANNUAL INCENTIVE ELEMENTS

Annual incentives exist in virtually every company. Incentives can be effective and useful in meeting a variety of purposes; however, our study shows that differences exist between higher- and lower-performing companies. Also, certain trends appear to be in the right direction and should be extended.

(a) Eligibility

Higher-performing companies take eligibility deeper into their organizations. Our Model extends eligibility to include all exempt personnel. This is consistent with and supportive of the fact that many companies are pursuing significant cultural changes where empowerment, greater delegation, decentralization, shared responsibility, quality initiatives, and a customer/shareholder orientation are all part of a new competitiveness.

(b) Size of Award

How big should the incentive opportunity be? Our Model's answer is consistent with the previously stated compensation strategy, calling for meaningful reward opportunities in return for superior performance and enhanced potential through increased proportional funding of above-target performance. Both concepts are reflected in the Model's higher and more leveraged award opportunities, as contrasted with those of the typical company.

This is illustrated in Exhibit 13.5, with all figures indexed to competitive salaries (100). Exhibit 13.6 displays the Model's Threshold, Goal, and Superior annual incentives as percentages of the Model's salaries.

(c) Funding Mechanism

A third major issue in annual incentive design is selecting the incentive funding mechanism and then determining how to measure it. There are four primary approaches to funding incentive pools:

1. *Goal attainment.* Rewards achievement of planned financial results.
2. *Fixed formula.* Rewards performance in excess of a predetermined and continuing threshold.
3. *Peer comparison.* Rewards relative to a group of comparable companies.
4. *Discretionary.* Rewards at the discretion of the compensation committee, Board, and/or CEO.

Our research shows a strong preference for using the goal attainment approach, as used in our Model.

Determining the right performance measure(s) is a crucial issue. Because companies and their business units differ, our Model does not recommend any specific financial measure or group of measures for all companies to use; however, and as noted by Exhibit 13.7, many choices are available. Most will use at least one element from the strategic/financial measures column. Of these, we think economic profit may be the least understood but would have significant

Exhibit 13.5   Annual Incentive Plans.[a]

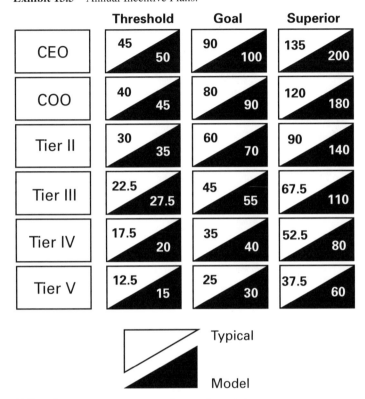

[a] All numbers represent percentages of competitve salaries.

Exhibit 13.6   Annual Incentives as a Percentage
of Model Salary.

	Threshold (%)	Goal (%)	Superior (%)
CEO	59	118	236
COO	53	106	212
Tier II	39	78	156
Tier III	30.5	61	122
Tier IV	21	42	84
Tier V	16	32	64

Exhibit 13.7   Frequently Used Performance Measures.

Strategic/Financial Measures	Operational Production Measures	Sales/Customer Service Measures
Market share	*Output:* volume, units	Customer satisfaction ratings
Operating earnings	produced, transactions,	Repeat or new business
Earnings before taxes	uptime, activity, reports,	from existing customers
and interest	tonnage	Customer retention
Earnings before interest,		Customer complaints,
taxes, depreciation,	*Input:* resources used, raw	response times,
and amortization	materials, tools and supplies,	resolution
Net income/earnings	labor hours, overtime,	Timeliness of processing
Economic profit	number of employees	
Earnings per share		Employee morale measures
Return on equity	*Effectiveness/efficiency*	Employee satisfaction
Return on assets	*ratios:* revenues per	Attendance
Return on sales	employee, volume per labor	Safety
Return on capital	hour, transactions per labor	Turnover
Cash flow	hour, cost per hire	Downtime
Revenue growth		Waste/rework/scrap

merit for many. In essence, it is the profit generated in excess of an enterprise's cost of capital and represents a higher standard than just being profitable (see Chapter 9, for a discussion of economic profit in greater detail).

(d)   Process Guidelines

Irrespective of what measure(s) is selected, several guidelines should be followed:

- Both top-down and bottom-up processes should be embraced. The top-down approach provides common direction for attaining goals by establishing priorities and links to performance measures. The bottom–up approach encourages buy-in and commitment from employees at the operating unit level and helps ensure that results support overall objectives.
- The choice of measure(s) should be limited to no more than two per funding pool.
- The measure(s) selected should be limited to those that participants can influence. They should have a clean line-of-sight attribute. Participants, however, may need direction on how to influence these measures.
- If either sales or revenues is used, it should always be coupled with a profit measure (e.g., return on sales).

- For any measure, the following points should be established:
  - *Threshold.* The level of performance deemed worthy of an incentive payment, below which no incentive is funded.
  - *Goal.* The goal or planned result—its attainment represents performance success worthy of funding at the targeted incentive levels.
  - *Superior.* The ideal result—represents performance excellence worthy of a maximum incentive award.
- The probability of attaining Threshold, Goal, and Superior results should be considered. A general guide and our Model recommendation is:
  - Threshold payout probability of 80%.
  - Goal payout probability of 60%.
  - Superior payout probability of 20%.
- Keep it simple. If those eligible for incentives do not understand a measure or how it relates to incentives, the plan will not fulfill its objectives.

Another consideration is the distance between Threshold and Goal and between Goal and Superior performance. The deviation from the Goal performance will depend on such things as the controllability, stability, and predictability of the financial results of the company, division, or unit for which funding is being established. In general, the spreads are broader for the less stable and less predictable.

(e)   The Corporate Pool

In establishing the corporate incentive pool, the Goal performance result should normally be the sum of its parts (i.e., the consolidation of the business units' goals), but the spreads between the corporate Threshold and corporate Goal, and corporate Goal and corporate Superior should be narrowed somewhat from what would be the sum of the business unit Thresholds and the sum of the business unit Superiors. In essence, the corporate incentive pool is the consolidation of its parts and is always in the middle of its business unit extremes. For better or worse, it can never be the outlier, unless the spreads between Threshold and Goal and Goal and Superior are narrowed. An example of this might be having the Thresholds and Superiors for the business units set at $\pm 20\%$ of their respective Goals, and the corporate Threshold and Superior set at $\pm 12\%$ of the corporate Goal.

(f)   Performance Mix

A final issue is the performance mix or the desired emphasis on corporate, business unit/division, and individual results. This will depend on an organization's goals, culture, structure, and management process. Our Model provides a starting point. For those eligible at the corporate level, it is a blend of corporate and individual results, with the former decreasing as one moves down through the tiers (Exhibit 13.8).

Line executives at the Tier II and III levels have a corporate stake, a more substantial division or business unit stake, and an individual piece. Because those in line Tiers IV and V are not expected to have much (or any) corporate impact, their incentives are composed of only division/business unit and individual pieces.

(g)   Employee Communication

Before incentives can really work, those eligible have to value the reward and believe that there is a high probability of receiving it. Before making such a judgment, they have to be able to see the relationship between the performance result and the incentive opportunity. This can be done graphically if a single criterion is used (Exhibit 13.9) or through the use of a matrix when two criteria are used to fund the incentive (Exhibit 13.10).

We now have completed a review of most of the design issues associated with the annual incentive element. Our Model helps narrow the choices of alternatives consistent with our compensation strategy. Once developed, the plan should be rolled out and communicated to all eligible employees. The communication itself need only deal with the adopted plan and not all of the alternatives that were considered.

Exhibit 13.8   Annual Incentives—Performance Mix at Goal as a Percentage of Competitive Salary.

| | Corporate | | Line | | |
	Corporate (%)	Individual (%)	Corporate (%)	Division (%)	Individual (%)
CEO	100	0	—	—	—
COO	90	0	—	—	—
Tier II	60	10	15	45	10
Tier III	45	10	10	35	10
Tier IV	30	10	0	30	10
Tier V	20	10	0	20	10

Exhibit 13.9 Single Criterion to Fund the Incentive Plan, Shown Graphically.

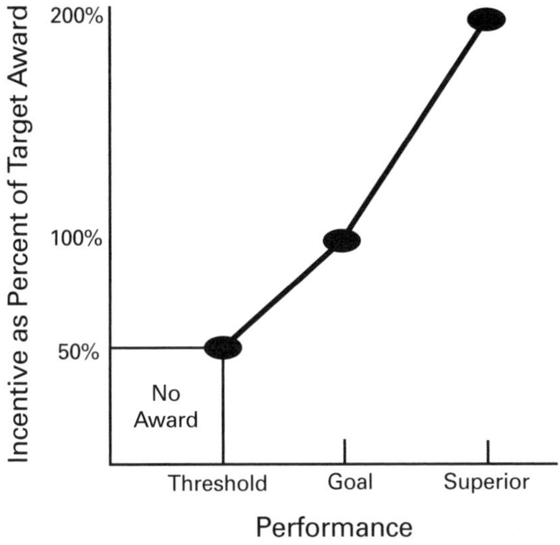

Exhibit 13.10 Two Criteria to Fund the Incentive Plan, Shown as a Matrix.

Volume Measure

Return Measure	Threshold		Goal		Superior
Threshold	.50	.62	.75	.87	1.00
	.62	.75	.87	1.00	1.25
Goal	.75	.87	1.00	1.25	1.50
	.87	1.00	1.25	1.50	1.75
Superior	1.00	1.25	1.50	1.75	2.00

Numbers represent multiples of the target incentive reward

13.5 LONG-TERM INCENTIVE ELEMENTS

Long-term incentives have attracted attention and criticism from the business press, academics, shareholders, the SEC, and politicians. Some of this criticism is deserved because there are examples of executives receiving substantial capital accumulation without creating a corresponding gain in shareholder value. One of the principles on which our Model is based is that poor performance will not be rewarded. This is not to say that wealth creation is to be avoided; on the contrary, significant personal gain is the goal to be achieved once the shareholder interest has been served.

Shareholder interest is the total return on the shareholder's investment. This is ultimately expressed as total shareholder return (TSR), which is the sum of the appreciation realized plus the dividends received divided by the shareholder's original investment. Later in this chapter we discuss how this measure can be used on a comparative basis.

Few areas are as dynamic as long-term incentives; however, their primary roles have remained relatively stable over time. These roles include:

- Aligning executive interests with those of shareholders.
- Communicating and reinforcing long-term performance objectives.
- Providing motivational balance to annual incentives.
- Providing performance-contingent capital accumulation.
- Helping retain management personnel.

Let's focus on how our Model can meet these longstanding primary purposes.

(a)   Eligibility

Over the past decade, we have witnessed an expansion in long-term plan eligibility from just executives to many more managers and professionals. This practice should be further expanded to include all exempt employees as owners. The rationale for this change is that if employees have a stake in the company, they will perform better and are more likely to stay.

(b)   Size of Award

How big should grants or awards be? They also have been getting bigger over the past decade, and our Model calls for substantial opportunities at all tier levels as compared to the typical company (Exhibit 13.11). As concerns the CEO and COO, many companies provide substantially larger long-term grants in relation to salary for their CEO than for their COO. The right answer for each company depends on the CEO/COO working relationship and the Board members' expectations of each.

(c)   Present Value Determination

Another complex issue involves determining the present value of stock options and other forms of long-term incentives. Two simple approaches are (1) multiple of pay and (2) percentage of ownership. These have often been replaced by more

Exhibit 13.11   Target Annualized Long-Term Incentives as a Percentage of Competitive Salary.

	Typical (%)	Model (%)
CEO	225	300
COO	170	225
Tier II	100	135
Tier III	50	75
Tier IV	35	50
Tier V	15	25

sophisticated and complex approaches, such as the Black Scholes Model, which yields a present value for projected option gains. Models of this type take into account such variables as option exercise price, stock price at date of grant, expected volatility, expected dividend yield, the risk-free interest rate during the expected option term, and the expected life of the option.

Calculating the present value of a stock option is potentially important for two separate purposes. One is to help guide companies in calculating award grant sizes; the other relates to complying with FASB Statement 123, "Accounting for Stock-Based Compensation" (see Chapter 18, "Accounting for Stock-Based Compensation" for a discussion of FASB Statement 123 and other accounting issues related to long-term incentives).

As relates to the first use, calculating award grant sizes, we think a few standards can be applied for making present value determinations:

Stock options = two-fifths (40%) the strike price × shares granted (or some other appropriate present value calculation)

Restricted shares = strike price × shares granted

Performance shares = strike price × shares contingently granted × the probability of goal attainment

We would also suggest that, as relates to the grant of stock options, recalculating the present value of stock options each time they are granted is neither necessary nor desirable. In fact, counterintuitive grants can result from an annually applied present value methodology. If the share value increases, then both the present value and the next grant's fair market value (FMV) increase; and the number of awarded shares would decrease. Conversely, if the share value decreases, then both the present value and the next grant's FMV decrease; and the number of awarded shares would increase.

In the first circumstance, the employee is penalized for having helped create a substantial increase in shareholder value and in the second circumstance, the employee would seem to be being rewarded for having contributed to a serious decrease in shareholder value.

Our suggestion for establishing stock option grants is to lock in on a present value based on an average of daily closing prices over a period of at least a month, and then stick with it for a three-year period. This allows the company to better manage the number of shares it will award each year. If the company expects more eligibles in the future, it should budget a growth factor to its pool of shares to be granted each year.

Most companies target individual grants and express them as a percentage of salary. Our Model calls for such and reflects a reduction in award size as one moves down through the tier levels. These grant targets, coupled with a set number of option shares budgeted for grant each year, provide the basis for a simple grant methodology. First, the dollar value of each individual's target stock option award can be calculated. Second, these dollar values can then be summed for the entire eligibility group. Third, the individual's dollar value can then be divided by the summed dollar value. This fraction can then be multiplied by the number of shares budgeted for award to determine the number of option shares to be awarded to the individual participant. In effect, each participant is the numerator and the entire participant population is the denominator. If the participant's target stock option award value is 1% of the entire group's target value, then the participant would receive 1% of that year's stock option shares. If a performance factor is desired, substitute actual cash compensation for salary (individual) and summed actual cash compensation for summed salaries (all eligibles) and run the same formula. Either way, our Model provides a simple way to grant all the option shares available each year.

(d)   Accounting and Treatment

Another consideration is the accounting treatment of the various plan alternatives. Issued in 1995, FASB Statement 123, "Accounting for Stock-Based Compensation," encouraged companies to adopt an accounting methodology based on the estimated fair value of employee stock options. However, companies were permitted to retain the accounting approach under APB Opinion No. 25 with increased disclosure. Because most companies have chosen to continue accounting under APB Opinion 25 with increased disclosure in the footnotes to financial statements, our Model will suggest programs that avoid, minimize, and/or control the expense associated with long-term incentives under these continuing rules (APB Opinion 25).

This means meeting the *measurement* date test of a known number of shares at a known price, as soon as is practical in order to attain fixed plan accounting treatment. The measurement date is the first date at which (1) the number of shares the employee is entitled to and (2) the option or purchase price the employee must pay are known. Today, nonqualified options at fair market value (FMV) meet the measurement date test at the time of grant and do not require any expensing, although they will be dilutive. Consequently, they are recommended.

(e)   Comparative Shareholder Value

One of the important findings of our research projects was the difficulty companies were having in setting fair financial performance measures for their performance share/unit plans. Our solution is to deemphasize long-term financial performance measures for compensation purposes and consider the issue from the perspective of the shareholder; that is, how the company is doing in comparison to a much broader sample of companies, such as the Standard & Poors (S&P) 500. While external conditions affect individual industries differently, all companies should have one common long-term goal—the creation of shareholder value. Outperforming a composite of many companies on a total shareholder return basis is the criterion that counts.

In addition to the frustration associated with setting finite longer-term performance targets, the use of comparative TSR results has been stimulated by the fact that all public companies must present in their proxy a graph comparing their five-year total shareholder return results to that of (1) a broad index such as the S&P 500 and (2) a publicly available industry index or a composite return for a selected group of companies.

A composite index (e.g., S&P 500) best reflects shareholder alternatives to the company's stock investment. There are five alternative ways to use a broad-based TSR comparative index:

- Company TSR greater than index TSR
- Quartile/decile placement among group
- Company TSR divided by index TSR
- Company TSR minus index TSR
- Company TSR against goal based on historic (i.e., five-year index TSR)

Paying out on the basis of these charted comparison results is certainly in keeping with rewarding executives according to what is being delivered to their shareholders. How we use the comparative data is discussed later when we describe the Model's long-term incentive alternatives.

(f)   Long-Term Incentive Alternatives

Our Model is composed of six different possible long-term incentive plan alternatives that could be used as supplements to, in combination with, or in lieu of nonqualified stock options. The underlying concept for each exists in one or more companies, but the use of all six does not exist in any company. Assuming a company has nonqualified options, and virtually all publicly traded companies should, it may choose to use only one or two of these long-term incentive elements. In any case, our Model represents an attempt to develop plans that blend the advantages of stock options, restricted stock, and performance shares/units while minimizing their disadvantages. The suggested plan elements and the possible tier levels to which they would apply are shown in Exhibit 13.12.

(i) Performance-Accelerated Restricted Stock (PARS) The performance-accelerated restricted stock plan concept can be attractively linked to TSR results. The concept is to provide a restricted stock award with a long vesting period, such as 5 years. The vesting period is then shortened or accelerated based on the company's TSR results as compared to the S&P 500, an industry index, or a selected group of peer companies.

If the company's TSR is better than its index or peer comparison group after three years, the granted PARS would vest and a new grant would be made. If not then ahead, a second comparison would be made after four years. If then ahead of the index or peer comparison group, the PARS would vest and a new grant would be made. If not then ahead, the shares would vest at the end of the fifth year and a new grant would then be made.

From the employees' perspective, winning is to get the shares to vest every three years since they will receive more shares over their careers. This is also what shareholders would like to have happen since it means they are getting a better return on their investment in the company than is being provided by the index or peer comparison group composite.

Because PARS are granted only every third, fourth, or fifth year, they are typically front-loaded fourfold when granted. In this way, a meaningful stake is established with each grant, and the plan will have strong retention attributes at all times.

(ii) Shareholder Value Units As an alternative to PARS, a company may want to consider the shareholder value plan concept (Exhibit 13.13), which

Exhibit 13.12   Long-Term Incentive Plan Elements.

Possible Elements	Possible Eligible Employees
Performance-accelerated restricted stock	All Eligibles
Shareholder value plan	CEO/COO, Tiers II, III, IV
Time-accelerated stock options	CEO/COO
Restricted stock performance plan	CEO/COO, Tier II
All-exempt employee plan	Tier V
Value-added plan	CEO/COO, Tiers II, III, IV

Exhibit 13.13   Shareholder Value Units Tied
to Shareholder Return.

	TSR Percentile Rank Among S&P 500	Contingent Unit Value
Threshold	**50th**	**$500**
	55	750
Target	**60**	**1,000**
	65	1,300
	70	1,600
	75	1,950
	80	2,300
	85	2,650
Maximum	**90 +**	**3,000**

provides performance units that have contingent value tied to a company's percentile ranking among the S&P 500 on a total shareholder return basis for a designated performance period (e.g., three years). For a participant to receive a payment, the company must be at least at the 50th percentile on a TSR basis. If the company is at the 50th percentile, participants receive one-half of a target award payment. A target award payment is earned if the company is at the 60th percentile on a TSR basis. If the company is at the 90th percentile or better on a TSR basis, the participants receive a payment of three times a target award. Thus, the payment schedule is progressive and potentially significant; however, shareholders should support a maximum payout because they will already have received a significant return on their investment in the company.

(iii) Time-Accelerated Stock Option   The time-accelerated stock option would pertain only to the most visible company executives (i.e., CEO/COO). This responds to the use of mega-grants to top officers and is an attempt to assure shareholders of a solid appreciation before significant gain to the executive. Options would be granted at either 100% of their fair market value on the date of grant for their full term or at a predetermined premium (e.g., 125%). Whether premium priced or left at their fair market value at time of grant, the options could only be exercised during their first five years, or some other preestablished timeframe, if the company's TSR results from date of grant is in excess of that for a broad index (i.e., the S&P 500).

   In order to ensure fixed, rather than variable, accounting treatment under APB Opinion 25, the options would need to be exerciseable for certain at some point in time within their exercise period. Factors used to determine the appropriate point of time include vesting periods in the company's other plans and whether it is more likely than not that the employee will still be employed at such point in time. The advantage of this approach is to hold the CEO/COO to a higher standard of shareholder appreciation before the CEO/COO can reap the benefits of this substantial longer-term incentive opportunity.

(iv) Restricted Stock Performance Plan   The restricted stock performance plan concept gets around the lack of a performance requirement inherent in most restricted stock programs by making the grant of restricted shares dependent on the prior year's performance, rather than prospectively, as is the case with performance shares. Each year, a pool of restricted shares is established for potential granting. The determinant of whether the shares are distributable can be tied to virtually any companywide financial or shareholder value measure (Exhibit 13.14). Since the measurement date test is met at the end of the performance year, subsequent appreciation occurring during the restriction period need not be expensed.

(v) All-Exempt Employee Plan   The all-exempt employee plan concept embraced by our Model is not as unique in plan design as it is in terms of its eligibility. It would apply to all exempt employees not included in the top four tiers. This practice has been adopted by a substantial number of corporations, and the trend is likely to grow rapidly. Our Model embraces the premise that all exempt employees should be owners so that they will identify with shareholder interests.

The plan concept is that eligible employees will receive a biannual restricted stock award equal to 10% of their salary with a 5-year vesting schedule. The long vesting schedule on the restricted shares is intentional—we want these employees to have a reason to stay with the company, remain as shareholders, and spread the expense of the awards.

Exhibit 13.14   Example: Funding Criteria.

Performance Measure	Restricted Shares Distributed (%)
15%ROE[a]	100
14%ROE	80
13%ROE	60
12%ROE	40
11%ROE	20
10%ROE	0

[a]ROE, return on equity.

They also will receive a biannual nonqualified stock option grant that is exercisable after three years and within 10 years from date of grant. These grants would be made alternatively to the biannual restricted stock awards, and they would receive 2.5 options for every restricted share. This has the effect of a 40% present value assumption as relates to the value of each stock option as compared to its fair market value at time of grant.

(vi) Value-Added Incentive Plan   Our final long-term incentive vehicle, the value-added incentive plan concept, does not require the use of actual stock. Thus, it can be used by both publicly owned companies for business units and private companies that desire a longer-term incentive vehicle that is directly linked to and earned based on the realized results.

In a sentence, it provides those eligible with an ownership interest in a long-term incentive pool that expands or contracts based on how the business unit performs in relationship to an annually adjusted return on the company's invested capital in the business unit. This is accomplished by using a sharing ratio of economic profits (a put) or shortfalls of economic profits (a take) above a self-adjusting threshold return on the company's investment in the business unit (i.e., 8% of the economic profit in excess of a 12% threshold return on capital). The threshold is annually adjusted based on the company's actual or desired debt-to-equity ratio and the cost of funds.

The value-added approach is fundamentally simple in concept and does not require establishment of long-term financial goals. It also can act as an excellent surrogate for stock when such is not available or desired.

13.6   OTHER COMPENSATION DESIGN CONSIDERATIONS

We have now covered a substantial number of design issues in the development of our Model's base salary, annual incentive, and long-term incentive elements. Our Model should also embrace the following two fairly contemporary considerations.

(a)   Stock Ownership Guidelines

Many companies have formalized stock ownership guidelines for executives. They believe, and we agree, that executives who invest in significant amounts of company stock are more inclined to focus on long-term growth, make decisions in the best interests of shareholders, and contribute to higher levels of shareholder value.

We suggest that target guidelines be established as a multiple of salary, depending on the level of the position within the company. For example: for the CEO, five times salary; for the COO, four times salary; for Tier II, three times salary; and for Tier III, two times salary. Typically, executives are given a period of time, such as three to five years, to fulfill their target ownership requirements.

If such a stipulation is met, the company should cease to frown upon, or put pressure upon, executives for disposing of some of their stockholdings. Some executives are paper wealthy but cash poor because they feel under pressure never to dispose of their stockholdings in the company. It is our belief that as long as executives meet or exceed the ownership requirement, they should be allowed to reap the benefits of their earned rewards in accordance with their personal needs and desires.

(b)   Stock Ownership Deferral Plan

We recommend that companies provide their employees an opportunity to defer current cash compensation by taking it in the form of a restricted stock grant with a premium. This concept could apply to base salaries, annual incentives, or cash payouts under a long-term plan. The employee would make an election to be paid in the form of restricted stock, without an IRC Section 83(b) election, rather than cash before taking receipt of the cash. To encourage participation and in light of the increased risk associated with taking the pay in the form of restricted stock, the company would provide a premium to those taking the restricted stock (i.e., 120% converted cash value in the form of restricted stock with a three-year restriction on the shares).

Advantages can flow both to the employees and to the company under such a program. Employees will receive a 20% increase in the amount earned and are able to invest this full amount in the company on a pretax basis. Like other shareholders, they can also vote these shares and receive dividends on them.

For the company, benefits include a workforce more likely to identify with shareholder interests; a workforce more likely to stay, since they would forfeit any unvested shares; retention of cash to be used for other purposes; a controlled and known amount to be expensed over the restriction period; and potentially enhanced tax deductions, assuming appreciation occurs while the shares are under restriction and/or dividends are paid on the shares while they are under restriction.

13.7   COMMUNICATIONS

If employees value the reward and believe that the probability that they will receive it is high, they will make the effort to attain it. But before employees can make such a judgment, they must understand how the program works and what it can mean to them. A "do this, get that" message must be conveyed to all employees.

Companies often do a good job of communicating when they are rolling out a new program; however, communication should continue on a regular basis. The compensation strategy, program components, and individual objectives should be reviewed annually with each program participant. Finally, communications on incentive performance and projected award levels should be provided on a regular basis. Knowing the score helps reinforce the purpose and the value of the compensation program.

13.8 CONCLUSION

Our goal has been to use the practices of higher-performing companies as a starting point to suggest a pay-for-performance model that would represent a better way to use compensation as an effective management tool. Starting with some guiding principles, we developed a compensation strategy and then suggested design concepts for each of the compensation components of salary, annual incentives, and longer-term incentives. Much must go into the design process in order to complete and communicate a fundamentally simple plan design. We hope our pay-for-performance Model will be useful as a means to tailor and improve compensation programs.

Chapter 14

Driving Organizational Change with Executive Compensation and Communication

Donald T. Sagolla and Donna L. DiBlase

Organizational change is not a new theme in business. In fact, every business is in a constant state of change, from adjusting to external competitiveness, changing leadership, and developing innovative ways to focus on delivering value to customers and shareholders. The challenge is to engage executives in behavior that will drive the business to meet or exceed performance objectives. Executive compensation practices and strategic communication about their link to business strategy are critical tools in managing and creating organizational change.

Traditionally, executive compensation practice is considered sound when it leads executives toward a reasonable set of expectations and when the compensation message is clear and intentional. This "message" has been typically based on annual quantifiable performance expectations understood to be part of the executive's responsibility to the organization. A challenge is to develop an executive compensation strategy that reinforces business strategy while communicating an organization's standards and expectations.

Although many organizations have designed compensation strategies to engage executives in managing organizational change, some fall short of transforming the organization into its desired state because of the lack of an effective communication and implementation strategy. A requirement for executives to manage organizational change has created shifts in compensation strategy, resulting in real and perceived gaps between pay and performance. These gaps are driven by changes in business conditions, performance expectations, and cultural values, as well as by a lack of clear and consistent communication about the cost of not changing and the rewards for success for both the company and the executive. A new challenge is to integrate executive compensation approaches with organizational change through a targeted communication and implementation strategy.

14.1 TYPES OF ORGANIZATIONAL CHANGE

There are numerous types of organizational change that Boards, chief executive officers (CEOs), and other key executives and managers must deal with in these times. Some of the major organizational changes have included the following:

- Reshaping the organizational structure, due to reengineering, merger/acquisitions, or shifts in business/product service focus.
- Reinforcing or redefining a leadership team or individual as the specifying influence on the business.
- Changing or refining the organization's cultural values.
- Creating a stronger focus on shareholder value creation.
- Reacting or proacting to competitive and economic changes.
- Complying with and/or anticipating the ongoing or changing needs of the Board and significant stakeholders.
- Integrating major internal business procedures, policies, and processes related to innovative new products and technologies.
- Responding/adapting to the continuous changes and requirements of current and prospective employees.

Certainly, other internal and external forces are generating organizational change, but those above, as well as others, have a couple of key themes related to them:

- Organizational change usually requires change in individual executives' and employees' performance and/or behaviors.
- Compensation management often influences the pace and the degree to which organization change is achieved.
- Effective communication of compensation and its link to organizational and individual performance is critical to creating organizational change.

While there are a multitude of compensation programs, systems, and considerations, this chapter focuses on the following factors. We believe they are having a major impact on organizational change today and that they will continue to do so in the foreseeable future:

- The relationship of compensation strategy and organizational change.
- Developing a communication strategy to drive behavior.
- The integration of executive compensation with organization and executive performance and, relatedly, the resultant *performance contract.*
- Linking compensation programs to characteristics of organizational change— a readiness assessment for compensation and organizational change.
- Communicating and implementing an executive compensation strategy.

14.2 THE RELATIONSHIP BETWEEN COMPENSATION STRATEGY AND ORGANIZATIONAL CHANGE

Compensation strategy is an overused, and often abused, term, not unlike such terms as *pay for performance, reengineering,* and *management by objectives.* These are quite often popularized but are seldom uniformly agreed to or fully defined. We would like to characterize *compensation strategy* along the following key dimensions, and thereby breathe some life into its application to organizational change. In doing so, as it is my belief that the subject of compensation strategy can be an entire book—and often is—we will focus on a few of the characteristics that have significant impact on organizational change:

- *Business assessment.* Compensation strategy begins with an unvarnished look at the business, its mission, where it's headed, and how it's doing. Relatedly, it also begins with an understanding about the standards and expectations of the key people in the organization and how they are doing.
- *Definition of competition.* An assessment of who the competition is for pay purposes, that is, *for attracting and retaining talent.* This is true, not just for today, but based on where (and when) the business is headed, the marketplace may need to be projected over the next several months or years, so that the desired competitive positioning doesn't atrophy.
- *Competitive positioning and mix of pay.* Basically, where the organization wants to position itself against the marketplace (e.g., 40th percentile, 50th percentile, 70th percentile) and how it is going to achieve this positioning based on the weight and relative role of salary, annual incentive/bonus, and/or longer-term compensation. This "positioning" and "mix" of pay often reflects related issues, such as risk/reward relationships, management style, incentive plan design features, recruiting, and selection criteria.

In the recent past there have been some meaningful revisions in rethinking compensation strategy and programs related to organization change. This has been particularly true in shaping compensation program mix and design related to the business stage of the organization. Many organizations have adopted a model that revises compensation program mix predicated on the required organizational changes and subsequent changes in performance measures and emphasis. Some organizations have enhanced the model and related performance measures to include executive/managerial focus, business strategy initiative(s), operating priority(s), and relevant performance measures (Exhibit 14.1 summarizes this model). While many organizations have employed a model like this one, there have been several stumbling blocks. For openers, an organization's top management may do a superb job at developing the appropriate compensation program and mix for its *current* business stage, yet fall short of proactively thinking through compensation design related to the company's strategic business unit's or division's anticipated or

Exhibit 14.1 Compensation Strategy and Business Stage: Change Management Implications.

Business Stage	Start-Up	Growth	Mature	Decline	Renewal
Organizational Characteristics					
Executive/Managerial Focus	*Entrepreneur*	*Marketeer*	*Operating/Administrator*	*Profiteer*	*Visionary*
Business Strategy Initiative(s)	• Heavy research and development • Technology • Market needs • Negative cash flow and profit	• Significant sales growth • Substantial investment • Improve competitive strength	• Sustain market position • Achieve optimal total shareholder value • Continuously improve productivity and quality	• Production capabilities optimized • Generate cash	• Rebuild business • Selective product/market focus • Increase market share/level sales growth
Operational Priority(s) and Performance Measures	• Completion of product/project implementation • Establish market share • Working capital	• Sales and return on sales • Market value and improve market share • Earnings	• Manufacturing and operating efficiencies • Cost control conscious • Profit margin • Cash flow	• Operating efficiencies (lean and mean) • Reengineering • Squeeze cash flow • Earnings	• Market penetration/share • Return on sales • Selective earnings measure
Compensation Strategy					
Base Salary	• Relatively Low	• Competitive	• Competitive–High	• Competitive	• Competitive
Short-Term Incentive	• Moderate	• High	• Moderate–High	• Moderate–High	• Moderate
Long-Term Incentive Capital Accumulation	• High	• Moderate–High	• Low–Moderate	• Low	• Moderate–High
Change Management and Communication Implications	• Create vision and cultural values • Reinforce acceptance of change • Solidify manager/professional selection criteria	• Build infrastructure • Efficiently use resources • Maintain organizational commitment and enthusiasm as organization is initially exposed to formalized policies and procedures	• Reinforce continuous improvement process and quality • "Reinvent" the business and reexamine core executive competencies • Infuse entrepreneurial characteristics into stable environment	• Create a sustained focus on value creation and free up assets that are not value creators • Focus on retaining and motivating organization "stalking horses"	• View the future through the present • See and build possibilities in chaos and decline • Achieve sustained commitments from top and middle management • Act boldly regarding "sideline players"

next most likely business stage. This leads to significant frustration among executives, managers, and the key employees in managing change because the reward system is tied to past priorities and values, while the current or prospective business stage suggests revised performance themes and values. This "shift" can further result in confusion related to performance expectations and cultural values and related low tolerance for ambiguity, consequently leading to resistance to change.

Related to the integration of compensation strategy to changing business stages, strategies, operation focus, and so on, what was necessary in the past is no longer sufficient for the future. That is to say, there is an emerging role of executives and managers in creating and managing change as characterized by organizational and managerial values, performance and change management focus, and on pay strategy itself, as summarized in Exhibit 14.2.

Exhibit 14.2   Emerging Role of Executive in Integrating Compensation and Communication Strategy with Organizational Change.

	Traditional	Emerging
Performance and Change Management Focus	• Implementing well-planned goals and objectives. • Superb professional/ technical skills. • Strong operationally or functionally. • Represents organization by professionalism and fairness.	• Leads by demonstrating organizational values and attributes in everyday work— a "stakeholder" mindset. • Creates and communicates cost of not changing (as changes are necessary) and articulates benefits and risks of changing. • Has a plan and knows where he or she is against that plan. • Understands, accepts, and demonstrates that *managing change* is at the top of the job description.
Compensation Strategy Management Focus	• Pay for achievement of performance goals and objectives related to company financial measures and individual "MBOs." • Integrate attraction, retention and motivation objective with compensation programs.	• Defining purpose of salary increase, annual and/or long-term initiatives to reinforce specific and separate "message." • Integrate "stakeholder" partnership, team, and cost-effectiveness objectives into compensation program. • Reinforcing change management with compensation element, meaningfully and *consistently.* • Using self-development as a basis and measure of reward. • Consistently and regularly diffuse entitlement.

14.3   DEVELOPING A COMMUNICATION STRATEGY TO SUPPORT AND DRIVE BEHAVIOR

Having a clear picture of the organization's desired state is critical in designing and implementing an executive compensation strategy that will create organizational change. Communicating the desired state, and the risks or costs associated with not achieving the desired state, is a requirement for effectively creating change.

Developing any communication strategy requires discussion and agreement on the following issues:

- Messages
  - What are the key messages?
  - What are the potential content points of the communication?
- Audiences
  - Who are the audiences?
  - What knowledge must be delivered to the audiences?
  - What existing attitudes and perceptions need to be addressed?
  - What are the desired behaviors as a result of the communication and change initiative?
- Media
  - What communication media will be used?
- Timing and resources
  - What is the timing of the communication rollout and the change? What are the key phases of the rollout?
  - What resources will be required to implement the communication strategy?

Effectively motivating people to change requires more than providing accurate and timely information, however. An effective communication strategy involves four critical components, all of which are required in order for change to occur successfully: Listening, Informing, Leading, and Involving [LILI] (see Exhibit 14.3):

1. *Listening* to the ideas and concerns of the executives is vital to learning about the current state and how it is perceived. Listening also helps in uncovering misunderstandings, missing information, or concerns about which the organization is unaware. Finally, listening is a valuable step in developing targeted messages and media that will motivate executives to behave in ways that will create the desired state of the business.

2. *Involving* executives in driving change makes them architects of change rather than bystanders. Involving requires building agreement or buy-in from

Exhibit 14.3   LILI: A Model for Effective Communication Strategy.

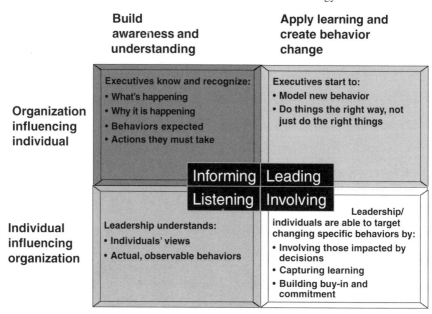

the executives on the rewards of changing and the cost of not changing. For example, a major technology company refocused its compensation strategy so that it was aligned with its business strategy of selling total technology services solutions. Executives who embraced this change and met the new performance targets received the monetary rewards paid by the incentive plan; however, these executives also received recognition from the CEO in streaming video featured on the company's Intranet. In this case, compensation and communication celebrating performance directly involved executives in making the change happen.

3. *Leading* is one of the most important components of a communication strategy. Leading is communicated primarily through actions and behaviors. Leaders and executives must demonstrate new behaviors in their work and in the ways in which they communicate with each other and the employees who report to them. As in the example noted under "Involving," tying executive compensation to the business strategy and then publicly recognizing executives whose performance supports the business strategy is a powerful way of highlighting leadership that helps drive change.

4. *Informing* is vital, but not sufficient to be successful in creating change; however, informing is where most communication efforts are focused and where many communication strategies stop. Opportunities to apply learning and create change are missed. Simply informing audiences without listening,

involving, and leading can lead to misinformation and misunderstanding by executives or employees regarding what they are expected to do. For example, a consumer products company implemented an employee stock option plan as a means to share company performance with employees while providing employees with an opportunity to build savings for the future. The company wanted employees to view the options as a long-term investment that could supplement their retirement savings. Unfortunately, employees were exercising their options and selling the underlying shares as soon as their options became vested.

In this case, listening helped the company to identify the reasons for this behavior and refine the communication strategy. In focus groups, employees said that they thought they were supposed to exercise their options and sell the shares as soon as possible. Employees drew this conclusion from communication that focused on "informing" about how stock options work, particularly on how the exercise process works. The company believed that the process of exercising options is complicated and therefore it felt compelled to thoroughly explain how to exercise options. The focus groups also revealed that employees viewed the stock option plan as a convenient source of cash, rather than as a retirement savings vehicle. The company refocused its communication efforts on positioning the stock option plan as a long-term investment and savings opportunity.

14.4   COMMUNICATING AND IMPLEMENTING AN EXECUTIVE COMPENSATION STRATEGY

In developing a communication strategy, it is important to leverage each of the four components of the LILI model to identify communication tactics to support each component. Exhibit 14.4 provides examples of tactics to support each component of the strategy.

At a minimum, a strategy for communicating executive compensation should inform executives of:

- The reason the compensation program or plan exists and how the plan supports the overall business strategy.
- How the plan works, complete with an example illustrating potential award amounts and how they might be affected by various performance achievements.
- What happens to plan participation and potential payments if an executive leaves the organization, transfers to another business unit not eligible for the plan, retires, or dies.
- Administrative governance issues.

Exhibit 14.4   LILI: Effective Communication Strategy at Work.

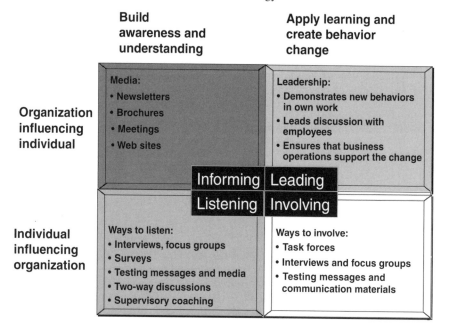

	Build awareness and understanding	Apply learning and create behavior change
Organization influencing individual	Media: • Newsletters • Brochures • Meetings • Web sites	Leadership: • Demonstrates new behaviors in own work • Leads discussion with employees • Ensures that business operations support the change
	Informing	Leading
	Listening	Involving
Individual influencing organization	Ways to listen: • Interviews, focus groups • Surveys • Testing messages and media • Two-way discussions • Supervisory coaching	Ways to involve: • Task forces • Interviews and focus groups • Testing messages and communication materials

While informing executives is critical, however, real change depends on the degree to which other components of the communication strategy are employed as well.

Executive compensation and an effective communication strategy go hand in hand in facilitating organizational change. For example, a major logistics and transportation company determined that to achieve its goals for long-term growth, the company needed to attract investors by focusing on and delivering long-term value to its shareholders. To support its new business strategy, the company implemented a new long-term incentive program for corporate and business unit executives that pays rewards based on measures linked to total shareholder return. The long-term incentive plan pays awards in a mixture of cash and company stock based on rolling three-year performance periods.

Rather than focusing its communication efforts only on informing executives about the new long-term incentive plan, the company took the opportunity to develop a strategy for communicating "total compensation" to its executives. The communication strategy focused key messages on the executive's value to the organization and the executive's critical role in making successful change happen for the company and its shareholders. The communication also rein-forced that executives are, in fact, shareholders as well. This communication also became an effective means of informing the Board of Directors and the compen-sation committee about the compensation strategy.

Along with communication about the compensation program, executives participated in training and ongoing meetings designed to help them develop business plans for their organizations that support the value creation business strategy. The business planning process and the performance measures in the incentive plan directly involved executives in driving organizational change.

Exhibit 14.5 illustrates some of the tactics included in the communication strategy for this particular company.

14.5 LINKAGE OF COMPENSATION TO THE ORGANIZATION'S CULTURE

Should the basis for compensation changes (a.k.a. rewards) relate exclusively to quantifiable business and individual performance? For all the superb progress made in recent years in tying pay to performance, shareholder, and economic value, as well as external organizational performance metrics/benchmarks, to say nothing of individual executive and manager achievements that integrate with a business plan, the answer to this provocative question is *not necessarily!* For example, certain qualitative dimensions of executive performance can, and

Exhibit 14.5   An Executive Compensation Communication Strategy.

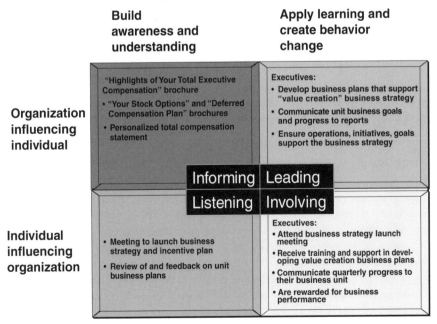

should, be quite significant. An executive who achieves substantial progress against revenue, market share, or profit goals at the risk of alienating subordinates, peers, and other important constituencies, such as Board members, may not be performing consistently with the organization's model for managerial success. It is imperative that the organization's formal and informal managerial success criteria be developed and communicated. These criteria are sometimes referred to as a managerial model "reflecting" the mission and cultural values of an organization. To create the desired behavior, it is imperative to tie some form of compensation to the "managerial model" or "cultural template" to both increase and enhance overall quantitative performance.

An example comes to mind of a likable, loyal, results-driven, overachieving, and very business-focused division head of a diversified company. This executive participated in a newly created, highly leveraged annual incentive program that paid out based on the division's achievement of profit and revenue targets. The division head surpassed all his goals, setting profit and revenue records along the way, and received the largest bonus of his life, virtually tripling his highest award of the past and maximizing the company's plan payout.

Several months later, after learning of his success, and as I was visiting his boss, the organization's CEO, I stopped by the division head's office to pay my respects (and to congratulate him on his past success). I found his office dark and virtually empty—he was being outplaced! Needless to say, I asked the CEO what happened, and he related the following saga.

It appeared that every other week the division head and a corporate functionary were at odds over one matter or another. One example found both the division head and the chief financial officer arguing about capital expenditures, which had a significant impact on the profit plan (the CEO had to intervene). The next month, the vice-president of Human Resources (HR) and the division head were "debating" about the division head's insistence on bringing in a key manager whose salary would be very close to, or as much as, the manager's boss and clearly higher than potential peers of similar standing and more experience (without a willingness on the division head's part to listen to alternatives). At any rate, it seemed to the CEO that he had to wear a striped shirt and whistle to these and other related "meetings" to referee the outcomes.

Two of the five key subordinates left the division, one of whom was the division head's identified successor, because they believed they were being too "quantitatively driven" to exceed monthly, quarterly, etc., plans.

A key member of the operating committee of the Board became alienated because the division head, while having positive results and fresh ideas, was not informed of significant planned policy and process changes before a Board meeting, as requested. And so the story went. The CEO was basically telling me two things: (1) The annual incentive plan worked too well. It achieved highly desirable short-term goals at the cost of longer-term goals but, more relevant to our pay strategy theme, (2) it did not reflect any assessment of the organization's cultural values. In fact, these values were changing due to "renewal" of the business, but were never fully communicated or tied to compensation.

Strategic communication and implementation of the plan can help increase the overall effectiveness of the compensation and business strategy. For example, the CEO was articulating a set of corporate values that could be captured in the following managerial model:

- Be capable of interpersonally stepping on someone's shoes without ruining their shine. That is, be able to influence others (e.g., colleagues) without abrading them (leading, listening, and involving, in our communication model, Exhibit 14.3).
- Bring in fresh talent without alienating key retainers (involving and listening).
- Represent yourself and the organization well to several important publics (e.g., the Board, the financial and local community, employees) (leading).
- Be successful and help others succeed in "institutionalizing" success (leading and involving).
- Have a plan, know where you are against that plan, but remember that "the package and the substance are important" (informing, leading).
- Be adaptive to different and changing business conditions and expectations (leading, listening).

To bring us up to date on the compensation side of the story, the CEO kept the annual incentive plan the same; however, he based salary increases and annual management development planning sessions on behavior/performance against the managerial model. In subsequent months, he modified the annual incentive plan to include a noticeable percentage increase (or decrease) based on implementation of major organization change initiatives. As changes in the business and company's cultural values occurred, the CEO used the compensation strategy to measure their progress and, in essence, leveraged managerial power in driving performance, culture, and change as appropriate.

14.6   THE MESSAGE OR PURPOSE OF COMPENSATION ELEMENTS

As significant as it is for a pay strategy to reflect the clarity or changes in an organization's cultural values, it is at least as important to define and reinforce the intention and the message of each compensation element—base salary increase, short-term/annual incentive, and longer-term/capital accumulation plans, such as stock options and performance unit plans. A pay strategy that "gives two or three bones for the same trick" (i.e., providing salary increase and bonuses for the same performance achievements) can produce unrealistic expectations. While it is important for executives to form a shareholder's point of view, it is also necessary to manage expectations and status. An incentive program can be used as a means of focusing executive attention on specific financial objectives or implementing a major organizational change initiative; however, if a "merit increase" is also used to reflect similar performance, mixed messages could result, as well as blurred expectations on the part of the executive.

Presuming that the intention of each element of pay is clear and separate, there is an additional and significant opportunity in using compensation strategy to deliver the appropriate message(s)—and that is in the area of organizational change. All too often, an organization attempts to undergo business or cultural change initiatives, or both, without tangibly reinforcing them through compensation. Those who embrace the change, whether reflective of a new organizational value, a restructuring of the company, a shift in business direction, launching a new or revised product, or even implementing a performance-oriented incentive plan, often feel used. These organizationally committed executives feel used because they often work alongside many contemporaries who are "sideline players." These sideline players understand that if the change is ignored, nothing will happen to them—that it's probably better to be a "late adapter," to wait until the momentum and *risk* are gone, and then get into the game and become a champion of change. The moral of the story is: The real champions of change get demoralized and the sideline players share in the reward of change without any risk. Worse yet, the more enthusiastic sponsors of change have to overcome the passive (and sometimes active) resistance to change.

Part of the problem or dilemma is that in most organizations today key players have to be permanently "change ready," and it is difficult for traditional compensation programs to "catch up" with organizational changes in dynamic companies, let alone be proactive. Therefore, there is no congruence between the organization's changing values, changing business goals, individual/team performance expectations, and pay. A workable, congruent *performance contract* is missing.

A sound pay strategy therefore can use the purpose or "message" of compensation, such as salary increase or bonus, to reward for implementing the change, even if it means more frequent performance planning and appraisal cycles and payouts, or prorating rewards on the basis of changing goals, performance expectations, and other factors. It presents a great opportunity to use the pay strategy to buttress or support the organizational changes and manage them, not the other way around.

The risk in not applying this concept is too great, because when the fundamental organizational direction and/or values change, so does the fundamental performance contract between the executive and the organization. Either the organization fails or the executives are weeded out. Defining and carrying out the necessary message of compensation can be an appropriate step or early warning sign (i.e., no salary increase and/or no bonus) before the weeding-out stage.

14.7   LINKING COMPENSATION PROGRAMS TO CHARACTERISTICS OF ORGANIZATION CHANGE— A READINESS ASSESSMENT

Organizational change has several key characteristics that compensation strategy and program design can facilitate. While there are a myriad of considerations for organizational change, for compensation purposes, most organizations have to deal with certain "givens" or "anchor points," which include the following:

- Organizational change usually results in unwelcomed and sometimes unanticipated cost(s) to the company.
- This cost is in the form of resistance to change. A company can try to control or dilute the cost, but the cost must be addressed.
- To be effective, organizational change requires a "cascading commitment" from top management, or the author of change, through the senior and middle leadership of the organization, to whomever or whatever the change is to affect. Without this "cascading commitment," implementation of a change will become dissipated or de minimus.
- Another cost, that of remaining the same (i.e., not changing), must be greater than the cost of changing. In time of stress (which organizational change often causes), many managers and employees will cling to historical values and resist change. Some will appear well intentioned, very active, and energized (not unlike a New York city cab driver whom I once asked to "step on it" to the airport, while I buried my head in a report that required my attention, without telling him which airport—he made great time, but didn't know where he was going, and I was delivered to the wrong airport). Organizational change causes this unfocused, high energy (often described as *active resistance*), which must be channeled.

The costs of resistance to change and not changing and the lack of a cascading commitment to implementing change result in numerous blockages to change and related problems (e.g., missed opportunities, poor morale, ineffective leadership).

Effective compensation management can facilitate organizational change such as revised emphasis on strategic focus and performance goals, reorganization, shifts in cultural value, and modification of managerial behavior. Exhibit 14.6 presents the compensation and compensation-related strategies, tactics, and tools that have proved helpful in companies that have successfully managed change.

Finally, while organizational change is being implemented, continuously acknowledge efforts made, recognize achievements/progress gained, and underscore value gained from implementing change versus the cost of not implementing change.

Exhibit 14.6   Effective Techniques for Managing Organizational Change.

Organizational Change Problem	Compensation/Communication Remedy/Tool
Resistance to change	• Define measurable criteria and tie incentive compensation to implementation of change. • Use communication tools such as plan highlights, brochures, and supervisory coaching (be definitive about measurable criteria). • Demonstrate that cost of not changing is greater than cost of changing. • Create team incentive and performance measurement to create positive peer pressure. • Include changed cultural values as part of salary review or management development process.
Sideline players won't positively or actively participate as change implementation team	• Develop longer-term incentive plan criteria to reinforce potential payout risks/opportunities. • Use 360-degree or peer assessment as performance appraisal program. • Use more frequent or "spot" incentive awards. • *Communicate* the design and purposes of compensation programs that measure change implementation. • Consistently and clearly illustrate compensation. • Ensure that "champions of change" have a meaningful stake, with significant compensation opportunities.
Real or fabricated confusion regarding change, lack of focus, increased defensiveness/ insecurity	• Communicate through top management and senior leadership, expected outcomes of change. • Clarify for employees roles/expectations through updated job descriptions. • Use focus groups to discuss and communicate long-term compensation value of program. • Discuss specifically what can be done to increase performance/ enhance value.

14.8   CONCLUSION

Modifying and communicating pay strategy to manage the ongoing reality and costs of change will facilitate the organization's ability to use the winds of change to navigate anticipated and extraneous business conditions. One of the keys to the success of a pay strategy and the desired organizational change is a communication strategy built on:

• Informing executives about the strategy.
• Listening for attitudes and perceptions.
• Involving executives in the change.
• Leading them in demonstrating the desired behaviors necessary for change.

Chapter 15

Transaction-Related Compensation Arrangements

Carol Silverman, JD

Companies in the midst of a transaction or restructuring—be it a merger, divestiture, spinoff, or reorganization—risk losing key employees and jeopardizing their ability to recruit critical talent. Employees may be reluctant to remain with the company through a disruptive process because they fear losing their jobs, and potential employees may be reluctant to accept job offers during uncertain times unless they are offered special incentives for doing so. Companies often seek professional advice regarding what is "reasonable" and "appropriate" to put in place to prevent a mass exodus and to protect those for whom there will be no position after the transaction or restructuring is consummated.

In such situations, there is a menu of possibilities to consider, including "parachute" (change-in-control) and severance programs, "stay" (retention) bonuses, and "sale" (transaction) bonuses. The decision about whether to implement all, some, or none of these programs should be based on the particular issues and challenges facing the company in question. In addition, companies need to decide how outstanding annual and long-term incentive awards should be treated.

This chapter provides guidance to companies that are either in the midst of or are planning ahead for the possibility of a transaction or restructuring. While some of the issues discussed, like retention, may seem more pressing in a booming economy, they are relevant in a down market as well because talented employees will almost always have alternative opportunities. Section 1 provides an overview of change-in-control and severance programs, retention and transaction bonuses, and alternative treatments for outstanding incentive awards. Sections 2 through 4 describe the specific provisions typically included in each respective type of arrangement. Section 5 covers corporate governance considerations.

15.1 OVERVIEW OF TRANSACTION-RELATED COMPENSATION ARRANGEMENTS

(a) Change-in-Control and Severance Programs

Change-in-control programs typically offer generous benefits to senior management in connection with a change in ownership or management of an organization. Usually, but not always, these so-called golden parachute benefits are contingent upon the executive's termination of employment (including "constructive termination").

Change-in-control programs may also offer benefits to less senior executives and nonmanagement employees in connection with a change in ownership or management. Because they are less generous than golden parachutes, these arrangements are commonly referred to as silver parachutes.

Broad-based severance programs, commonly referred to as tin parachutes, offer more modest benefits to all employees or to all nonunion employees. These benefits often cover employment terminations whether or not there is a change in ownership or management, although they are often enhanced if there is a change in ownership or management.

(b) Retention and Transaction Bonuses

When a transaction or restructuring is on the horizon or when, for some reason, a company is facing turbulent times, special incentive programs are often implemented. They may be adopted when a company "puts itself on the block" for a possible sale, at the request of an acquirer after a deal is signed, or by an acquirer after a deal is consummated. This is very different from the optimal timing for adopting change-in-control and severance programs, which is *before* a transaction is imminent. These special—transaction-related—incentives include retention bonuses, commonly referred to as "stay" bonuses, and transaction bonuses, commonly referred to as "sale" bonuses. For purposes of this chapter, the goal of a stay bonus is retention of key employees through, and possibly after, a sale, and the goal of a sale bonus is to provide incentives for key employees to help make a sale happen.

When stay bonuses are necessary, they are usually extended to critical employees at all levels of an organization. Unlike parachutes, they are not geared toward senior management. In fact, if senior management is adequately protected by change-in-control programs, they may not also be covered by stay bonus programs. This is a company- and individual-specific decision.

Sale bonuses are usually targeted toward executives who have a real ability to influence the sale process.

(c)   Treatment of Incentive Awards

In addition to evaluating the need for transaction-related incentives, companies also need to think about how outstanding incentive awards should be treated. For annual and long-term cash incentive plans, companies need to make decisions such as whether award payments should be accelerated, whether they should be prorated, and whether performance goals require adjustment. For equity plans, the issues typically center on whether vesting of awards should be accelerated, whether awards should be cashed out or "rolled over," and, if they are "rolled over," whether the number of shares and exercise prices need to be adjusted to keep employees "whole." Obviously, the nature of the transaction influences the range of alternatives available to the employer.

15.2   CHANGE-IN-CONTROL AND SEVERANCE PROGRAMS

(a)   Executive Change-in-Control Programs

Of all of the transaction-related arrangements discussed in this chapter, executive change-in-control programs have become the most formulaic. Consequently, "typical" market practice is easy to identify and describe.

(i) Purpose   Change-in-control programs offer benefits to executives in connection with a change in ownership or management of an organization. Initially such protections were motivated by a desire to decrease the risk of a hostile takeover by making an acquisition of a company more expensive. Thus, they were considered to be an adjunct to a "poison pill"; however, events have shown that change-in-control programs rarely, if ever, prevent an acquisition from occurring. Instead, in the current environment of frequent, often friendly, mergers and acquisitions, such programs sometimes result in a windfall and substantially increase the bargaining power vis-à-vis the acquirer of executives who are viewed as critical to the success of the surviving company.

Supporters of change-in-control protections believe that they serve the following purposes:

*   During periods of uncertainty, they encourage executives to direct their attention to the company's affairs and reduce the possibility that executives will direct their attention toward seeking other employment.
*   They enable executives to evaluate acquisition proposals more objectively without regard to personal considerations, such as continued employment with the acquirer.
*   They improve the likelihood of recruiting new executives because they guarantee a level of protection even if the company is sold shortly after the executive is hired.

- They help preserve shareholder value in cases where management team continuity through a transition period is important.

Opponents of change-in-control protections believe that they simply entrench management at considerable expense to shareholders.

(ii) Triggers   Change-in-control protections can be:

- "Single trigger"—Provide payments and benefits automatically upon a change in control or upon a voluntary termination by the executive for any reason after a change in control.
- "Double trigger"—Require that there be both a change in control and a subsequent termination of employment, either by the company without "cause" or by the executive for "good reason" (i.e., a constructive termination).
- "Modified single trigger"—Like a double trigger except that the executive also has the right to terminate for any reason during a limited window period after a change in control (e.g., anytime during the 30-day period after the first anniversary of the change in control).

Typically, definitions of "cause" are drafted extremely narrowly, rarely include failure to perform properly on the job and, in the case of the most senior officers, often require a finding of cause by a "super majority" (e.g., two-thirds) of the Board of Directors before termination. A typical definition might read as follows:

> A written resolution of two-thirds of the Board of Directors to the effect that one of the following conditions is met:
>
> (1) Executive's willful and continued failure substantially to perform his duties under the agreement (other than as a result of total or partial incapacity due to physical or mental illness or as a result of termination by executive for Good Reason) after notice and opportunity to cure;
>
> (2) any willful act or omission by executive constituting dishonesty, fraud or other malfeasance, and any act or omission by executive constituting immoral conduct, which in any such case is injurious to the financial condition or business reputation of the company or any of its affiliates;
>
> (3) Executive's conviction of a felony, or a plea of *nolo contendere* to a felony charge, under the laws of the United States or any state thereof or any other jurisdiction in which the company conducts business; or
>
> (4) breach by executive of any restrictive covenant to which executive is subject.
>
> For purposes of this definition, no act or failure to act shall be deemed "willful" unless effected by the executive not in good faith and without a reasonable belief that such action of failure to act was in or not opposed to the company's best interests.

Executives are often given a limited period to "cure" the behavior that triggered the termination after receiving written notice of the behavior.

In contrast to definitions of cause, definitions of "good reason" for senior executives tend to be drafted broadly. A typical definition might include all or almost all of the following:

- Material diminution in the executive's title, position, status, duties or responsibilities, or the assignment to the executive of duties that are inconsistent, in a material respect, with the scope of duties and responsibilities associated with the executive's position
- Removal from, or failure to reelect, to current position
- Reduction in base salary
- Failure to continue existing incentive, retirement, and welfare plans or to provide equivalent plans or failure to maintain the executive's level of participation in such plans
- Relocation of principal workplace without consent to a location more than a specified number of miles from its current location
- Failure to obtain the consent of a successor to assume the agreement
- Material breach by the company of any of its obligations under the agreement

Contracts particularly favorable to executives will specify that a good-faith determination by an executive that he or she has good reason is sufficient to trigger rights to severance upon termination. Companies are often given a limited period to "cure" the behavior that led to the termination after receiving written notice of the behavior.

Practically speaking, for a chief executive officer (CEO) there may be no difference between a single trigger and a double trigger if the transaction is a merger. That is because a merger or acquisition will almost always result in good reason—triggering the right to terminate employment and collect severance—for at least one of the two CEOs unless he or she becomes the CEO of the successor company and the successor company is at least comparable to the acquired company. With other senior executives, this will be more of a facts-and-circumstances test and could very well turn on the good reason definition. For example, if you are a CFO of a public company that is acquired and operated as a subsidiary, this could be considered an adverse change in responsibilities or a demotion that constitutes good reason and triggers the right to terminate employment and receive severance.

(iii) Severance Payments and Benefits   Change-in-control protections typically provide for the following payments and benefits:

- Accrued unpaid salary and benefits (e.g., accrued vacation) to date of termination
- Any prior-year bonus earned but not paid
- Pro-rata bonus for current year (based on target bonus, maximum bonus, prior years' bonus, average bonus over three prior years, etc.)
- Payment equal to a multiple of base salary plus bonus (based on either target bonus, maximum bonus, prior years' bonus, average bonus over three prior years, etc.)
- Payment equal to a multiple of annual defined contribution plan matching contributions
- Accelerated vesting, and sometimes "cashing out" of options, restricted stock, and other long-term performance awards
- Accelerated vesting, and sometimes "cashing out," of deferred compensation and supplemental executive retirement plan (SERP) benefits
- Additional age and service credit during the "severance period" for purposes of pension calculation under SERP plus recognition of severance payment for purposes of calculating "pay"
- Welfare benefit continuation during the severance period (subject to mitigation if subsequently employed by another employer)

In the case of both large and small companies and across industries, with the exception of the technology sector, for senior executives (e.g., proxy-named executive officers), the typical multiple used to compute severance is three times, and the period during which benefits are continued is three years. For other executives and key employees, one times or two times is fairly standard, with benefit continuation paralleling the severance multiple (e.g., a one times multiple and continuation of benefits for one year). In the technology sector, where equity compensation has been emphasized, a two times multiple is more typical than a three times multiple even for senior executives. This has also been true for highly cyclical companies for a long time, such as the semiconductor and personal computer (PC) businesses. It will be interesting to see if this trend changes in reaction to the recent market downturn.

(iv) Change-in-Control Definitions   "Change-in-control" definitions typically include:

- The acquisition by a third party of a specified percentage of the company's voting stock
- A merger or acquisition
- A change in a majority of the composition of the Board of Directors of the company

- A sale of all or substantially all of the assets of the company
- Adoption by the company's shareholders of a plan of liquidation

The following is a discussion of potential issues surrounding the definition of a change in control:

1. *When should an acquisition by a third party constitute a change in control?* Change-in-control protections should take effect when there is a true shift in the balance of power. For most public companies, that is a percentage below 51%, whereas, for many private companies, the percentage is 51% or above. For public companies, third-party acquisition triggers are fairly equally divided between 20%, 25%, and 30%; however, public companies with a controlling shareholder tend to require a significantly higher acquisition percentage. The appropriate percentage in such a situation should be determined on a case-by-case basis, based on a reasonable assessment of how many shares a third party would need to acquire to be able to exercise significant influence over management.

2. *What to do in a "merger of equals" situation.* Companies should carefully consider whether a "merger of equals" or other similar transaction should trigger a change in control or whether there should be exceptions for transactions where the existing shareholders continue to control the company following the transactions. For example, a definition might exclude a transaction where no third party has acquired more than the specified percentage of the company (as discussed previously), and the shareholders of the company will control the Board of Directors and maintain a controlling percentage of the voting securities of the post-transaction company. For this exception, the most common percentages are 51% and 60%.

3. *Shareholder approval versus consummation of the transaction.* Some companies provide that shareholder (or Board) approval of a transaction (as opposed to consummation of the transaction) is sufficient to trigger a change in control. While this definition may not be a problem in a change-in-control program with a double trigger, it can lead to serious retention issues and windfalls to employees if equity vests upon the shareholder approval, particularly where regulatory approval is required, and there is a real risk that the transaction could fall through. In fact, this exact situation was highly publicized and criticized when the intended merger of Sprint and Worldcom was called off (this issue is discussed in greater detail in Section 4).

4. *Potential change in control.* Another question is whether executives should be protected if their employment is terminated in the event of a *potential* change in control such as the announcement of a tender of offer or the acquisition by a third party of a smaller percentage of the company's stock than is necessary to constitute a change in control. Justifications for this include the risk

that employees can be vulnerable to losing jobs long before a transaction is consummated, especially in bitter and hotly contested contests culminating in protracted litigation or in industries where there are significant regulatory hurdles to closing.

5. *Inadvertent triggers.* Companies should also be aware that, in this age of holding companies, reverse triangular mergers, and the like, unless definitions are drafted with care, a change in control might be triggered inadvertently by the form (as opposed to the substance) of a transaction (i.e., the target appears to be the surviving company). Under some circumstances, change-in-control protections at both the target and the acquirer could be triggered.

(v) Golden Parachute Tax Penalties   Section 280G of the Internal Revenue Code (IRC) applies to "parachute payments." Parachute payments are any payments made to "disqualified individuals" that are contingent upon (i.e., occasioned or accelerated by) a change in control and that do not qualify as reasonable compensation for services actually rendered *after* the change in control. "Disqualified individuals" are employees, independent contractors, or service providers who are also officers (limited to 50 individuals), significant shareholders (shareholdings valued at $1,000,000 or more), or highly compensated individuals (highest paid 1% of employees or, if less, among the highest paid 250 employees, earning at least $75,000). For purposes of determining whether an employee holds shares with a value of $1,000,000, the full value of the shares underlying vested options are counted and, in most companies, options vest upon a change in control.

If the aggregate present value of all parachute payments equals or exceeds three times the disqualified individual's "base amount" (average annual compensation includable in gross income in the five most recent taxable years), then any amount in excess of the sum of (1) the base amount and (2) all amounts qualifying as reasonable compensation for services rendered *before* the change in control, is an "excess parachute payment." Excess parachute payments are nondeductible to the company and are subject to a nondeductible 20% excise tax imposed on the executive.

Artful drafting (e.g., including requiring significant noncompetition covenants and consulting agreements in exchange for change-in-control benefits) can significantly mitigate the adverse tax consequences of Section 280G, but many companies that offer change-in-control protections do not require noncompetes from their executives. In fact, some companies explicitly provide that noncompetes expire upon a change in control.

Prevalent practice for senior executives outside of the technology sector is to provide for nondeductible "gross-ups" for the federal excise taxes imposed on excess parachute payments. The purpose of the gross-up is to put the executive in the same after-tax position he or she would have been in had Congress never adopted the excise tax, thus defeating the purpose of the legislation. This is accomplished by providing the executive with sufficient additional amounts (the "gross-up amount") to pay (1) the excise and income taxes on the gross-up amount, plus (2) the excise (but not the income) tax on the severance benefits specified in the contract. (The executive is left to pay the income taxes on the severance amount, as would normally be the case.) If an employment agreement provides for a gross-up for the excise tax, the effect can be to almost double the financial liability of the company when the severance payments are triggered.

Alternatives to a full gross-up include:

- *Cap:* Limiting payments to the maximum amount that will *not* trigger the excise tax (the "safe harbor").
- *Modified cap:* Limiting the payments only if the net after-tax amount the executive would receive, after applying the cap, exceeds the net after-tax amount the executive would receive if he or she received the entire amount and paid the excise tax; otherwise, doing nothing.
- *Modified gross-up:* Limiting the payments only if they exceed the safe harbor by less than a specified percentage; otherwise, providing a gross-up.

It is important to realize that a change in control as defined in a company change-in-control program will not necessarily be a change in control under Section 280G and vice versa. Also, payments made by private companies that obtain shareholder approval of change-in-control programs will not be subject to the excise tax.

(vi) Funding and Security Arrangements Some companies prefund change-in-control payments through the use of irrevocable nonqualified trust arrangements of some kind. The most popular kind of nonqualified trust is the so-called rabbi trust. Under a rabbi trust, contributions are neither taxable to covered executives nor deductible by the employer until paid because trust funds remain subject to the claims of the company's creditors in insolvency or bankruptcy proceedings. For the same reason, trust investment income is taxable to the employer. Alternatively, some companies provide that funding through a trust shall take place upon a change in control or that a previously funded but revocable trust shall become irrevocable upon a change in control.

(vii) Silver Parachutes Change-in-control protections for less senior executives and middle management are commonly referred to as silver parachutes. They tend to be similar to the golden parachutes described earlier, except that the multiple of salary and bonus used to compute severance is generally smaller (e.g., one to two times base and bonus instead of two to three times base and

bonus), and single triggers and modified single triggers are less prevalent (with the former being quite rare). In addition, silver parachutes are not as likely to provide for gross-ups and may have somewhat less generous good reason definitions. If golden parachute benefits are funded or secured, the same is generally true for silver parachutes.

(b) Broad-Based Severance Plans

Typically, broad-based severance plans cover employment terminations whether or not a transaction occurs. Most companies use formulas to calculate severance pay. Formulas are most often driven by length of service, salary level, organization level, or a combination of any of these factors. The most common driver is length of service, with salary level and organization level following as distant seconds.

Of those companies that base severance on years of service, one week's pay per year of service is most often used. The next most prevalent formula is two weeks per year of service. Some companies increase payments (e.g., from one to two weeks per year of service) if the employee's length of service exceeds a specified number (e.g., five) years. Another method by which companies calculate severance is to pay a fixed multiple of pay, regardless of length of service or other factors. Most companies consider only base pay in severance calculations. The companies that do include bonus or other incentive pay in the severance package typically prorate the targeted incentive amount. Companies often impose limits regarding the minimum and maximum payouts an employee may receive under the severance program.

Transactions increase the need for severance programs if they will place multiple employees in the job market within a relatively compressed period. Companies that do not have a formal severance policy may want to think about adopting one if a transaction is a real possibility. Other companies might want to amend their existing severance policies to provide for enhanced severance payments if the employment termination is in connection with a change in control. At a minimum, companies should consider negotiating with a potential buyer for severance protection for employees terminated within a specified period (e.g., two years) following a merger or acquisition, and include it as part of the transaction agreement. Broad-based change-in-control severance programs are commonly known as tin parachutes.

15.3 RETENTION AND TRANSACTION BONUSES

(a) Purpose

Special transaction- or restructuring-related retention bonus programs may be adopted under a variety of circumstances. They may come as early as a company deciding to put itself up for sale and as late as the consummation of the sale. They may be targeted at employees who could otherwise trigger lucrative parachute or severance benefits under single trigger, modified single trigger, or good reason provisions. They are provided in addition to normal annual incentives and may, or may not, be based on performance.

The most common justifications for implementing special incentive programs in the face of an actual or potential transaction or restructuring are to:

- Retain key employees before, during, and after a transaction or a restructuring.
- Provide continuity of management.
- Assure employees that their services are valued.
- Reward employees for tolerating turmoil.
- Lend a measure of certainty to an uncertain situation.
- Provide financial security to individuals who may ultimately be terminated.
- In the case of a sale bonus, reward key employees for assisting in the sale and maximizing the proceeds to the company.

Basically, meaningful retention and transaction bonuses allow employees to forego other available job opportunities during uncertain times and concentrate on getting the deal done and the transition complete.

Often, if there are change in control benefits that are applicable to the transaction, covered executives don't need retention or transaction bonuses. However, this will not be true under at least two scenarios. The first is where the transaction won't trigger a change in control (i.e., change in control is defined at the parent level but a subsidiary undergoes a spin-off or a divestiture) and uncertainty runs rampant. The second is where an executive who is needed to stay has a single trigger or modified single trigger change in control agreement that will permit him or her to terminate employment and collect generous severance benefits. Under such circumstances, special incentive programs are likely to be needed to maintain management continuity or retain key contributors, even for the short term. In situations where an excise tax could be triggered under Section 280G and the executive is entitled to a gross-up, companies might also want to "convert" change in control protections into retention bonuses in order preserve the deduction and to avoid triggering the excise tax and gross-up payment discussed in Section 2(e). Executives might waive rights under single triggers, modified single triggers or good reason provisions in their change in control agreements in exchange for incentives that require them to perform certain services following the change in control. The clear economic rationale for doing this is that, while severance could trigger an excise tax obligation, *reasonable* compensation for services rendered *after* a change in control, if properly designed, should not.

(b) Design Considerations

There is no clearly identifiable "market practice" for retention and transaction bonuses and no "one size fits all" approach. This is in stark contrast to golden parachutes, which, as discussed previously, have become fairly formulaic for top executives. In fact, examples can almost always be found to support any type and magnitude of award, no matter how large or small. Consequently, although competitive practices should be considered, success requires tailoring features to meet the company's needs, as well as employee expectations and needs.

Retention and transaction bonuses provide employees who are key to the transaction's success with a compensation opportunity tied to continued service in order to encourage such employees to stay around and make the deal happen. If they are to accomplish this purpose, bonuses should:

*   Offer compensation opportunities that are significant, logical within the context of past practices, and sufficiently large to offset the uncertainty and risk associated with the transaction.
*   Be linked to the expected timing of the transaction or restructuring.
*   Consider pre- and post-transaction organizational culture issues.

The structure may be based on past, current, or future service.

(i) Retention Period   The retention period is the length of time that the employee must remain with the company in order to receive the bonus. It commences on the date the retention program is initiated and extends either for a specified absolute period (e.g., two years)—a retention bonus—or for a period relative to the occurrence of an event or transaction—a transaction bonus. In the latter case, the relative period might be until the occurrence of the transaction (e.g., merger, acquisition, divestiture, emergence from bankruptcy) or for some specified period after the event.

Retention periods should balance the need of an employer to retain an employee for a certain length of time with the risk that too long of a time horizon will cause employees to place too small a value on the benefit. Retention periods typically range from less than one to five years, with most being one to three years. Executives are more likely to be paid benefits over longer periods, with other employees seeing their rewards sooner.

(ii) Who Should Be Covered?   The number of employees receiving retention/transaction bonuses varies widely. At one extreme, only one executive might be covered. At the other extreme, all employees might be covered. Generally, companies fall in the middle, although because public filings require only the disclosure of executive bonuses, the number of nonexecutive employees receiving such bonuses may be significantly understated in public disclosures. Companies

that cover a large number of employees sometimes disclose the aggregate amount allocated for retention bonuses to nonexecutives.

In selecting individuals who should be covered, companies should first segment the employee population to identify who they need to keep and for how long. Then they should think about what vehicles are available and which of these are most likely to work. Companies tend to pick and choose the individuals who will receive them and the amount to be offered, based on considerations such as:

- How critical the employee is to the successful completion of the transaction or a successful transition period
- The likelihood of resignation
- The existence of an employment contract or severance agreement

Companies might find it surprising that CEOs are often excluded, usually because they are adequately protected by change-in-control agreements.

(iii) Cash versus Equity Although many people tend to associate restricted stock with general retention incentives, cash is actually the favored medium when the incentives are transaction-related, particularly for lower-level employees. Executives are more likely to see stock awards or a combination.

(iv) Individual Retention Amounts Individual retention award opportunities range widely in size (e.g., from 25% of salary to 300% of total annual compensation), depending primarily on organizational level and, in certain sectors like technology, skill set. For senior executives, however, it is becoming increasingly common for retention bonus amounts to mimic golden parachute severance multiples. Transaction bonuses that increase in size as the sale price increases may be appropriate for those who can really influence how well the transaction goes and what value/savings can be achieved.

(v) Service versus Performance Requirements Most retention programs are based on service alone, particularly if they are aimed at a large number of employees; however, many companies also include a performance component, particularly for more senior executives. Performance goals could be tied to things that need to be accomplished for a successful transition. There could be target payments for satisfactory performance and maximum payments (e.g., two times target) for exceptional performance. Nonetheless, in the post-Enron environment they are unlikely to be adopted by public companies because they may be perceived as an incentive for management to manipulate financial statements.

(vi) Payment Schedules Pure transaction bonuses are generally paid in a lump sum upon consummation of the transaction. Companies are fairly equally

divided about whether retention bonuses are paid in a single lump sum or in installments. In our experience, retention bonuses tend to be paid out over one-, two-, or three-year periods. The longer the total retention period, the more likely that a significant portion of the bonus will be paid in installments commencing before the total retention period expires. For example, one-third might be paid on each of the transaction consummation, the six-month anniversary, and the one-year anniversary.

A question that companies might grapple with is whether all or any portion of the bonus should be paid if the transaction or restructuring falls through and, if so, when that payment should be made. In the case of a pure transaction bonus, no amount should be paid. In the case of a retention bonus, companies could consider paying at least one-third of the bonus on a fixed date whether or not the transaction or restructuring has occurred. The date selected should be past the anticipated consummation of the transaction or restructuring at the time the arrangement is entered into.

(vii) Termination of Employment Provisions   Retention bonuses almost always pay out if an executive is terminated without "cause" before the scheduled payment. In some cases, this may also be true of pure transaction bonuses. In addition, companies should consider what types of constructive terminations should also trigger a payment. For executives, the constructive termination triggers are likely to be the same as those described in the discussion of "good reason" provisions in Section 15.2(a)(ii). For other employees, constructive termination is likely to be limited to a decrease in salary and a significant relocation.

Companies that cover executives under both retention and change-in-control programs should consider carefully whether executives should be able to receive payments under both if their employment terminates before the end of the retention period. For the most part, the answer will be no, and the documents should be drafted carefully to include offsets or other provisions that avoid "double dipping."

15.4   TREATMENT OF CASH AND EQUITY INCENTIVES

At the time of a transaction, companies are likely to be in the middle of annual and long-term plan performance cycles. As a result, decisions will need to be made regarding how outstanding annual and long-term incentive awards are to be treated. These decisions are sometimes made when there is no transaction on the horizon and are written into the plan document (as is typical with equity plans and some long-term performance cash plans). Other times, the company decides what to do at the time of the transaction (as is typical in annual incentive plans and some long-term performance cash plans). Although change-in-control programs often address how incentive awards will be treated, certain transactions (e.g., the sale of a division or a subsidiary) that affect the operation of incentive plans may not be covered under change-in-control programs because they do not fall within the definition of a change in control, and of course, most incentive plan participants will not be covered by change-in-control programs.

The following discussion assumes that outstanding awards have value (i.e., in the case of options, they are not underwater and in the case of cash plans, they will pay out at least at minimum). In a down market, companies also need to deal with the possibility that existing awards have no value. Under this scenario, companies should emphasize retention incentives and post-transaction compensation.

(a)   Cash Incentives

For annual incentive plans and cash-based long-term incentive plans, some of the key issues to be addressed (either when the plan is being designed or when the company is facing a potential transaction) include:

- Whether to accelerate awards when the transaction occurs in the middle of the performance cycle or wait until the end of the performance cycle.
- Whether awards should be prorated or paid in full.
- Whether payments should be based on the actual level of period-to-date performance (assuming that can be measured) or a presumed level of performance (e.g., target performance or average of last three incentives).
- If actual period-to-date performance is to be measured, whether goals should be adjusted to reflect the transaction.

Companies in financial difficulty that put themselves up for sale might want to translate annual incentive goals into quarterly goals to provide incentives for employees even if performance in the early quarters is poor.

Usually, cycles are terminated as of the transaction and prorated awards are paid out, based on actual period-to-date performance, if measurable, or target performance if not. Executives covered by change-in-control agreements are often treated more generously under those agreements.

(b)   Equity Incentives

The treatment of equity awards upon a change in control is generally considered when a plan is initially designed and included in the plan document. Conversely, the treatment of equity awards in a transaction that might not be a change in control, such as a spinoff or a divestiture, is rarely covered by the plan document and often results in unfortunate results for employees of the spunoff/divested entities unless special provisions are made for them at the time of the transaction.

(i) Change in Control   If there is a change in control, prevalent practice is to vest stock options, restricted shares, and other long-term incentive awards automatically upon the change in control and not to require a termination of employment (single trigger). As discussed in Section 15.2(a)(iv), if the definition of change in control includes a potential change in control (like the announcement of a transaction) or shareholder approval of a transaction, employees may enjoy windfalls if their options trigger and the transaction is not consummated. It also makes it more difficult to retain employees through the consummation of the transaction because they have the ability to cash in on their awards and go work for a competitor.

In addition to drafting definitions carefully, companies should also think about whether single-trigger vesting, which is a traditional approach with its roots in the "hostile" acquisition era of the 1980s, continues to be appropriate at all. The increasing number of mergers of equals, where companies wish to retain executives after the deal, calls into question the practice of making executives rich at the time of the deal. As a result, particularly in the high-tech arena, there is a growing movement toward double-trigger vesting. With double-trigger vesting, options would continue to vest in their ordinary course and would accelerate only if an employee loses his or her job (which might include a constructive termination). Options would also accelerate if the acquirer refused to "roll over" or "assume" the options post-transaction.

The most desirable provision from a company viewpoint is to give discretion to the committee administering the plan to determine whether to accelerate awards and whether to cash out awards; however, companies were historically advised not to make vesting discretionary and not to provide for cashouts of awards because both the exercise of discretion and payment of cash in exchange for an award would disqualify the transaction from "pooling" treatment for financial accounting and reporting purposes. Although pooling has been effectively eliminated from generally accepted accounting practices (GAAP), companies are still being advised not to make vesting discretionary because of unfavorable accounting treatment under FIN 44 (the new interpretation of APB 25 by the Financial Accounting Standards Board). Discretionary vesting would be considered a "modification" of an outstanding award that could potentially result in a charge to earnings. In the case of options, the charge would be equal to the difference between the exercise price of the option and the fair market value of the shares (i.e., the "spread") on the date of the modification.

Whether or not options are accelerated, if they are assumed by the acquiring company, it is common to adjust outstanding options held by employees to keep them "whole." This is typically done by converting existing options on the acquired company's stock to options on the stock of the acquirer with an equivalent aggregate "spread." Companies should also be aware that, under FIN 44, in a purchase business combination, the accounting treatment of outstanding options that are assumed by an acquirer depends on whether they are vested or unvested at the date of the transaction. See Chapter 18 for a discussion of the accounting treatment.

Generally, options that are significantly underwater (i.e., the exercise price is greater than the fair market value) will not be assumed by an acquiring company. Companies should consult with counsel about whether they can cancel these options without penalty or if some payment (e.g., based on Black-Scholes value) would need to be made.

(ii) Non−Change-in-Control Transactions—Spinoffs It is rare for a plan to provide for automatic vesting upon a spinoff, divestiture, or other restructuring that does not fall within the definition of a change in control. On the contrary, what often happens is that employees of the spunoff or divested entity are treated as having terminated employment at closing under the terms of the plan. This results in the loss of unvested awards and forces them to exercise vested awards within limited post-termination exercise periods. Much depends on the plan's definition of an "eligible participant." For example, eligible participants might be limited to employees of the company or 50%-owned subsidiaries.

In addition, even if the plan would permit the employees to continue to hold shares in the parent company, it might be undesirable from a compensation perspective. From a compensation perspective, the interests of the employees should probably be tied to the success of the spunoff or divested entity.

For all of these reasons, as with mergers, in the case of a spinoff, it is typical to convert outstanding options of the parent company into options on the spunoff entity with an equivalent aggregate spread. This can generally be done without incurring any accounting charges if certain conditions are met. (See Chapter 18 for a discussion of the "ratio and spread" test.) For companies that decide that accelerated vesting is also appropriate (not a majority practice), as discussed in Section 15.4(a) above, this is likely to result in an accounting charge unless the acceleration was provided for in the plan document.

15.5 CORPORATE GOVERNANCE ISSUES

When approving the terms of the types of plans and agreements described in this chapter (particularly if they affect senior executives), directors are exercising fiduciary duties. The compensation committee may retain outside consultants to provide competitive market data in order to assess the appropriateness of the package being offered and to make recommendations based on consulting experiences with other similarly situated companies. Competent legal counsel is also advisable to avoid ambiguity in contract terms that can lead to subsequent unintended misinterpretations and to advise the committee on the process to follow in discharging its fiduciary duties.

The implementation of change-in-control parachute protections in particular should be the subject of careful Board consideration because of the heightened scrutiny they receive from shareholders, investor activists, and potential acquirers. Generally, protections that are implemented at a time when no transactions are on the horizon survive a litigation challenge because of the "business judgment rule," which prevents courts from interfering with the good faith and careful decisions of a company's directors. Conversely, protections implemented in the face of a hostile acquisition are suspect because of the possibility that the requisite good faith and due care may be missing from the Board's deliberations. Directors may be justifiably reluctant to approve parachute protections under such circumstances because of the excessive cost to the company and the fear that such approval may constitute a violation of their fiduciary duties and result in personal liability.

Lawyers and consultants often talk about a general "rule of thumb" based on market practice that payments linked to a transaction (e.g., change in control, retention, severance) should not exceed a certain percentage of the value shareholders receive as a result of a transaction. For a long time, this percentage was 2% to 3%; lately the talk is 3% to 5%.

15.6 CONCLUSION

All of these topics need careful consideration. Some of it can be the subject of careful advance planning and drafting (i.e., change-in-control programs and change-in-control incentive plan provisions). Some of it will, by its nature, have to be dealt with "in the heat of battle" (i.e., retention/transaction bonuses). The common denominator to both situations is having the right team of advisers, combining both experience and technical knowledge, at the table whenever decisions are made.

Chapter 16

Director Compensation

Peter J. Oppermann

In 1995, the National Association of Corporate Directors (NACD) issued a report on Director Compensation. In this report, guidelines for director compensation plans were developed that suggested aligning the interests of shareholders and directors, while providing value to directors for value received from those directors. In 1996, Section 16(b) of the Securities and Exchange Commission (SEC) regulations was amended, allowing directors to make discretionary grants of equity to themselves, removing the restrictions that had most plans granting stock options under a formula approved by shareholders. Since those two events, the stock market has risen sharply, but remained volatile, compensation for chief executive officers (CEOs) and other senior executives (who make up the bulk of directors) has continued to rise, and the demand for qualified independent directors has intensified.

It is no surprise then that director compensation programs have evolved from retainer and meeting fees to sophisticated plans based heavily on equity, with Board and individual director discretion that allows both attraction and reward for talented individuals who guide ever-larger public companies. Add to the uncertain economic times the activism of shareholder groups and the job of director not only entails more time but also intense scrutiny of all decisions. Compensation for that increased time commitment and reward for increasing shareholder value have become the benchmarks of good compensation programs for directors.

16.1 TRENDS IN DIRECTOR COMPENSATION

Based on Mercer studies over the past few years, some important trends in director compensation have arisen:

- Cash compensation (cash retainer, stock retainer, and meeting fees) has risen at a rate similar to the increase in salaries of top executives, around 6% per year. Companies do not change their cash compensation plans annually, but the value of any retainer or meeting fee paid in stock has risen with the market.

- Equity compensation has gone from a minor percentage to a major component of the director package. The value of equity awards, apart from equity granted as replacement for retainer or fees, exceeds 50% of a total package for directors.

- Increased flexibility in plan choices for individual directors, allowing deferrals, payment alternatives in cash, stock, and even options help balance the need for current cash with the desire for greater ties to shareholders.

- Benefit plans, including retirement programs, do not meet the criteria for tying director pay to the interests of shareholder. Consequently, these plans comprise a very small portion of director compensation value, with greatly diminished prevalence.

- The movement of pay for performance in the boardroom has started, with a small but ever-growing contingent tying equity grants to financial or shareholder performance targets.

16.2   NACD GUIDELINES AND CHANGES IN SECTION 16(b)

(a)   NACD Guidelines

The NACD established a Blue Ribbon Commission on Director Compensation in 1995. The guidelines that came out of that commission's report encouraged companies to align shareholders' and directors' interests in the compensation program for directors. In addition, the Commission developed a series of principles to determine best practices of director compensation plans. These five principles are the following:

1. Director compensation should be determined by the Board and disclosed completely to shareholders.

2. Director compensation should be aligned with the long-term goals of shareholders.

3. Director compensation should be used to motivate director behavior.

4. Directors should be adequately compensated for their time and effort.

5. Director compensation should be approached on an overall basis rather than as an array of separate elements.

As a result of these guidelines being published, the alignment of shareholders' and directors' interests have become the focal point of compensation program changes.

(b)   Effect of Section 16(b) on Director Compensation

The acquisition of a stock award by an insider is exempt under Rule 16(b) if the grant meets any one of the following requirements:

- The grant is approved by shareholders.
- The grant is approved by the entire Board of Directors or a committee of the Board composed of two or more nonemployee directors (most typical).
- The grant is not approved at all, but the recipient holds an equity security for six months from the date of grant to the date of its disposition, or in the case of a stock option or other derivative security, the disposition of the underlying security.

A nonemployee director under Rule 16(b) is an individual who is not:

- Currently an employee of the issuer (or affiliate)
- Receiving compensation other than as a director, which would require SEC disclosure (currently $60,000)
- Involved in a business relationship or have an interest in any transaction that would trigger SEC disclosure

Retired executives may serve on the compensation committee. This exemption allows Boards broad discretion in determining the terms of stock compensation to directors. Thus, directors have control over their own awards, including an ability to dispose of the awards either by sale or through a gift transfer. In addition, directors are able to modify provisions of existing plans without seeking shareholder approval. This makes it possible for Boards to make frequent changes to previously adopted plans, whether or not the plans were approved by shareholders.

16.3   ELEMENTS OF DIRECTOR COMPENSATION

(a)   Retainer

Almost all companies in our studies pay an annual retainer to directors, a practice that has been consistent over time. The major determinant of retainer amounts is company size (see Exhibit 16.1).

The greatest change in retainers is not the size but the form; stock has become common in the retainer portion of compensation programs. While only a small percentage of companies pay the entire retainer in stock, almost 40% pay part in cash and part in stock. In the administration of these plans, the equity portion

Exhibit 16.1 Median Annual Retainer
by Company Size.

Sales/Revenues	Annual Retainer
$1.0 to 1.99 billion	$25,000
$2.0 to $4.99 billion	27,750
$5.0 to $9.99 billion	35,000
$10.0 billion or more	42,995
All companies	**34,000**

Source: © Mercer 350-Company Study, 2001.

is most often stated as a dollar amount, with the number of shares changing each year based on the stock price at the time the retainer is paid. While this results in a smaller number of shares when the stock price increases, this arrangement helps to shelter directors from market fluctuations year to year. In addition, these awards are generally made in one of three ways:

1. Unrestricted shares, with the cash portion used to pay any taxes due upon receipt, making the retainer a true equity award. These shares may also be paid quarterly.
2. Restricted stock with a one- to three-year vesting
3. Deferred stock, with payout deferred until retirement

(b) Meeting Fees

While retainers vary by company size, meeting fees are fairly consistent by company size and industry, generally between $1,000 and $1,500 per meeting. The practice of paying a fee to attend a meeting has a twofold purpose: (1) to induce a director to actually attend a meeting and (2) to differentiate pay for those who contribute more versus those who contribute less. A recent trend is to eliminate meeting fees altogether, and instead to increase retainers by an amount equivalent to the annual fees as if all meetings were attended. This additional amount could be paid in cash or stock and is intended to move away from the notion that a director's time is only worth the $1,500 fee.

(c) Committee Pay

Fees for committee membership and committee chairs are common in all industries and company revenues. More than half of the companies Mercer surveyed pay a retainer for committee chairperson and more than 80% pay a fee for attendance at meetings. This practice is intended to help the idea of equal pay for equal work differentiating pay among directors by the amount of time and responsibility they shoulder. Committee work and committee chairs involve substantially more time and, in some cases, greater fiduciary responsibility, requiring larger compensation packages to help induce participation. The amount of retainer paid for committee chairs, however, only ranges from $2,000 to $8,000, with most between $3,000 and $5,000. Committee fees range from $480 to $1,350, with most paying $1,000 per meeting. The differentiation of committee and chair work is not great, and considering the spotlight trained on members of the audit, compensation, and nominating committees by shareholder groups, the compensation may not justify the responsibility. We will begin to see changes regarding this issue in the coming years.

The total amount of cash paid for both Board and committee service will obviously depend on the number of Board meetings and committee memberships and meetings a director may participate in. Exhibit 16.2 gives examples of total annual compensation (TAC) by company sales/revenues. TAC consists of retainer, Board meeting fees, committee meeting fees, and additional chairperson service fees.

(d)   Equity Compensation

As stated earlier, the most noticeable trend, and the element that has had the greatest impact on director compensation is the use of equity in the form of options, restricted stock, or stock units.

Equity in director compensation programs is usually used in any of three ways:

1.   As a stand-alone grant, with the primary purpose of tying a portion of compensation to shareholder returns. In most cases, options are used for this purpose.

2.   As a substitute for some other form of compensation, usually retainer, meeting fees, or committee chair fees or retainers.

3.   As the basis for increased stock ownership by directors.

Exhibit 16.2   Median Total Annual Cash Compensation by Company Size.

Sales/Revenues	Annual Retainer	TAC
$1.0 to 1.99 billion	$25,000	$43,000
$2.0 to $4.99 billion	27,750	48,000
$5.0 to $9.99 billion	35,000	56,000
$10.0 billion or more	42,995	66,500
All companies	**34,000**	**54,000**

Source: © Mercer 350-Company Study, 2001.

(i) Stand-Alone Grants   The use of stock options as an add-on to existing cash programs is typical, with most companies now having stand-alone plans. Stock grants now constitute the majority of directors' pay (see Exhibit 16.3).

Not surprisingly, nonqualified options are the core long-term vehicle, granted under a shareholder-approved plan, generally granted with a fixed number of options each year and possibly a larger number granted upon joining the Board. Vesting is usually short, typically one year, with the only controversy being how far past retirement or resignation a director is allowed to exercise the option. In a few cases, there is no limit other than the term of the option. The rationale is that the director's influence on the performance of the company extends beyond the time he or she serves on the Board, and the director should recognize the rewards for a period of time. Most companies, however, do not extend the exercise period beyond one year.

The percentage of total compensation for a director that comes from stand-alone equity plans varies by industry (see Exhibit 16.4). Those industries that typically compensate executives heavily in equity follow that trend with directors.

While the increase in annual compensation for directors does not increase that dramatically as companies get larger, the size of equity awards does leverage the total compensation package in larger companies (see Exhibit 16.5).

The use of options in smaller private companies continues to be a strong reward for service and a reward for increasing the value of the company. Good examples are in the biotechnology and e-commerce sectors. Many of these start-ups, especially those with venture backing, pay all or most of the compensation value to their directors in the form of options. This method is effective because with no charge to earnings, options represent a cost-effective way of attracting some key Board members. As with any option, however, the value received by a director depends on the stock price increasing, and with these two sectors as good examples, directors may find themselves with no pay for a period of time due to a fluctuating stock market. In contrast, less than 5% of larger public companies pay 100% of their retainer in options.

Exhibit 16.3   Prevalence of Stock for Directors.

Percentage of Companies Offering Any Kind of Equity	1996	1998	2000
	89%	92%	94%
Unrestricted Stock	30	37	36
Restricted Stock	27	29	28
Deferred Stock	26	30	27
Other	1	1	2
Multiple Award Types	40	52	58

Source: © Mercer 350-Company Study, 2001.

Exhibit 16.4   Equity as a Percentage of Total
Direct Compensation (TDC).

	Equity % of TDC[a]
Computers, office equipment	89%
Health care, pharmaceuticals	62
Electronics, electrical equipment	70
Insurance	70
Diversified financials	64
Chemicals	56
Petroleum refining	50
Commercial banking	46
Food, beverages	53
Industrial, farm equipment	61
Retailers	66
Publishing, printing	56
Transportation	51
Forest, paper products	38
Utilities	42
Metals	36
All industries	**57**

[a] Total direct compensation (TDC) is the sum of total annual compensation plus long-term incentives, including the value of grants in the form of restricted stock, unrestricted stock, deferred stock, and stock options (valued using a binomial option-pricing model). Includes equity stock retainer.

Source: © Mercer 350-Company Study, 2001.

Exhibit 16.5   Median Total Compensation
by Company Size.

Sales/Revenue	TAC	TDC
$1.0 to 1.99 billion	$43,400	$ 79,622
$2.0 to $4.99 billion	48,000	84,892
$5.0 to $9.99 billion	56,000	103,363
$10.0 billion or more	66,520	139,000
All companies	**$54,000**	**$105,032**

Source: © Mercer 350-Company Study, 2001.

(ii) Substitute for Other Compensation   A second reason for using equity in directors' programs is as a substitute for another form of compensation. If equity is used as a substitution for cash, three methods are most typical:

1. Paying the entire cash compensation in stock, typically options or restricted stock.
2. Paying part in cash and part in stock.
3. Deferring part of compensation in stock or deferred stock.

While it is not typical practice, the use of stock options only to compensate directors for service has a powerful attraction for some companies and their shareholders. First, it says to shareholders that the directors are willing to be rewarded for the direction and the decisions made by the management they oversee. Further, it says that the directors this organization wants on its Board are willing to accept the consequences of their decisions and are not joining just to receive a compensation package or recognition as a Board member.

While there are benefits of paying directors entirely in stock—tying directors to enhancing shareholder value and increasing director share ownership—some concerns accompany this course of action. With options, there is a real chance that directors will focus more on the short-term performance of the stock, to increase the value of their options, and not on the long term where the greater potential gain could be realized. A simple way around that objection might be to vest the options over a three-year period, the term of their directorship, or to have the vesting based on the stock price reaching a certain level, with vesting in effect accelerated from a longer period, say six years.

Another concern is evident whenever options are granted: What happens when the price of the stock declines? A director typically receives options each year, and if the price continues to decline over a period of time, then the real value of the options is much less than any model would show.

A second typical use of stock is paying in a combination of cash and stock. This type of arrangement allows companies to emulate the type of programs that are available to executives; that is, to have some of their compensation paid in a nonvariable form and some in variable compensation. In our studies, about 25% of companies split the Board retainer between cash and stock. Stock retainers typically take one of four forms:

1. Unrestricted shares, paid once a year.
2. Restricted shares with one- to three-year vesting.
3. Deferred stock with payout deferred until retirement.
4. Deferred stock units, where the amount to be deferred is converted into units, whose value rises or falls with the company's stock price. At the end of the deferral period, the amount is paid in stock.

A third type of substitution is to defer part of current compensation into some stock vehicle, in effect deferring the receipt of some compensation until a later time, and (hopefully) enjoying the appreciation in the stock price over that time. Half of the companies that Mercer studied offer this type of deferral. The most typical of these is the deferral into stock units. The amount to be deferred is converted into units, whose value then rises or falls with the company's stock price. At the end of the deferral period, the amount is paid in company shares. In offering deferral of retainer or fees in company stock or stock units, the company may offer an inducement to mitigate the risk of stock versus the certainty of cash. A premium of 10% to 20% in the number of units or shares over the current value of cash may be offered for deferral into stock. Similarly, the number of options offered in exchange is increased by 20% over a Black-Scholes value to induce deferral.

(iii) Stock Ownership While both of these reasons for using stock in a director plan are valid, probably the most compelling reason for using stock is to support a stock ownership policy for the directors. This trend of encouraging directors to own stock follows the stock ownership policy trend for executives. The link between these two is important because it puts the directors in the same boat as the executives they oversee. The use of stock ownership guidelines is on the increase, growing from 1% to more than 20% of companies surveyed in five years.

The importance of stock ownership by executives is not generally disputed; the amount, however, is. There is a central tendency to have guidelines that approximate three to five times annual retainer. But as stated earlier, annual retainer does not increase as rapidly as the size of a company, so the dollar amount of ownership required in a small company may be similar to the ownership in a large company. A better method is to relate the amount of ownership to some measure of capitalization (number of shares) or to the amount of total compensation (retainer plus meeting fees) for the director.

(e) Coping with Volatility

Between receiving over half the value of their compensation through stand-alone equity grants, usually options, possibly receiving stock as part of a retainer, and having the ability to defer other forms of cash into equity, the volatility of the stock market can cause havoc with director compensation programs. To be sure, the voluntary election into stock or stock units as a replacement for cash, or the choice of deferring cash into some form of deferred equity can enhance the competitiveness of some pay programs—and those choices are the individual directors'. But some choices are available to help lessen the effects of this market volatility over time.

With most stand-alone stock option grants expressed as a specific number of shares, the value of option grants declines when the market value of a company's stock declines. To prevent this, a company could delineate the option grant as a Black-Scholes value, say $30,000. If the price in one year declines, more options are granted; if the price increases the following year, fewer options are granted.

Another alternative to decrease the effects of stock price volatility involves the use of both stock and stock options. If a company were to grant a fixed dollar amount of shares as part or all of its retainer, price fluctuations would result in higher numbers of shares when the price falls, but fewer when it rises. If this plan were coupled with a typical option plan that grants a fixed number of options each year, then an increase in price one year would not reduce the number of options. These would increase in value at the time that fewer shares of stock were being granted as part of the retainer. The opposite is also true.

(f) Pay for Performance

True pay-for-performance plans are few and far between in director compensation programs. Less than 5% of companies that Mercer studied had plans for directors that were based on performance. They fall within these areas:

- The number of stock options granted was based on the extent to which the company reached a certain level of performance the prior year.
- Performance-contingent stock option vesting (vesting occurs upon the company reaching a performance hurdle).
- Performance-accelerated stock option vesting (vesting accelerated from a service date to an earlier date based on performance).
- Performance units.
- Performance shares.
- Annual incentive.

Interestingly, all of the companies that have these pay-for-performance plans use them in addition to either typical options or restricted stock plans.

With the flexibility handed to directors with the 1996 change in the SEC regulations, and further encouragement from the NACD's study of director compensation, it is surprising that more plans that award options based on performance or stock based on performance are not more evident.

(g) Special Situations

Directors are often asked to take on specific tasks or responsibilities that go beyond the normal scope of Board participation. These special services could include special assignments or inspection trips made on behalf of the company, additional meetings involved with mergers or acquisitions, or other special meetings as representatives of the company. In most cases, compensation for these services comes in the form of cash payments, typically $1,000 to $2,000 per day or per meeting. This would be the case of extraordinary Board meetings as well, where the number of meetings exceeds the normal 12 or so meetings. This type of meeting is not usually compensated with stock grants or option awards, although the ability of directors to choose the form of payment would apply to these fees.

(h)   Non-CEO Chairperson

The concept of a company having a non-CEO chairperson is not unusual in other countries, with Great Britain having these arrangements as the regulatory norm. In the United States, less than 10% of the companies we studied have a nonexecutive chairperson, and the range of compensation for this position is wide. Most receive compensation under a special arrangement in amounts that can range from $40,000 to $400,000 per year, based on the time commitment and the chairperson's prior experience. In addition, the non-CEO chairperson also receives stock or options typically granted to other nonemployee Board members, and sometimes even larger amounts than those directors.

16.4   DEVELOPING A DIRECTOR COMPENSATION PROGRAM

The role of directors continues to change as shareholders, especially institutional shareholders, demand more from corporations. Director compensation should help in attracting the type of director that a company wants, it needs to reflect the overall pay strategy of the company, and it should be an adequate reward for the results, over the long term, of the decisions that the Board and the company make.

(a)   Director Compensation Strategy

To develop a program that addresses these needs, a company must begin by developing a compensation strategy for its directors, not too dissimilar from the compensation strategy adopted by many organizations. In this sense, a director's strategy should follow the same tenets as the executive's strategy when addressing similar issues.

Such issues would include the following:

- *What companies should be in a peer group for developing competitive levels of director compensation?* With the development of total shareholder return graphs in proxy statement, many companies have developed compensation peer groups that mirror or closely resemble those used as comparison indices in the shareholder return graph. The concept of demonstrating the relationship of performance and pay by using the same group for determining appropriate levels of senior executives' pay and the performance that leads to that pay is logical. Using the same group of companies to determine "competitive" pay for directors is also logical. The types of data that should be reviewed include:

— Board retainers

— Board meeting fees and the typical numbers of Board meetings

— Committee fees and the number of meetings that such common committees as Audit and Compensation have per year

— How many committees each director participates in

— Committee retainers

— Stock option grants, both annual and one-time awards, and how they are determined

— Other benefits including retirement plans

— Total value of compensation, including retirement plan

— Stock ownership policy

• *What level of competitiveness does the company want to maintain for its directors?* Generally, the overall level of compensation will be a range based on such items as the number of committees, the number of committee chairs, and the number of meetings that a committee may hold. While all of these issues are important, probably the more important issues are what elements are used, the total amount paid in cash given a consistent set of meetings and chairs, and how this compares to the amount of stock compensation used. The degree of competitiveness that a company should target should be not the competitiveness of each element but rather the competitiveness of the overall program.

• *Should there be a relationship between company performance and director pay?* A typical executive compensation philosophy would relate competitive total cash compensation to competitive performance, with superior (75th percentile) pay for comparable performance. It may also emphasize long-term compensation, based on shareholder value creation, over annual incentives, based on short-term financial performance. The degree to which directors' pay varies based on annual performance would typically be very little, if at all, because directors do not generally affect, on an annual basis, the financial performance of a company; however, the degree to which a company wants its directors tied to long-term performance could closely parallel the same strategy used for executives. With the changes to Section 16(b), directors have much greater latitude in determining the amounts of options granted to each other annually. If the importance of increasing shareholder value is heavily weighted in the executives' plan, then it would be appropriate to carry that weight to the directors' plan.

• *What role do benefits such as retirement plans, charitable bequests, etc., play in attracting, retaining, and rewarding directors?* For directors, the concept of providing income after Board service is certainly not one of providing a living wage. Rather, it is one of deferring income until after retirement. The concept of providing deferral vehicles, rather than retirement plans, helps differentiate employees from directors and allows directors the flexibility to manage their own current and retirement cash.

The use of other benefits such as charitable bequests or health benefits also needs to be discussed in context of their relevance to the role of directors in a company. Most directors have jobs other than the Boards on which they serve, and the companies they work for will provide health benefits. Charitable bequests, however, generally are not available to employees and may not be in shareholders' best interests.

As part of a comprehensive executive compensation strategy, many companies are adopting a policy requiring executives to own a certain amount of shares, generally related to their levels of salary and their positions in the company. This policy helps more closely tie the interests of executives with the interests of shareholders. Based on our recent studies, this is an increasing trend among U.S. companies, with somewhat less than 50% of the companies that we studied having these guidelines.

In companies that instituted these policies, it would be appropriate for their directors to also have requirements for stock ownership. These policies base the amount of stock owned on some multiple of retainer, or retainer plus Board meeting fees. Most are in the range of three to five times retainer, and directors have three years to reach those amounts. In some cases, a fixed share amount regardless of price is used, and the number may be based on a price when the director joins the Board.

(b)   Suggested Compensation Model

Based on the changes in Section 16(b), and the atmosphere surrounding directors' pay, Mercer suggests the following model for companies to use in setting up their compensation programs.

(i) Cash   Based on the competitive analysis completed as part of the compensation strategy development, companies should look at the total value of the compensation package for peer companies and approach setting levels and components from a total compensation prospective. Each element should be viewed as follows.

Retainers for Board service are an appropriate mechanism for compensating directors for their availability and participation in the Board process; however, the use of meeting fees for Board service may not be the most appropriate method for compensating directors for participation in meetings. With the typical meeting fee at approximately $1,300, directors are not attending meetings because of the financial reward for their attendance. And $1,300 does not represent the value that the company receives for a director's participation at a meeting. With the frequent attendance of meetings by telephone, the concept of attendance at a meeting has a different meaning than it once did. Therefore, companies should move from paying for attendance to paying for contribution. Instead of paying meeting fees, companies should determine the annual amount of meeting fees it would pay based on a historical number of meetings or a planned number of meetings for the year, and pay that amount in additional retainer.

The same concept can be applied to committee fees. Because most companies will pay a retainer for committee chairs, it is only logical that companies should convert an annual amount of meeting fees to a committee retainer. This could continue to be supplemented by committee chair retainers to reflect their additional responsibility.

(ii) **Stock**   *Develop stock ownership guidelines for directors that are based on the ownership guidelines for executives.* Stock ownership by directors is desirable from both a company and a shareholder standpoint. The controversy that appears to exist is whether the payment of compensation in stock is enough to ensure that the behavior of the directors is in the best interest of the shareholders, and that their decisions will be influenced, not by the amount of cash they receive, but by the amount of increase in shareholder value they will be influencing. Mercer suggests that the amount of ownership be approximately five times the annual retainer. Because most director share ownership guidelines are expressed as a percentage of salary, it is logical to express guidelines for directors in the same manner. Even with the increased amount of retainers that essentially replace director fees, for a $40,000 total cash compensation director, the amount of ownership would be $200,000. If the director in addition receives stock compensation equal to only half, or $20,000, of that retainer, over a five-year period more than half of the requirement would be satisfied. Should the stock increase in value over that period, most of the requirement would be satisfied from the stock compensation portion of director compensation.

Grant stock options or restricted stock to executives on an annual basis. With the changes in Section 16(b), directors have the ability to grant much more market-competitive options or restricted stock grants. In order to determine the appropriate amount of long-term compensation, companies need to review their director compensation strategy and the peer data to determine the percentage of stock that is competitive. In addition, the mix of compensation that a company has for its executives helps develop an appropriate percentage of the total package that should be delivered in stock. If, for example, a CEO has half of his total package in long-term compensation, it may be appropriate for directors to have a large percentage of their compensation in stock as well. Our recent studies have found that high-performing companies put a significant emphasis on long-term compensation for executives.

To determine the amount of options to give a director, companies should set a dollar value and use Black-Scholes or some equivalent option-pricing model to develop a range of options for grant each year. The range should stay the same for a number of years so as not to penalize nor overly reward directors for the increase or decrease in the stock price each year. One of the biggest problems with the formula-driven stock plans that some companies instituted is that the value of, say, a 5,000-share grant today may be two or three times as high as its value was only a few years ago, due to the increase in the stock market over the past few years. At some point, the value may seem too high compared to the amounts that executives and other directors are receiving.

Directors should not receive different individual grants based on individual performance. Stock compensation for directors is a way to create a level of overall corporate teamwork. It would be inappropriate for directors to receive individual awards of options or stock because their focus is on overall corporate performance, created by both directors and executives. Individual contribution to performance may not have a place in director compensation at all, other than through larger retainers for committee chairmanships.

Allow directors the ability to receive some portion of their cash in stock or options. Allowing directors this elective ability can help increase director share-holding, while not precluding the ability to attract either retired executives or members of academia to Boards who might not appreciate or afford an all-stock plan.

Increased Board discretion over the terms of awards to nonemployee directors raises key strategic issues for Boards. Boards will now have the opportunity to align director stock compensation with company performance; however, non–formula-based plans could raise questions about directors' ability to maintain their objectivity in the exercise of their respective duties as Board members. It is essential that consideration be given to the impact of the proposed compensation program on the Board's ability to fulfill its fiduciary obligations to shareholders in the exercise of its duties. Directors implementing compensation programs without adequately assessing the balance between pay-for-performance considerations and fiduciary concerns may find that well-intentioned programs could adversely affect shareholder relations and lead to poor decision making by the Board.

(iii)   Eliminate Other Benefits   The use of benefit plans in director compensation has seen a dramatic downturn. Shareholder activists have attacked the use and importance of retirement plans and charitable bequests for directors as not being in the best interests of shareholders, and many companies have acted in advance of shareholder inquiries. Instead, companies should allow deferral opportunities in stock or deferred stock to allow build-up of retirement assets.

Payout of Current Cash in Stock   The accrued benefit to date could be paid out to directors in either restricted stock or unrestricted shares. Since shareholders are concerned about directors owning more stock, paying out the cash value of retainers or fees in shares would be sensitive to these concerns and consistent with current trends in directors' compensation.

Restricted Stock   Restricted stock is compatible with the concept of delayed payment and results in deferred taxation until the shares vest, presumably at retirement or termination from Board service. At this time the director would be taxed at ordinary income tax rates, and the company would receive a corresponding deduction. Restrictions should be so structured that forfeiture would occur only under limited circumstances. For example, it would generally be sufficient to stipulate that the restricted shares would vest only if the director continued as a director until reaching a mandated retirement age or failed to win election to the Board. Director termination for other reasons (e.g., resignation or termination for cause) would subject the restricted shares to forfeiture. Exhibit 16.6 illustrates the financial benefits of deferral compared to current receipt of the accrued amounts.

Unrestricted Stock   The advantages of unrestricted stock are that it requires no new vesting restrictions, entails no risk of forfeiture, requires no ongoing administration, and ends the plan once and for all. The directors would, however, be taxed on the fair value of the shares. This approach would have less appeal to shareholders because the directors would be free to sell the shares at any time. Also, over time this approach may yield a lesser financial reward than restricted shares (see Exhibit 16.6).

Deferred Stock Plan   A deferred compensation plan that pays out wholly or partially in stock would be more sensitive to shareholders than one that pays out solely in cash. The cash value would be converted into stock units by dividing the amount by the fair market value of the company's stock as of the date of transfer. Deferred stock units are fundamentally a bookkeeping entry, and the individual remains an unsecured creditor of the company with regard to the deferred compensation balance. Over the vesting period, the value of the units would be booked as compensation expense on the income statement. At retirement or termination, the units would be paid out in shares of stock.

16.5 SUMMARY

As with most issues of top management compensation, director compensation is coming under the watchful eye of the SEC. In the next few years, we will probably see compensation tables, similar to those required for executives, that will detail all aspects of director compensation, including performance plans and stockholdings. This will make it easier for companies to compare the value of their plans with those of a peer group and will also allow new ideas and concepts to be more available.

Exhibit 16.6   Comparison of Pretax Deferred Payment and Current Payment.

Assumptions:

Value of cash retainer	$40,000
Fair market value on 1/1/ × 1	$35.00
Fair market value on 1/1/ × 6	$50.00
Individual income tax rate:	
Federal	38.6%
State	6%
Medicare	2.9%
Federal benefit of state taxes paid	(2.3%)
Total	45.2%
Individual capital gains tax rate:	
Federal	20%
State	6%
Federal benefit of state taxes paid	(1.2%)
Total	24.8%
Director exceeds the Social Security tax threshold based on other income	

	Deferral Elected	No Deferral Elected
Value of retainer	$40,000	$40,000
Current payment to director	—	$40,000
Income tax liability	—	($18,080)
After tax payment to director	—	$21,920
Fair market value on 1/1/ × 1	$35.00	$35.00
Shares to director	1,143	626
Fair market value on 1/1/ × 6	$57,150	$31,300
Income tax liability	($25,832)	—
Basis	—	($21,920)
Long-term appreciation	—	$9,380
Capital gains tax	—	($2,326)
Net to director	$31,318	$28,974

Some companies are taking the following steps now to refresh their plans:

- Develop a strategy for directors' compensation, using the executives' strategy as a basis.
- Consider changing meeting fees to retainers.

- Grant stock options to directors annually, but with a valuation based on the current stock price and not as formula driven, as has been the case in the past. Use another form of equity as payment or partial payment for retainer or fees to mitigate market volatility.

- Include stock ownership guidelines as part of the program.

- Limit retirement programs, but offer deferral opportunities for current cash payments.

As director compensation reflects the pay-for-performance philosophy that most companies have adopted for executives, the value of these packages will begin to better reflect the time, effort, and performance of the companies whom they serve.

Chapter 17

The Role of the Compensation Committee

Steven L. Cross and Donald T. Sagolla

The role of the compensation committee is vital to the effective management of a company's executive pay practices and can be viewed as the linchpin in an effective executive compensation program. This chapter focuses on the role and structure of compensation committees in companies that have successful pay practices. We will examine some of the influences that have caused dramatic changes in the role of the compensation committee and the factors that contribute to an effective compensation committee.

17.1   BUSINESS/COMPETITIVE ENVIRONMENT

Although U.S. business has always been competitive, the intensity of the competitive environment has accelerated significantly, resulting in shorter product design cycles, reduced inventories, and quicker responses to changing consumer demands. These accelerating forces dramatically increase the importance of the human element to company success. Innovation is driven by people, and the competition for quality leadership is fierce. There is also mounting pressure on executives to perform in the short term while continuing to build for the long term, thereby increasing the emphasis on quality leadership. This great balancing act has put increasing pressure on the executive compensation programs, and the pressure is felt at the level of the compensation committee. The result is that compensation committees are dealing with more innovative and substantive pay programs, while considering the effects of a demanding shareholder environment.

17.2   SHAREHOLDER AND REGULATORY BACKDROP

During the past 10 years, there has been a substantial increase in shareholder and regulatory activity related to executive compensation. Much has been made of "excessive" executive compensation compared to general employee pay and shareholder return. Often the focus is on the Board of Directors and, in particular, the compensation committee.

Compensation committees began to proliferate in the 1970s, when the Securities Exchange Commission (SEC) determined under Section 16(b)3 of the Securities Exchange Act of 1934 that certain stock compensation programs were exempt from some of the short-swing profit rules imposed on most transactions when the plans were administered by "independent and disinterested" Board members or committees of the Board. In 1993, the SEC adopted rules related to proxy disclosure for executive compensation, which require that the compensation committee of the Board (or the full Board in the absence of a formal committee) provide a written report to shareholders on executive compensation policy and practices regarding the chief executive officer (CEO) specifically, and the other named officers in general. These requirements place the compensation committee in a position to be second-guessed by shareholders and nonshareholders alike. Not only must amounts of compensation be disclosed but also general information about the performance measures and the strategies underlying the programs. This means that the compensation programs and pay levels must be rational and appear so in the disclosure documents.

The Internal Revenue Service (IRS) and the Financial Accounting Standards Board (FASB) have also influenced trends in executive compensation. See, for example:

- Internal Revenue Code (IRC) Section 162(m) limitation of deductibility for compensation in excess of $1,000,000
- IRC Section 280G and 4999 dealing with limitations of deductibility on "golden parachute" payments
- IRC Section 415 and 401 dealing with limitations on the amounts of compensation related to qualified retirement plans
- FAS 123, APB 25, and FIN 44 on accounting for stock compensation, in particular the rules regarding cancelling and reissuing stock options

As a result, compensation committees have begun to exert greater effort, expend more time, and be involved in more decisions than ever before.

(a)   Purpose of the Compensation Committee

The purpose of the compensation committee is to oversee the compensation policy of a company. While oversight and policy-making activities may vary, some responsibilities are common to all compensation committees:

- *Setting compensation policy.* Setting compensation policy includes adopting compensation programs designed to support the business strategy of the company. The adoption of many plans must have the approval of, or be administered by, the full Board or a committee of the Board, in order to qualify under certain securities or tax rules.

- *Reviewing company performance and compensation levels.* The relationship between company performance and incentive compensation is critical to validating the effectiveness of the compensation programs as well as validating the senior management compensation in light of shareholder expectations. (The issue of performance validation is covered in more detail later in this chapter.)

- *Setting compensation levels for senior management.* Practices vary widely among companies as to how deeply in the organization the oversight of the committee goes. In some organizations, the committee may make hands-on decisions about pay levels for three to four levels of direct reports to the CEO. In other companies, the committee may set the pay levels for the top one or two executives only and delegate the decision process to the CEO. The committee, for example, may ultimately approve all officer compensation but leave the deliberations on individual compensation to the CEO. In either case, the committee should make individual pay decisions based on its ability to evaluate the salient factors affecting the compensation of those individuals. If the committee has no working knowledge of the performance of certain executives, it cannot make realistic and meaningful decisions on pay for those individuals.

- *Influencing management development and succession planning.* In many instances, the compensation committee will be charged with overseeing and evaluating management development. This should include the performance evaluation of the CEO as well as the company's ongoing management development program. The succession planning responsibilities for the CEO are often the purview of the compensation committee. This is especially fitting for committees whose involvement in assessing the performance of the executive management team is significant. Up-to-date information on key employees and their performance and background makes the job of succession planning more effective.

- *Communication with the full Board.* The compensation committee should communicate significant issues and actions to the full Board. Where issues cannot be resolved, the committee should advise the Board of the issues and actions to be taken within a specified timeframe. It is usually the charge of the chairperson of the committee to handle this communication.

- *Recommending compensation of the Board.* Many of the same fundamental processes of evaluation are applied to director compensation as are applied to executive pay. In making decisions regarding its own compensation, the committee should exercise diligence in evaluating the competitive environment and assure that proper deliberations respecting reasonableness take place. Often the committee will rely on outside consultants to help evaluate and establish the Board compensation program.

• *Auditing the compensation program.* The committee should assess the executive compensation strategy and compensation programs (e.g., the annual incentive and long-term incentive plans) annually or at least every two years. This is often done with an outside consultant. Typical issues and questions to be addressed in an audit can be found in Section 5 of this chapter.

(b) Compensation Committee Process

The process of overseeing and administering the pay policies of an organization varies widely depending on the style and culture of the committee and the relationships of the various directors with senior management and the Board. For example, in a mature organization with well-communicated compensation policies, the need for radical changes to the compensation structure and therefore the need for committee involvement is less. In an environment of rapid change, more committee involvement is needed, for example, in a merger, acquisition, or major restructuring. The process by which the policies are carried out may also evolve as members of the Board, the committee, or senior management may change. For example, if there is a new CEO as a result of a merger, the committee may require more deliberation and more information or may rely more heavily on third-party support than before the merger.

The following are general guidelines for compensation committees:

• *Adopt a compensation committee charter.* The committee should work closely with the CEO to clearly establish the role and responsibilities of the committee in overseeing the compensation program. If this is done in open dialogue, each party will be comfortable in the ongoing relationship in dealing with the sensitive issues surrounding executive pay. The committee and senior management should work closely with the company's attorneys to ensure that the charter is consistent with the company's constitution and bylaws, as well as securities rules and any other state or federal legislation. Exhibit 17.1 is a sample charter.

• *Formalize the compensation philosophy and strategy.* The company should commit time and resources to develop a coherent compensation philosophy and strategy that it can communicate to the committee. The adoption of the strategy should be an interactive process between senior management and the committee. A compensation philosophy and strategy will evolve with the business plan and changes in the marketplace. It should include the following:

— Assessment of the company's short- and long-term business objectives

— Review of the economic environment

— Mix and balance of fixed and variable compensation elements

Exhibit 17.1 Sample Compensation Committee Charter.

The Compensation Committee of the Board of Directors shall consist of not less than three or more than six outside members of the Board of Directors, one of whom shall be the chairman. The committee and its chairman shall be elected annually by the Board of Directors.

The Board of Directors delegates to the Compensation Committee strategic and administrative responsibility on a broad range of issues. The committee's basic responsibility is to assure that the Chief Executive Officer, other officers and key management of the Company are compensated effectively in a manner consistent with the stated compensation strategy of the Company, internal equity considerations, competitive practice, and the requirements of the appropriate regulatory bodies. The committee shall also communicate to shareholders the Company's compensation policies and the reasoning behind such policies as required by the Securities and Exchange Commission.

More specifically, the committee shall be responsible for the following:

1. Review annually and approve the Company's stated compensation strategy to ensure that management are rewarded appropriately for their contributions to company growth and profitability and that the executive compensation strategy supports organization objectives and shareholder interests.

2. Review annually and determine the individual elements of total compensation for the Chief Executive Officer and communicate in the annual Board Compensation Committee Report to shareholders the factors and criteria on which the Chief Executive Officer's compensation for the last year was based, including the relationship of the Company's performance to the Chief Executive Officer's compensation.

3. Review and approve the individual elements of total compensation for the executive officers and key management other than the Chief Executive Officer and communicate in the annual Board Compensation Committee Report to shareholders the specific relationship of corporate performance to executive compensation.

4. Ensure that the annual incentive compensation plan is administered in a manner consistent with the Company's compensation strategy and the terms of the plan as to the following:

   - Participation
   - Target annual incentive awards
   - Corporate financial goals
   - Actual awards paid to senior management
   - Total funds reserved for payment under the plan
   - Qualification under IRS Code Section 162(m)

(continued)

5. Approve for submission to shareholders all new equity-related incentive plans for management and administer the Company's long-term incentive programs in a manner consistent with the terms of the plans as to the following:
   - Participation
   - Vesting requirements
   - Awards to senior management
   - Total shares reserved for awards

6. Fix the terms and awards of stock compensation for members of the Board in accordance with the rules in effect under Section 16 of the Securities and Exchange Act of 1934.

7. Approve an annual aggregate amount that may be used by the Chief Executive Officer for special incentive awards.

8. Approve revisions to the Company's salary range structure, salary increase guidelines, and executive promotions.

9. Review with the Chief Executive Officer compensation matters relating to management succession.

10. Review the Company's employee benefit programs and approve changes, subject where appropriate, to shareholder or Board of Director approval.

— Alignment of performance measures with business strategy

— Link with the cultural or qualitative goals of the organization

— Role of benefits, perquisites, severance, and change-of-control agreements

— Link of pay design with attraction and retention of talent

- *Establish the level and nature of support to the committee.* Access to certain technical specialists such as legal, financial, and human resources specialists, will facilitate the decision process for the committee. To the extent possible, the individuals dealing with the committee should be consistent over time, so that they can better understand their role and anticipate the needs of the committee. Similarly, the committee will gain a higher comfort level with the staff specialists, thus enhancing the efficiency of the process. (The role of compensation consultants is discussed in more detail later in this chapter.)

- *Develop the flow of information needed for the committee to do its job.* The committee should identify the kinds and frequency of information it needs, including financial results, competitive benchmarking (compensation and financial), and relevant external market information. This should be done on a predetermined basis. Each supporting staff specialist should be aware of his or her responsibility to provide relevant and regular information in a timely fashion.

- *Establish the format and frequency of meetings.* The committee should schedule at least one regular meeting per quarter and endeavor to keep the agenda as manageable as possible. Most committees schedule their meetings to coincide with regularly scheduled Board meetings. It is advisable to develop a schedule of issues to be addressed over the course of the year. Often the timing of certain issues is dictated by reporting requirements or competitive forces. In these cases, the company should move other, more flexible issues to different meeting dates.

- *Review and analyze executive compensation against the market.* In order for the committee to understand the market context for its decisions, it should periodically review competitive pay and performance standards within its competitive market. This should be done at least annually but more frequently if warranted by changes in the strategy or compensation programs.

- *Report to the full Board.* After each meeting, the committee should communicate the status of the committee's actions to the full Board.

(c) Practice Concerns for Compensation Committees

Too often, companies allow the external environment to dictate their compensation strategies or levels. The compensation strategy must reflect the culture of the organization as well as the competitive environment. For this reason, the compensation committee should have practical knowledge of the compensation philosophy and management style of the company. Committee members need not share the management style of the organization they serve, but they should have a solid understanding of the strategy and the rationale for whatever programs are involved. They should also clearly understand their role in the process and the market forces at work in the industry in which the company operates.

Communication of information to the committee should include the general trends of the industry for compensation practices, strategies, levels, vehicles, and rationale. It will not suffice for them to simply understand, for example, that pay is going up or that there is a general increase in long-term compensation. They need to be educated about why these changes are taking place and what the implications are to the company and its programs. To the extent these issues are clearly communicated, the committee will have an easier time addressing each element of the pay program.

If company management and the committee differ on compensation philosophy, the CEO should address the issue from a practical and strategic basis. One of the primary objectives in the relationship between senior management and the compensation committee is to establish the prudent application of shared philosophical principles.

The following are barriers to creating a shared compensation philosophy:

- *Lack of trust between senior management and the compensation committee (or the Board as a whole).* Lack of trust may be based on perceived misuse of the compensation program or a simple lack of communication. Sometimes the committee may be perceived as having reneged on promises made to executives. Where there has been a breakdown in trust between the members of the committee and the CEO, committee members may be hesitant to subscribe to aggressive or innovative compensation programs or strategies, however legitimate they may be. The reestablishment of trust should become a priority of the committee and senior management.

- *Lack of understanding of the role of compensation in today's competitive environment.* There are times when members of the committee lack experience in dealing with the administration of compensation programs. There are also times when members are chosen from industries in which compensation practices vary widely from the environment of the company. In either case, the committee members should be educated about the forces at work in the company's industry, which may require or lend themselves to certain approaches to compensation. Practically, it would be desirable if the committee members already had a good working understanding of compensation management before their assignment to the committee.

- *Differences in opinion on the effectiveness of compensation elements.* For example, the view that focuses on the dilutive effects of equity compensation clashes with the view that equity compensation is a primary vehicle to align the interests of executives with shareholders and drive long-term performance. These differences should be anticipated during the strategy development phase of the committee's involvement, or members may develop an overall discomfort with the policies or strategy.

17.3   PERFORMANCE BENCHMARKING

The market can be a vast resource for compensation information, if used properly. It can provide a useful guideline for establishing a basis for compensation packages, or it can be misinterpreted to develop an unrealistic view of pay practices.

Performance benchmarking is the continuous process of comparing company performance to its competitors in the market. It helps identify new ideas, processes, and methodologies that may improve company practices and reveal a company's strengths and weaknesses in the industry. This may be particularly important when forming a compensation package to attract an executive from another company, or to retain and motivate an incumbent. It also reminds the compensation committee and the executives that company performance and therefore executive compensation is judged relative to the competition. Evaluating a company against its peers is a primary source of meaningful input into the evaluation, provided the composition of the peer group is appropriate and the data is accurate and timely.

In reviewing performance benchmarks, the committee should avoid over-reacting to short-term shifts in company or peer performance. If the strategy is well conceived, the short-term variance in performance indicators may be easily explainable and therefore not warrant radical changes to the approach.

Performance benchmarks should also be chosen carefully so that the data are accepted as reliable and verifiable. In some industries, data are simply not widely published or otherwise available. Multiple peer groups may be needed for various reasons such as marketplace for talent, products and services, and invested capital. Inconsistent and uncertain performance benchmark data can dramatically affect the perceived integrity of the compensation programs and cause employees to lose confidence in the compensation process.

Companies often use several performance measures to indicate how well they are performing—either against plan, against peers, or against historical performance. As far as the compensation committee's analysis is concerned, it is important that the performance indicators used by the company include those by which compensation is evaluated, and that the relationship between pay and performance be reviewed. Also, it is vital to remember that peer group analysis by itself does not paint a complete picture. Rather, other salient factors such as the company's position in the business cycle and the company's individual strategy, must be considered in the analysis.

Compensation committees also need to determine which factors drive competitive compensation practices in their industry or market. Industries often have their own performance indicators that are unique to that industry. For example, commodities companies are subject to price fluctuations in the underlying commodity. For this reason, net income is not always viewed as the mark of short-term success or failure. Rather, indicators dealing with productivity and operating efficiency may be more applicable in evaluating annual performance.

The committee should recognize the effect of various performance indicators on the different elements of compensation. In most industries, revenue size is the strongest influence of base salary for the top executive jobs (asset size in financial institutions). This assumes that the larger the company, the broader the scope of the job and therefore the higher the base compensation. This is generally true even though there are other factors to consider. By contrast, the sensitivity between revenue size and bonus payment is not strong. Annual bonus payments are often driven by measures of annual profitability. Another example is the fact that grants of long-term incentives are not generally tied to annual profitability. While some companies do make grant determinations based on annual results, most do not.

(a)   Compensation Analysis

Compensation benchmarking enables the compensation committee to take an analytical look at the competitiveness and appropriateness of the compensation and benefits package. It can be used to validate various facets of a program, such as the individual pay elements, the performance objectives, and the desired behavioral responses.

Market compensation data are often presented in a disaggregated manner that enables a committee to evaluate the efficacy of each pay component, such as base salary, annual incentive plans, long-term incentive plans, and benefits. Moreover, the market acts as a standard through which the committee may compare not only the array of separate elements of a package, but also the feasibility of performance targets, given the state of the industry and economy.

In addition to understanding the measures on which performance is based, it is important to identify those factors that will influence behavior. Pinpointing those companies in a similar stage of development may enable the committee to identify those relevant factors that will help meet the objectives of the company. Observing past compensation practices of these companies will also illustrate whether the committee's proposed pay philosophy will likely evoke the desired response.

(b) Shareholder Return and Related Performance Measures

Increasingly, the compensation committee is charged with ensuring the relationship between executive compensation and the creation of shareholder value. Shareholders depend on management to increase the market value of their investments and to secure the financial position of the company. In achieving this goal, the committee needs to consider those instruments that will align the executive's motives with increasing shareholder return. A positive message will be carried to management and shareholders by creating stronger links between executive pay and corporate performance. These actions should include finding a balance between lower-risk pay components, such as salary, benefits, and perquisites, which generally favor management, and higher-risk pay components, such as annual bonus and longer-term incentives that favor shareholder interests.

The committee may find it necessary to challenge management's current performance focus and suggest a focus more geared to future needs. For example, shareholder return and related financial metrics, such as net income and cash flow, may need to be balanced with measures such as market share, product development, product innovation, and managing human capital.

Other chapters in this book discuss the trends in measuring the relationships between shareholder returns and certain performance benchmarks. In today's environment, the company should communicate clearly with the committee those measures that strongly correlate with increasing shareholder value. In many cases, some measure of economic profit correlates strongly to the creation of shareholder wealth. This measure should indicate management's ability to efficiently employ company assets. The specific application of these economic profit measures may differ by industry and position in the business cycle; however, the committee must be aware of the importance of the link between various measures and shareholder value.

17.4   USE OF THIRD-PARTY RESOURCES

(a)   Compensation Consultants

Committee members and management possess specific knowledge of the company's organization, strategies, and key strengths. Such knowledge helps shape a compensation package that aligns company objectives with compensation instruments. Although internal representatives may be viewed as possessing more hands-on experience, they are often perceived as being too sympathetic or having a conflict of interest.

Outside compensation consultants can bring value to the executive compensation process in several ways. Most important, they give unbiased assessments of the company's pay programs and provide access to competitive pay information. They can also bring the committee up to date on various accounting, tax, and securities issues affecting executive compensation. Because outside consultants spend their time designing and evaluating compensation plans, they can bring the latest thinking on incentive plan design.

With the growing complexity of executive compensation and the increasing number of compensation instruments, external consultants may minimize the learning curve, reducing the considerable costs associated with implementing a new or revised compensation plan. With access to tax specialists, accountants, health benefits professionals, actuaries, and legal professionals, consultants will be better equipped to consider the latest compensation vehicles and regulatory requirements and their impact on overall operations. Apart from their expertise and specialized knowledge, the use of third-party consultants may provide some degree of protection and alleviate the tension aroused by a conflict of opinions. Working from clearly articulated goals, the committee, with help from consultants, can administer a program that will align compensation and benefits programs with overall business strategy, and gain the confidence of the participants.

In selecting the outside consultants, the best approach is for senior management to involve the committee in the decision-making process. In many cases, senior management will identify qualified consultants and request proposals or statements of qualifications from some of them. Senior management may then conduct a prescreening in which a manageable list of "finalists" is determined. At that point, the finalists would be asked to present their qualifications to the committee and field questions regarding their views and experiences. The committee and senior management would then meet to decide jointly on the consultant.

(b) Compensation Surveys

Compensation surveys provide a vast amount of information, including executive and nonexecutive salary and bonus levels, long-term incentive levels, compensation programs, and benefits programs. Because data gathering is often costly and time consuming for the company, these reports provide compensation data in a cost-effective and precise manner. Surveys enhance the usefulness of compensation data to create and evaluate an individual company's compensation program by presenting fundamental elements of comparable companies. Moreover, conductors of compensation surveys are likely to gain more cooperation from competitors, take advantage of economies of scale, and identify when atypical responses occur, contributing to reliable and objective data. Essentially, surveys can be a useful resource, if handled with care.

One factor to bear in mind is the methodology used to conduct the survey. Base salary and annual bonus information are not normally stratified by performance of the individuals or the companies responding to the survey. Therefore, the reader must assume that the middle of the pay range represents an average tenured and average-performing employee. The data are often reported by statistical range such as 25th, 50th, and 75th percentiles. This pay range helps the reader understand the breadth of pay practices for each benchmark job. Too often, the user assumes that if the company is paying above or below the market midpoint that they are either over- or underpaying the incumbent. Some surveys are beginning to deal with the effect of performance on pay and report the differences in pay practices by high performers versus low performers.

Knowing how to use the comparative data surveys provide is important. The committee needs to bear in mind that surveys apply to general situations and identifying relevant data may not be easy. Most often, the committee will rely on third parties, such as compensation consultants or staff human resources professionals, to analyze the survey data. These professionals generally have more survey data available to them and the time to analyze the findings to ensure validity and applicability of the data. It is generally accepted in most industries that published survey sources are the best source for available comparative data; however, there are certain industries or market segments in which the data are less reliable or available. In these cases, the committee and company should endeavor to agree on the most appropriate methodology for gathering and analyzing competitive compensation data.

17.5 QUESTIONS AND ISSUES FOR THE COMPENSATION COMMITTEE

The committee should periodically assess the company's compensation programs and strategy. In doing so, the committee will rely on company management to provide information and insight and may also seek the services of outside consultants. The following questions and issues should be addressed:

- Does our compensation strategy support company and shareholder objectives?
- How do financial performance and senior management pay levels compare to our competitors?
- To what key internal performance measures are the executive incentive programs linked? What is the link to shareholder value?
- Have we identified performance criteria within the control of senior management?
- Is the senior management performance appraisal process working effectively?
- Have we achieved a desired balance between annual and long-term plans?
- Does each incentive plan element play a specific role in motivating and retaining management?
- Do senior management employment contracts reflect the interests of shareholders?
- How do long-term incentives impact the company's earnings and dilution?

The committee's ongoing assessment should include the following issues regarding annual and long-term incentive plans:

- Purpose of the plans
- Relation to the business strategy and company, division, or business unit goals
- Bottom-line impact of the plan
- Criteria for eligibility and participation
- Timing of plan awards
- Opportunities for nonparticipants to participate
- Consistency of performance measures with the business and product cycles
- Weighting of individual and company performance
- Integration of participants' and business plan objectives
- Degree to which plan objectives reflect organizational culture
- Process for plan approval and assessment
- Parameters for exceptions and discretion
- Use of performance "floor" or "ceiling" and degree of "stretch" in assigning targets
- Appropriateness of performance-accelerated features in long-term plans

- Effectiveness of participant communications materials and workshops
- Effect of proposed changes on institutional shareholders and other outside constituencies

17.6 SUMMARY

The role of the compensation committee has increased in importance and exposure over the last decade, following the trends in executive compensation. The committee has the opportunity to be a strategic contributor to the company's success through thoughtful and meaningful input in the process of administering compensation and benefits programs.

The committees that fill that role will be those that work closely with senior management to understand the strategies of the organization and the link to compensation philosophy. They will also work closely to understand the link between pay, performance, and the creation of shareholder value. They should avail themselves of meaningful resources in carrying out their duties and should stay abreast of market conditions.

Chapter 18

Accounting for Stock-Based Compensation

Susan Eichen

18.1 BACKGROUND

(a) Who Sets Accounting Rules?

The Financial Accounting Standards Board (FASB) is responsible for establishing the generally accepted accounting principles (GAAP) to which financial reporting by U.S. corporations must conform. FASB, organized in 1973, is an independent organization composed of seven Board members, headquartered in Norwalk, Connecticut. It is the successor to the Committee on Accounting Procedure of the American Institute of CPAs (AICPA) (1936–1959) and the Accounting Principles Board (APB), another arm of the AICPA (1959–1973). Pronouncements of the predecessor organizations remain in force except to the extent amended or superseded by FASB.

FASB develops accounting standards and concepts based on research by its staff, contacts with foreign and international accounting standard-setting bodies, and input from public accounting firms, companies, and other constituents. The typical process for any significant question is to deliberate issues over a period of months, publish an Exposure Draft, receive public comment on the Exposure Draft, redeliberate the issues, and publish a final Statement of Financial Accounting Standards.

In 1984, FASB formed the Emerging Issues Task Force (EITF). EITF members are drawn primarily from public accounting firms but also include representatives of large companies and associations, such as the Financial Executives Institute and the Institute of Management Accountants. The chairman of the EITF is FASB's director of research and technical activities. The chief accountant of the Securities and Exchange Commission (SEC) participates in EITF meetings as an observer but also has floor privileges.

As the name of the task force implies, the EITF's mission is to deal with emerging issues before numerous questions and divergent practices with respect to those issues arise. The EITF operates by consensus. If a consensus is reached on an issue, that issue typically will not be addressed by the full Board. If no consensus is reached, the full Board may deliberate the issue.

Publicly held companies must also follow accounting rules established by the SEC. The SEC and FASB generally work together to ensure consistency in accounting rules.

In recent years, efforts have been made to establish a global set of accounting standards that will be accepted by many countries. Those efforts are currently being conducted by the International Accounting Standards Board (IASB), which consists of representatives from the accounting rule makers in eight countries. The IASB was formed by the International Accounting Standards Committee (IASC), which represents accounting organizations throughout the world.

(b) Where Can I Find the Accounting Rules Governing Stock-Based Compensation?

There are two principal standards governing accounting for employee stock compensation:

- Accounting Principles Board Opinion No. 25 (APB 25), "Accounting for Stock Issued to Employees," published by FASB's predecessor in 1972.
- Statement of Financial Accounting Standards No. 123 (FAS 123), "Accounting for Stock-Based Compensation," published by FASB in 1995.

(i) APB 25   APB 25 requires that the cost of stock-based compensation be measured using the "intrinsic value" method. The intrinsic value of an equity award is equal to the spread between the market value of the stock less the amount, if any, that the employee is required to pay. For most employee stock options, the intrinsic value at the date of grant is zero, resulting in no compensation cost. This is one of the reasons stock options have been so popular as incentives.

As stock-based compensation has evolved over the years since APB 25 was issued, many questions have arisen regarding the application of APB 25's standards to various transactions and issues. FASB has responded by providing additional guidance in the form of the following:

- *FASB Interpretations (FIN)*
  - FIN 28: "Accounting for Stock Appreciation Rights and Other Variable Stock Option or Award Plans, an interpretation of APB Opinions No. 15 and 25," December 1978.
  - FIN 44: "Accounting for Certain Transactions involving Stock Compensation, an interpretation of APB Opinion No. 25," March 2000.

- *EITF issues.* The EITF has considered many issues regarding stock-based compensation, some dating back to the mid-1980s. Some have been superseded by FIN 44. The most noteworthy issue currently in effect is Issue 00-23, a lengthy series of questions intended to illuminate the accounting treatment of specific situations not clearly addressed in FIN 44 or APB 25. The EITF began deliberations on Issue 00-23 in 2000.

(ii) FAS 123   In the early 1990s, FASB attempted to replace APB 25 with a different standard for stock-based compensation that would measure the value of stock options using economic "fair value" models. For employee stock options, this means using an option-pricing model such as the Black-Scholes or binomial model "that takes into account as of the grant date the exercise price and expected life of the option, the current price of the underlying stock and its expected volatility, expected dividends on the stock . . . , and the risk-free interest rate for the expected term of the option." FAS 123 provides specific guidance regarding selection of appropriate assumptions for each of these variables.

FASB's attempt to require companies to book an expense for stock options, in contrast to APB 25's far more favorable treatment, was thwarted by vociferous protests from companies and some members of Congress. As a result, FASB issued a new standard in 1995 in the form of FAS 123, which *permits* companies to adopt the fair value method of valuing employee stock options, but *requires* only pro forma (footnote) disclosure of the fair value cost. Decades-old APB 25 thus continues to reign as the "bible" of stock-based compensation issued to employees.

For most companies, FAS 123 has been relevant only because of its mandated footnote disclosure. Since the issuance of FIN 44, however, companies have been clearly required to use FAS 123 to value stock-based grants to nonemployees. FIN 44 clearly specifies the scope of APB 25: It may be used only to account for stock-based grants to common-law employees and outside directors elected to the company's Board. Stock-based awards to all nonemployees (except outside directors) must be accounted for under FAS 123.

Additional guidance regarding the implementation of FAS 123 has been issued since 1995. This includes:

- EITF 96-18, "Accounting for Equity Instruments That Are Issued to Other Than Employees for Acquiring, or in Conjunction with Selling, Goods or Services."
- FASB Technical Bulletin No. 97-1, "Accounting under Statement 123 for Certain Employee Stock Purchase Plans with a Look-Back Option."

As of this writing, the IASB is considering a proposal that would require FAS 123–type accounting for all countries that follow its standards. The IASB's deliberations on this issue and an overall set of international accounting standards are expected to extend over several years. It is uncertain at this time what those standards will look like, as well as whether they will be acceptable to the countries that constitute the IASB and its parent body, the IASC.

18.2 UNDERSTANDING THE BASICS OF APB 25

Please note that all information included in this chapter is intended to serve as general background information for the nonaccountant. The rules governing accounting for stock-based compensation are complex and detailed, and a full description is beyond the scope of this chapter. In addition, as the EITF continues to consider various topics related to stock-based compensation, some of the material in this chapter may be modified. Specific accounting treatment will depend on the facts and circumstances of a particular transaction or situation and should be discussed with the company's auditors before reaching a conclusion.

(a) The Three Fundamental Questions

Under APB 25, the accounting treatment of a stock-based compensation plan depends on the answers to three questions:

1. Is the plan *compensatory* or *noncompensatory*?
2. If the plan is compensatory, are awards under the plan *fixed* or *variable*?
3. How is compensation cost measured and recognized?

Exhibit 18.1 provides an overview of the structure of APB 25 and how answers to the three questions determine the accounting treatment of a stock-based award.

(i) Is the Plan Compensatory or Noncompensatory?   A plan that is *noncompensatory* does not result in any charge to earnings; however, four criteria have to be met for a plan to fall into this category:

1. Substantially *all full-time employees* meeting specified employment qualifications may participate. (Employees owning a specified percentage of the company's outstanding stock and certain executives may be excluded.)
2. Stock is offered to eligible employees *equally* or on the basis of a uniform percentage of salary or wages (although the plan may limit the number of shares that an employee may purchase under a plan).
3. The *time* permitted for exercise of an option or purchase right is limited to a reasonable period.
4. The *discount* from the market price of the stock is no greater than would be reasonable in an offer of stock to stockholders or others.

Exhibit 18.1   Taxonomy of Stock Plan Accounting Under APB 25.

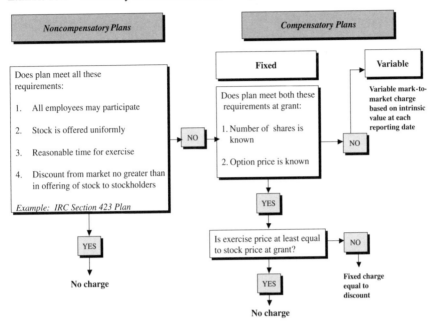

APB 25 specifies that a Section 423 employee stock purchase plan is an example of a noncompensatory plan. As a practical matter, a plan that meets the criteria to qualify under Section 423 is the only common type of stock compensation arrangement that can qualify as noncompensatory.

FIN 44 clarifies the size of the discount permissible to qualify a plan as non-compensatory. A discount of up to 15% of the stock price, determined as of the grant date, is acceptable, since this is permitted under Section 423. FIN 44 further clarifies that even so-called look-back plans—those where the employee can purchase stock at a discount from the stock price at the beginning or end of the term, whichever is lower—can be deemed noncompensatory, since this provision is also permitted under Section 423.

(ii) If the Plan Is Compensatory, Are Awards Under the Plan Fixed or Variable?   Any plan that does not qualify as noncompensatory is compensatory. Compensation cost in a compensatory plan must be measured. The measurement date may be fixed or variable.

The measurement date for a *fixed* award is the date of grant. An award is fixed if the following two features are known at the date of grant:

1.   The number of shares that an individual is entitled to receive under that award

2.   The exercise or other purchase price

For example, a classic stock option award, under which the number of shares that can be purchased and the exercise price are set as of the date of grant, is a fixed award. The measurement date is the grant date, and compensation cost (if any) is measured as of that date.

The measurement date for a *variable* award does not occur until both of the elements under 1 and 2 above are known. For example, an option that has an exercise price that increases or decreases according to the movement of an index, such as the Standard and Poor's (S&P) 500, would be a variable award because the exercise price is not known at the grant date. Similarly, an option that may not be exercised until specified corporate performance targets are met would be a variable award because the number of shares the option holder is entitled to receive is not known at the grant date.

For a variable award, "mark-to-market" accounting is required during the period beginning on the grant date and ending on the measurement date—that is, value must be estimated at each reporting date, with any increase since the last reporting date recorded as cost. A simplified example of variable accounting, which assumes the option is fully vested at the grant date, is shown in Exhibit 18.2.

Typically, a variable award will result in greater cost than a fixed award, as well as greater administrative burden. Most companies find that plans with variable accounting treatment are unacceptable because of their impact on earnings: the amount of expense is both uncontrollable and unpredictable, as shown in the example in Exhibit 18.2. Annual expense swings from $2,000 in the first year to − $2,000 (a reversal of the prior year's expense) in the second, up to $4,000

Exhibit 18.2   Illustration of Variable Accounting: 100% Vested.

Assumptions:

1,000 shares under option, granted 12/31/00

$10 exercise price (equal to stock price on grant date)

Options fully vested at grant date

Options are exercised on 12/31/04

				Compensation		
Date	Stock Price	Per Share	Total	Total Accrued at Beginning of Year	Current Year Expense	Total Accrued at Year-End
12/31/01	$12	$2	$2,000	$ 0	$2,000	$2,000
12/31/02	$ 9	$0	$ 0	$2,000	($2,000)	$ 0
12/31/03	$14	$4	$4,000	$ 0	$4,000	$4,000
12/31/04	$15	$5	$5,000	$4,000	$1,000	$5,000

in the third, and down to $1,000 in the fourth. In addition to the difficulty of forecasting financial results because of these variations, in many cases the final measurement date depends on when the option holder decides to exercise—an event beyond the company's control. For this reason, performance-contingent awards—those where the number of shares or exercise price are contingent upon specific performance criteria—are used infrequently.

A requirement that a minimum service period be completed for awards to be exercisable does not trigger variable accounting by making the number of shares issuable unknown at the grant date. For example, stock option awards typically have vesting provisions that specify the schedule under which the option is "earned": if the option holder's employment terminates before the vesting date(s), he or she will forfeit the option, and the option cannot be exercised until vesting occurs. A common vesting schedule for a stock option is 33% per year starting one year after the option has been granted. This suggests that the number of shares to be issued might, in fact, not be known at the grant date, since there is uncertainty about whether the option holder will actually remain employed and earn the right to receive the shares under the option; however, APB 25 specifically states that this type of service requirement does not convert an otherwise fixed award into a variable one.

The difference in accounting treatment between plans that condition exercisability only on completion of a minimum service period and those that condition exercisability on satisfaction of specified performance targets is ironic, given modern compensation practice. Although institutional shareholders and certain tax and legal rules encourage companies to adopt performance-based plans, these plans receive less favorable accounting treatment under APB 25 than non–performance-based plans. Thus, the accounting rules encourage companies to adopt plans that are not necessarily the most effective at either motivating and rewarding employees, or linking their interests with those of shareholders.

Furthermore, application of the rules under APB 25 yields contradictory results. A performance-contingent plan, whose value is uncertain until the performance outcome is known, is generally less valuable to the option holder, and potentially less costly to the company, than a conventional service-based plan, whose value is dependent only on the option holder's continued service; however, APB 25 results in a higher cost for the less valuable award, compared with zero cost for the more valuable award.

A compromise award design has arisen from this inconsistency. "Performance-accelerated" awards vest at some time in the future based solely on continued service; however, the awards may vest earlier, that is, vesting is accelerated if certain performance goals are achieved. Thus, these awards meet the two requirements for fixed accounting: The number of shares that may be issued is fixed and known at the grant date, as is the exercise price. The only variable is the timing of the vesting.

Note that the ultimate vesting date for a performance-accelerated award must generally be no more than seven to eight years from the grant date. If it is longer than that, the company runs the risk of triggering variable accounting, since it becomes less likely that the employee will actually vest in the award, and the award will be deemed performance contingent, rather than performance accelerated.

One additional note regarding variable accounting: Companies often find themselves in the situation where their stock plans have too few shares remaining available for their regular annual grant. They may consider awarding options in advance of obtaining shareholder approval that is required for the underlying shares. It is important to note that variable accounting is triggered if the company makes such awards before obtaining the required shareholder approval. The measurement date is considered the date that shareholder approval is obtained. If the stock price has increased since the options were initially granted, the company will have to recognize compensation cost. Note that this applies not only when shareholder approval is required, but also when it is voluntarily sought.

An exception is made if management and the members of the Board of Directors control sufficient votes to approve the plan. In that case, the measurement date may be deemed to occur on the initial grant date, and fixed accounting would apply.

In addition, note that this requirement may inadvertently convert an otherwise noncompensatory stock purchase plan into a compensatory plan, if the company makes grants under the plan before approving shareholder approval for the underlying shares. Since the shareholder approval date is the measurement date, the resulting discount may be greater than the 15% "safe harbor" provided for under APB 25 and FIN 44.

(iii) How Is Compensation Cost Measured and Recognized? APB 25

measures compensation cost using the *"intrinsic value"* method: Compensation cost is equal to the quoted market price of the stock at the measurement date minus the amount, if any, the individual is required to pay for the stock. This is also called the "spread" or, if the option has not yet been exercised, "paper gain."

The intrinsic value method produces a favorable result for most commonly used stock options. If the exercise price is at least equal to the stock price at the date of grant (as is the case with most stock options), the intrinsic value of the option is zero. Thus, "premium" options, where the exercise price is set higher than the stock price on the grant date, will create no accounting charge. "Discount options," however, which set the exercise price below the stock price on the grant date, will generate an expense equal to the amount of the discount (i.e., the intrinsic value).

Most types of stock compensation awards, other than stock options, result in compensation cost. For example, assume that an employee is awarded 1,000 restricted shares, and the value per share is $50 at the grant date. The employee is not required to pay anything to receive the stock. The intrinsic value of the award is $50,000 (1,000 times $50).

Compensation cost is *recognized* over the service period to which the award relates—typically, the vesting period. The amortization schedule used to recognize the accounting cost depends on the vesting schedule and whether the award is fixed or variable. The most typical vesting schedules include:

* *Cliff vesting.* A cliff vesting schedule provides for 100% vesting on a specified future date, with nothing vesting before that date—for example, an award that vests 100% on the third anniversary of the grant date. The cost (if any) of such an award would be recognized in equal installments over the three years of the vesting period: 33% each year. For example, if an employee vested in the restricted stock grant described above at the end of three years, the $50,000 total compensation cost would be recognized equally over the three-year vesting period ($16,667 per year).

* *Pro-rata vesting.* A pro-rata vesting schedule, also called serial, graded, ratable, or installment, provides that the award will vest in installments over a period of years, such as 33% per year starting one year after the grant date. The award thus becomes vested 33% at the end of the first year, 67% at the end of the second year, and 100% at the end of the third year.

FIN 28 requires that a variable award with this type of pro-rata vesting schedule is accounted for by treating each tranche as if it were an individual grant. Thus, for an award that vests in thirds over three years, the first tranche is assumed to be earned over one year, and 100% of its cost would be recognized in that first year. The second is assumed to be earned over two years, with 50% of its cost recognized in each of those two years. The third is assumed to be earned over three years, with 33% of its cost recognized in each of the three years. This is illustrated in Exhibit 18.3.

A variable award with pro-rata vesting *must* be amortized as shown in Exhibit 18.3; however, EITF 00-23 specifies that a fixed award with a pro-rata vesting schedule *may* be amortized using either the FIN 28–type of amortization schedule or in equal installments. Exhibit 18.4 illustrates the difference between these two approaches for a fixed award of restricted stock.

In the exhibit, the cost of the restricted stock is fixed and known at the grant date. The amortization schedule, whether it is equal installments or in accordance with FIN 28, is also fixed and known at the grant date. Changes in the stock price have no impact on the cost of a fixed award. In comparison with the equal installment vesting, the FIN 28 amortization schedule "front-loads" the expense—$6,050 for the FIN 28 schedule in the first year versus only $3,333 for the equal installment method.

If the award vested 100% at the end of three years (cliff vesting instead of pro rata), the equal installment method would be the only one permissible.

Exhibit 18.3   Illustration of Variable Accounting: 33% (Pro Rata) Vesting Per Year.

Same assumptions as Exhibit 18.2, but with 33% per year vesting starting on first anniversary of grant.

			Compensation				
Date	Stock Price	Per Share	Aggregate	Percent Accrued*	Total Accrued at Beginning of Year	Current Year Expense	Total Accrued at Year-End
12/31/01	$12	$2	$2,000	60.5%	$0	$1,210	$1,210
12/31/02	$9	$0	$0	88.0%	$1,210	($1,210)	$0
12/31/03	$14	$4	$4,000	100%	$0	$4,000	$4,000
12/31/04	$15	$5	$5,000	100%	$4,000	$1,000	$5,000

* See chart below

		Aggregate Percentage of Compensation Accrued by End of Each Year of Service		
For Options Vesting In:	Service Period	2001	2002	2003
2001	1 year	33%	33%	33%
2002	2 years	16.5%	33%	33%
2003	3 years	11%	22%	33%
Aggregate percentage accrued at end of each year		60.5%	88%	100%

Once a company chooses an amortization method for awards that vest on a pro-rata basis, it must adhere to that method for all awards that vest pro rata.

(b)   Whose Awards Are Covered Under APB 25?

The title of APB 25 specifies that it applies to stock-based grants to employees only. In practice, however, many companies used to follow APB 25 when accounting for stock-based grants to almost any type of service provider, including outside consultants, independent contractors, and members of the Board of Directors.

FIN 44 changed this practice by specifying that APB 25 is applicable only to "common law" employees, which is generally the same as the definition of "employee" for payroll tax purposes, and elected members of the Board of Directors.

Exhibit 18.4   Illustration of Fixed Accounting.

Assumptions:

1,000 restricted shares awarded on 12/31/00

$10 stock price on 12/31/00

Shares vest 33% per year starting on first anniversary of grant

Total cost fixed at grant: $10,000

		Equal Installment Amortization		
Date	Percent Accrued	Total Accrued at Beginning of Year	Current Year Expense	Total Accrued at Year-End
12/31/01	33%	$0	$3,333	$3,333
12/31/02	67%	$3,333	$3,333	$6,666
12/31/03	100%	$6,666	$3,334	$10,000

		FIN 28 Amortization		
Date	Percent Accrued*	Total Accrued at Beginning of Year	Current Year Expense	Total Accrued at Year-End
12/31/01	60.5%	$0	$6,050	$6,050
12/31/02	88.0%	$6,050	$2,750	$8,800
12/31/03	100%	$8,800	$1,200	$10,000

*See table in Exhibit 18.3.

In addition, when a company prepares consolidated financial statements, stock-based awards to employees of any entity within the consolidated group, whether based on the parent's stock or the stock of any of the subsidiaries, are accounted for under APB 25. Note that this is only true in the consolidated financial statements (and the separate financial statements of the subsidiaries if their employees have received awards based on the parent's stock). In cases where the awards are based on the stock of one or more of the subsidiaries, and separate financial statements are prepared, different rules apply—generally, FAS 123 rules (see following discussion).

In general, stock-based grants to any nonemployees are accounted for under FAS 123, discussed in Section 18.3. This typically includes grants to independent contractors and consultants. It also applies to grants made to employees of a joint venture, when the grants are based on the stock of one of the joint venture partners.

(c) What Happens If the Terms of an Outstanding Award Are Changed?

As described previously, an award can be considered "fixed" if both the number of shares and purchase price, if any, are known at the grant date. In practice, companies often modify the terms of an award for a variety of reasons.

The accounting rules governing modifications to stock-based awards are detailed and cumbersome. The most important thing to know about modifications is that any change to an existing award, no matter how minor it may appear, can trigger potentially unfavorable accounting treatment. In some cases, the result is a new measurement date: The change effectively creates a new award with a new fixed measurement date. In other cases, the result is that a fixed award is converted into a variable award, since the number of shares or purchase price are deemed uncertain as of the original grant date.

In most cases, compensation cost that arises from a modification to an award that triggers either a new measurement date or variable accounting is amortized over the remaining vesting period of the award. If the award is fully vested, any additional compensation cost to be recognized is recognized in full immediately.

This section includes a description of the accounting treatment of some of the most common types of modifications. These are:

- Renewal or extension of the life of an award
- Reduction of the exercise price
- Increase in number of shares to be issued

(i) Renewal or Extension of the Life of an Award   This category includes extension of the term of an award upon termination of employment and acceleration of vesting. APB 25 specifies that a renewal of a fixed award or extension of the award's life results in a new measurement date, as if the award were newly granted. FIN 44 provides guidance on this requirement.

Term Extension   One of the most common examples of the application of this rule is a situation where an executive is about to terminate service as a result of retirement. Option agreements typically provide that an option will expire within a specified period following retirement—say, one year, or the end of the option's contractual term, whichever is shorter. Many companies find that there are circumstances when they would like to extend the expiration date relating to retirement, possibly restoring the full remaining contractual term of the option, to provide the retiring executive with a longer opportunity to exercise. Sometimes this is because the options are currently underwater or because the post-retirement provision was established long ago and market practice has become more generous.

The accounting treatment is to remeasure the option's intrinsic value at the date the modification to the award is made. Any intrinsic value in excess of the amount measured at the original measurement date (which is generally zero for options with "at-the-money" or premium exercise prices) must be recognized as expense; however, the expense need not be recognized unless the termination (retirement, in this case) actually occurs.

As an example, assume that a company has decided to modify all of its outstanding option agreements by increasing the post-retirement exercise period from one year to three years (but not beyond the remaining term of the option). On the date the modification is made, the intrinsic value of all affected options is measured and fixed; however, the company need only recognize an expense for those employees who actually retire and can therefore benefit from the extension by having a longer period in which to exercise. Any options that are exercised or expire before the optionee's retirement will not generate any expense.

From a practical standpoint, if the options are underwater, the intrinsic value at the modification date is zero, and the company will not incur any expense, regardless of whether the option holder retires and therefore can benefit from the term extension.

Another common situation where companies might like to extend the post-termination exercise period occurs when there is a reduction in force or divestiture. A typical option agreement might specify that the employees have 90 days in which to exercise following termination of employment. But if a reduction in force or a divestiture occurs, the company may wish to be more generous, possibly extending the 90-day period to the full remaining contractual term.

The accounting treatment is similar to that described previously for extension of the term in the case of retirement. The intrinsic value is measured on the modification date, and an expense is recognized only if the employees terminate service.

In practice, the company may need to estimate the expense before the actual termination date, if it is likely that the employment termination and associated term extension will occur. If the option vests and is exercised before employment termination, any previously recognized expense may be reversed because extension of the option's term that would have been triggered by separation did not occur.

Note that if the term of an option is extended beyond the original contractual maximum (10 years for most stock options), cost must be remeasured and recognized for any employee who *could* benefit from the extension, regardless of whether there is a termination associated with it. The cost would be recognized over the remaining vesting period, if any, or immediately, if the award were fully vested.

Acceleration of Vesting A modification of a fixed award to accelerate its vesting will be considered a renewal of the award if, after the modification, an employee is able to exercise or vest in an award that, under the original terms, would have expired unexercisable or unvested.

The accounting treatment here is similar to the treatment for an extension of the term. The new measurement date occurs when the modification is made, and is recognized if and when the acceleration actually occurs. For example, an option agreement might specify that any unvested options are forfeited upon early retirement. The company might wish to accelerate vesting on the options to encourage early retirement, as part of a reorganization. The date the award is modified to change the vesting provision becomes the new measurement date. Any intrinsic value in excess of the amount measured at the original measurement date would be recognized as compensation expense—if the option holders do, in fact, take early retirement and the vesting accelerates.

Similarly, whether an accounting charge is triggered by modifying an outstanding award to provide for acceleration of vesting while an employee remains in service depends on whether the employee actually benefits from the modification. For example, a company might choose to accelerate the vesting on an option that is scheduled to vest in three years. Compensation expense would be recognized only if the option holder terminates employment before the end of three years, resulting in restoration of an award that would otherwise have been forfeited were it not for the modification. No charge would be necessary if the employee remains in service.

Our discussion of vesting acceleration has so far focused on options. Note that these rules apply to all awards, including restricted stock. For example, assume that a restricted stock grant that has not yet vested will be forfeited upon involuntary termination. The company decides it wants to terminate employment of the executive holding the stock as a result of a change in its business strategy, rather than for performance issues. The company would like the executive to be able to retain his or her unvested restricted stock upon termination. If the company accelerates the vesting, the value of the stock on the modification date is measured. If the stock has appreciated in value since the grant date, there will be additional compensation expense to recognize if the executive's employment is terminated and the vesting accelerates. Exhibit 18.5 illustrates the impact of this type of vesting acceleration.

In the situation illustrated in Exhibit 18.5, the total cost to be recognized increased from $10,000 to $11,333 ($3,333 plus $8,000 due to acceleration of vesting). The stock price on the date the acceleration was triggered (6/30/02) may have been lower than it was on the modification date (12/31/01), but the value on 12/31/01 was used to measure the cost because it was the new measurement date.

(ii) Reduction of the Exercise Price

This covers the typical "option repricing" situation that occurs when stock options are underwater. It triggers variable accounting until the option is exercised, forfeited, or expires. The rationale is that once a company has reduced the exercise price of an option, it can no longer claim that the exercise price was known at the initial grant date. In addition,

Exhibit 18.5   Impact of Vesting Acceleration.

Assumptions:
1,000 restricted shares awarded on 12/31/00
$10 stock price on 12/31/00
$12 stock price on 12/31/01
Shares vest 33% per year starting on first anniversary of grant
Total cost fixed at grant: $10,000
Cost amortized in equal installments (first table in Exhibit 18.4)

12/31/01:	Company recognizes $3,333 in expense (33% × $10,000). Company then modifies the award to provide for acceleration of vesting in event of retirement. The new measurement date is 12/31/01. The total value of the award on 12/31/01 is $12,000, of which $8,000 (67% or 667 shares) is unvested. This represents the cost at the modification date that must be recognized if the executive retires and the vesting accelerates on those shares.
6/30/02:	Executive retires and vesting accelerates on 667 unvested shares. The company must recognize the additional $8,000 of expense.

FASB believes that there is no practical way to determine whether future exercise price reductions may occur.

The most common method of repricing an option consists of canceling the original option and replacing it with a new one with a lower exercise price. Canceling an option, or settling it for cash ("buying" it back), and immediately replacing it with a new one will trigger variable accounting. In addition, a repricing will be deemed to have occurred if an option is canceled or settled for cash or other consideration and replaced with a new option to the same employee at a lower exercise price, within six months before or six months after the cancellation/settlement—a 12-month window. This "six-month" rule has resulted in many companies canceling underwater options with a promise to grant new ones in six months and a day ("six and one" grants).

Note that, from a practical standpoint, the six-month look-back period counts backward from the date the company offers employees the opportunity to cancel their options. The six-month look-forward period, however, begins on the date the option is legally canceled. Depending upon the length of the offering period, the 12-month window may, in fact, be longer.

Cancellation of the option can occur directly or indirectly. This is one of the more insidious features of FIN 44, which states that "any modification to the terms of an option award to reduce the likelihood of exercise by the grantee shall be considered a cancellation of that award." For example, an increase in the exercise price or curtailment of the remaining life, including lengthening the vesting schedule, is likely to be considered a cancellation.

Note, however, that if an option is cancelled and replaced with a restricted or unrestricted stock grant, the stock grant will not be subject to variable accounting because the grant has a purchase price of zero, and the exercise/purchase price could not be reduced below it.

An option's exercise price can be reduced indirectly without changing the terms of the initial award. An indirect repricing will occur if, for example, an award is modified to provide that a cash bonus will be paid only if the option is exercised. (A cash bonus payment that is contingent on the vesting of an option, however, will not trigger variable accounting for the underlying option.) The cash bonus indirectly reduces the exercise price based on the total consideration the company will receive when the option is exercised, even though the stated exercise price of the option itself has not been changed. The same reasoning applies if the company allows the option to be exercised with a full recourse note that bears a nonmarket interest rate. The inclusion of the nonmarket interest rate will make the associated option subject to variable accounting, whether this feature was part of the original award or added later.

An exercise price can be reduced directly or indirectly contingent upon the occurrence of a specified future event or condition. For example, an option can be modified to provide that the exercise price will be reduced if a certain earnings target or stock price is reached in the future. This will trigger variable accounting until the award is exercised, forfeited, or expires. Note that if the contingency feature has been added and the contingent event does not occur, the company *cannot* reverse any charges previously accrued, whereas the charges *could* be reversed if the contingency feature were part of the original option terms.

(iii) Increase in Number of Shares to Be Issued   This will also trigger variable accounting until the option is exercised, forfeited, or expires. The most common example of this would be the addition of a reload feature after the option is already outstanding. A reload feature provides for the grant of a new option upon exercise of an existing option if specified conditions are met (generally, that the exercise price is satisfied using previously owned shares of the company's stock). If the reload feature is included in the original terms of the grant, the option will be fixed. If a company adds a reload provision to an outstanding option, the option will be subject to variable accounting. If the reload feature provides for multiple subsequent grants through further reloads, variable accounting is required for each additional grant with a reload feature.

(d)   How Are Options and Stock Awards Accounted for If They Contain a Put, Call, or Other Type of Repurchase Feature?

The rules regarding puts, calls, and rights of first refusal are complex. As with all information included in this chapter, the specific accounting treatment will depend on the facts and circumstances of a particular transaction or situation and should be discussed with the company's auditors before reaching a conclusion.

The rules regarding repurchase features depend on whether an entity is publicly or privately held. For these purposes, a public company is one that has publicly traded equity securities, including "thinly traded" stock, or has filed with a regulatory agency in preparation for a sale of equity securities to the public. A subsidiary of a public company is also considered public. If only debt is publicly traded, the company is considered private.

If a stock-based award issued by a public company contains a put, call, or right of first refusal, the award will generally be variable only if the shares are expected to be repurchased within six months after issuance. Note that this assumes that the repurchase right is based on the fair value of the stock at the repurchase date. If the repurchase feature is a put that allows the employee to sell the shares back to the company based on a formula price or a variable premium over the fair value at the repurchase date, the award will be variable until the put is exercised or expires.

For nonpublic companies, awards with puts, calls, or rights of first refusal are variable unless either:

- The repurchase price equals fair value at the repurchase date, and the shares are not expected to be repurchased within six months of issuance (note that this would make the award equivalent to that of a public company with a repurchase feature), or
- The repurchase price does not equal fair value at the repurchase date, but the employee has made a substantial investment (defined as 100% of the purchase price), and bears risk and rewards of ownership.

For private company stock options with a repurchase feature, variable accounting would generally be required only until the option is exercised, as long as the underlying shares are not expected to be repurchased within six months after the exercise date.

If shares were "unexpectedly" repurchased within six months of issuance or exercise (and thus variable accounting had not been applied), the company would need to recognize a charge equal to the spread between the exercise price and the price paid by the company to repurchase the shares.

The EITF has issued extensive guidance regarding the term *expected* to be repurchased (Issue 00-23). This guidance states that repurchase provisions that are essentially related to forfeitures of the underlying awards will not make an otherwise fixed award variable. An example of this would be a requirement that a company repurchases shares for an amount equal to the option's original exercise price if the option holder terminates employment within a specified period, equivalent to a vesting period.

An exception to the repurchase rules is made for shares that are withheld by the company to satisfy withholding tax requirements upon exercise of an option, vesting of a restricted share award, or any other event that triggers a requirement for the company to withhold taxes for the employee; however, variable accounting will apply to all of a company's awards granted under a plan if:

- The plan permits the employee to elect withholding in excess of the employer's statutory minimum, or
- The plan is silent or the employer may decide the amount of withholding, and there is a pattern of withholding in excess of the employer's statutory minimum.

Even if there is no pattern of excess withholding, if there is excess withholding with respect to an individual award, an accounting charge must be taken equal to the intrinsic value of the award.

(e)   What Are the Special Rules That Apply to Options Granted in Connection with Business Combinations?

It is common in certain kinds of business combinations to adjust any outstanding options held by employees of the acquired company to keep them "whole." This is typically done by converting existing options on the acquired company's stock to equivalent value options on the stock of the acquirer. The adjustment of outstanding options in connection with a business combination may result in no accounting charge, a new (fixed) measurement date, or variable accounting, depending on both the type of combination and the nature of the adjustment. Some alternative approaches include:

- *Spinoffs.* A special rule applies to options that are granted or exchanged as part of a spinoff transaction or other so-called nonreciprocal equity transactions. This is the "ratio-and-spread" test. There is no accounting consequence for changes made to the exercise price, number of shares, or both as a result of a nonreciprocal equity restructuring if:
  - The aggregate intrinsic value of the award immediately after the change is not greater than the aggregate intrinsic value of the award before the change, and
  - The ratio of the exercise price per share to the market price per share is not reduced.

  If these two criteria are not met, the modified award is accounted for as variable until it is exercised, forfeited, or expires unexercised.

- *Purchase business combinations.* The accounting treatment of outstanding options depends on whether they are vested or unvested at the date of the transaction. It does not matter whether the conversion of the options meets the ratio-and-spread test.
  - *Vested options.* The fair value (e.g., Black-Scholes) of vested options or awards that are issued by an acquirer in exchange for outstanding awards

held by employees of the acquired company are accounted for as part of the purchase price in accordance with FAS 141 and 142.

— *Unvested options.* As with vested options, the fair value of unvested awards is also accounted for as part of the purchase price; however, the company must also measure the intrinsic value of the replacement awards at the consummation date of the transaction. The portion of the intrinsic value attributable to the unvested portion of the options is recognized as compensation cost over the remaining future vesting period and deducted from the fair value allocated to the purchase price. The unvested portion is based on the remaining vesting period divided by the original total vesting period.

An example is shown in Exhibit 18.6.

Note: We have excluded discussion of rules regarding pooling-of-interests since this accounting alternative for business combinations has been eliminated for transactions initiated after June 30, 2001.

18.3   UNDERSTANDING THE BASICS OF FAS 123

(a)   General Information

Unlike APB 25, FAS 123 requires that equity-based awards be valued at their "fair value," rather than intrinsic value. Under the fair-value method, compensation cost is measured at the grant date based on the value of the award and is

Exhibit 18.6   Options Exchanged in a Purchase Business Combination.

Assumptions:

Company A acquires Company B on July 1, 2003, in a purchase business combination. Company A exchanges 10,000 options with a fair value of $100,000 for 5,000 options held by the employees of Company B before the exchange. The options held by Company B employees were granted on June 30, 2001, and provided for cliff vesting on June 30, 2004. Company A options granted in the exchange vest according to the same schedule (cliff vest on June 30, 2004). The intrinsic value of the Company A options granted at the date of the exchange is $4 per option.

Accounting treatment:

The $100,000 fair value of the options granted in the exchange is part of the purchase price paid for Company B; however, $13,333 is allocated to unearned compensation and is deducted by Company A from the cost of Company B. The unearned compensation of $13,333 is determined as the total intrinsic value of the awards ($4 × 10,000, or $40,000) multiplied by the fraction (one-third) that is the remaining vesting period over the total vesting period. The unearned compensation of $13,333 must be recognized by Company A as compensation expense over the remaining vesting period.

---

recognized over the service period, which is typically the vesting period. This means that most stock options, which have zero intrinsic value when granted and therefore no compensation cost under APB 25, will require recognition of compensation cost under FAS 123. For this reason, nearly all companies have opted for the "disclosure-only" provisions of FAS 123, continuing to use APB 25 as the basis for recognizing compensation costs in the financial statements themselves; however, companies are required to use FAS 123 when accounting for stock-based grants to nonemployees (other than outside directors).

For stock options, fair value is determined using an option-pricing model, such as the Black-Scholes model, that takes into account the following:

- Stock price at the grant date
- Exercise price
- Expected life of the option
- Volatility of the underlying stock
- Expected dividends on the underlying stock
- Risk-free interest rate over the expected life of the option

Nonpublic entities are permitted to exclude volatility (i.e., set it equal to zero) in estimating the fair value of their stock options, which results in measurement at "minimum value."

The fair value of restricted stock or other full-value grants is generally measured at the market price of the stock on the grant date, similar to APB 25.

(b) Noncompensatory Treatment

FAS 123 effectively eliminates the noncompensatory treatment afforded to employee stock purchase plans (Section 423 plans) under APB 25. It does include a noncompensatory exclusion, but the requirements are virtually impossible to satisfy if a company wishes to implement an employee stock purchase plan that will actually be attractive to employees.

(c) Transactions with Employees

(i) What Is "Fair Value"?   The six variables used to calculate the fair value of an option are listed previously. FAS 123 provides fairly explicit guidance on how to estimate the value of those variables. For example, the expected life of the option is generally not the same as its full term. It represents the time when employees are expected to exercise the options. FAS 123 suggests that companies consider several factors in estimating an option's expected life, including the vesting period, the company's historical exercise experience, and the expected volatility of the stock.

Based on the guidance included in FAS 123, companies are expected to choose the best estimate within a range of possible amounts; however, if no "best guess" is possible, companies are permitted to use an estimate that will result in the lowest option value. "If no amount within a range is a better estimate than any other amount, it is appropriate to use an estimate at the *low* end of the range for expected volatility and expected option life, and an estimate at the *high* end of the range for expected dividends." Exhibit 18.7 summarizes the impact on the option's value of changes in each of the variables.

The fair value of an award to an employee is not adjusted for subsequent changes in any of the variables—once it is fixed at the grant date, it does not change, providing there is no change in the option's terms. The number of awards, however, is "trued up" based on the actual number that vest. This actual number is the basis for the recognition of the total amount of compensation cost.

(ii) How Are Performance Conditions Accounted for Under FAS 123?
No compensation cost is recognized for awards that are forfeited by employees either because they fail to satisfy a service requirement for vesting (i.e., terminate employment before full vesting) or because the company fails to achieve a performance condition. This is one of the key conceptual advantages of FAS 123 versus APB 25: FAS 123 includes certain provisions regarding performance-based plans that differ from APB 25 and, in fact, are far more logical, as described in Section 18.2(a)(ii). Unlike APB 25, FAS 123 treats awards with service-based and performance-based vesting in essentially the same way. For both types of awards, the value of the award is fixed at the grant date and reversed if the vesting requirement is not met.

Note that FAS 123 excludes from "performance condition" any requirements that are based on stock price, such as total return or a target stock price. For these awards, compensation cost is recognized for awards to all employees who satisfy any associated service requirement, regardless of whether the stock price performance condition is met.

To illustrate how performance conditions are accounted for under FAS 123, let us look at two different performance-based options at the same company,

Exhibit 18.7 Impact of Change in Assumptions on Black-Scholes Value of a Stock Option.

Increase in:	Impact on option value:
Stock price	Increase
Exercise price	Decrease
Expected life	Increase
Volatility	Increase
Expected dividends	Decrease
Risk-free interest rate	Increase

granted at the same time. Option A vests if the company's *earnings per share growth* meets or exceeds the median of a group of peer companies at the end of three years. Option B vests if the company's *stock price appreciation* meets or exceeds the median of a group of peer companies at the end of three years. The fair value of the options at the grant date is identical. The cost of each option would be spread over the three-year potential vesting period. The accounting treatment is as follows:

- *Interim cost estimates—Option A:* Based on the company's estimate of the likelihood of meeting the EPS goal, plus an estimate of the number of employees still employed at the end of three years.

- *Interim cost estimates—Option B:* Based only on an estimate of the number of employees still employed at the end of three years.

- *Final cost—performance goals met:* Option A and Option B will have the same final total cost: Fair value of the options at grant date, times number of options vested due to fulfillment of both performance and service requirements.

- *Final cost—performance goals missed:* Option A will result in zero total cost—all interim accruals would be reversed at the end of the three years. Option B, however, would result in a cost equal to the full fair value as if the performance condition had actually been met—fair value of options at grant date times number of options that would have vested based solely on the service requirement.

Interim costs may be accrued either by estimating a forfeiture rate and then adjusting it to reflect actual forfeitures or simply by recognizing forfeitures as they occur.

(iii) How Are Modifications Accounted for Under FAS 123?   The accounting treatment for modifications of existing awards under FAS 123 is quite different than APB 25—and much simpler. A modification that makes an award more valuable is treated as if the original award was exchanged for a new award. Compensation cost must be recognized for any incremental value. The incremental value is the difference between (a) the fair value of the modified option and (b) the value of the old option immediately before its terms were modified, based on the shorter of (1) its remaining expected life or (2) the expected life of the modified option.

(d)   Transactions with Nonemployees

Because APB 25 can only be used to account for stock-based awards to employees and elected members of a company's Board of Directors, FAS 123 is used to account for awards to all nonemployees. FIN 44 and various EITF issues help define a "nonemployee." This includes:

- Independent contractors
- Consultants
- Other nonemployees who provide goods or services
- Employees of an unconsolidated subsidiary who receive grants from the parent
- Employees of a parent company who receive grants from an unconsolidated subsidiary
- Employees of a joint venture who receive grants from one or more of the investors in the joint venture

The provisions of FAS 123 that apply to nonemployees are similar to those for employees, with two key exceptions:

- Use full term, not expected life—In computing the fair value of an option awarded to a nonemployee, the full contractual term is used, rather than the expected life.
- Variable until committed—EITF 96-18 specifies that the value of awards to nonemployee service providers, such as independent contractors, is not fixed under FAS 123 until either:
  - The date at which the nonemployee's performance is complete, or
  - The date at which a "performance commitment" is reached. A performance commitment exists when performance by the nonemployee to earn the equity award is probable because of sufficiently large disincentives for nonperformance.

For example, an option granted by a company to employees of an unconsolidated subsidiary that carried a three-year cliff vesting schedule would have a measurement date at the end of the three-year period. The fair value of the option at the end of the vesting period would be the compensation cost. During interim reporting periods, the cost is estimated by calculating the fair value and recording any changes from the prior period as expense.

(e)   Disclosure Requirements

Although most companies continue to use APB 25 to recognize accounting costs for stock-based compensation in their financial statements, the footnotes to all financial statements must include certain FAS 123 disclosures. For companies that continue to apply APB 25, the footnotes must disclose the pro forma income and pro forma earnings per share, as if FAS 123 had been used to account for stock-based compensation. The pro forma amounts must reflect the difference between compensation cost included in net income according to APB 25 and the related cost measured according to FAS 123.

For all stock-based plans, regardless of whether the company uses APB 25 or FAS 123 to recognize costs in its financial statements, required disclosures include:

- General description of the terms of the plan(s), including vesting requirements, maximum term, and number of shares authorized
- Number and weighted-average exercise prices of options for each of the following:
  - Outstanding at beginning of year
  - Granted, exercised, forfeited, or expired during the year
- Weighted-average grant-date fair value of options and other stock-based awards granted during the year
- Description of method and assumptions used to estimate fair value, including:
  - Risk-free interest rate
  - Expected life
  - Expected volatility
  - Expected dividends
- Total compensation cost recognized in income for stock-based awards
- Any significant modifications made to outstanding awards

In addition, for options outstanding at the end of the year, disclosure must include the range of exercise prices, weighted-average exercise price, and weighted-average remaining contractual life.

18.4 IMPACT OF STOCK-BASED AWARDS ON EARNINGS PER SHARE

FAS 128, Earnings per Share, was issued in 1997 and governs the calculation of earnings per share (EPS). We will briefly describe the role played by stock-based awards in EPS, since they contribute to dilution for accounting purposes.

(a) Overview

There are two types of EPS:

1. *Basic EPS:* Takes into account only dilution from common shares outstanding.
2. *Diluted EPS:* Takes into account dilution from common shares outstanding and from "potential common stock" from stock options, stock warrants, written put options, and forward purchase contracts (i.e., where a company is required to buy back its own stock) and convertible securities (e.g., debentures and preferred stock that may be converted to common stock).

(b)   Calculation of Basic EPS

The numerator for basic EPS is "income available to common stockholders," so dividends on preferred stock are subtracted. The denominator is the "weighted-average number of common shares outstanding"—shares issued or reacquired by the company during the reporting period are weighted for the portion of the period that they were outstanding.

(c)   Calculation of Diluted EPS—In General

The numerator for diluted EPS is the same as the earnings number used for basic EPS, except that a few adjustments are required for the income or loss that would result if convertible securities were converted to common shares during the reporting period. More important for our purposes, the denominator for diluted EPS includes the number of additional common shares that would have been outstanding in the reporting period if the "potential common shares" that would have a dilutive effect had in fact been issued during the reporting period. As is the case for actual shares, potential common shares are weighted for the portion of the reporting period that they were outstanding.

Only potential common stock that would have a dilutive effect is considered. A good example is stock options: only options that are in the money have a potential dilutive effect and, thus, are taken into account in computing the denominator. Options that are underwater have a potential anti-dilutive effect: They are assumed not to be exercised and are excluded from the denominator.

(d)   How Stock Options Are Taken into Account in Diluted EPS

FAS 128 has different rules for performance-based options (vesting is based on meeting specified performance goals) and options that are not performance-based (vesting is based on a factor other than performance—typically the passage of time).

In the case of options that are not performance-based, dilution is deemed to occur from all in-the-money employee stock options regardless of whether they are vested. FAS 128 requires that the "treasury stock method" be used to determine how many shares would result from exercise of in-the-money options. Under this method, the exercise price paid by employees is assumed to be used by the company to reacquire its own shares at the average market price for the period. The result is that only the difference between market price and exercise price (the intrinsic value) is taken into account in determining the number of additional shares in the diluted EPS denominator.

The treasury stock method is illustrated by the following example (Exhibit 18.8):

- Both the exercise of all outstanding options that are in the money and the resulting issuance of shares of common stock are deemed to occur at the beginning of the reporting period (or when the options were granted, if later).

• The proceeds from exercise is deemed to be used by the company to purchase its common stock at the average market price during the reporting period.

• The hypothetical tax benefit that the company would realize from the assumed exercise (corporate tax rate times the intrinsic value, using the average market price for the year minus the exercise price) is added to the exercise proceeds in determining the number of shares that could be repurchased (this is not shown in our simplified example).

• The difference between the number of shares deemed issued and the number of shares deemed purchased is added to the denominator of the diluted EPS calculation.

If the vesting of stock options is subject to performance-related conditions, the treatment of those shares in calculating diluted EPS depends on whether the performance conditions have been satisfied, and is more complex.

(e)   Treatment of Restricted Stock in Computing Diluted EPS

Restricted stock that is unvested is excluded from basic EPS but included in the denominator in diluted EPS; it is treated comparably to performance-based and non–performance-based stock options in computing diluted EPS. The treasury stock method is used. The hypothetical proceeds used to repurchase shares is equal to the average unamortized deferred compensation balance for the period. From a practical standpoint, this often means that restricted stock is dilutive only to the extent that it is vested.

Exhibit 18.8   Illustration of the Treasury Stock Method.

100,000 options outstanding with $25 exercise price

Average stock price during the year = $30

Shares "issued": 100,000

Shares "repurchased":

    Proceeds from exercise = $2,500,000 ($25 × 100,000)

    Shares repurchased at average stock price = 83,333 ($2,500,000/$30)

    Number of shares added to denominator = 100,000 − 83,333 = 16,667

Note: The net result of this calculation is that the in-the-money value of the options is used to repurchase shares:

    In the money value of the options = $500,000 (($30 − $25) × 100,000)

    Number of shares added to denominator = 16,667 ($500,000/$30)

Selected Tax Aspects of Executive Compensation Plans*

Howard J. Golden, JD

This chapter addresses selected tax aspects of executive compensation plan design and implementation. The subjects discussed include U.S. taxation of equity devices, the limits on deductibility under Section 280G of the Internal Revenue Code of 1986, as amended ("IRC"), and the limits on deductibility under Section 162(m) of the IRC.

The information in this chapter is current as of the date of writing and is provided by Mercer in its capacity as a consultant in the area of executive compensation. Matter of a legal or accounting nature should be reviewed by tax counsel or an accounting firm.

19.1 TAXATION OF EQUITY DEVICES

(a) Background

There are four possible methods of providing equity compensation to the employees of a corporation. The variables include the decision to grant real equity versus equity equivalents, as well as the decision to grant a whole share value versus the value of appreciation only. The effect of these decisions is portrayed in the following chart:

	Equity	Equity Equivalents
Whole Share Value:	Restricted Stock	Phantom Stock
Appreciation Only:	Stock Options	Stock Appreciation Rights

---

* The author wishes to thank his colleague Randall S. Fast, who provided comments and review on much of this chapter. The author also thanks his colleague Carol S. Silverman, who provided material that was helpful in the development of this chapter.

This section discusses the tax treatment of these four compensation devices from both an employee and employer perspective. Additional strategic considerations are also reviewed.

(b) Description of Devices

A brief description of each of the four devices follows.

(i) *Restricted Stock*   Restricted stock generally consists of a grant of shares of the company's common stock, subject to specified vesting provisions and possible limitations on sale. Vesting in such awards is typically made contingent upon an employee's continued employment for a specified period ("service-based restricted stock"). However, vesting may also be related to the achievement of specified goals, which may be an additional condition precedent to vesting ("performance-contingent restricted stock"). In the alternative, attainment of the goals may merely result in vesting at an earlier point in time ("performance-accelerated restricted stock").

(ii) *Stock Options*   Stock options give employees the right to purchase shares of the employer's stock at a specified price during a defined period. There are two types of options: incentive stock options and nonqualified stock options.

Incentive Stock Options (ISOs)   ISOs satisfy the requirements of various provisions of the IRC (including those of Section 422, which are discussed below) and therefore receive preferential tax treatment: allowing the employee to postpone the recognition of taxable income until the underlying shares are sold, and taxing the resulting gain at long-term capital gain rates (although the alternative minimum tax may apply to certain taxpayers on exercise of the option).

Nonqualified Stock Options (NQSOs)   NQSOs do not receive preferential tax treatment but are also not subject to the stringent requirements of IRC Section 422.

Typically, both ISOs and NQSOs have an exercise price equal to the fair market value of the underlying stock on the date of grant. However, they may be granted at a premium (the exercise price is greater than the fair market value of the stock on the grant date of the option), and NQSOs may be granted at a discount (the exercise price is less than the fair market value of the stock on the grant date of the option).

Vesting in stock option awards is generally made contingent upon an employee's continued employment for a specified period of time ("service-based vesting"). However, vesting could be made contingent upon the achievement of specified goals ("performance-contingent vesting") or may be accelerated by achievement of such goals ("performance-accelerated vesting"). Market prevalence indicates that ISOs almost always employ service-based vesting.

(iii) Phantom Stock Phantom stock consists of an award in the form of hypothetical shares or units that approximate the way real shares of the company's nonvoting common stock would be valued on the open market. Award payments may be made in cash, stock, or both, generally on a date or dates previously specified at the time of grant.

Phantom stock arrangements are designed to provide compensation directly related to the value of company stock without actually issuing shares to employees. These arrangements are generally intended to supplant more traditional awards (such as stock options or restricted stock) and are sometimes used by privately held or foreign employers who are unwilling or unable to grant actual stock to employees.

As is the case with restricted stock, vesting in phantom stock may be service-based, performance-contingent, or performance-accelerated.

(iv) Stock Appreciation Rights A stock appreciation right (SAR) is a contractual right entitling employees to receive the appreciation in value of a specified number of shares of the company's common stock over a specified period of time. Payment of the appreciation may be in the form of cash, stock, or both.

SARs enable employees to participate in any increase in the market value of company stock without actually owning the underlying shares. SARs may be granted alone or in tandem with stock options. In a tandem arrangement, if the SAR were exercised, the company would pay the employee cash, stock, or a combination thereof equal in value to the gain on the underlying stock's appreciation, and the stock option would be cancelled. Alternatively, the option could be exercised and the SAR surrendered, in which case the employee would receive shares of the company's stock.

As is the case with NQSOs, vesting in SARs may be service-based, performance-contingent, or performance-accelerated.

(c) Tax Treatment of Devices

(i) Restricted Stock

Employee The employee is generally taxed at the time the restricted stock vests (i.e., restrictions lapse) and not at the time of grant. Once the restricted stock vests, the employee recognizes ordinary income equal to the difference between the fair market value of the stock at the time of vesting and the amount, if any, paid for the shares (e.g., par value). Upon a subsequent sale of vested shares, the employee would recognize long-term capital gain or loss (provided the holding period requirement is met) in an amount equal to any difference between (1) the amount received on sale and (2) the amount of ordinary income recognized upon vesting plus the amount paid, if any. The holding period for a capital asset (e.g., stock) to obtain long-term capital gain or loss treatment is a period of more than one year. It should also be noted that Congress changes the capital gains tax provisions frequently.

In the alternative to recognizing income when the restrictions lapse, the employee might elect (under IRC Section 83(b)) to be taxed on the value of the restricted stock award at the time of grant. If the employee makes this election and files the election with the IRS in a timely manner, taxation of any subsequent appreciation would be deferred until the stock is sold. If the stock were forfeited before vesting, the taxes previously paid would not be recoverable.

Employer   The company is entitled to a tax deduction equivalent to the amount of ordinary income realized by the employee, provided that the company collects the appropriate withholding taxes on the ordinary income. Recipients of restricted stock are typically entitled to receive any dividends declared before vesting (and to exercise voting rights, if any). Dividends on unvested restricted stock would generally be treated as additional compensation to the employee and be deductible by the company. Dividends on vested shares, and on unvested restricted shares subject to a Section 83(b) election, would not be tax deductible by the company.

(ii) Stock Options—Incentive Stock Options   An option qualifies as an ISO only if it meets the following requirements:

- The option is issued pursuant to a written plan (approved by shareholders within 12 months before or after the date of adoption by the Board of Directors) stating the maximum number of shares that may be subject to option grants under the plan, and the employees or class of employees eligible to receive option grants.
- The option is granted within 10 years from the time the plan is adopted by the Board, or approved by the shareholders, whichever is earlier.
- The option is not exercisable more than 10 years from the date of grant (5 years for holders of more than 10% of the company's stock).
- The exercise price is not less than 100% of the fair market value of the underlying stock at the time of grant (110% for more-than-10% shareholders).
- The option is not transferable except by will or the laws of descent and distribution.
- The value of the employee's options that first become exercisable in any given calendar year may not exceed $100,000. In calculating this amount, the value of the stock is determined at the date of grant. Any purported ISOs that exceed the $100,000 limit are treated as nonqualified stock options on a pro-rata basis.

Employee   In the case of ISOs, taxation of the employee is deferred until the shares acquired on exercise are sold (although the "spread" at exercise may well be subject to alternative minimum tax at that time),[1] and any appreciation above the exercise price receives long-term capital gain treatment, if:

- The stock acquired upon exercise is not sold within two years from the date of grant of the ISO and one year from the date of exercise of the ISO, and
- The employee remains in the employ of the company up to three months before exercising the option (one year if termination is due to disability).

If the holding period requirements are not met (i.e., there is a "disqualifying disposition"), the employee must recognize as ordinary compensation income at the time of sale the difference between the option exercise price and the fair market value at the time of exercise. Any remaining income is taxed as long-term or short-term capital gain. Special rules apply to transactions wherein the stock is sold at a price below the fair market value of the stock on the date of exercise.

Employer   If the holding period requirements are met, the company would not receive a tax deduction. If they are not met, the company would be entitled to a corresponding deduction equal to the compensation income realized by the employee at sale.

(iii) Stock Options—Nonqualified Stock Options

Employee   In the case of NQSOs, the employee is generally not taxed when the option is granted, but, upon exercise, the employee recognizes ordinary income equal to the excess of the fair market value of the stock acquired (at exercise) over the exercise price paid. Upon sale of the acquired shares, the employee recognizes long-term capital gain or loss (provided the more than one-year holding period requirement is met) in an amount equal to any difference between the amount received on sale and the fair market value of the stock at exercise.

Employer   At the time of exercise, the company is entitled to an income tax deduction corresponding to the amount of ordinary income realized by the employee.

Because NQSOs are not subject to the requirements applicable to ISOs, wide flexibility exists in plan design:

- There are no express limits on the amount of stock that may be optioned.
- There are no express limits on the length of the exercise period, although the maximum exercise period is often limited to 10 years.

---

[1] Recent tax law changes make it particularly important for the ISO recipient to investigate whether the alternative minimum tax will apply.

- There are no restrictions on the exercise period after termination of employment, except for the term of the option, although time limits on post-termination exercise are sometimes imposed.

(iv) Phantom Stock

Employee   Generally, the employee is not taxed on an award of phantom stock at the time of grant. Income taxation is deferred until the time when an award of phantom stock is converted into shares of company stock and released to the employee or cash is paid to the employee. The IRS generally treats such an award as taxable at the earliest time the employee could be entitled to receive such payment unless the employee had made an election, substantially in advance of that time, to defer payment.

Once stock or cash is delivered, the employee is taxed at ordinary income tax rates on the fair market value of the shares released or the entire amount of cash paid. However, if the distribution is in shares of stock subject to additional restrictions, creating a substantial risk of forfeiture, taxation is deferred until the shares vest (i.e., the risk of forfeiture no longer exists).

Employer   The employer would be entitled to a tax deduction at the same time and in the same amount as the employee recognizes ordinary income.

(v) Stock Appreciation Rights

Employee   At the time the SAR is granted, the employee is not taxed. Upon exercise of the SAR, the employee is generally subject to ordinary income tax on any cash or the fair market value of any stock received. If payment is in stock and the shares are subject to additional restrictions, creating a substantial risk of forfeiture, taxation is deferred until the shares vest. If a maximum limit is placed on the appreciation the employee may receive under a stand-alone SAR, the IRS generally would consider the employee to be in receipt of taxable income at the time the ceiling is reached, unless the employee had made an election, substantially in advance of that time, to defer receipt.

Employer   The employer would be entitled to a tax deduction at the same time and in the same amount as the employee recognizes ordinary income.

(d)   Strategic Considerations

(i) General Considerations   The key features of real stock that distinguish it from phantom stock are:

- Dividends
- Voting rights

- Minority rights of dissent (in merger situations)
- A claim on assets of the business (in liquidation and reorganization situations)
- Potential tax advantages to the employee

Phantom stock can replicate the economic value of real stock, along with the value of dividends, but it does not replicate the voting or equitable shareholder rights, or the potential tax advantages attendant upon the issuance of real stock to the employee. It may not be necessary or desirable to replicate all of these characteristics when designing an equity compensation plan.

(ii) Restricted Stock

Advantages

- The employee is entitled to receive dividends (subject to tax) and could receive long-term capital gain treatment on all or some of any appreciation in the value of the shares subsequent to grant.
  - The Section 83(b) election provides the employee with flexibility to fix the ordinary income tax liability at the time of grant or defer such liability until the restrictions on the stock lapse.
- Generally, the employee would not have to invest any of his or her money to obtain restricted stock (unless state corporate law required cash payment for par or stated value).
- The employer gets a tax deduction for the prevesting dividends when paid.
- The accounting charge to earnings for service-based or performance-accelerated restricted stock is based on the initial grant value, while the tax deduction is based on the value at the time the shares vest, which should be higher (assuming the stock value appreciates), although the time of the deduction is postponed until the vesting date.
- For the employer, service-based restricted stock, and to a lesser extent performance-accelerated or performance-contingent restricted stock, are powerful retention devices.
  - Unlike underwater stock options, restricted stock will not become a disincentive if the company's stock value should decrease.

Disadvantages

- Restricted stock awards require a charge to earnings, which can be substantial, particularly in the case of performance-contingent awards, if the stock appreciates in value.

- Once an award of restricted stock, and to a lesser extent performance-accelerated restricted stock, has been made (even if the award is based on previous performance), it carries little additional performance incentive because the link between performance and reward is more tenuous than with other award types.

- If overly onerous, the forfeiture provisions (e.g., a particularly long vesting period) attached to an award of restricted stock can make the award unattractive.

- There can be a substantial income tax liability associated with the vesting of restricted stock, which will likely lead to the sale of at least a portion of the shares which vest.

- If the employee makes a Section 83(b) election and subsequently forfeits the stock before it vests, the income tax paid at the time the election is made cannot be recovered.

(iii) Stock Options

Advantages

- The amount of the award is tied directly to future appreciation in the value of company stock.

- For options with service-based or performance-accelerated vesting, there is no charge to earnings under APB No. 25 as long as the options are granted at or above fair market value.

- ISOs

  — Taxation of the employee is deferred until the underlying shares are sold, and the executive's entire gain on the sale of the shares is taxed at capital gain rates if the ISO holding period requirements are met. (However, the alternative minimum tax may well apply.)

- NQSOs

  — The company receives an income tax deduction equal to the gain at exercise realized by the employee.

  — NQSO plans are flexible and may be designed in a variety of ways.

Disadvantages

- Options create economic dilution to existing shareholders to the extent that they are "in the money."

- The employee must invest his or her own money in order to exercise the option and realize any gain. (Opportunities to tender previously owned shares or to participate in broker-assisted exercise programs may be available to deal with this issue.)

- — The company may institute a loan program to reduce this disadvantage, but in order to avoid unfavorable accounting treatment, the employee would have to be personally liable for loan principal and interest and hold the shares for at least six months before selling them.

- ISOs
  - — The company does not receive a corresponding tax deduction unless the employee fails to meet the ISO holding period requirements before selling the shares.
  - — The spread at exercise may well be considered alternative minimum taxable income for the employee.
  - — ISOs generally may not be exercised more than three months after the employee's retirement.
  - — ISOs are not as flexible as NQSOs and must follow the requirements of IRC Section 422 in order to receive favorable tax treatment.
  - — ISOs do not generally provide for performance-based or even performance-accelerated vesting.
  - — Shareholder approval is required for ISOs.

- NQSOs
  - — NQSOs do not receive the preferential tax treatment ISOs receive and, thus, may be less attractive to the employee than ISOs. However, this concern may be addressed in employee communications.

(iv) Phantom Stock

Advantages

- A phantom stock arrangement may be designed in a variety of ways to mirror the value derived from a restricted stock arrangement. The program may be designed to include internal as well as external performance measures, and the final payout may be made in cash, stock, or a combination of the two.

- The employee may realize large gains without investing any of his or her own money.

- The employee can be afforded flexibility to make advance elections about when the award will be settled and taxes will be imposed.

- The company receives a tax deduction equal to any ordinary income realized by the employee from the phantom stock award.

- For service-based and performance-accelerated awards paid in stock, the accounting charge to earnings is based on the initial grant value, while the tax deduction is at a higher value (assuming the stock value appreciates), although it is postponed until the vesting date.

Disadvantages

- Phantom stock awards require a charge to earnings under APB No. 25, which can be substantial, particularly in the case of performance-contingent awards, if the stock appreciates in value.

- Once an award of phantom stock has been made (even if based upon previous performance), the link between performance and reward is relatively tenuous unless the award is performance-contingent, or at least performance-accelerated.

- If overly onerous, the vesting provisions attached to an award of phantom stock can make the award unattractive (e.g., a particularly long vesting period).

(v) Stock Appreciation Rights

Advantages

- The amount of the award is tied directly to future appreciation in the value of company stock.

- The employee does not need to raise cash to exercise an SAR, which eliminates downside risk and the need for any special financing arrangements.

- The company receives a tax deduction equal to the gain realized by the employee, which, if the award is paid in stock, represents a net cash savings (at the cost of shareholder dilution).

- SARs are flexible and may be designed in a variety of ways.

Disadvantages

- SARs require a charge to earnings, which can be substantial, if the stock appreciates sharply in value.

19.2 GOLDEN PARACHUTES

This section discusses tax aspects of golden parachute payments. These issues arise in connection with a change of control of an employer.

(a) Definition of a Golden Parachute

A golden parachute is an arrangement that guarantees payment contingent upon a change of control of the company to some of an employer's employees. IRC Section 280G and the regulations thereunder further define the term *parachute payment*. Excess parachutes are nondeductible by the employer and result in an excise tax on the recipient.

Golden parachutes have traditionally been used as a "poison pill" and are increasingly included in employment agreements as a matter of general practice.

(b) Benefits of a Golden Parachute

The benefits include attracting and retaining key executives before a change of control by assuring fair treatment should the event occur, and retaining key executives during the actual takeover. A golden parachute also ensures that management can address a potential takeover offer without concern about personal situations.

(c) Definition of Excess Parachute Payment

As Section 280G describes it, an "excess parachute payment" is the excess of any parachute payment over the "base amount." The base amount is defined as the individual's includible compensation for the "base period." This is generally interpreted to mean the average of the taxable wages reported on the individual's W-2 income for the past five years (the base period). Certain other detailed rules are described in the regulations.

The compensation for the base period is compared with amounts received that are contingent on the change of control. Such amounts include payments under contracts or plans, including (1) cash, (2) the value of the acceleration of vesting in equity or SERPs, and (3) the value of continued welfare benefits.

If the aggregate amount of the present value of all the parachute payment equals or exceeds *three* times the base amount, then the excess parachute payment is the amount in excess of *one* times the base amount. If there is an excess parachute payment, the company may not deduct the amount of the excess parachute payment, and the individual is taxed on the income received and is also subject to an excise tax of 20% on the excess parachute payment. The amount equal to three times the base amount is sometimes called the *trigger amount.*

Other requirements:

- *Special rules for nonpublicly traded companies:* If no stock in the corporation was publicly traded before the change of control, the nondeductibility and excise tax penalties do not apply if the parachute payment is approved by persons who owed more than 75% of the voting power of all outstanding stock of the corporation after adequate disclosure of all material facts.

- *In order for Section 280G to apply to a change-of-control payment, the payment must be to a "disqualified individual":* A "disqualified individual" is an employee or independent contractor who is a shareholder who owns an amount equal in value to the lesser of $1 million or 1% of the total fair market value of the outstanding shares of all classes of the corporation's stock. The term also includes an employee or independent contractor who is an officer (subject to certain limitations described in the regulations) or a "highly compensated individual" as defined in the regulations.

(d) Design Considerations

- *What is the window period?* This is the period after the change of control during which the executive is protected and entitled to change-of-control payments or benefits. The period is usually two to three years but varies with position level and reporting relationships.

- *Should the change-of-control payout triggers be single, double, or modified?* Under a *single trigger,* the executive is entitled to a change-of-control payment if there is a change of control. The executive can voluntarily terminate at any time within the window period and receive the change-of-control payments or benefits. Under a *double trigger,* two things must occur for the change-of-control payment to be made:

  — A change of control, *and*

  — Termination without cause, or constructive termination.

  Constructive termination or termination for "good reason" is generally defined in the change-of-control agreement or in plan provisions dealing with a change of control. The term usually relates to a demotion or any other material change in position. A double trigger is the most prevalent type of arrangement.

  A *modified trigger* is a combination of the single and double trigger. The executive can leave by choice within a specified window (e.g., 12 months after the change of control) and receive severance payments.

- *What are the elements of pay for which change-of-control payments may be made?* These include:

  — Base salary

  — Bonus

  — Welfare benefits

  — Perquisites

  — Acceleration of unvested equity grants (e.g., options or restricted stock)

  — Acceleration of SERP payments (with or without additional service or age credits)

- *What arrangements should be made with respect to potential taxation of the excess parachute payment?* There are at least three possible designs:

  — Cutback of change-of-control payments or benefits

  — Gross-up payments

  — A modified cap

Under a *cutback,* the parachute payment is cut back to $1 less than the trigger amount (i.e., $1 less than three times the base amount). Since the cutback parachute payments are less than the trigger, all amounts are deductible by the company, and no excise taxes need be paid by the individual.

In a *gross-up* situation, the company increases the parachute payment by an amount such that after payment of income, social security, and excise taxes on the gross-up payment, the executive is made whole.

A *modified cap* varies by individual agreement. Usually, the executive is given the greater of (1) receiving the cutback parachute or (2) receiving the full parachute amount and paying all applicable taxes.

(e) Calculations

- Elements included in the parachute payment are explicitly stated in the change-of-control agreement or plan document.
- The payment usually includes items such as:
  - Salary
  - Annual incentive
  - Perquisites (continuation of club membership, automobile, etc.)
  - Outplacement payments or service
  - Welfare benefits (continuation of medical, life, or disability coverage during the severance period)
  - Acceleration of vesting of, or additional benefits in, SERPs
  - Acceleration of vesting of options, restricted stock, and other equity programs
- Amounts specified in the change-of-control agreement are paid for a "severance period," generally defined in the contract, usually one to three years.
- The sum of all these elements is the "Total Change-of-Control Value."
- Total change-of-control value is compared with the trigger amount to see if there is an excess parachute payment. If such an excess payment exists, the payment will be afforded the appropriate treatment:
  - Cutback
  - Gross-up
  - Modified cap
- The trigger equals three times the base amount.
- The base amount is the average W-2 taxable income for the past five years preceding the calendar year of the change of control.
- If the total change-of-control value is greater than the trigger, the trigger has been tripped.

(i) Example 1: Cutback

- Elyse has a change-of-control agreement that includes current base salary, most recent bonus, welfare benefits, perquisites, and option acceleration upon the change of control. The severance period is three years.
- Change-of-control agreement requires payment to be cut back.
- The change of control occurs in 2001.

Current base salary	$ 250,000
Most recent bonus	100,000
Cost of welfare benefits	2,500
Cost of perquisites	500
	$353,000
Times severance period	3
	$1,059,000
Plus option acceleration*	250,000
Total parachute payment	$1,309,000

*Discussed below

Base amount	
2000 W-2 taxable wages	$ 300,000
1999 W-2	250,000
1998 W-2	225,000
1997 W-2	220,000
1996 W-2	125,000
Average	$ 224,000
Trigger = $224,000 × 3 =	$ 672,000
Parachute payment	$1,309,000
This is greater than the trigger.	

- Since the payment must be cut back pursuant to the agreement, the parachute payment to Elyse will be $1 less than the trigger, or $671,999 (a cutback amount of $637,001).

(ii) Example 2: Gross-Up

- Greg has a change-of-control agreement that includes current base salary, most recent bonus, welfare benefits, perquisites, and option acceleration upon the change of control. The severance period is three years.

- The change-of-control agreement requires a gross-up payment. (For purposes of simplicity, only federal income and excise taxes are considered for this example; usually, FICA taxes, and sometimes state taxes, are also grossed-up.)

Current base salary	$ 200,000
Most recent bonus	1,000,000
Cost of welfare benefits	7,500
Cost of perquisites	20,000
	$1,227,500
Times severance period	3
	$3,682,500
Plus option acceleration*	1,250,000
Total parachute payment	$4,932,500

*Discussed below

Base amount	
2000 W-2	$1,000,000
1999 W-2	850,000
1998 W-2	900,000
1997 W-2	700,000
1996 W-2	650,000
Average	$820,000
Base amount	$820,000
Trigger = $820,000 × 3 =	$2,460,000
Total parachute payment	$4,932,500

- Since the total parachute payment is greater than the trigger, the excess over the base amount is nondeductible by the company, and the excess over the base amount is also subject to an excise tax of 20% paid by the employee.

- Amount subject to excise tax:

$$4,932,500 - \$820,000 = \$4,112,500.$$

- Excise tax $= 20\% \times \$4,112,500 = \$822,500.$

- An amount must be paid to Greg such that after payment, he retains an amount equal to the excise tax, taking only federal income tax and excise taxes into account in the gross-up.

- This amount, after calculations, is = $2,035,891.

- Final change-of-control value = $4,932,500 + $2,035,891 (or $6,968,391).

- Gross-up can be costly, especially with senior executives.

(iii) **How Is Equity Acceleration Treated?** This is the most complicated piece of the parachute payment. It is composed of two pieces:

- The first number is the amount by which the spread on the change of control date exceeds the present value of the projected spread at the date the options were originally scheduled to vest. The discount rate used in determining the present value is also prescribed by the IRC.
- The second number is an amount used to reflect the lapse of the obligation to perform future services as a condition of exercising the option. A minimum amount of 1% is used as prescribed by the regulations.
- Details of both calculations are contained in Treasury Regulation Section 1.280G-1, Q&A-24.

19.3 SECTION 162(m) COMPLIANCE

For publicly traded companies, compensation in excess of $1 million paid to the CEO and the next four highly compensated officers is not tax deductible to the company unless the amount paid meets certain statutory exceptions. This treatment is required by IRC Section 162(m). Treasury Regulation Section 162-27 explains the requirements of Section 162(m).

(a) Application

The limitation on the deduction applies to "covered employees" of a "publicly held corporation." A publicly held corporation means one that, on the last day of its taxable year, is subject to the reporting requirements of Section 12 of the Securities Exchange Act of 1934. A "covered employee" is determined as of the last day of the year and is a person reported in the summary compensation table of the proxy statement and who is employed on the last day of the year.

(b) Performance-Based Compensation

An exception to the Section 162(m) rules applies to "qualified performance-based compensation" if the requirements of the exception are met. These requirements are:

- Objective performance goals
- An independent Compensation Committee
- Shareholder approval
- Compensation Committee certification

(i) Objective Performance Goals   Compensation must be paid solely on account of the attainment of one or more preestablished, objective performance goals:

- "Preestablished" means established by the Compensation Committee in writing not later than 90 days after the commencement of the performance period.
- "Objective" means that a third party having knowledge of the relevant facts could determine whether the goal is met.
- Preestablished goals must state, in terms of an objective formula or standard, the method for computing the amount of compensation if the goals are attained. The formula must also specify the individual employees or class of employees to which it applies.
- The formula must preclude Compensation Committee discretion to increase the amount of compensation payable. It may permit Compensation Committee discretion to decrease the amount ("negative discretion").
- The compensation must be contingent on attainment of the goal.

(ii) Independent Compensation Committee   The Compensation Committee must consist of two or more "outside directors." Outside directors are individuals who are *not:*

- Current employees of the company
- Former employees receiving compensation for prior services during the taxable year
- Officers of the company either currently or at any time in the past
- Currently receiving "remuneration" (broadly defined), either directly or indirectly, in any capacity other than as a director

(iii) Shareholder Approval   The material terms under which the remuneration is to be paid must be *disclosed to and approved by shareholders* before the payment of such remuneration. Material terms include:

- A description of eligible employees
- A description of the business criteria on which the performance goal is based
- The maximum amount of compensation that could be paid to any employee

(iv) Compensation Committee Certification   The compensation committee must certify in writing that the performance goals established were in fact satisfied. This requirement does not apply to stock options.

The regulations spell out the details of these requirements.

(c) Implementation Guidelines

To maximize deductibility, a company might consider the following actions with respect to its compensation programs:

*   Set annual base salaries for named executives at less than $1,000,000. If salaries are set above $1,000,000, pay the excess on a deferred basis (e.g., deferred until retirement).

*   Annual and long-term cash incentive plans

    — Obtain shareholder approval of "material terms" described above.

    — Specify maximum dollar value of potential payout.

    — Have the plan administered by a compensation committee consisting of two or more outside directors.

    — Make payouts contingent upon achievement of objective performance results calculable using a formula/standard.

    — Set goals during the first 90 days of the performance period.

    — Prohibit upward adjustments to payouts (downward adjustments are permitted).

    — Obtain committee certification of goal achievement before making any payments.

*   Many companies create separate annual incentive plans for their named executives because plans that do not include named executives do not have to be approved by shareholders and do not have to comply with the other requirements described in this section.

*   Stock option plans

    — Obtain shareholder approval.

    — Specify maximum annual number of options that may be granted to an individual.

    — Have the plan administered by a compensation committee consisting of two or more outside directors.

*   Performance share plans

    — Same as for long-term incentive plans except that maximum could be expressed as a maximum number of shares.

*   Restricted stock

    — Restricted stock that vests solely on the basis of time can never qualify as performance-based compensation.

*   Special rules apply to companies that were privately held and become public companies.

*   Note also that some companies may forego tax deductions to pay compensation in excess of the 162(m) limitations.

Index

A

Accounting for stock-based compensation
Accounting Principles Board Opinion No.
25 (APB 25). *See* APB 25
accounting rules
establishment of, 329–330
sources of, 330–332
FAS No. 123. *See* FAS No. 123,
"Accounting for Stock-Based
Compensation"
FAS No. 128. *See* FAS No. 128, "Earnings
per Share"
FIN 28. *See* FIN 28, "Accounting for
Stock Appreciation Rights and Other
Variable Stock Option or Award
Plans"
FIN 44. *See* FIN 44, "Accounting for
Certain Transactions involving Stock
Compensation"
sources of standards, 330–332
Accounting issues
Accounting Principles Board. *See*
Accounting Principles Board (APB)
business combinations and treatment of
outstanding stock options, 294
earnings per share, effect of stock-based
awards on, 352–354
Financial Accounting Standards Board. *See*
Financial Accounting Standards Board
(FASB)
long-term incentives, pay-for-performance
model, 256–257
stock options and spinoffs, 295
variable accounting, performance-based
grants and performance-contingent
vesting, 215

Accounting Principles Board (APB), 329–330,
362
Opinion No. 25. *See* APB 25
Action plan and developing reward strategy
program, 12
Administration
elective deferral plans, 234
401(k) mirror plans, 230
not-for-profit organizations, incentive plans,
146
sales administration
methods of, spreadsheets and software,
127
perspective on compensation, 110
Affordability and variable pay programs, 22
All-exempt employee plan, 260–261
Annual incentive plans
guidelines for plan design, 242
management. *See* Annual management
incentive plan
pay-for-performance model, 247–252
treatment of and corporate transactions or
restructuring, 279, 281, 292–295
value-based management. *See* Value-based
management (VBM) and incentive
plans
Annual management incentive plan
checklist, 167–168
cost/benefit assessment
due diligence, 165–166
self-funding concept, 165
deferrals, mandatory and voluntary, 167
holdbacks, 167
individual performance, assessing
assessment approaches, 164–165
funding, 164
goal setting, reliance on, 164

Annual management incentive plan *(continued)*
  line-of-sight relationship, 154–155
  management incentive plan and profit-
    sharing plan compared, 155
  as motivator of management behavior, 153
  not-for-profit organizations. *See*
    Not-for-profit organizations
  participation criteria, 158–159
  pay-for-performance linkage, 154
  performance measurements
    Balanced Scorecard, 157
    characteristics of, 154
    financial measures, 155–156
    long-term incentive plans, integration
      with, 157–158
    nonfinancial measures, 156–157
  performance scales, developing
    external validation process, 162–163
    incentive formulas, 163–164
    standards, establishing, 160–161
    target awards, threshold and superior
      levels, 162
  target award opportunities, 159–160
  tax considerations under IRC Section
    162(m), 166
  variability of compensation cost, 153–154
APB 25
  accounting for stock compensation, 316
  business combinations, options granted in
    connection with, 346–347
  compensation cost measurement and
    recognition, 336–338
  compensatory and noncompensatory plans,
    332–333
  coverage issues, 338–339
  EITF issues, 331
  exercise price, reduction of, 342–344
  FASB Interpretations, 330
  fixed and variable awards, 333–336
  fundamental questions, 332
  increase in number of shares to be issued,
    344
  intrinsic value method, 330
  life of award, renewal or extension of,
    340–342
  outstanding awards, change in terms of,
    340–344
  phantom stock awards, 364
  puts, calls, and other repurchase features,
    344–346
  stock options, treatment of, 191, 199
Assessments
  candidates, 93–94
  employees. *See* Employees
Auditing
  compensation committee's responsibilities,
    318
  sales compensation plan, 127–129

B

Balanced Scorecard
  key performance indicators, identifying, 21
  not-for-profit organizations, 143
  performance measurement, 44, 46, 157
    example of framework, 47
  variable pay programs, 28
Base pay. *See also* Pay
  competency linkage
    design alternatives, 70
    guideline salary, 78–80
    within job grade structure, 70–71
    models for, 69
    salary increase factor within broadband
      structure, 71–74
    salary placement factor within broadband
      structure, 74–80
  management, 153
  not-for-profit organizations, 140
  pay-for-performance model, 246–247
Behavioral competencies, 83
  and performance management, 47
Benchmarks. *See* Performance benchmarking
Benefits
  executive benefits. *See* Executive benefits
  flexible benefits, 4
  hospitality company example, 1, 8–9
  and reward strategy, 2, 4
Binomial pricing model, 208, 331
Black-Scholes option-pricing approach,
  191–192, 208, 346, 348
  director compensation, 305–306
  and FAS 123, 331
Blue Ribbon Commission on Director
    Compensation, 297–298

Board of directors
director compensation. *See* Director
compensation
National Association of Corporate Directors
(NACD), 297
not-for-profit organizations, approval of
compensation plan, 136–137
stock-based awards, accounting issues,
338–339, 350–351
transaction-related compensation
arrangements, corporate governance
issues, 295–296
Broad-based equity plans
accounting issues, 207–208
advantages of, 210–214
all-exempt employee plan, 260–261
allocation formulas, 209
disadvantages of, 215–219
generally, 205
global stock plans
eligibility, 220
generally, 220
high- and low-paying countries, effects in,
222
labor and data issues, 221
local nationals' pay, impact on, 222
locally tax-qualified plans, use of, 220
regulatory issues, 222
satisfaction with plans, 220
securities laws, 222
tax issues, employee perspective, 221
grant frequency and size, 209–210
incentive stock options (ISOs), 207–208
increased use of, 205–207
mechanics of making grants, 208
regulatory issues, 207–208
share allocation, 208–209
shareholder approval, 207
tax considerations, 207–208
value drivers, 209
Business combinations, accounting issues, 294,
346–347
Business design, assessing, 12
Business environment
review of, 11
and variable pay programs, 22
Business judgment rule, 296

Business model and reward strategy, 3
Business plan
economic profit compared to MVA, 182–183
multiyear business plans and performance
award plans, 198
Business stages and compensation strategy,
266–268
Business strategy
changes in, 113
sales model, alignment with, 116–117
and talent strategy, 88
Business unit performance
annual management incentive plan, funding,
164
goal setting, 164

C

Career advancement
buying versus building talent, 10
career path programs and development
planning, 58, 95
hospitality company example, 1, 9
importance of, 4
and reward strategy, 2, 4–5
Cash
director compensation model, 309–310
long-term incentives, 187–188
Cash flow return on investment (CFROI), 170,
176
Change-in-control agreements
broad-based severance plans, 288
cause, definitions of, 282
chief executive officers, 283
definitions, 284–286
funding, 287
generally, 279–280
golden parachutes. *See* Golden parachutes
good reason, definitions of, 283
incentive plans, treatment of, 293–295
not-for-profit organizations, 150–151
poison pills, 281, 365
purpose of, 281–282
rabbi trusts, 287
severance payments and benefits, 284
silver parachutes, 280, 287–288
tin parachutes, 280, 288
triggers, 282–283

Charitable organizations. *See* Not-for-profit
    organizations
Chief Executive Officer (CEO)
    and compensation committee, 317
    compensation in excess of $1 million, tax
        considerations, 370–372
    compensation model, 244–245
    involvement in pay-for-performance design,
        242
    mergers and acquisitions and
        change-in-control agreements. *See*
        Change-in-control agreements
    non-CEO chairperson and director
        compensation, 307
    retention and transaction bonuses, 291
    talent management, role in, 91, 94
Chief Operating Officer (COO), compensation
    model, 244–245
Clawbacks and post-termination exercise of
    stock options, 193
Coaching
    performance management, 53–55
    situational, 53
Committee on Accounting Procedure of the
    American Institute of CPAs (AICPA),
    329
Committee pay, director compensation,
    300–301, 310
Communications
    broad-based equity plans, 217–218
    compensation committees, 321
    guidelines for plan design, 243
    organizational change and executive
        compensation, 269–273, 278
    pay-for-performance model, 262–263
    strategy model, 269–271
    variable pay programs, 28, 34–35
Comparability data, not-for-profit
    organizations, 135–136
Compensation committees
    CEO, role of, 317
    committee charter, 318–320
    communication, 321–322
    compensation consultants, 325
    compensation strategy, 321
    compensation surveys, 326
    considerations, 326–328

effect of business competitive environment,
    315
    generally, 315
    involvement in pay-for-performance design,
        242
    performance benchmarking
        compensation analysis, 323–324
        generally, 322–323
        shareholder return and related measures,
            324–325
    process, guidelines, 318, 320–321
    purpose of, 316–318
    regulatory issues, 315–316
    role of, generally, 315, 328
    shareholder concerns, 315–316
    transaction-related compensation
        arrangements, 295
Compensation strategy, 241
    compensation committee process, 318
    defined, 266
    and organizational change. *See*
        Organizational change
    statement, 23–24
Competencies
    and candidate assessment, 93
    models, 93
    role of in talent management, 88–90
Competency assessment
    behavioral competency, 67–68
    multisource (360-degree) approach, 66
    ratings, 66
    strategy visioning process, 68
    technical competency, 67
    and variable pay programs. *See* Variable pay
        programs (pay for results)
Competency-based incentives and variable pay
    programs, 24
Competency-based rewards
    base pay linkage, 65
        base pay design alternatives, overview, 70
        base pay linkage models, 70–80
        generally, 69
    current practices, 65
    design approaches generally, 63–64
    generally, 85
    readiness assessment, 65–66
    recognition awards, 84

role of, 64–65
strength of competency assessment system,
66–69
variable pay/incentive applications
award modifier, 81–82
competency acquisition, special bonuses
for, 82–83
design model elements, 83–84
generally, 80–81
Conflicts of interest, not-for-profit
organizations, 137, 139
Consultants
compensation consultants, use of, 325–327
stock-based awards, accounting issues,
350–351
stock-based grants to, accounting for,
338–339
Corporate culture, linkage of compensation to,
273–275
Cost effectiveness
cost/benefit analysis and due diligence,
165–166
cost/benefits of annual management
incentive plan, assessing, 165–166
long-term incentives, 189
not-for-profit organizations, incentive plans,
145–146
sales compensation plan
cost of sales curve, 121
key drivers of individual performance and
earnings, 121
performance and pay distributions,
120–121
Cost of capital, weighted average (WACC),
178, 180
Customers
changes in buying and decision-making
processes, effect on sales
compensation plan, 113
and designing sales compensation plan, 110

D

Data collection
employee access to data, 23
feasibility data, 22
performance data, 23
Deferred compensation, nonqualified

director compensation, 312
elective deferral plans
administration and financing issues, 234
cost of, 233
generally, 224, 231
plan designs, 231–232
proxy disclosures, 234
tax and legal issues, 232
401(k) mirror plans
administration issues, 230
eligibility for, 229
financing issues, 230
generally, 224, 229
plan designs, 229–230
tax and legal issues, 230
not-for-profit organizations, 139–140
supplemental executive retirement plans
(SERPs)
generally, 224–225
rabbi trust, 228–229
restoration plans, 226
target plans, 226–227
tax and legal issues, 227–228
Deferred incentive plan awards, 167
Dilution, stock. *See* Stock
Director compensation
cash payments, 306–307, 309–310
committee pay, 300–301, 310
compensation committee recommendations,
317–318
compensation model
benefit plans, elimination of, 311–312
cash, 309–310
stock, 310–311
compensation strategy, 307–309
equity compensation
deferred stock plan, 312
generally, 301, 310–311
restricted and unrestricted stock, 312
retainers, 299–300, 309
SEC regulations, 297, 299
special services, 306–307
stand-alone grants, 302
stock ownership, 305
as substitute for other compensation,
304–305
trends, 297–298

Director compensation
  equity compensation *(continued)*
    volatility concerns, 305–306
  generally, 297, 312, 314
  meeting fees, 300, 310
  National Association of Corporate Directors
    (NACD), 298
  non-CEO chairperson, 307
  pay-for-performance plans, 306
Disability benefits. *See* Executive benefits
Disclosure requirements, FAS 123, 348,
  351–352
Due diligence, cost/benefit analysis, 165–166

E

Earnings before interest and taxes (EBIT), 170
Earnings per share (EPS)
  accounting issues, 352–354
  basic, 352–353
  diluted, 352–354
  disclosures under FAS 123, 351–352
  FAS 128, 352–354
  value-based management performance
    metrics, 170–171
Economic profit (EP)
  defined, 178
  value-based management performance
    metrics, 176, 178
    performance targets, establishing, 178–183
    and stage of readiness, 183–184
Economic Value Added (EVA) and value-based
  management performance metrics,
  170–171, 176
Education
  talent development, 93
  variable pay programs, educating employees
    on, 28
Elective deferral plans
  administrative issues, 234
  cost of, 233
  ERISA requirements, 231–232
  financing issues, 234
  generally, 231
  plan design, 231–232
  and proxy disclosures, 234
  tax and legal issues, 232
Emerging Issues Task Force (EITF), 329–330

  EITF 96-18, 331
  Issue 00-23, 331
Employee
  retention
    reward system and business model, 3
Employee readiness diagnostic, 22–23
Employees
  aligning interests of shareholders and stock
    options, 210–211
  evaluations. *See* Performance management
  retention. *See also* Retention incentives
    reward system and business model, 3
  use of stock options, 213
  stock options for rank and file employees.
    See Broad-based equity plans
  turnover, determining causes of, 11
Equity-based compensation. *See also* Long-
  term incentives
  accounting for. *See* Accounting for stock-
    based compensation
  broad-based plans. *See* Broad-based equity
    plans
  global equity plans. *See* Broad-based equity
    plans
  stock appreciation rights (SARs). *See* Stock
    appreciation rights (SARs)
  stock options. *See* Stock options
ERISA
  elective deferral plans, 231–232
  401(k) mirror plans, 230
  supplemental executive retirement programs
    (SERPs), 227
Executive benefits
  core benefits, 223–224
  disability benefits
    generally, 224, 237
    other considerations, 238
    plan design, 237–238
    tax and legal issues, 238
  generally, 223, 240
  life insurance
    generally, 224, 234
    other considerations, 237
    plan design, 234–235
    reasons for providing, 234
    tax and legal issues, 236
  medical benefits

generally, 224, 238–239
plan design, 239
tax and legal issues, 239
nonqualified deferred compensation. *See*
  Deferred compensation, nonqualified
not-for-profit organizations, 140, 149
perquisites, 224–225
  generally, 239–240
  reasons for providing, 240
Executive compensation
change-in-control programs. *See* Change-in-
  control agreements; Golden parachutes
and driving organizational change. *See*
  Organizational change
guidelines for plan design, 243

F

Fair value method, 347–348
valuing employee stock options, 331
variables used in calculating, 348–349
FAS No. 123, "Accounting for Stock-Based
  Compensation," 216, 256, 316, 347–352
disclosure requirements, 348, 351–352
fair value defined, 348–349
fair value method, 347–348
generally, 347–348
modifications, accounting for, 350
noncompensatory treatment, 348
nonemployee transactions, 350–351
performance conditions, accounting for,
  349–350
FAS No. 128, "Earnings per Share"
basic EPS, 352–353
diluted EPS, 352–354
generally, 352
FAS No.123, "Accounting for Stock-Based
  Compensation"
further guidance, 331
generally, 331
Feasibility assessment and variable pay
  programs, 22
FIN 28, "Accounting for Stock Appreciation
  Rights and Other Variable Stock
  Option or Award Plans," 330
FIN 44, "Accounting for Certain Transactions
  involving Stock Compensation," 294,
  330

accounting for stock compensation, 316
compensatory and noncompensatory plans,
  333
repricing outstanding option grants, 203
valuation of stock-based grants, 331
Financial Accounting Standards Board (FASB)
establishment of accounting rules, 329–330
FASB Technical Bulletin No. 97-1, 331
Financial Interpretation Number 28. *See* FIN
  28, "Accounting for Stock
  Appreciation Rights and Other
  Variable Stock Option or Award Plans"
Financial Interpretation Number 44. *See* FIN
  44, "Accounting for Certain
  Transactions involving Stock
  Compensation"
Statement No. 123. *See* FAS No. 123,
  "Accounting for Stock-Based
  Compensation"
Statement No. 128. *See* FAS No. 128,
  "Earnings per Share"
Focus groups
reality testing, 27
variable pay, employee readiness for, 22–23
401(k) mirror plans
administration issues, 230
distributions, 230
ERISA requirements, 230
financing issues, 230
generally, 229
nonqualified plans, 230
plan designs, 229–230
qualified plans, 230
tax and legal issues, 230
Funding trigger, not-for-profit organizations,
  145

G

Gainsharing
case study
  approach to variable pay program, 31
  background, 30–31
  communication, 34–35
  cost analysis, 34
  design team role, 35
  incentive plan design, 31–32
  key performance indicators, 32

Gainsharing
    case study *(continued)*
        modifying factors, 32
        other design criteria, 33
        performance thresholds, 32–33
        plan funding formulas, 32–33
        plan results, 35–36
        plan testing, 34
        plan trigger, 33
        participation and frequency policies, 26
        variable pay programs, 24
Generally Accepted Accounting Principles
    (GAAP)
    and FASB, 329
    pooling treatment, 294
    value-based management performance
        metrics, 170, 178
Global equity plans. *See* Broad-based equity
    plans
Goals, objective setting and performance
    management, 49–51
Goalsharing and variable pay programs, 24
Golden parachutes. *See also* Change-in-control
        agreements
    benefits of, 365
    calculations, 367–369
    cutbacks, 367–368
    defined, 364–365
    design considerations, 366–367
    equity acceleration, 370
    excess parachute payment defined, 365–366
    gross-up payments, 366–369
    modified cap, 366–367
    as poison pill, 365
    triggers, 366
Greenfield operations and variable pay
    programs, 27

H

Holdbacks, incentive awards, 167
Holistic approach, 1–2
Housing loans and executive benefits, not-for-
    profit organizations, 149–150
Huddart, Steven, 219
Human capital
    approaches to, 10
    and business strategy, 12

measuring reward practices, 12
    and optimal rewards mix, 12
    scorecard, 12
Human resources
    role of in sales compensation, 109
    and salespeople, 109
    and talent management, 91
    and technology, 101
Huselid, Mark A., 86

I

Incentive stock options. *See* Stock options
Incentives, performance-based
    annual management incentive plan. *See*
        Annual management incentive plan
    not-for-profit organizations. *See*
        Not-for-profit organizations
    value-based management. *See* Value-based
        management (VBM) and incentive
        plans
Independent contractors, accounting for stock-
    based awards, 338–339, 350–351
Individual incentives
    case study, individual and team incentives
        for relationship management
        background, 39–40
        incentive plan design features, 40–41
    variable pay programs, 24
Insider trading rules
    and stock appreciation rights, 195
    and stock options, 195
Internal Revenue Code (IRC)
    Section 401, qualified retirement plans, 316
    Section 415, qualified retirement plans, 316
    Section 422, 356, 363
    Section 4999, golden parachute payments,
        316
    Section 83(b), 358, 361
    Section 280G, 364–365
        golden parachute payments, 286–287,
            289, 316
    Section 162(m), compensation in excess of
        $1 million
        deductibility limitations for
            compensation, 316
        performance-based exemption, 166,
            370–372

International Accounting Standards Board
(IASB), 330
Intrinsic value method of measuring
compensation cost, 336–337, 341,
347
Invested capital and value-based management
performance metrics, 179

K

Key performance indicators (Kpis)
gainsharing plan, 32
identifying, 21
metrics, 25
variable pay programs, designing the plan,
25–26

L

Lang, Mark, 219
Life insurance, executive benefits. *See*
Executive benefits
Line-of-sight concept, 154–155, 159, 164, 215,
242
Long-term incentives
and compensation strategy, 189–190
and corporate transactions or restructuring,
279, 281
defined, 187–188
generally, 187
guidelines for plan design, 242
increased participation in, 199–200
increased value of, 200
investor concerns, 201–202
market volatility, responses to, 202–203
objectives, 188–189
pay-for-performance model, 253–261
performance award plans, 197–198
private companies, 199
restricted stock, 195–196, 199
salary levels and incentive awards,
189–190
stock appreciation rights. *See* Stock
appreciation rights (SARs)
stock options. *See* Stock options
successful plans, features of, 204
treatment of and corporate transactions or
restructuring, 292–295
value-added incentive plan, 261

value-based management. *See* Value-based
management (VBM) and incentive
plans
Look-back plans, 333

M

Management
annual incentive plan. *See* Annual
management incentive plan
involvement in pay-for-performance design,
242
performance management. *See* Performance
management
sales management, perspective on sales
compensation, 110
senior management and attitude toward
sales, 109
talent management. *See* Talent management
value-based. *See* Value-based management
(VBM) and incentive plans
Market value added (MVA)
business plan approach, 182–183
defined, 181
value-based management performance
metrics, 181–182
Medical benefits, supplemental executive. *See*
Executive benefits
Meeting fees, director compensation, 300, 310
Mergers and acquisitions
change-in-control and severance programs
broad-based severance plans, 288
executive programs, 281–288
generally, 280
corporate governance issues and
compensation programs, 295–296
incentive awards, treatment of
cash incentives, 293
equity incentives, 293–295
generally, 281, 292–293
retention and transaction bonuses
design considerations, 290–292
generally, 280
purpose of, 288–290
sales compensation plan, effect on, 117–119
Metrics. *See* Key performance indicators
(KPIs); Performance measures
talent management, 102

N

National Association of Corporate Directors
(NACD), Blue Ribbon Commission on
Director Compensation, 297–298
Net operating profit after tax (NOPAT),
171–179
Nonemployees and stock-based awards,
accounting issues, 338–339, 350–351
Not-for-profit organizations
annual management incentive plans, 166
charitable organizations, 131
compensation
defined, 134
generally, 130–131
planning, 130–131, 152
deferred compensation, 139–140
disqualified person, 132
executive compensation programs,
components of, 140–141, 149–152
factors impacting compensation, 130
incentives
administrative guidelines, 146
cost/benefit relationship, 145–146
developing pay-for-performance culture,
148–149
eligibility, 142
funding trigger, 145
generally, 141–142
incentive opportunity, 142–143
long-term incentive plans, 146–148
performance measures, 143–144
performance/payout scale, 144–145
indirect compensation
change-in-control agreements, 150–151
generally, 149
relocation expenses and housing loans,
149–150
retention incentives, 151–152
severance protection, 150–151
subsidiary organization, compensation
provided by, 152
supplemental executive retirement
program (SERP), 151
initial contract exception, 134–135
pay-for-performance culture, developing,
148–149
presumption of reasonableness, 133–135
approval by independent board, 136–137
comparability of data, 135–136
documentation of decision, 137–138
private foundations, 131, 139
public charities, 131
reasonableness of compensation and tax
rules
approval by independent board, 136–137
comparability of data, 135–136
determining reasonableness, 138–139
documentation, 137–138
tax-exempt status
generally, 131
sanctions, 132–135
tax rules and sanctions, 131–132
unreasonable compensation and federal tax
rules, 132

O

Objective setting and performance
management, 49–51
On-the-job learning and talent development,
95–96
Organizational change
communication strategy, 269–271, 278
and compensation strategy, 266–268
costs of, 277–278
executive compensation
communicating and implementing
strategy, 271–273
generally, 264
linkage to organization's culture, 273–275
linking to characteristics of organizational
change, 277–278
purpose of, 275–276
generally, 264, 278
readiness assessment, 277–278
techniques for managing, 278
types of, 265

P

Parachute programs. *See* Change-in-control
agreements; Golden parachutes
Pay
base pay. *See* Base pay

broad pay bands
"core" and "stretch" pay zones, 73–74
development of, 71–72
guideline salary, 78–79
salary placement within, 74–80
hospitality company example, 1, 8
and reward strategy, 2–4
variable pay programs. *See* Variable pay
programs (pay for results)
Pay-for-performance
annual incentives, 247–252
base salary, 246–247
communications, 262–263
director compensation, 306
guidelines, 241–243
long-term incentives, 253–261
alternatives, 257–261
purpose of model and strategy, 244–245
stock ownership
deferral plan, 262
guidelines, 261–262
Performance-accelerated restricted stock
(PARS), 258
Performance award plans
annual awards, 197
long-term incentives, 197–198
performance targets, 198
problems with, 197
stock options compared, 197
Performance benchmarking
compensation analysis, 323–324
generally, 322–323
shareholder return, 324–325
Performance cash plans, long-term incentives,
197
Performance management
appraisal interviews, 57–58
balanced performance measurement, 44, 46
behavioral competencies, 47
cyclic nature of, 48–49
development planning, 58–59
evaluation and development, 48–49, 55–57
feedback, 48
and appraisal interviews, 57
and coaching, 53–55
multisource appraisal process, 51–53
framework for success, 44–45

generally, 43
objective setting, guidelines for, 49–51
as ongoing process, 48
performance planning, 48
performance rating scales, 55–56
reward linkage example, 60
self-assessment, 56–57
success factors, 60–62
technical and functional knowledge, 46–47
Performance measures
Balanced Scorecard. *See* Balanced
Scorecard
comparative measures, 243
financial measures, 155–156
long-term incentive plans, integration with,
157–158
nonfinancial measures, 156–157
not-for-profit organizations, 143–144
value-based management metrics, 170–171
Performance scales
external validation process, 162–163
standards, establishing, 160–161
target awards and threshold and superior
levels, 162
Performance share plans, 157
long-term incentives, 197–198
Performance unit plans, 157
long-term incentives, 197–198
Perquisites, executive benefits, 224–225,
239–240
Phantom stock, 357, 360, 363–364
Poison pill, golden parachutes as, 281, 365
Private companies
broad-based equity plans, advantages of,
212
director compensation, stock options, 302
golden parachutes, special rules, 365
long-term incentives, cash and equity
alternatives, 199
stock options with repurchase feature,
accounting issues, 345–346
Private foundations. *See* Not-for-profit
organizations
Profit sharing
management incentive plan distinguished,
155
variable pay programs, 24

Project design teams
   business environmental assessment, 22
   variable pay programs, 21
   compensation strategy statement, 23
   plan design, 24–26
Proxy disclosures
   elective deferral plans, investment earnings
      on, 234
   SEC rules for executive compensation, 316

Q

Qualitative measures and goals, 50
Quantitative measures and goals, 50

R

Rabbi trusts, 228–229
   funding change-in-control payments, 287
Readiness assessment
   competency-based reward programs
      generally, 65–66
      strength of assessment system, 66–69
   organizational change and executive
      compensation, 277–278
Recognition awards, 84
Relocation expenses, executive benefits and
   not-for-profit organizations, 149–150
Restricted stock. *See* Stock, restricted
Retainers and director compensation, 299–300,
   309
Retention incentives
   design considerations
      cash or equity payments, 291
      coverage, 290–291
      generally, 290
      individual retention amounts, 291
      payment schedules, 291–292
      retention period, 290
      service and performance requirements,
         291
      termination of employment, 292
   executive benefits, not-for-profit
      organizations, 151–152
   generally, 279–280
   purpose of, 288–289
Retirement plans
   elective deferral plans. *See* Elective deferral
      plans

401(k) plans. *See* 401(k) mirror plans
   supplemental executive retirement program
      (SERP). *See* Supplemental executive
      retirement program (SERP)
Return on investment (ROI)
   and employee turnover, 11
   and reward strategy, 9–10
   rewards ROI, 11
   value-based management performance
      metrics, 170–171
Reward strategy
   case examples
      global manufacturer, 17–19
      mergers and acquisitions and workforce
         integration, 15–17
      technology industry, 13–15
   competency-based rewards. *See*
      Competency-based rewards
   components of
      benefits, 4
      careers, 4–5
      generally, 2–3
      pay, 3–4
   data collection
      employee histories, 10–11
      focus groups and surveys, 10–11
   data leveraging
      data collection, 9–10
      generally, 9
   developing an effective program, 11–12
   effectiveness of, 5
   focus groups and surveys, 10–11
   hospitality company example
      background, 1
      benefits, 8–9
      careers, 9
      data collection, 8
      performance-based pay, 8
   human capital, 10
   importance of, 2
   indications of problems with reward system,
      18
   management of
      and benchmarking, 7
      and best practices, 7
      cost management, 6
      data, importance of, 7

importance of, 5
internal review, 7
political and departmental influences, 7

S

Sales compensation
administration of plan, 127
auditing the plan, 127–129
case example, 112
customers' needs and perspective, 110
design and implementation of plan
case example, 126
elements of plan, 122–125
planning, early involvement of key
parties, 125
tips for design, 129
tips for implementation, 126–127
disguised base salary, 108
human resources, role of, 109
impact of modifying sales compensation
plans, study results, 105–106
importance of effective sales force, 107
indications of problems with pay plan
lack of motivation, 122
mergers and acquisitions issues, 117–119
not cost effective, 120–121
sales model, elements of misaligned,
113–117
key parties, including in plan design, 109
management and sales, opposing positions
of, 104–105
modifying the plan, 127–128
myths, 128
objectives of pay plan, 111–112
pay elements, summary of, 124
problems with, 107–108
purpose of, 108
sales administration, role of, 110
sales force perspective, 110–111
sales management's perspective, 110
senior management's perspective, 109
shadow base salary, 108
software, 127
as a strategic tool, 107
top performers
lack of pay for performance, 107
and motivation, 122

too much pay for wrong or limited
performance, 107–108
top territories or inherited territories, 108
Sales management process, roles and key
elements of, 115
Sales model and compensation, 113–117
Scorecard. *See* Balanced Scorecard
Securities and Exchange Commission (SEC)
Emerging Issues Task Force, role in,
329–330
insider trading rules, 195
Rule 16(b), 297, 299
Securities Exchange Act of 1934
Section 12, reporting requirements, 370
Section 16(b)3, 316
Self-funding, management incentive plans, 165
Severance protection
broad-based severance plans, 288
executive benefits, not-for-profit
organizations, 150–151
generally, 279–280
Shareholder value plan, 258–259
Shareholders
employees as, 210–211
shareholder approval, stock option plans,
207
shareholder value and long-term incentives,
188, 214
guidelines for plan design, 242
shareholder value and stock options, 204
stock options, 201–202
Short-swing profit rules, 316
Silver parachutes, 280, 287–288. *See also*
Change-in-control agreements
Spinoffs
business combinations, options granted in
connection with, 346–347
stock options, treatment of, 295
Staff role in talent development, 94
Statements of Financial Accounting Standards
No. 123. *See* FAS No. 123, "Accounting for
Stock-Based Compensation"
No. 128. *See* FAS No. 128, "Earnings per
Share"
Stock
dilution, 201–202, 216, 218
overhang concerns, 201–202, 216, 218

Stock *(continued)*
  phantom stock, 357, 360, 363–364
  puts, calls, and other repurchase features,
    344–346
  reload options, 194
  underwater, 218, 340, 342
Stock, restricted
  diluted earnings per share, computing, 354
  director compensation, 301, 312
  long-term incentive plans, 188, 195–196
  performance-accelerated (PARS), 258
  stock performance plan, 260
  tax considerations. *See* Tax considerations
Stock, unrestricted and director compensation,
    313
Stock appreciation rights (SARs)
  long-term incentives, 195
  tax considerations, 357, 360, 361, 364
Stock options. *See also* Accounting for
    stock-based compensation
  annual grants of, 191–192
  APB 25. *See* APB 25
  binomial model for option pricing, 331
  Black-Scholes option-pricing approach,
    191–192, 208, 331
  broad-based plans. *See* Broad-based equity
    plans
  change in control and vesting, 293–295
  clawback features, 193
  and creating shareholder value, 204
  director compensation. *See* Director
    compensation
  discounted options, 190
  earnings per share, diluted, 353–354
  exercise price, 190
  fair value method of valuing, 331
  generally, 190–193
  global equity plans. *See* Broad-based equity
    plans
  incentive stock options (ISOs), 191, 207
    nonqualified stock options compared, 191
    tax considerations. *See* Tax considerations
  increased participation in, 199–200
  increased value of, 200
  insider trading rules, 195
  long-term incentives, 190
  market volatility, responses to, 202–203

  nonqualified stock options, 188, 191, 208
    incentive stock options compared, 191
    tax considerations. *See* Tax considerations
    tax deductions and smaller companies,
      191
  number of shares to grant, approaches, 192
  performance award plans compared, 197
  post-termination exercises, 193
  premium-priced options, 190
  reduction of exercise price, 342–344
  reloading, 344
  renewal or extension of life of award,
    accounting issues, 340–342
  spinoffs, 295
  stock ownership deferral plan, 262
  stock ownership guidelines, 261–262
  tax considerations. *See* Tax considerations
  term of, 191
  termination of employment due to death,
    disability, or normal retirement, 193
  time-accelerated, 259–260
  underwater options, 202–203
  variations on basic stock option
    generally, 193
    performance-accelerated vesting, 194
    performance-contingent options, 194
    premium-priced options, 194
    reload options, 194–195
  vesting
    acceleration of, accounting issues,
      341–342
    change in control issues, 293–295
    schedules, 192–193
    spinoffs, 295
Supplemental executive retirement program
    (SERP)
  ERISA requirements, 227
  executive benefits, not-for-profit
    organizations, 151
  generally, 151, 225
  rabbi trusts, 228–229
  restoration plans, 226
  severance pay and benefits, change-in-
    control agreements, 284
  target plans, 226
  tax and legal issues, 227–228
  top hat group, 227

Suppliers as strategic partners, 107
Surveys on compensation, use of, 326

T

Talent development. *See also* Talent
    management
    buying versus building talent, 10
    managers, role of, 96–97
    on-the-job learning, 95–96
Talent management
    and business strategy alignment
        competencies, role of, 88–90
        talent management system, 87–88
        talent strategies and business strategies, 88
    economic benefits of, 86–87
    high potentials, assessing, 98–99
    importance of, 86–87
    metrics, 102
    potential and promotability ratings, 99
    systems, 87
    talent planning and development
        as business process, 91–93
        candidate assessment, 93–94
        career path options, 95
        forward-looking nature of, 93
        managers, role of, 96–98
        multiple talent pools, need for, 94–95
        on-the-job learning, 95–96
        organizational and individual needs, 94
        role of CEO, 91, 94
        staff and process support, 94
        talent reviews, 96–101
        techniques, 90–91
        technology and success measurement,
            101–103
    talent pools, importance of, 94
    talent strategy, 88
    business strategy linkage, 92
    underperformers, 100–101
Tax considerations. *See also* Internal Revenue
    Code (IRC)
    Alternative Minimum Tax, 199
    401(k) mirror plans, 230
    golden parachutes
        benefits of, 365
        calculations, 367–369
        cutback example, 368

defined, 364–365
    design considerations, 366–367
    equity acceleration, 370
    excess parachute payment, 365–366
    gross-up example, 368–369
    tax penalties, 286–287
IRC Section 162(m), compensation in
    excess of $1 million
    deductibility limitations, 316
    generally, 370
    implementation guidelines, 372
    performance-based compensation, 166,
        370–371
    performance-based exemption, qualifying
        for, 166
    phantom stock, 357–360, 363–364
    restricted stock, 356–358, 361–362
    and performance-based compensation,
        196
    retention and transaction bonuses, 289
    stock appreciation rights (SARs), 357,
        360–361, 364
    stock options, 189
    incentive stock options (ISOs), 356,
        358–359, 362–363
    nonqualified stock options (NQSOs),
        191, 356, 359–360, 362–363
    supplemental executive retirement programs
        (SERPs), 227–228
Tax-exempt organizations. *See* Not-for-profit
    organizations
Taxpayer Bill of Rights, 132
Team/group incentives
    case study, individual and team incentives
        for relationship management
        background, 39–40
        incentive plan design features, 40–41
        participation and frequency policies, 26
        variable pay programs, 24
Technical competency and bonus awards, 83–84
Technology
    high-technology industry and stock options,
        211
    and talent management, 101–102
Termination of employment
    retention and transaction bonuses, 292
    and stock options, 193

Tin parachutes, 280, 288. *See also*
    Change-in-control agreements
Total business return (TBR) and value-based
    management performance metrics,
    170, 176
Total shareholder return (TSR) and guidelines
    for plan design, 242–243
Training and variable pay programs, 29
Transaction bonuses
    design considerations
        cash or equity payments, 291
        coverage, 290–291
        generally, 290
        individual retention amounts, 291
        payment schedules, 291–292
        retention period, 290
        service and performance requirements,
            291
        termination of employment, 292
    generally, 279–280
    purpose of, 288–289
Treasury Regulations
    Section 162-27, 370
    Section 1.280G-1, Q&A-24, 370

U

Unrestricted stock, 313

V

Value-added incentive plan, 261
Value-based management (VBM) and incentive
    plans
    annual incentive plans, 184–185
    commitment to positive change, 173–175
    communication, 173–175
    compensation plan design
        design features, 176–177
        principles of, 175–176, 186
    implementing VBM, 173–175, 185–186
    long-term incentives, 184–185
    performance measurements, 170–171
    performance targets
        approach to setting and numerical
            example, 178–183
        evaluation of target-setting approach, 183
        stage of readiness, impact on incentive
            plan design, 183–185

    readiness for VBM, 171–173
        level of and plan design, 183–186
        risks and rewards, 175–176
        value-based management defined, 169–170
    Value drivers and broad-based equity plans,
        209
Variable pay programs (pay for results)
    adjustments to plan, 30
    affordability, 22
    business environmental assessment, 22
    case study
        individual and team incentives for
            relationship management, 39–42
    communications and education program, 28
    compensation strategy statement, 23–24
    competency assessment linkage
        approaches generally, 81
        competency acquisition, special bonuses
            for, 82–83
        incentive award modifier, 81–82
        models for, design elements, 83–84
    competency-based incentives, 24
    employee readiness diagnostic, 22–23
    feasibility assessment, 22
    gainsharing, 24, 26
        case study, 30–36
    generally, 20, 42
    goalsharing, 24
    greenfield operations, 27–28
    individual incentives, 24
    integration of plan, 29–30
    monitoring and feedback, 30
    objectives, developing
        Kaplan and Norton Balanced Scorecard,
            21
        key performance indicators, 21
        project design team, 21
    phases of implementation, 20–21
    pilot program, 27–28
    plan design
        financial factors, 25
        generally, 24–25
        participation and frequency, 26–27
        productivity factors, 25
        quality factors, 25–26
    plan implementation, 28–29
    profit sharing, 24

required elements for success, 23
team/group incentives, 24, 26
    changes in team membership, 38
    communication and education, 38
    defining the team, 36–37
    differences in individual performances,
        37–38
    distributing awards to team members, 37
    "free ride" employees, 38
    implications for management, 38–39
    individual and team incentives, 39
    plan design, 36
    transition approach, 27–28
    types of plans, 24
    "what-if" testing, 27
Vesting
    acceleration of, accounting issues, 341–342
    cliff vesting, 337
    director compensation, 311–312

lower level employees and likelihood of
    cashing out, 219
performance conditions, accounting for,
    349–350
pro-rata vesting, 337–338
restricted stock, 196
stock options, 192–194, 213
    acceleration, 341–342
    change in control issues, 293–295
    spinoffs, 295
variable accounting issues and stock options,
    215

W

Weighted average cost of capital (WACC)
    value-based management performance
        metrics, 178, 180
"What-if" testing and variable pay programs,
    27